photos Sylvain Margaine texts David Margaine

ABANDONED FRANCE

photos Sylvain Margaine texts David Margaine

ABANDONED FRANCE

JONGLEZ PUBLISHING

Contents

Introduction

Why publish another book on urban exploration?

After several publications on our travels to forgotten places around the world, we realised that we had only just touched on the industrial wastelands of France; yet there is a growing awareness of this endangered heritage.

Through these pages, we seek to present these places – whether ancient or modern, and from the seemingly trivial to the most important – as reflections of the country's rich history.

This project has taken us back to several sites already covered in previous books. Some of these places have changed or evolved, others have disappeared for ever. In addition to these old acquaintances, we have made several new discoveries.

Through these twenty-two places, chosen from our explorations over the last fifteen years, we take you to the four corners of France to share the beauty and tell the story of this forgotten heritage.

Enjoy *your* explorations!

David and Sylvain Margaine, October 2017

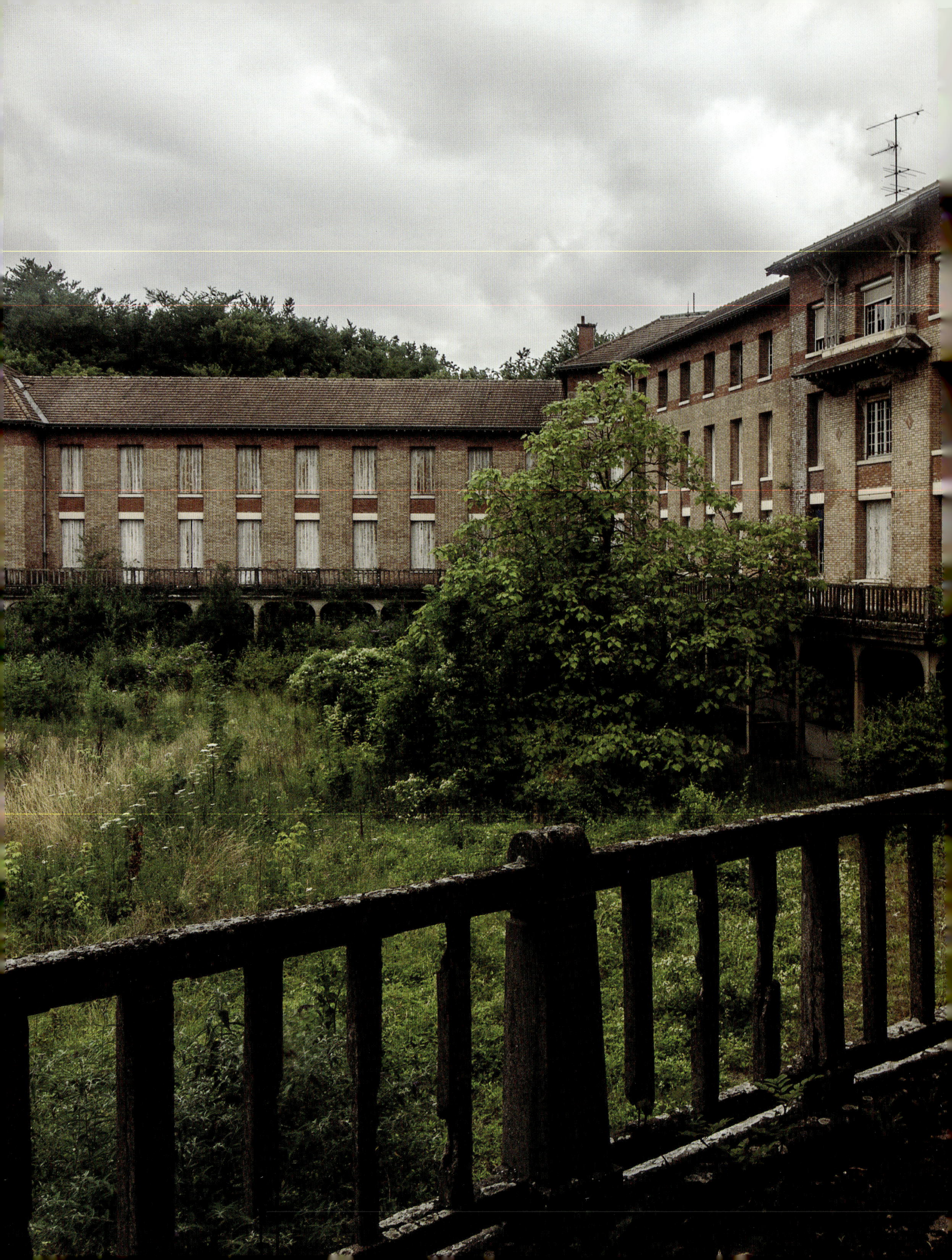

Sanatorium d'Angicourt, Oise

In the 19th century, there was as yet no effective treatment for tuberculosis. However, efforts were being made to avoid air-borne contagion by isolating patients who had the disease in dedicated care units.

The Assistance Publique (welfare services) of Paris, for example, founded an institution for the city's TB patients. In 1892, the general administration department acquired the Verderonne estate, 336,000 square metres of land on a hill next to Angicourt, about 60 kilometres north of Paris. Henri Belouet, one of the architects, was commissioned to design a sanatorium like those he had seen in Germany. As a pioneer in the hospital management of tuberculosis, Germany was a reference for medical specialists and architects throughout Europe.

Belouet drew up plans for a stone and rubble building with a main body flanked by two identical wings – one for men and the other for women – forming an angle of 110°. The pavilions, which faced south for maximum sunlight, stood on a hillside sheltered from the wind. Staff were housed on the third and top floors.

The administration and general services were located in a building at the top of the hill. Underground cellars and galleries provided good ventilation and housed a network of pipes. Carrying out this work required a major investment, especially since the ground had to be levelled to create an artificial plateau mid-slope.

Despite funding from Pari Mutuel, the money ran out. In theory, each wing was to hold 150 beds, in rooms for one to eight patients. At the end of 1900, only half of the main building was functional.

In 1903, the hospital was named Sanatorium Villemin as a tribute to the doctor who had demonstrated the contagious nature of tuberculosis.

It was in those years that the head physician, Georges Küss, perfected the therapeutic technique of the artificial lung, which was to remain the basic TB treatment in the pre-antibiotics era.

The triage of prospective Villemin patients depended on the stage of their disease. After a month's observation, only those who seemed to have a favourable prognosis were admitted.

After admission, their stay lasted until a complete and lasting cure ... or death. In which case, a funeral service would be discreetly held next to the stables.

During the First World War, the sanatorium was requisitioned as a military hospital before reverting to its original vocation in the 1920s. In 1928, the second pavilion, in brick and stone, was finally built, doubling the reception capacity.

Due to its isolation, the site had to be self-sufficient in water, heating and electricity. Some of its food supplies were grown on site.

Because of the risk of bombing, the sanatorium was evacuated at the beginning of the Second World War, during which it took in the wounded. From the Liberation to the 1960s, and the general availability of antibiotics, Villemin sanatorium resumed its primary functions. From 1963, as Hôpital Villemin, it admitted only welfare recipients and women with chronic diseases. The following year, the hospital's role changed again, when it became a dedicated centre for dependent elderly people. It was finally closed down in 1997, as the facilities were no longer suited to modern care techniques.

The property was put up for sale by the Assistance Publique des Hôpitaux de Paris, but has lain abandoned ever since.

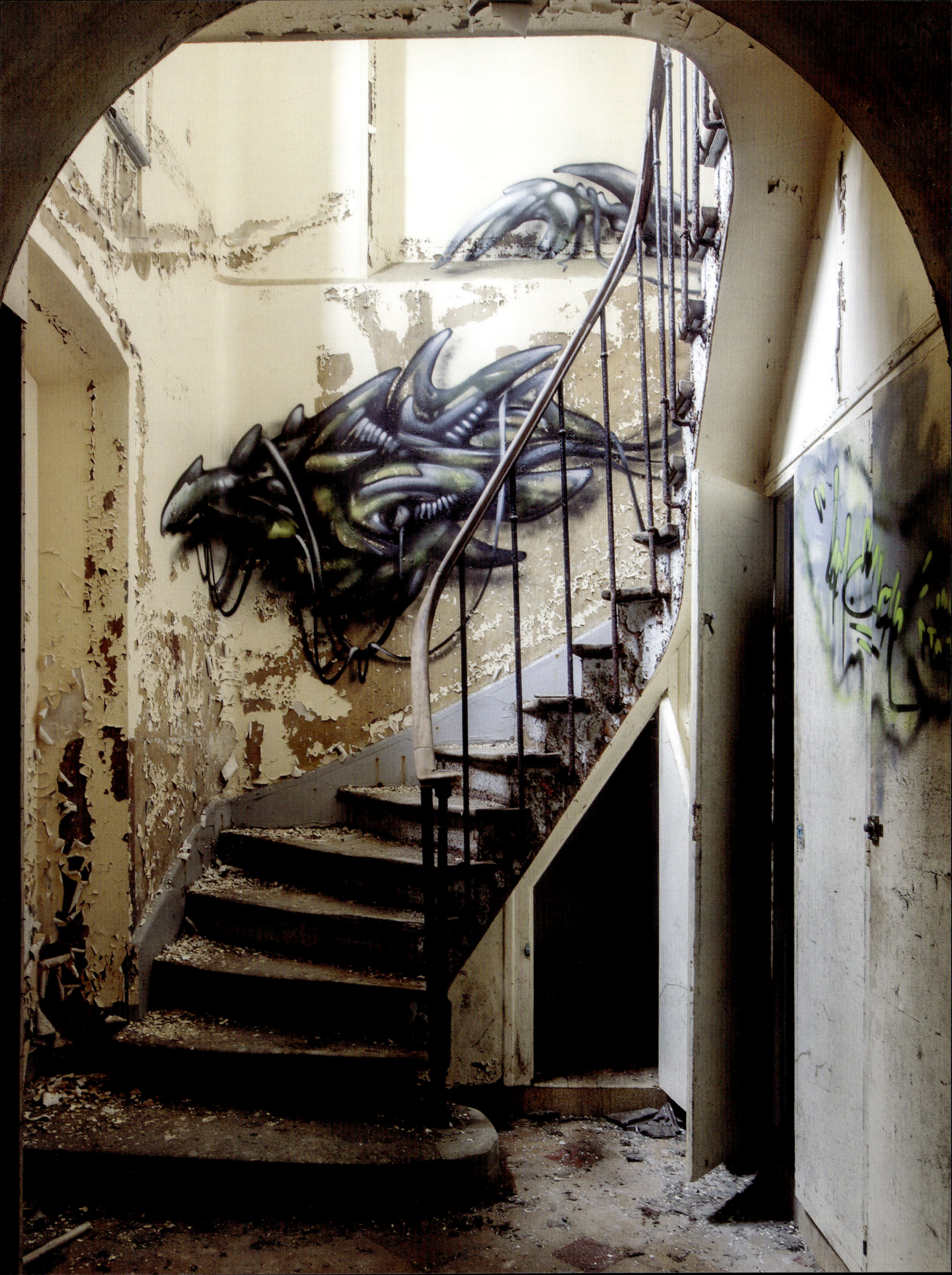

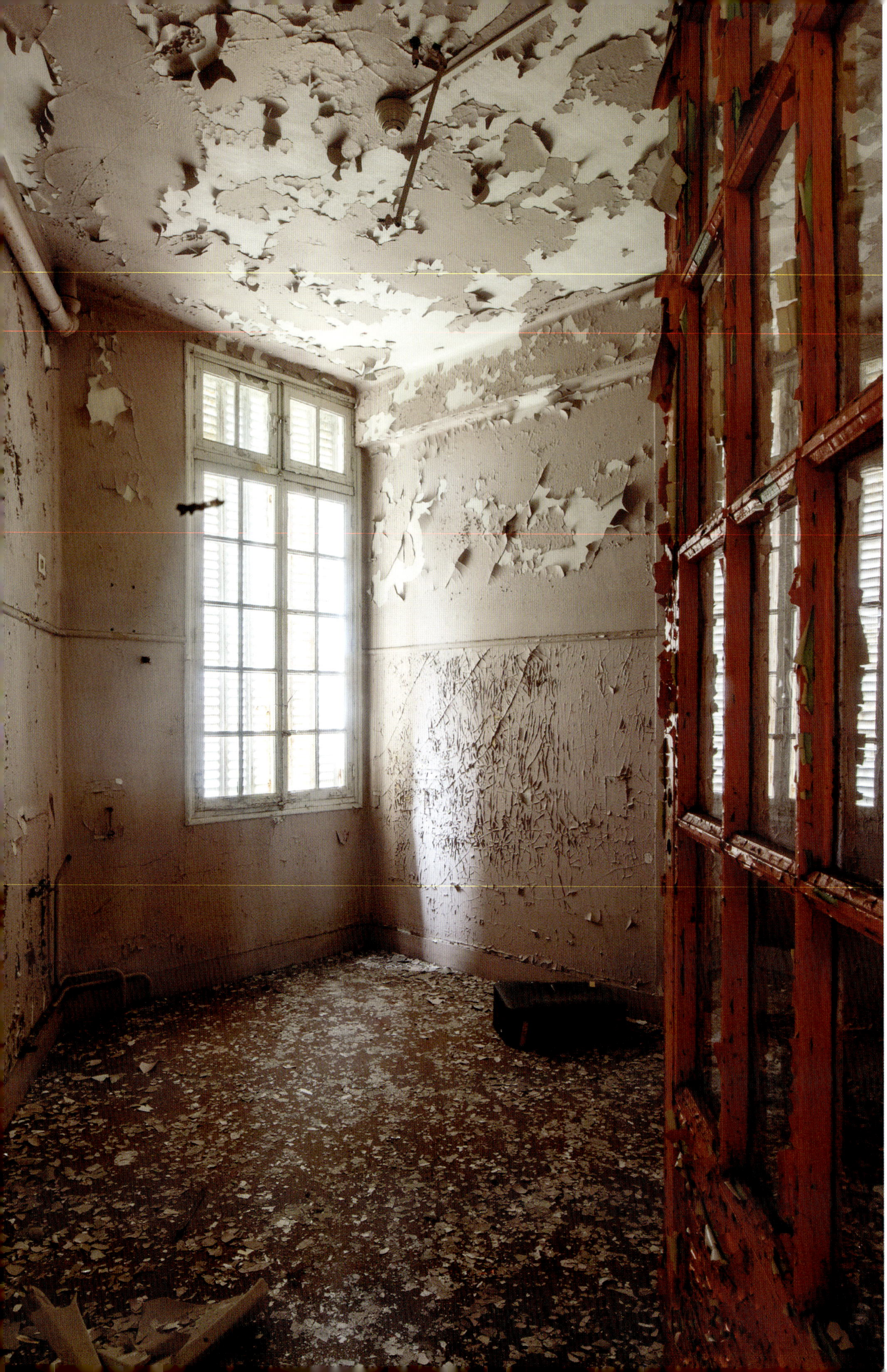

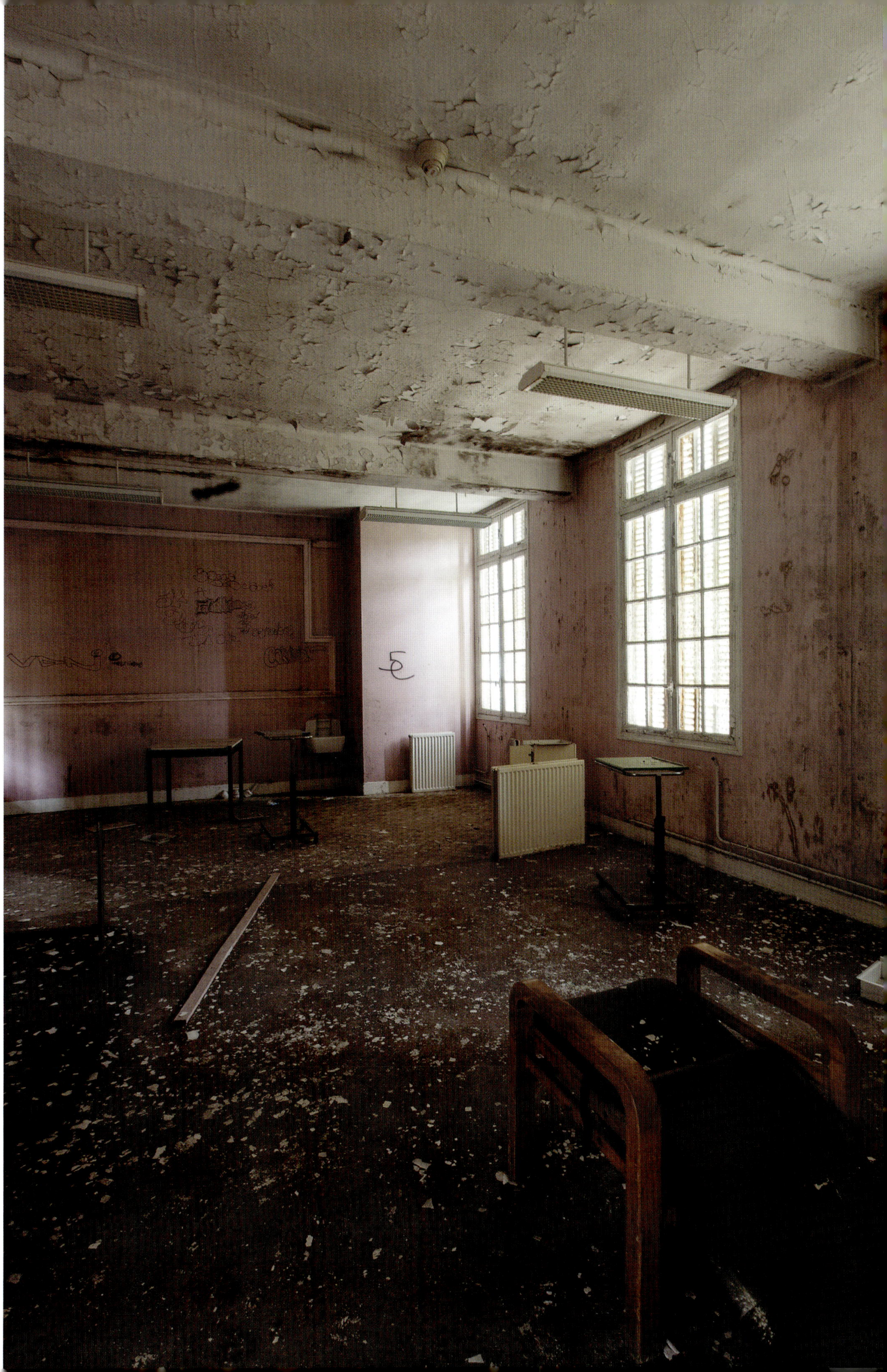

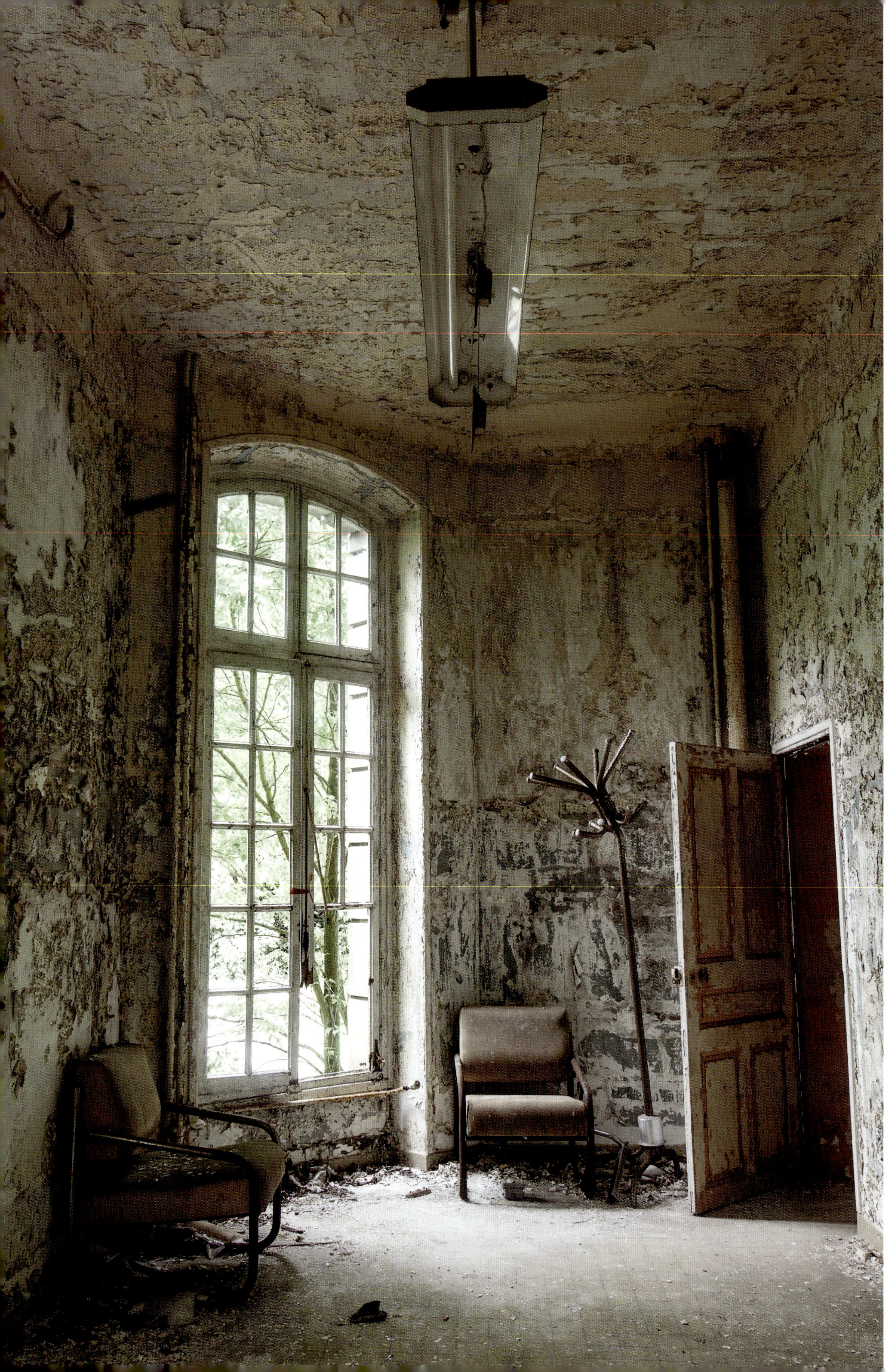

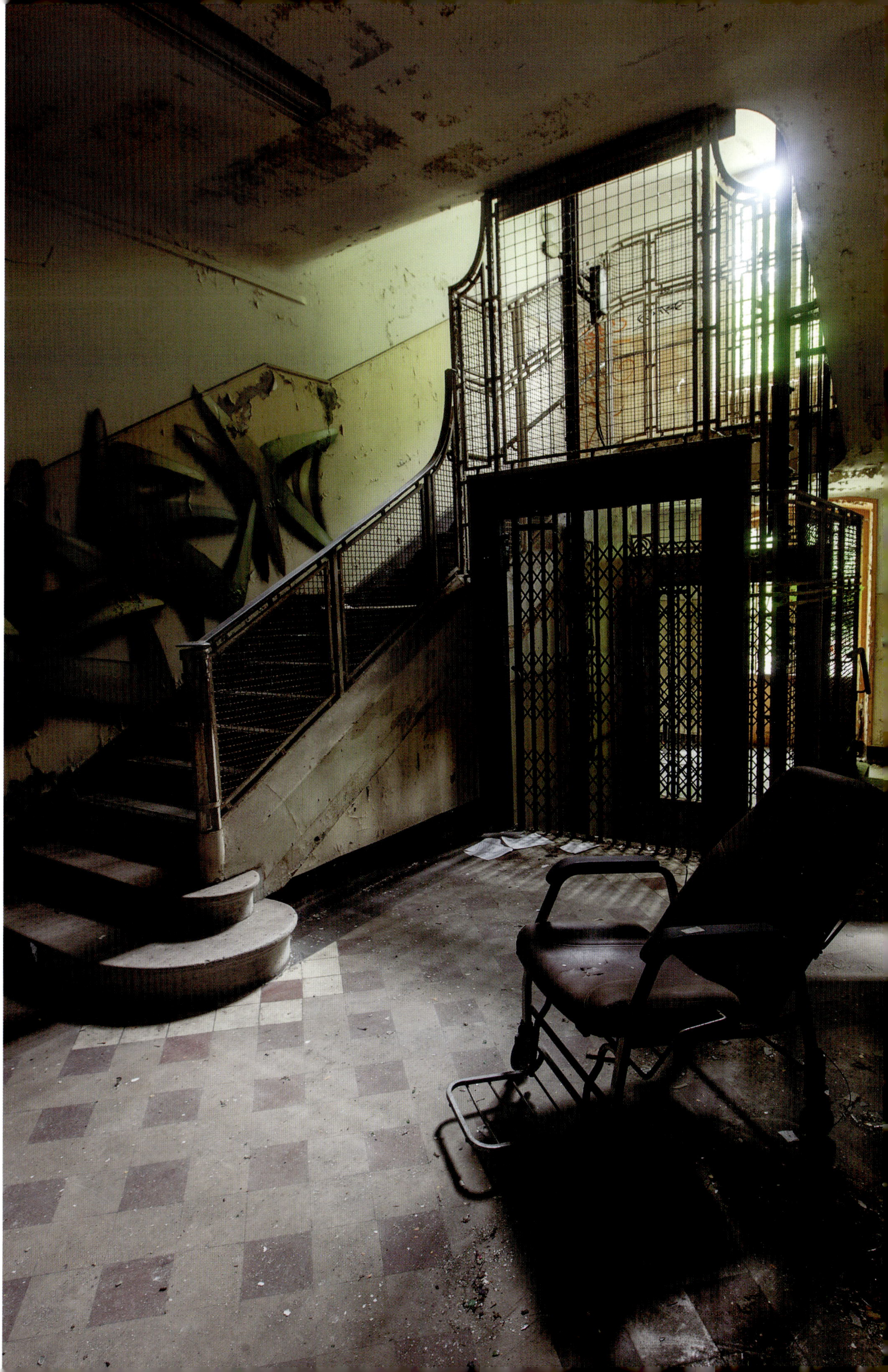

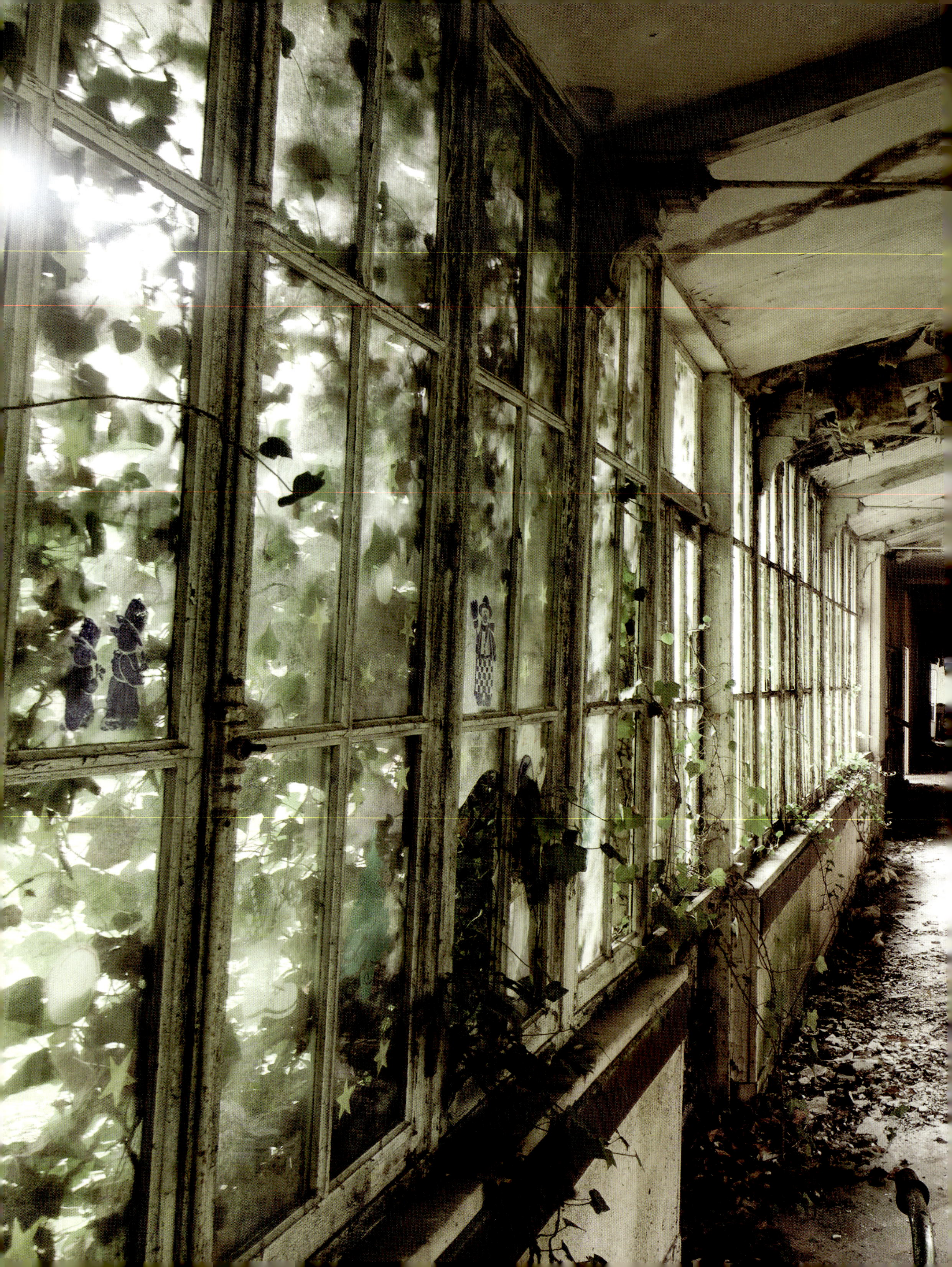

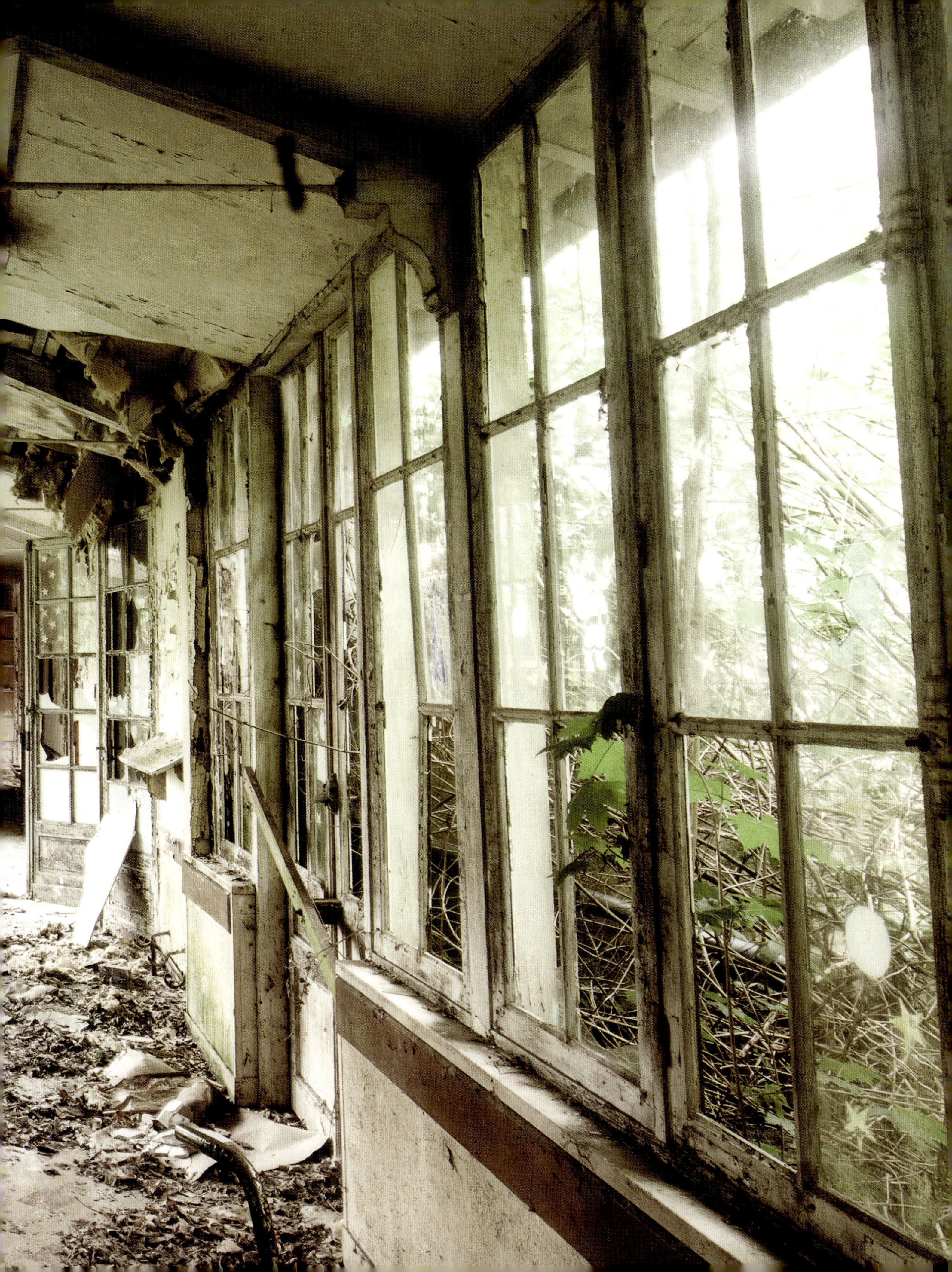

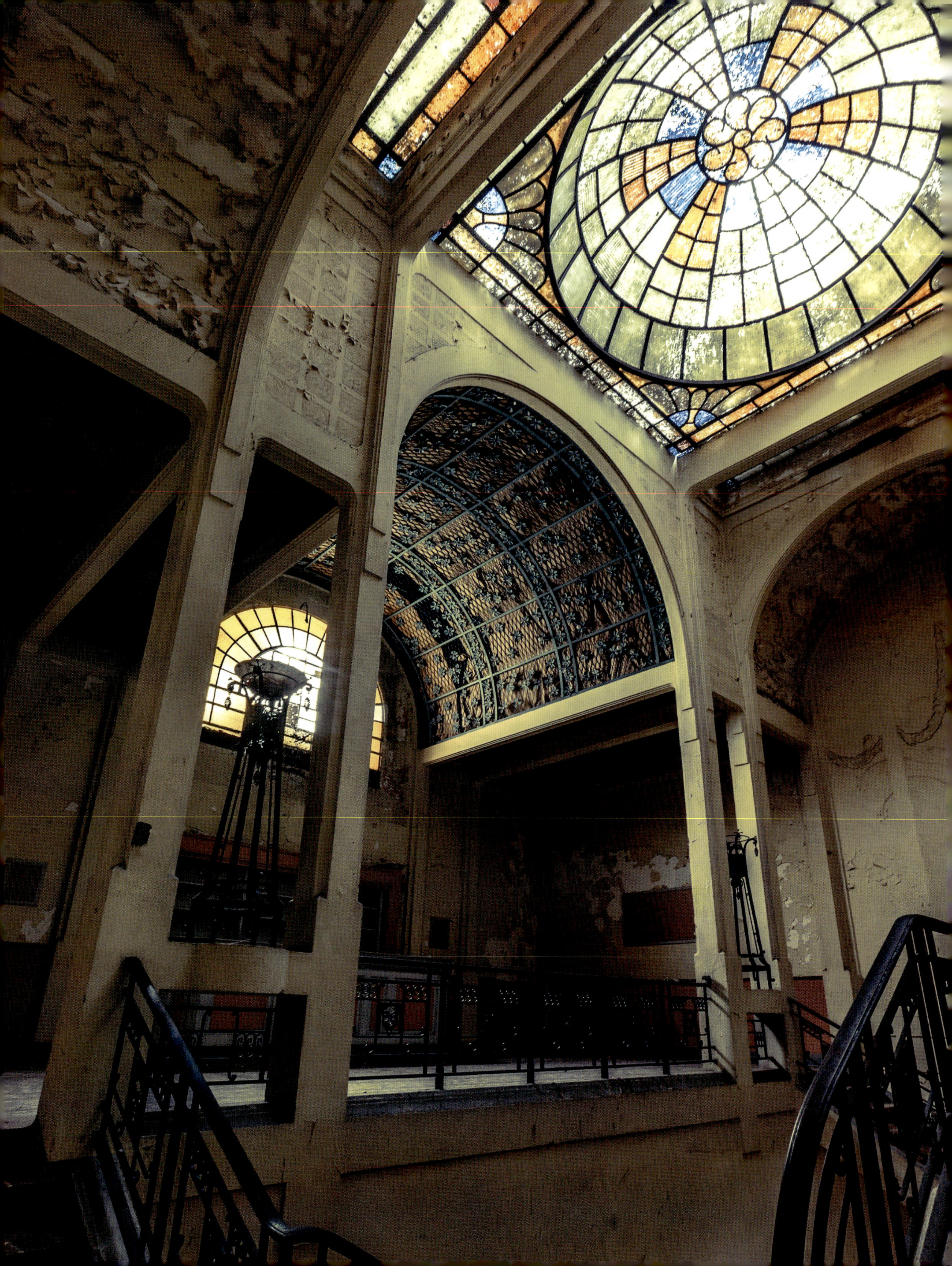

Salle Sthrau, Maubeuge

The town of Maubeuge in northern France grew up around a monastery built in the 7th century by Saint Aldegonde.

The story of Salle Sthrau, in the heart of the city, also has religious origins. Dating from 1624, this brick and stone building in Baroque style was originally the chapel of the Jesuit college.

Deconsecrated during the French Revolution, the building was renamed in honour of a young military drummer and hero called Sthrau. He fell at the battle of Wattignies in 1793, when the Revolutionary conscript troops defeated the Austrian army and put an end to the siege of Maubeuge.

Salle Sthrau has been used as a stable, ballroom, museum, library and music room.

It did not escape the bombing in the First World War, and only the outer walls and gable remained. Three men were put in charge of its restoration: two architectural engineers, Jean and Henri Lafitte, and Jean's son Jean-Paul, a painter and decorator. Funds granted in 1923 launched six years of work. The result was the embodiment of Art Deco. With the exception of the original sections that had survived, the whole structure is of reinforced concrete.

The chapel is built on two levels, connected by a curved staircase with open balusters. On the ground floor is a rectangular music room, decorated with paintings and stuccowork. On the first floor, a ballroom with an ellipsoidal vaulted ceiling and two galleries. Jean-Paul Lafitte's paintings cover the walls. Stained-glass windows in the gable end illuminate the ballroom foyer. Many of the wrought-iron fittings are inspired by nature or the dramatic arts, typical Art Deco motifs.

Despite the initial registration of the façades and roof as historical monuments, and then of the interior in 1997, lack of maintenance led to the building's closure for safety reasons in 1998. The cost of restoration was beyond the town's means.

In 2016, the local investment support fund joined forces with the municipality and the regional office of cultural affairs, to vote for the first of three stages in the restoration of Salle Sthrau. Work began in March 2017.

To complete the work, a subscription for individuals and companies was launched under the auspices of the Fondation du Patrimoine (National Heritage Foundation). Half of the 5-million-euro restoration cost has still to be found.

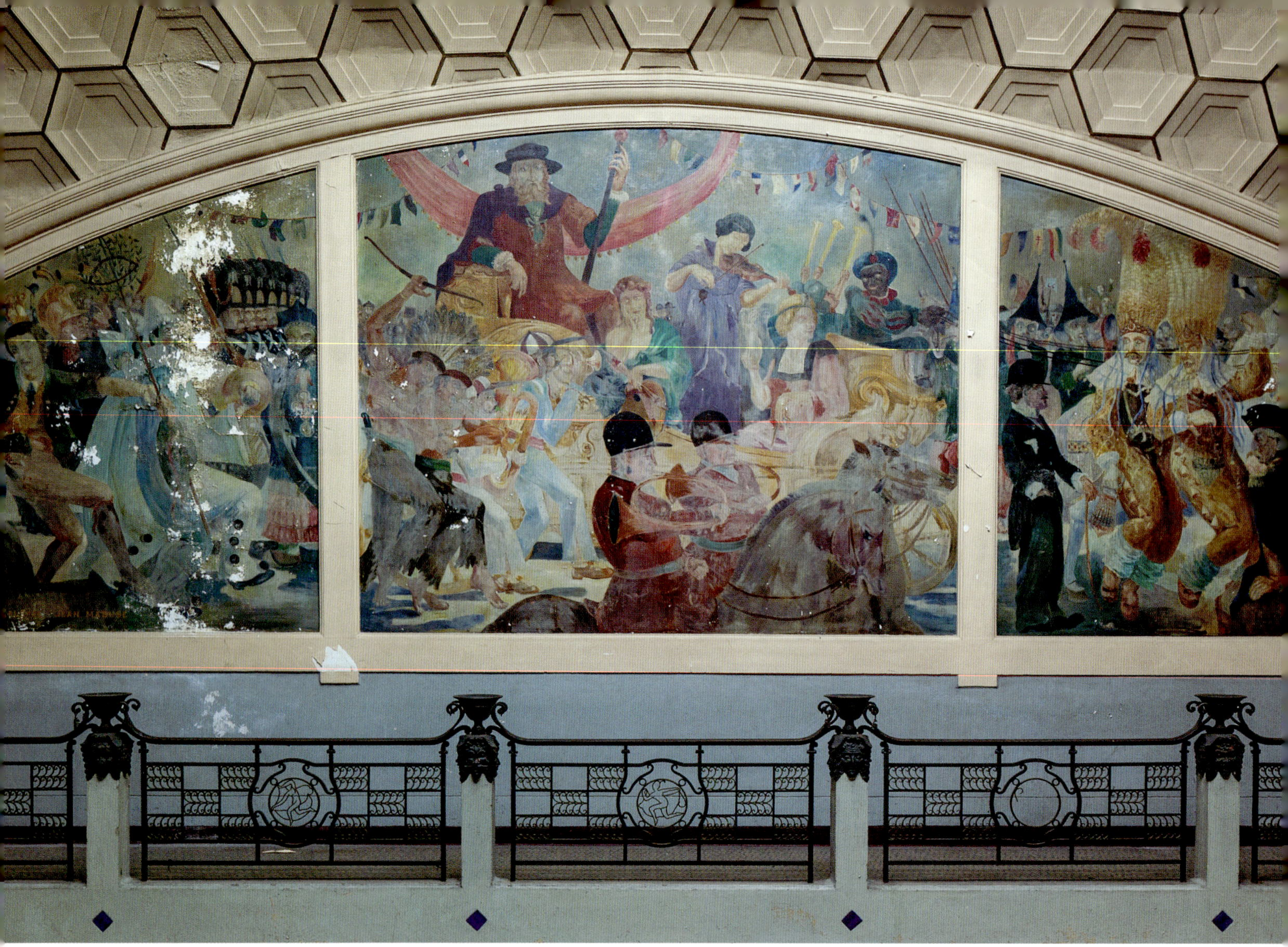

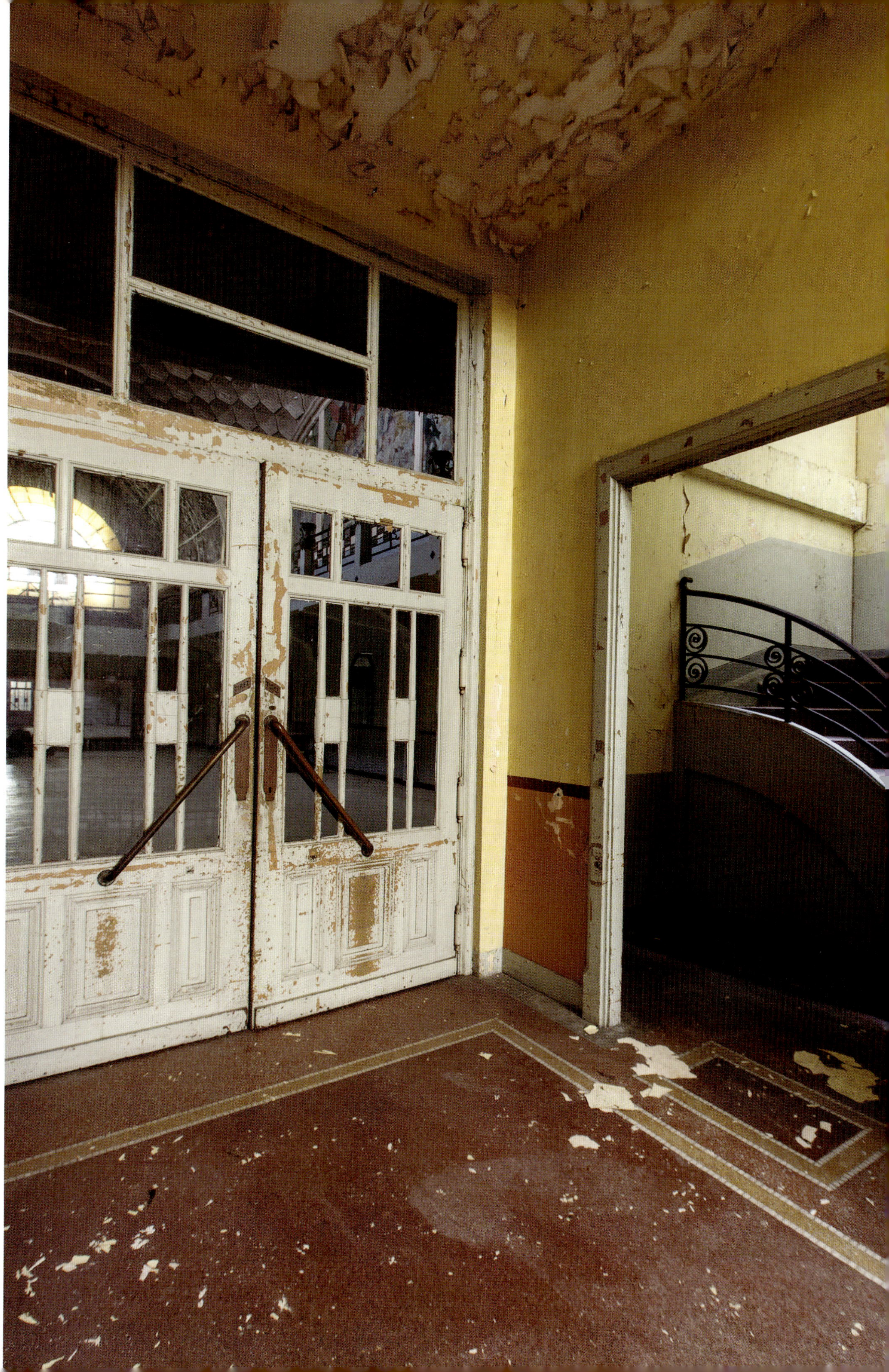

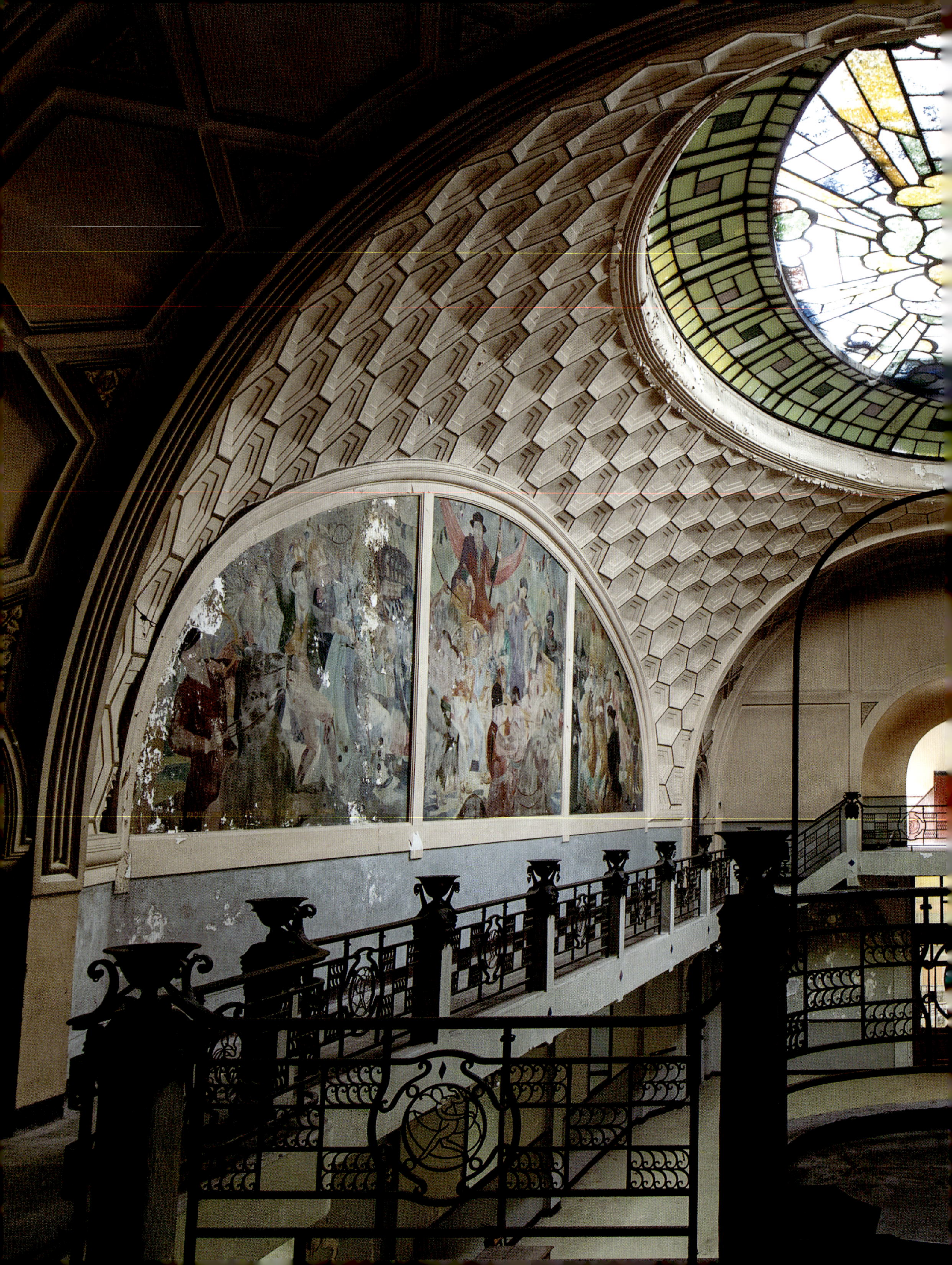

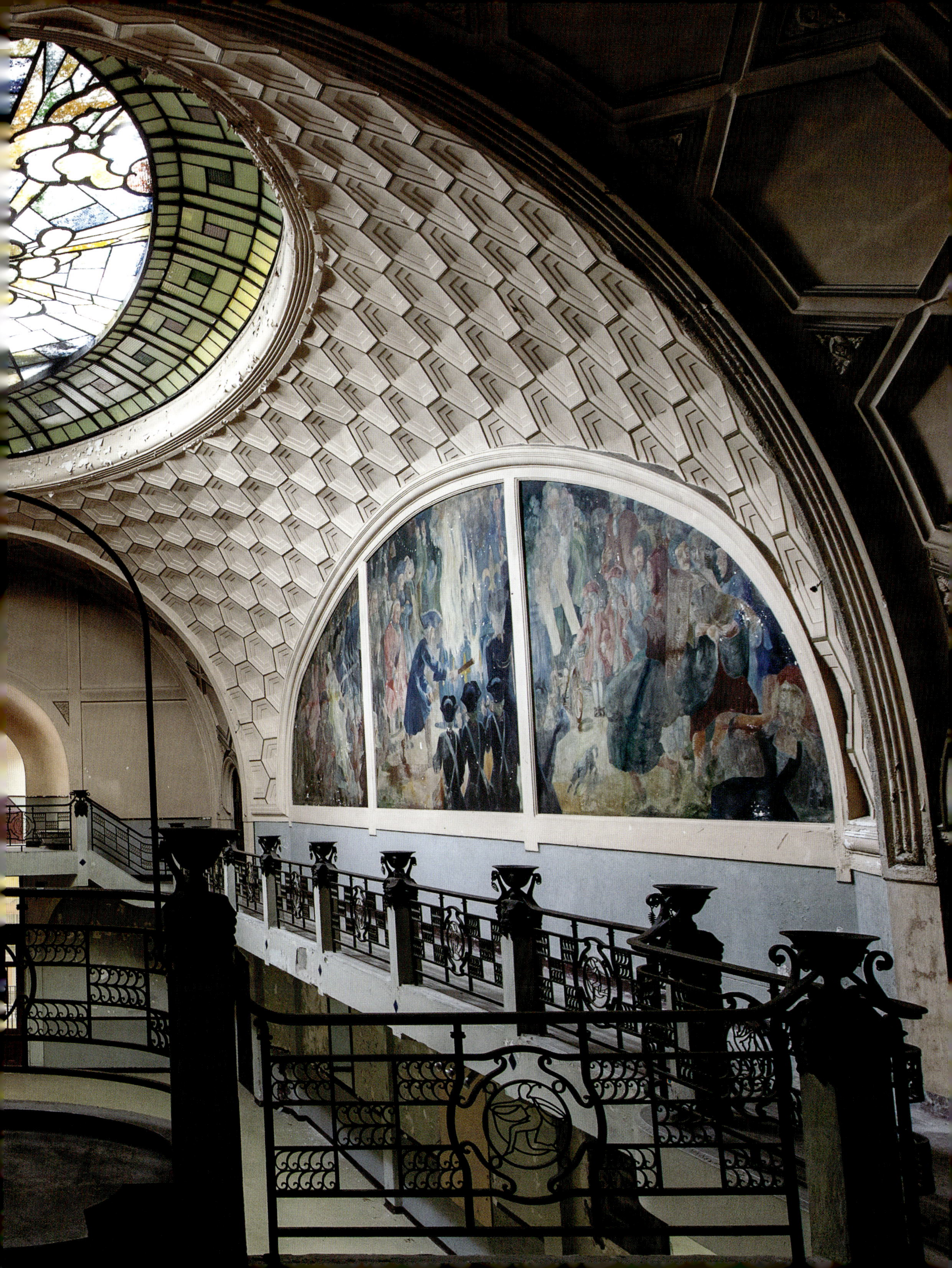

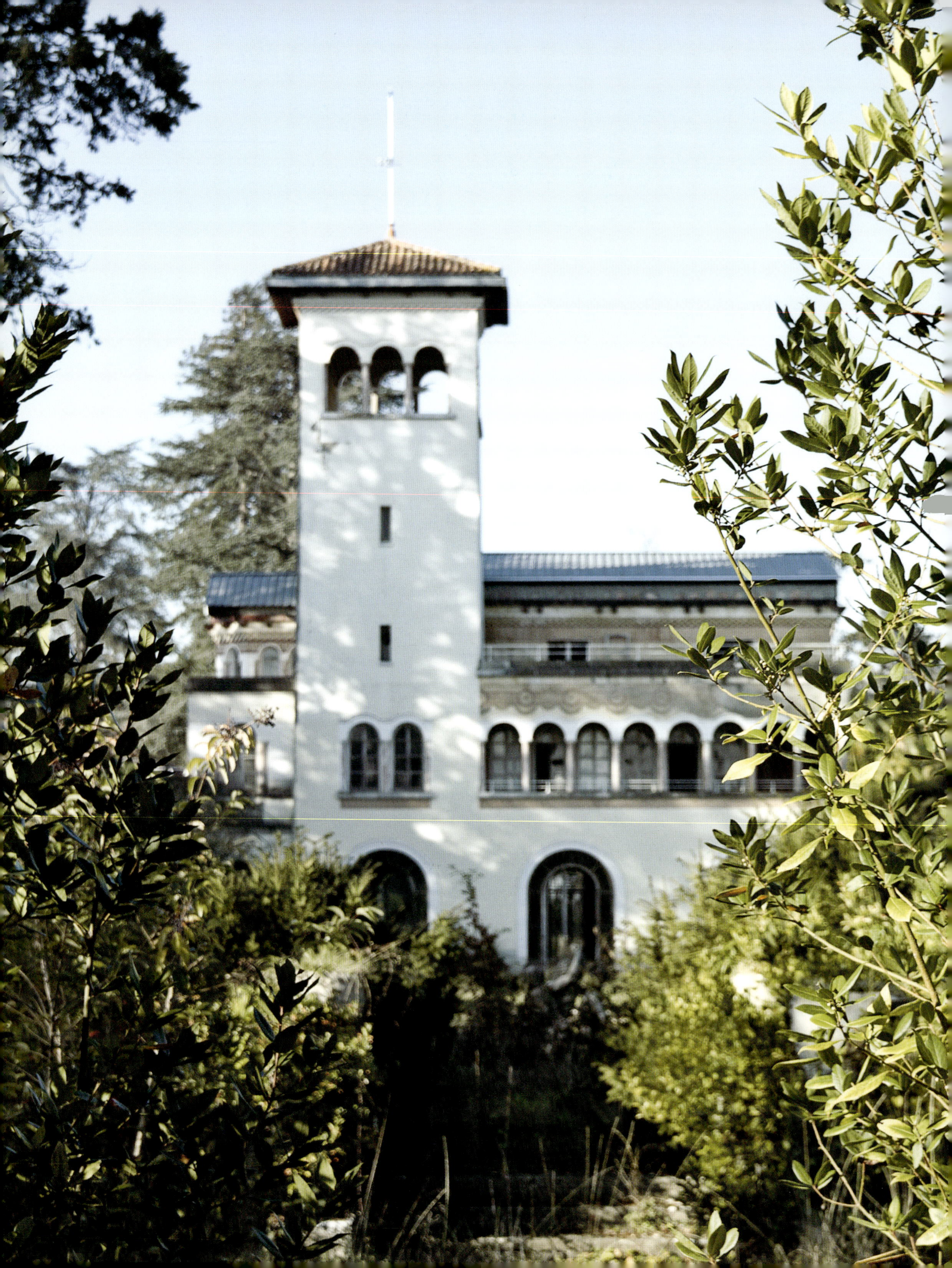

Château Bijou, Labastide-Villefranche

At the outbreak of the French Revolution, Béarn in south-western France was a prosperous traditional province.

The solid bourgeois residence built by a nobleman in the Béarnaise commune of Labastide-Villefranche is evidence of the relative local wealth of the time. This is the house that would become Château Bijou, thanks to the efforts of Charlotte Combe Saint-Macary.

Charlotte was the daughter of Eugène Saint-Macary, a local merchant who came home to France in 1881, having made his fortune over twenty years spent in Chile. She devoted her life to charitable work and finance and became involved in setting up several hospitals, orphanages and associations in the region, as well as in Paris.

She also invested some of her wealth in converting the Labastide-Villefranche home into a country house in a completely different style. From 1913 to 1924, she commissioned the architect Régin to oversee her restoration project. Jules Vacherot, landscape architect-in-chief of the city of Paris, and landscape architect André Riousse were also in her service. The three of them completely revamped the building and the adjoining 17-hectare park.

The main entrance now opened onto a courtyard bordered by vast lawns, closed off to the south-east by a 12th-century Romanesque cloister, which had been reassembled stone by stone. The slope down to a lake was transformed into a Hispano-Moorish garden. A tree-shaded avenue led to the landing stage, raised on columns. The park featured an orangery and carved fountains. It also had greenhouses, a vegetable garden and nurseries. The interior of the chateau is no less spectacular. There are numerous frescoes, marble pillars and even a neo-Gothic chapel.

The owner, who in 1927 was recognised as a *chevalier* of the highest French order of merit, the Légion d'Honneur, for her various activities, remained at Château Bijou during the Second World War. Arrested by the Germans for supporting the Resistance, she was released in 1943 and returned to her home in Béarn. In 1950, she commissioned the chief architect of civic buildings and national palaces, Albert Laprade, to restore the fresh water reservoir in the tower.

After Madame Combe's death, maintenance of the villa became a problem.

In 1971, the estate and its fixtures and fittings were sold to the Ministry of the Interior, which had announced its intention to buy. Château Bijou became a holiday retreat for police officers. In the 1980s, a restaurant and bungalows were built in the park, but the whole place slowly and inexorably deteriorated.

In 1991, the Basque nationalist paramilitary organisation Iparretarrak ("the Northerners") claimed responsibility for an attack aimed at the occupants of the chateau. Then in 2000 the roof was ravaged by fire, perhaps also due to Iparretarrak, and it was patched up with a zinc covering.

The following year, the police mutual insurance company sold Château Bijou to a Dutch landowner, who left it to decay further.

Nevertheless, the entire estate was registered as a historical monument in 2008. The same year, an association was formed to restore the gardens to their former glory. The plan was to organise cultural events and set up a camping site.

In 2009, Basque investor Bruno Vidalenc bought Château Bijou with a restoration project in mind. He consulted JGArchitects practice on the feasibility of opening a hospice for dependent elderly people. By early 2017, however, nothing had changed.

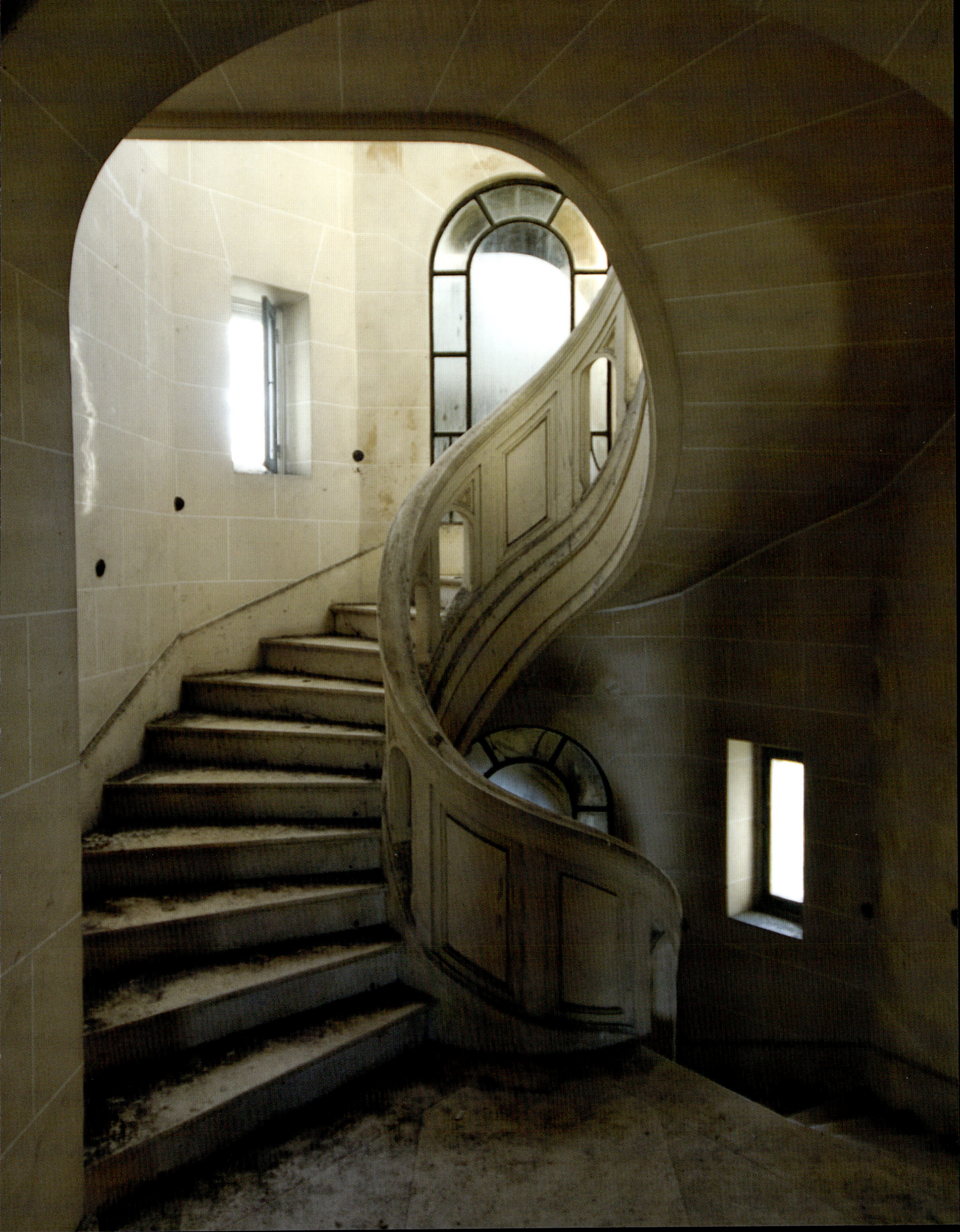

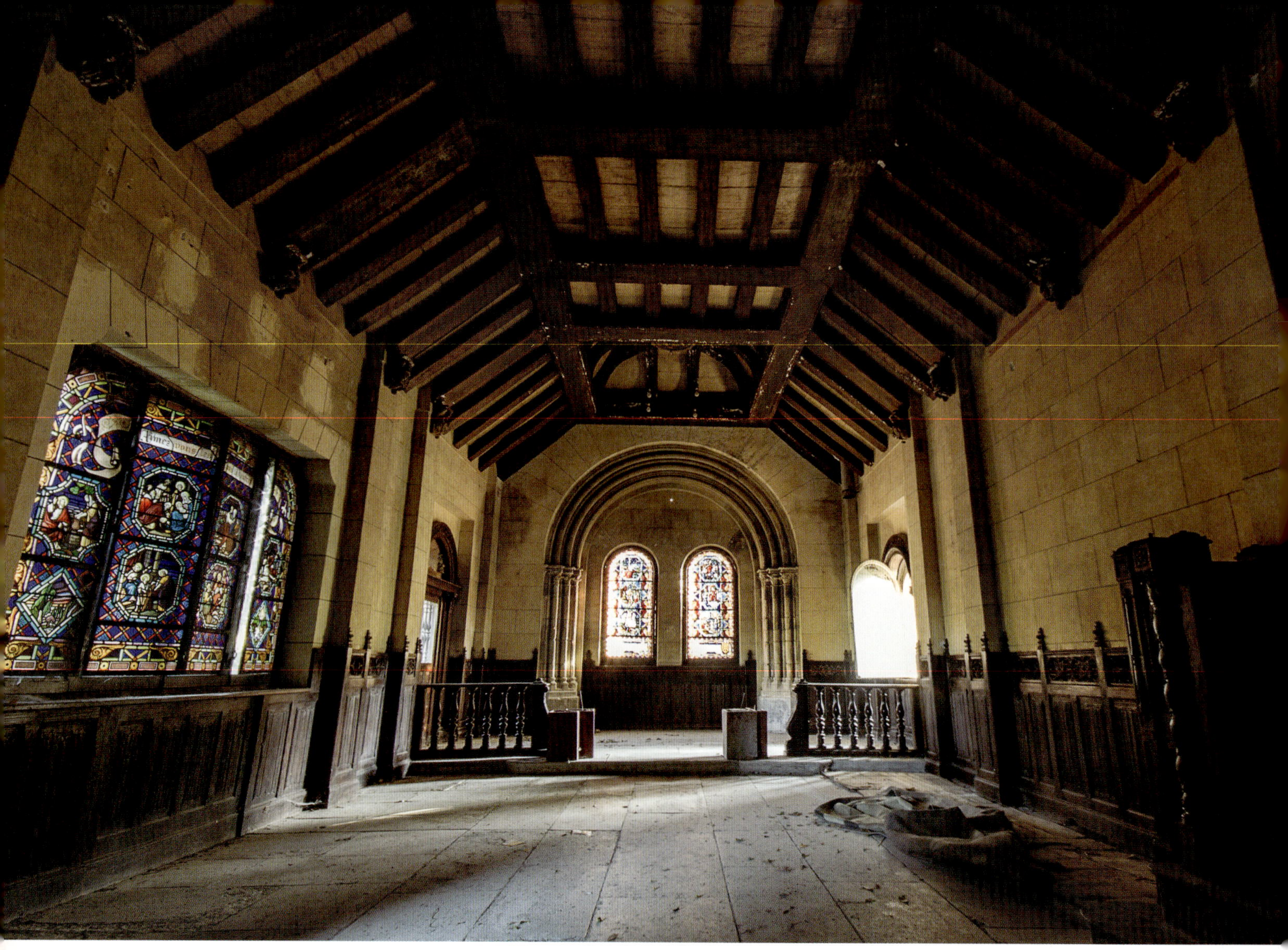

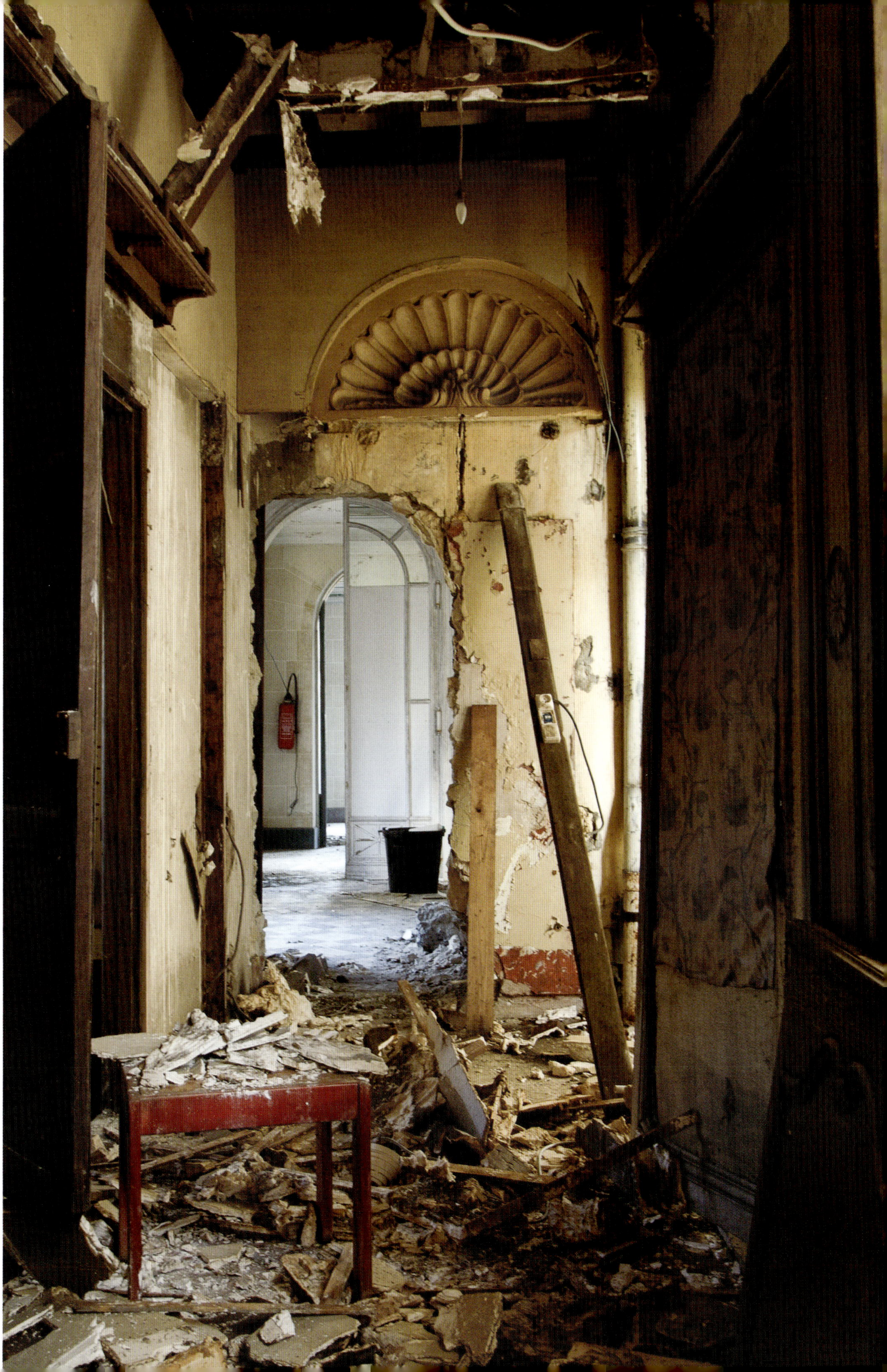

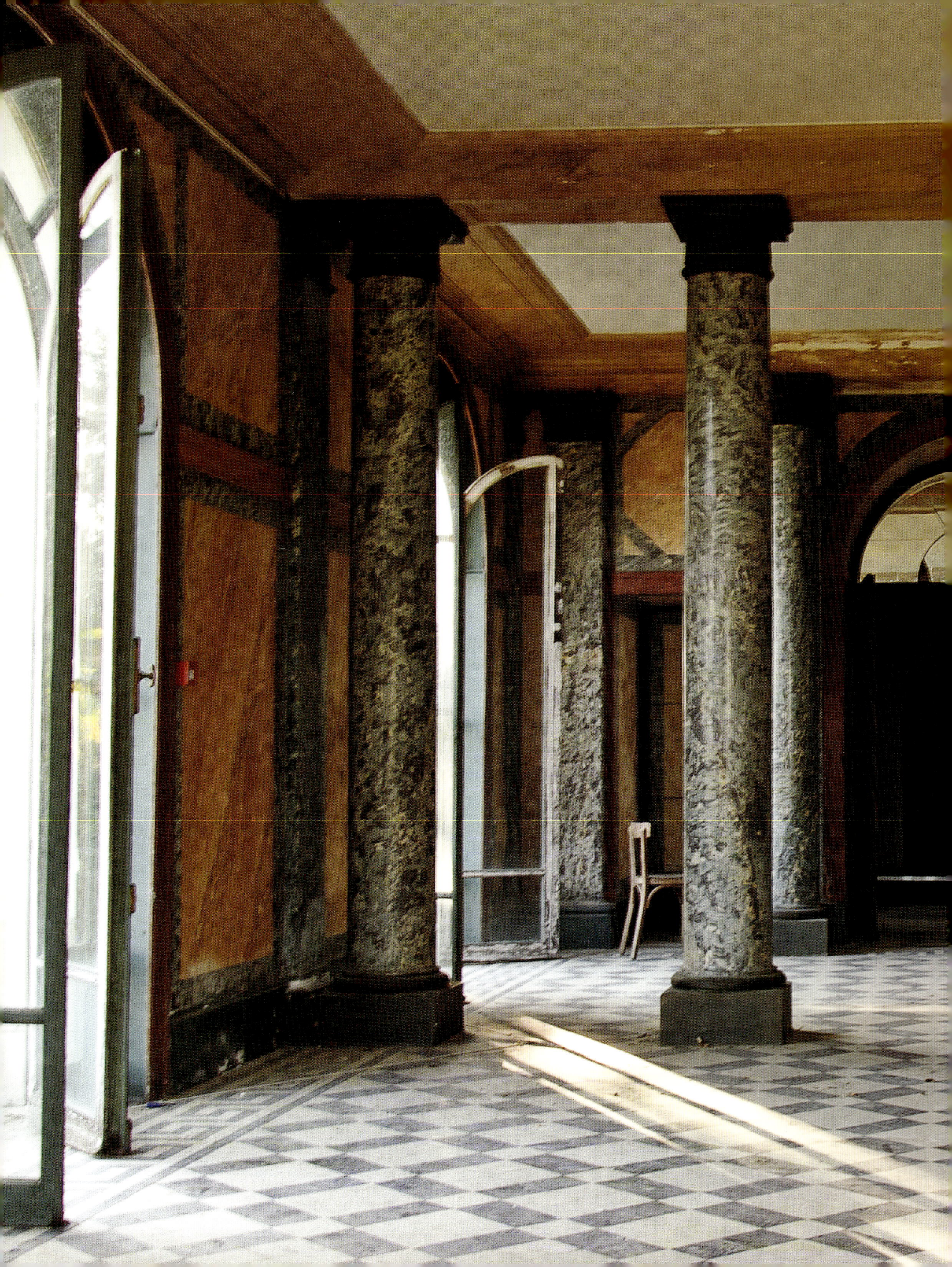

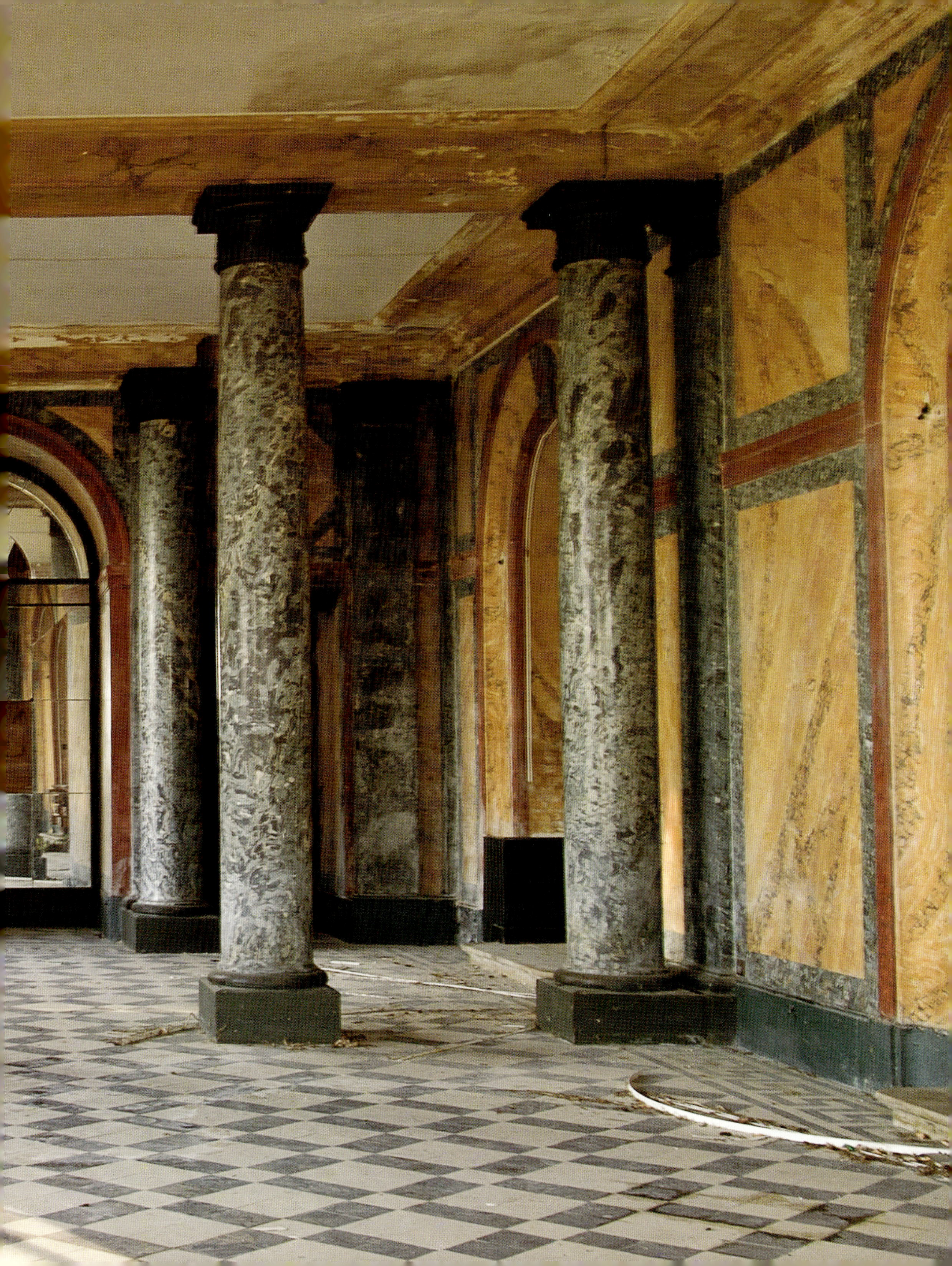

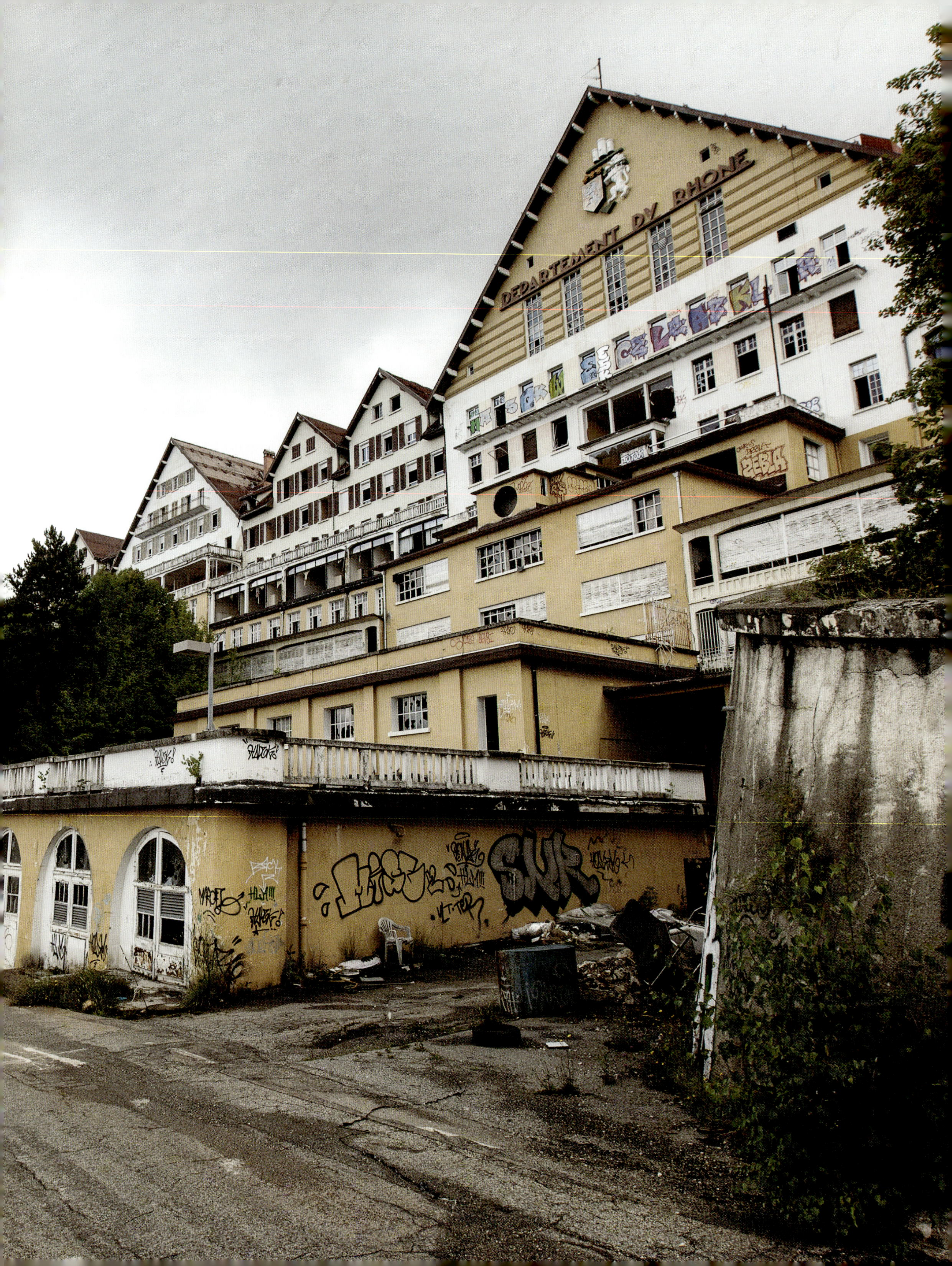
DEPARTEMENT DV RHONE

Three sanatoriums, Saint-Hilaire du Touvet, Isère

The Isère commune of Saint-Hilaire du Touvet, set on a sunlit plateau framed by alpine forest and overlooked by the peak of the Dent de Crolles, has everything it takes to make a remote village the ideal place to build a sanatorium. Eventually there would be three of them.

In 1900, the Société Anonyme des Sanatoriums des Montagnes de la Grande Chartreuse was the first to select this village as a treatment centre for TB patients.

But when that project came to nothing, the local branch of the metalworkers union decided to launch a scheme to help its employees. With union backing, the Association Métallurgique et Minière contre la Tuberculose strove throughout the 1920s to build a 300-bed sanatorium, equipped with the most up-to-date facilities. But first a route had to be opened up to a site without electricity or water supplies. To achieve this, the association launched a successful appeal to the union fund, Caisse Syndicale d'Assurance Mutuelles des Forges de France, to build a funicular railway on the mountainside in order to transport materials to the construction site.

The minister of labour, health and welfare declared the new Sanatorium de Rocheplane open in 1929. The eight-storey building was designed by architect Robert-Alexandre Fournez. Two wings arranged in tiers flank a gable-roofed main section.

Four years later, the Sanatorium des Petites Roches, managed by Rhône regional council, opened with a capacity of around 650 beds. It was the largest of its kind in France at the time.

Petites Roches, also designed by Fournez, is built around two symmetrical pavilions of eleven storeys with gabled roofs. One for men, the other for women. A higher central building was subsequently added.

In addition to the general services, a second flurry of work begun in 1937 adding an operating block serving the three buildings, plus a chapel. Subterranean galleries were excavated where patients could take a cure. These single-sex facilities were originally intended for the local population but later took patients from all over France.

Two years after Petites Roches, the Sanatorium des Étudiants de France was opened to the south of the other two facilities. Funded by the Fondation Santé des Étudiants de France, it had 150 beds reserved for students who had contracted tuberculosis. Its U-shaped design recalls the first types of sanatorium. In his plans, the architect Antoine Gavet included facilities to allow the patients to continue their studies. The assignment of teachers, organisation of conferences and the well-equipped auditorium are evidence of a rich and varied cultural life. Further extension work increased the capacity to 250 beds.

Despite their imposing size – the site covers 70,000 square metres – these three buildings embrace the Alpine landscape and integrate relatively well with the mountainous backdrop.

The local population also gave the development a positive reception. The admittance of a thousand or so patients to these sanatoriums gave an unexpected boost to the economic, industrial and demographic development of a depopulating region.

In addition, the association set up and ran the services required by a sanatorium, which employed many local people.

The years 1960–1970 marked a turning point in the treatment of tuberculosis.

Antibiotics had proved their worth and the isolation of tuberculosis patients was no longer necessary.

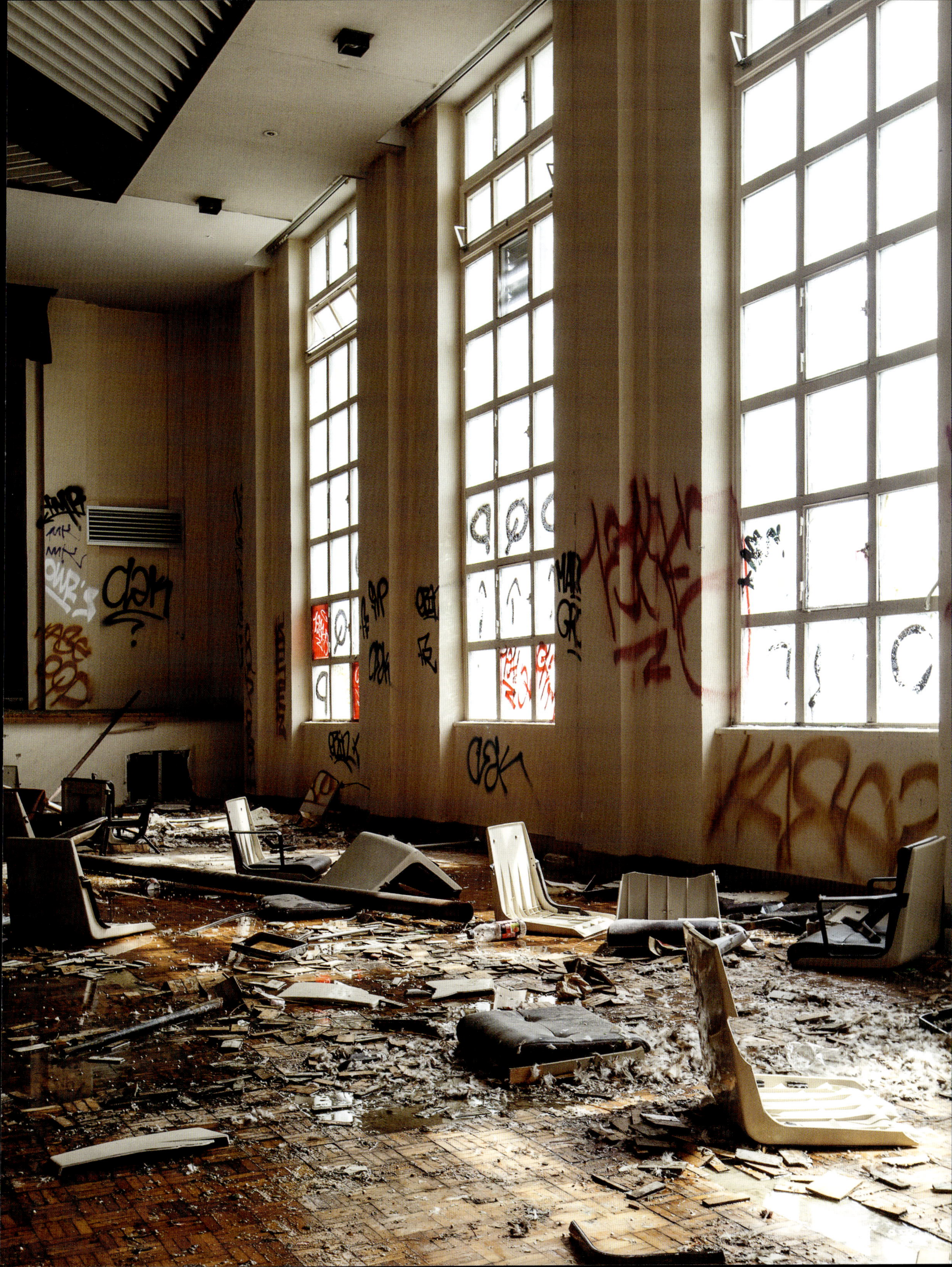

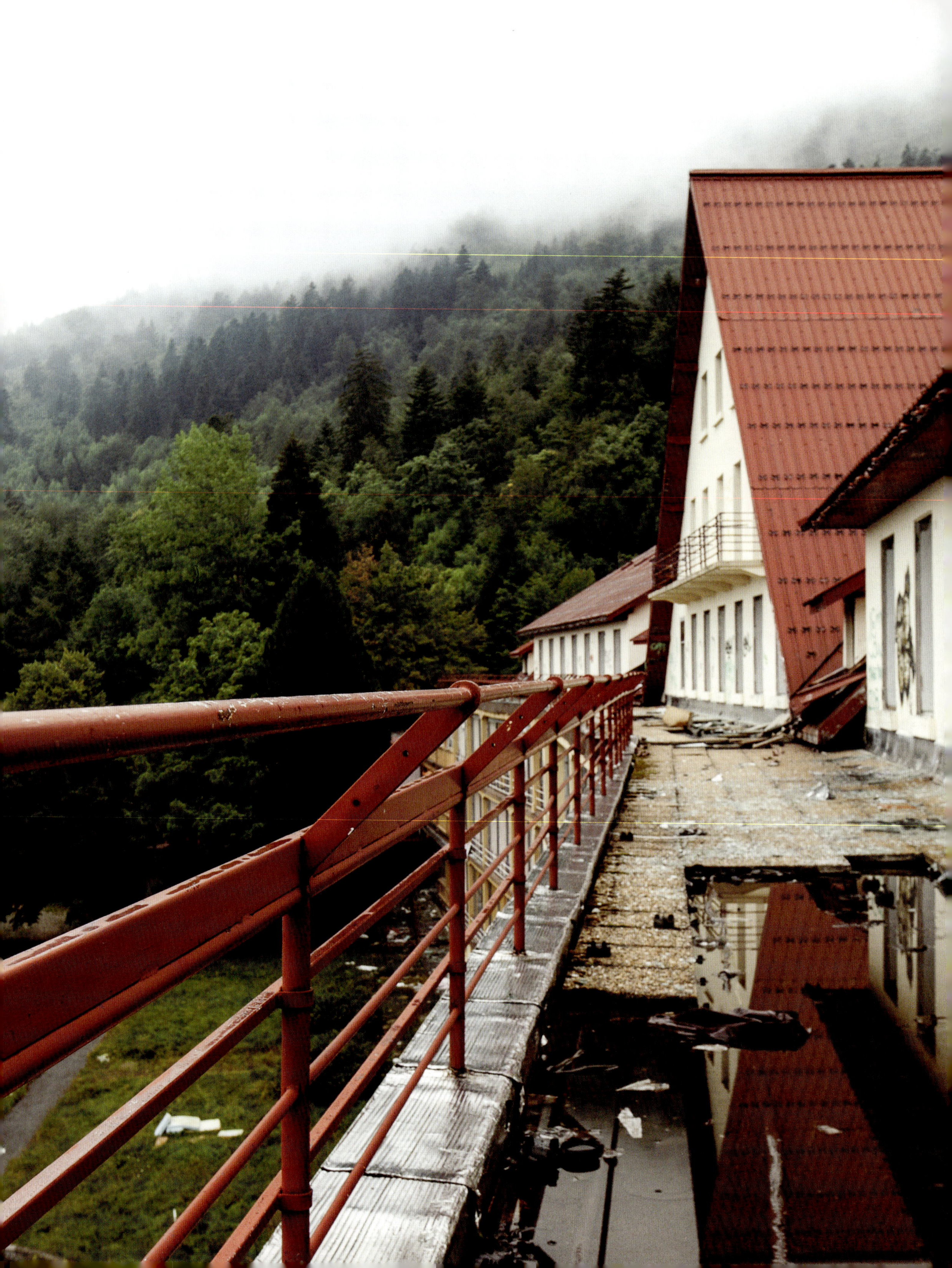

These three facilities then had to adapt to new specialities.

The sanatorium belonging to the Association Métallurgique et Minière became the Centre Médico-Chirurgical Rocheplane and offered follow-up care and rehabilitation services. The public sanatorium converted to the Petites Roches medical and surgical centre was to be used for orthopaedics. The Étudiants de France building, for its part, admitted seriously ill or disabled students and gave them the opportunity to study while recuperating. In 1983, as a tribute to one of the doctors who had died a year earlier, the students' building was renamed Centre Médico-Universitaire Daniel Douady.

Despite these reconversions, the constant modernisation of the facilities and the increased pooling of services, their remoteness from major urban centres called their viability into question. A series of avalanches damaged the buildings during the 1970s and 80s and placed them in the red zone (no planning permission permitted) of the local Risk Prevention Plan. Because of the very high cost of securing the site, the work of the sanatoriums was gradually transferred to the valley in the first decade of the 21st century. The centres that had lost their patients were left to the mercy of vandals, who soon ransacked them.

The three properties, redeemed by the state in 2014 for a symbolic euro, are scheduled to be demolished. An environmental authority notice of July 2016 foresees the complete demolition of the buildings after cleanup. The site will then be returned to its natural state with softwood, hardwood and grassland plantations in harmony with the contours of the valley.

The overall estimated cleanup cost of 17 million euros may explain why, in early 2017, the empty shells of the three sanatoriums were still standing.

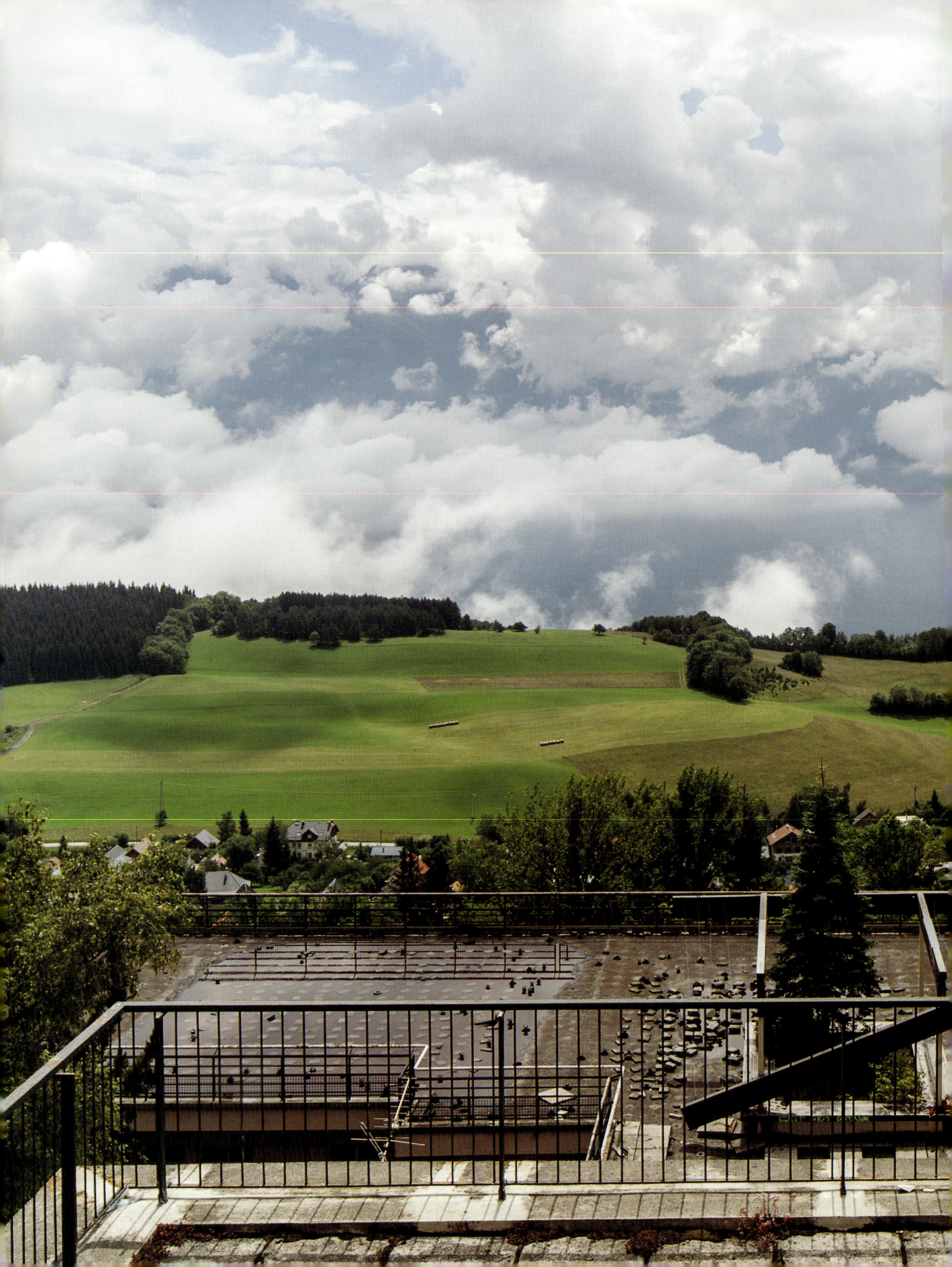

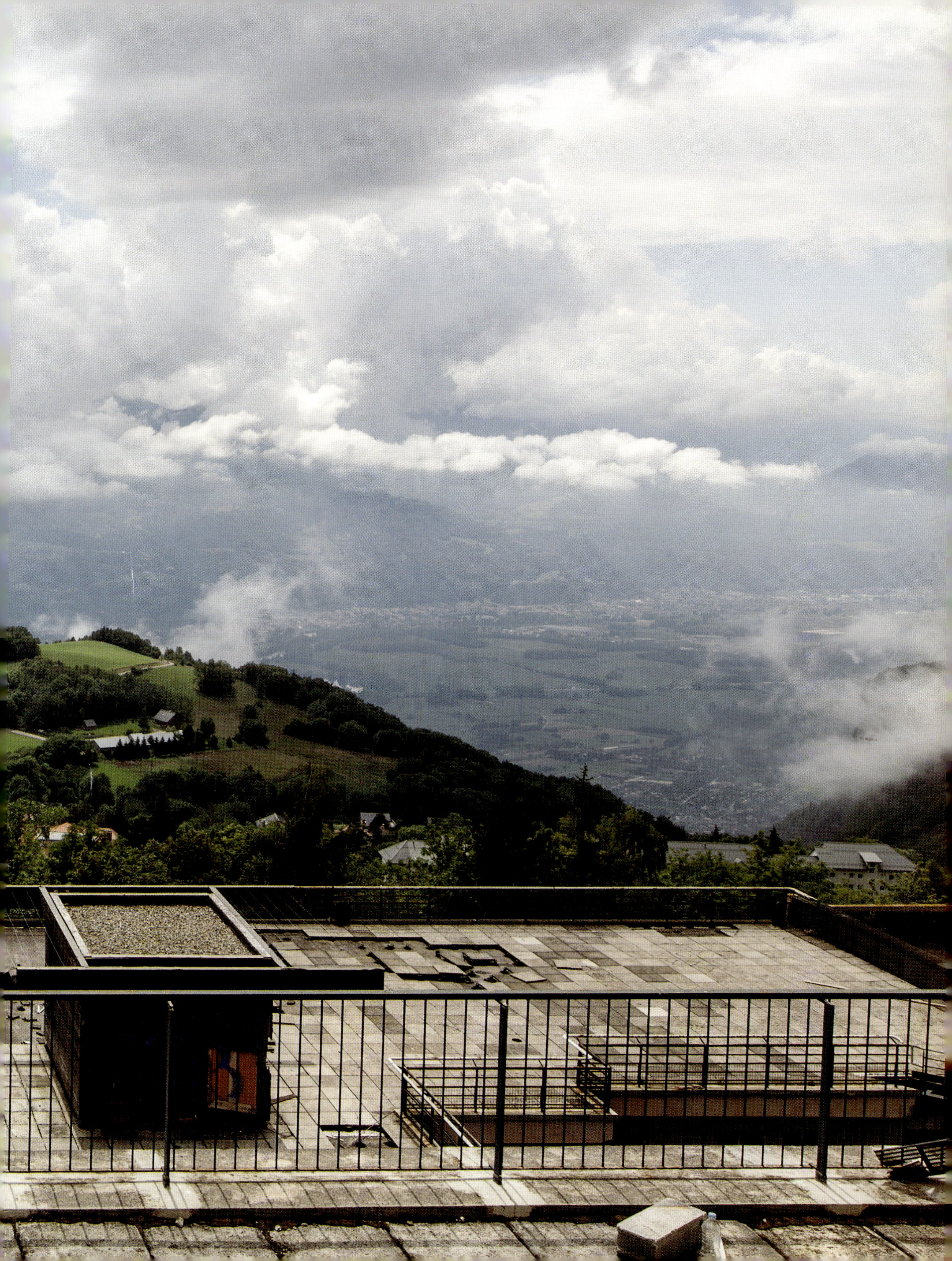

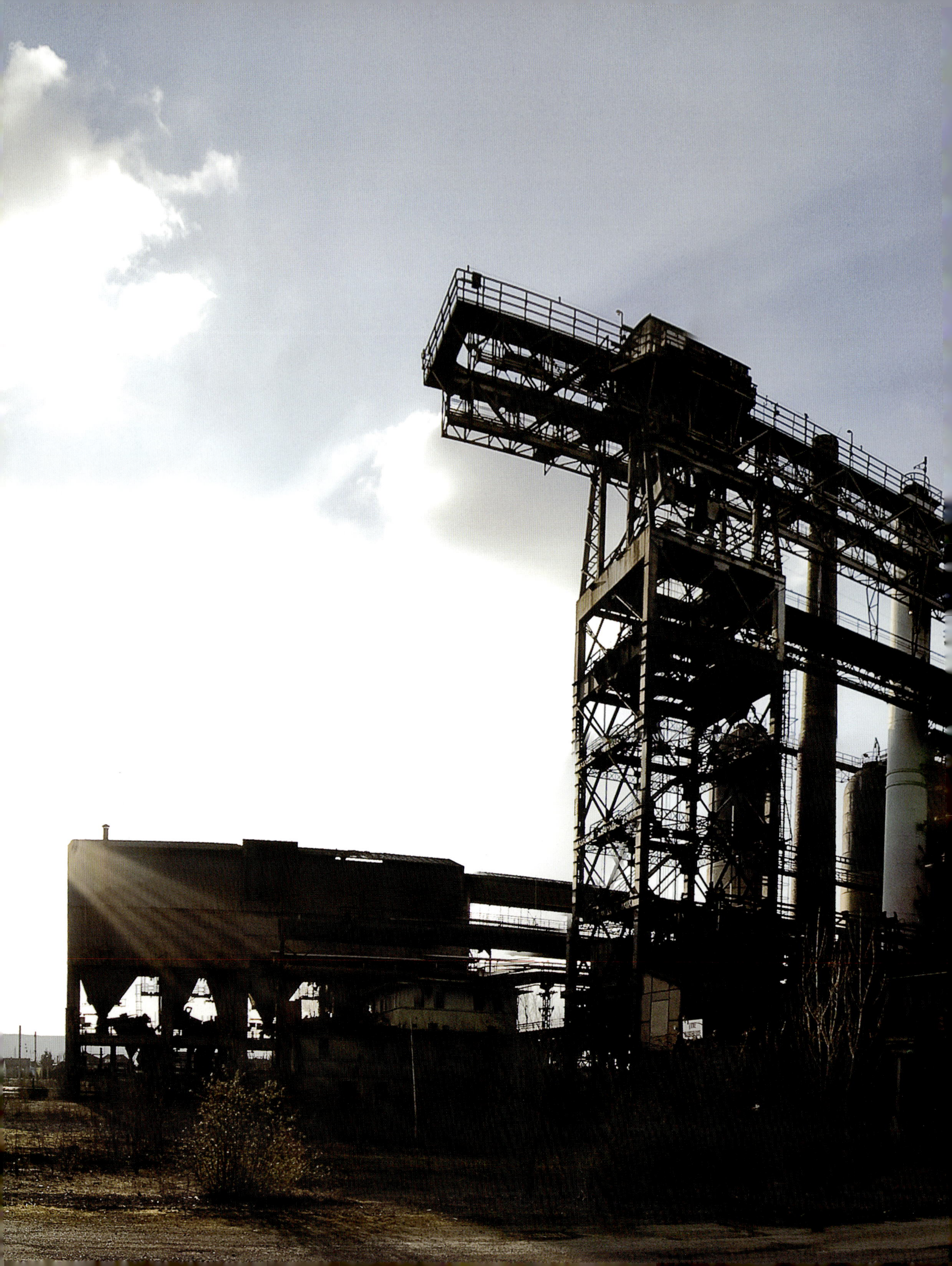

Uckange blast furnaces, Moselle

Until its decline in the 1980s, the Lorraine steel industry remained in the hands of large families who passed on their heritage from generation to generation.

The Wendel dynasty is one of the best-known examples. Its German equivalent may be the Stumm family, owners of the Saar blast furnaces. In 1878, the Stumm brothers opened a cast-iron factory at Uckange in the Moselle department of north-eastern France, which was annexed by the German Empire at the time.

Over the twenty-seven years until 1905, the Stumms built a line of six blast furnaces numbered I to VI. The furnaces fed the adjoining plant with minette, iron ore from the Lorraine subsoil. The site covers a strip of land some 2 kilometres long by 300 metres wide.

After the German defeat of 1918, the site was sequestered by the French state before being taken over by the Société des Forges et Aciéries de Nord et de Lorraine. As the blast furnaces were repaired, they were first renumbered A to F and subsequently given the letter U and a number from 1 to 6.

During the 1930s, U3 and U4 were completely redesigned with a so-called mantle – a circular iron beam supporting the upper part of the furnace in such a way that the brickwork could easily be replaced. U5 and U6 were dismantled.

From then on, the general appearance of the site did not change.

It produced cast iron for moulding, which had multiple applications and was initially intended for the Saar industries, which Uckange turned away from during the Second World War.

From the end of the war until the 1970s, the blast furnaces were repeatedly modernised as foundry techniques advanced.

In 1965, the Société des Forges et Aciéries de Nord et de Lorraine joined forces with the factory in the commune of Saulnes to found the Société Hauts-Fourneaux Réunis de Saulnes et Uckange.

Around this time the company took advantage of its proximity to the Moselle to ship in better-quality minerals from abroad. In 1976, U4 underwent a major renovation as the iron and steel crisis severely affected the Lorraine basin. The furnace was not fired up again until 1989, and then only for two years.

Meanwhile, the decline of the industry led to the closure of a number of sites.

Despite its acquisition by the French steel-making group USINOR and a final redevelopment programme, the plant was shut down once and for all on 17 December 1991, then abandoned.

At the same time, some former employees and local historians set up the MECILOR association, with the aim of preserving their regional industrial heritage.

Ten years later, blast furnace U4, the only survivor of Uckange, was registered as a historical monument.

Following protracted negotiations, the Val de Fensch association of local authorities, supported by the Ministry of Culture, acquired U4 and opened a tourist and arts venue in 2007, enlivened by the light show of visual artist Claude Lévêque.

The venue formed part of the Jardin des Traces, "Gardens with Memories", to upgrade the brownfield site of the former plant.

The 12-hectare site should be completely revamped by 2020 through "Evolu'4", a 20-million-euro project with an ambitious mix of housing, green spaces, cultural venues and commercial zones.

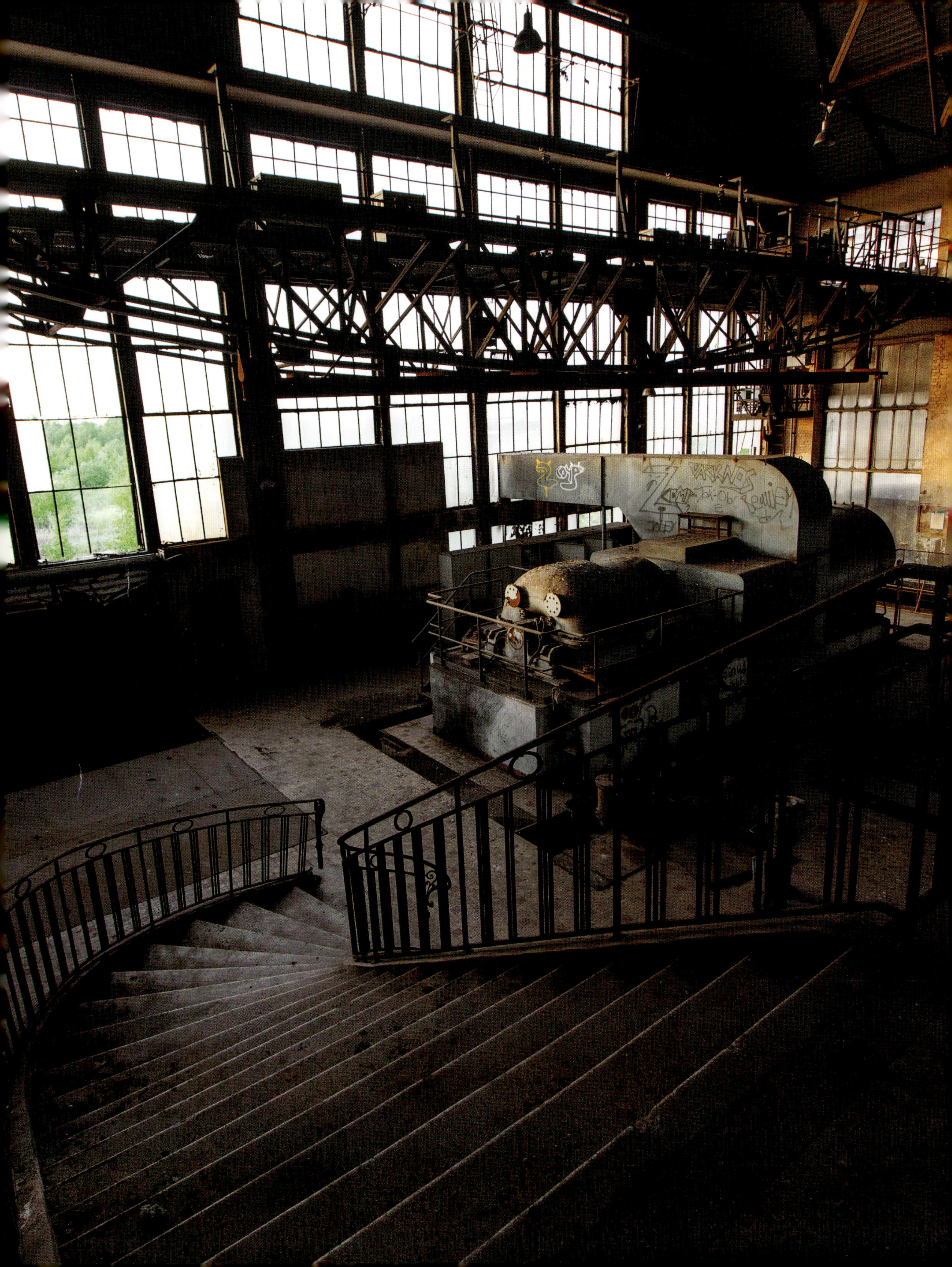

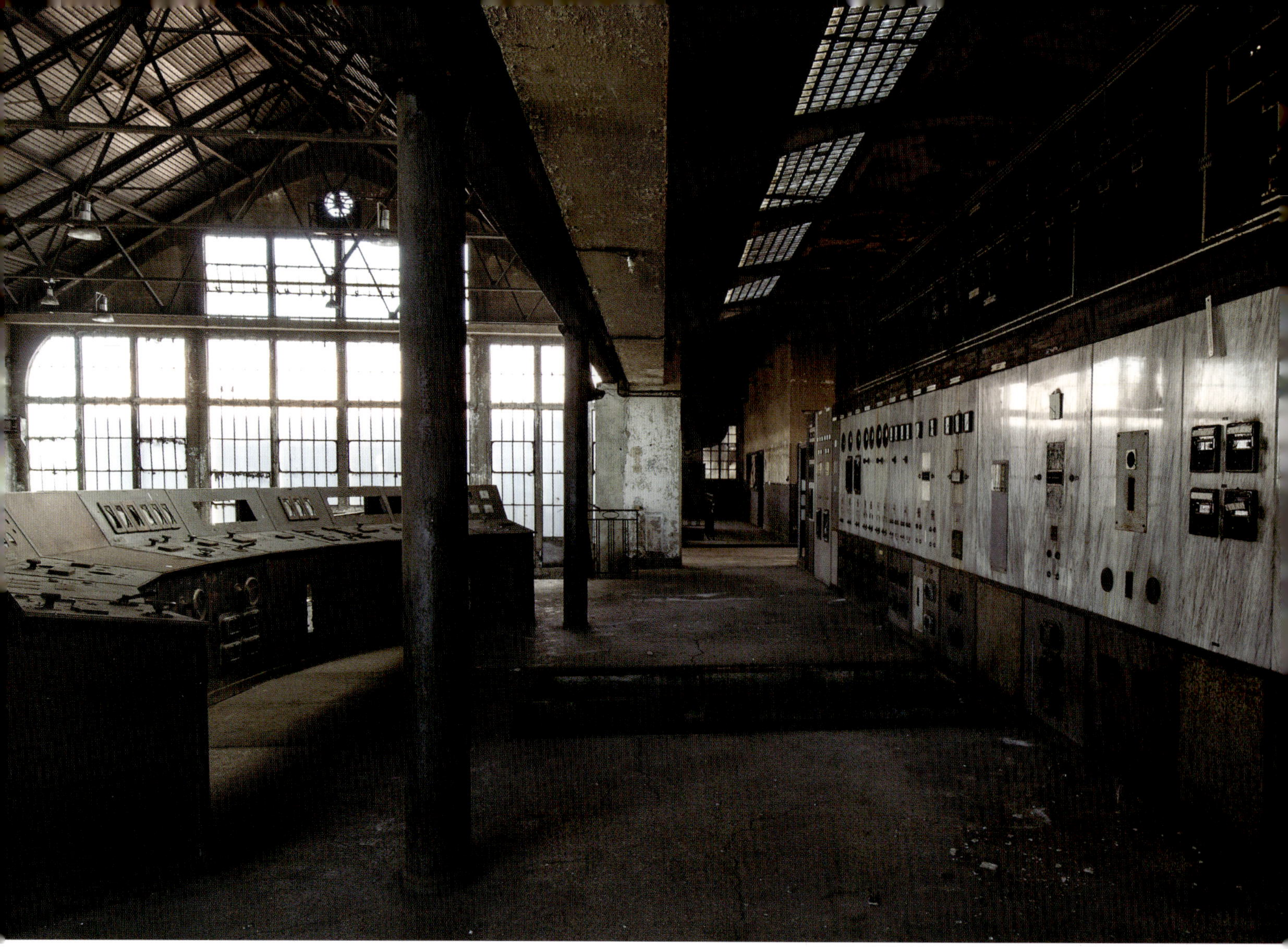

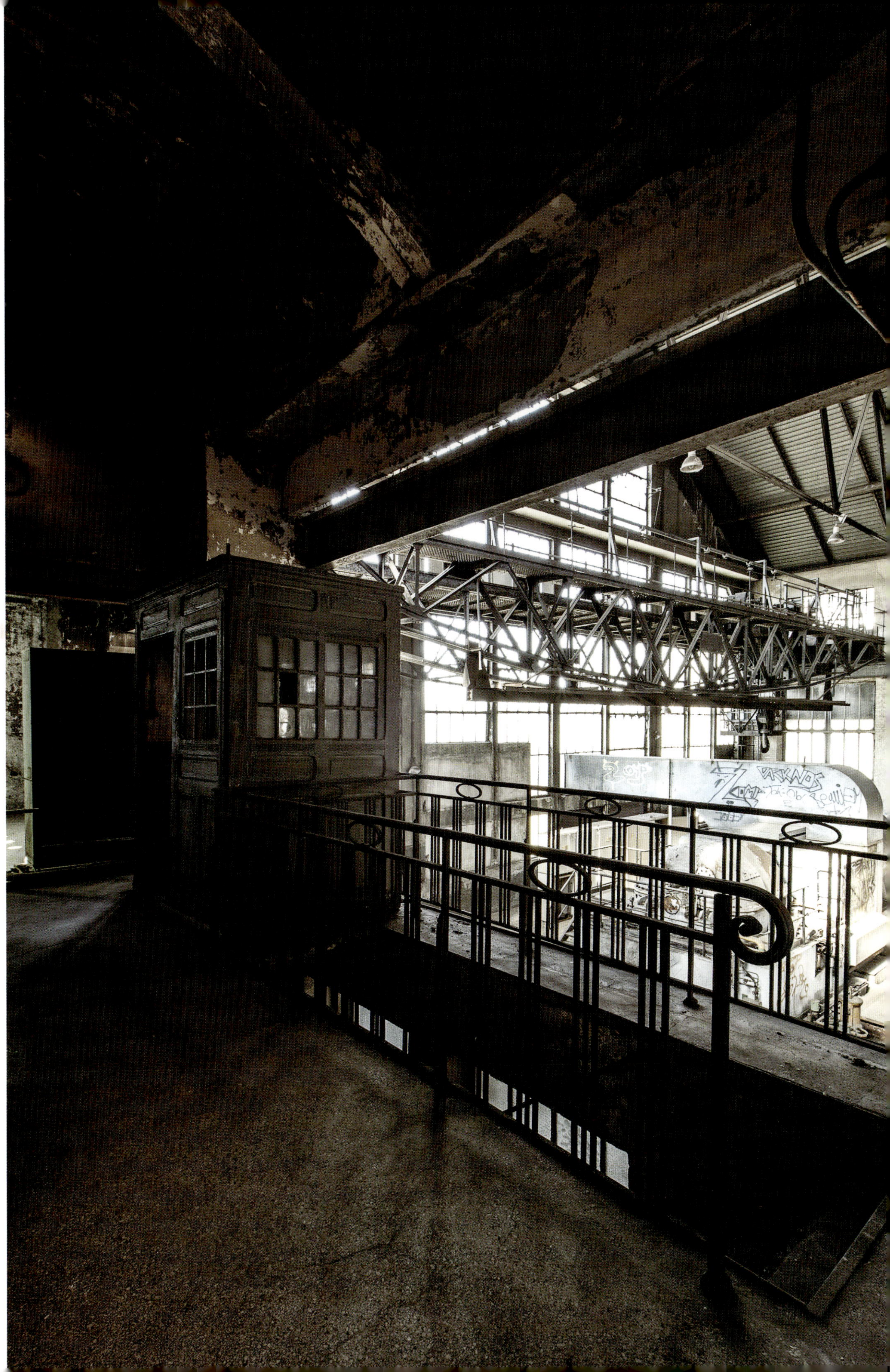

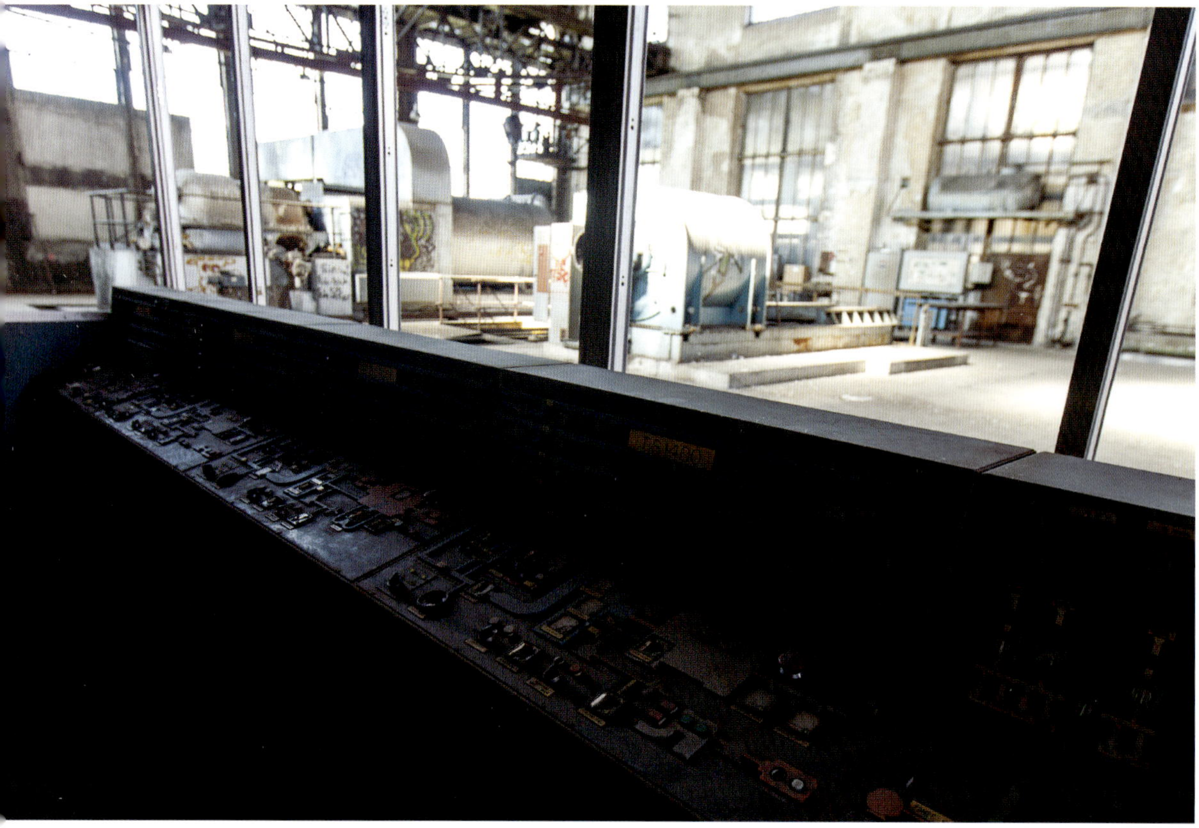

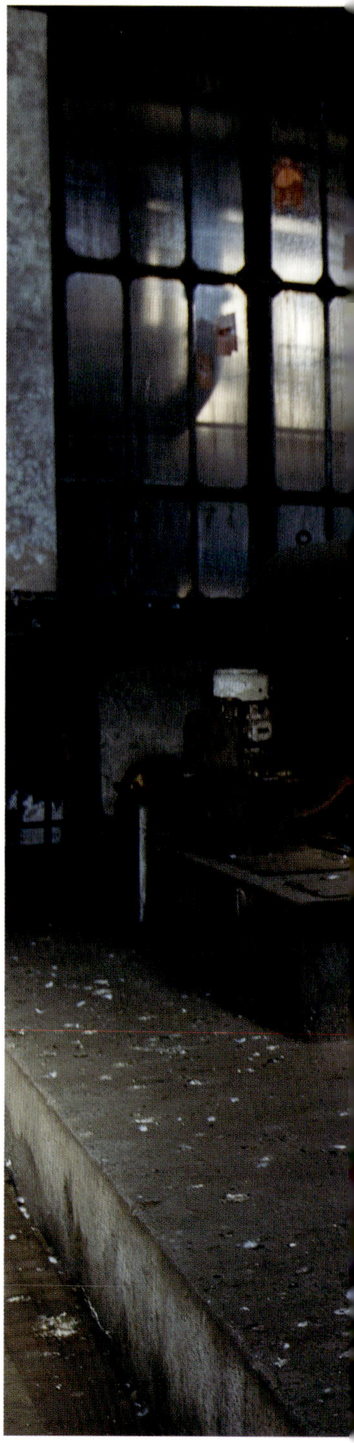

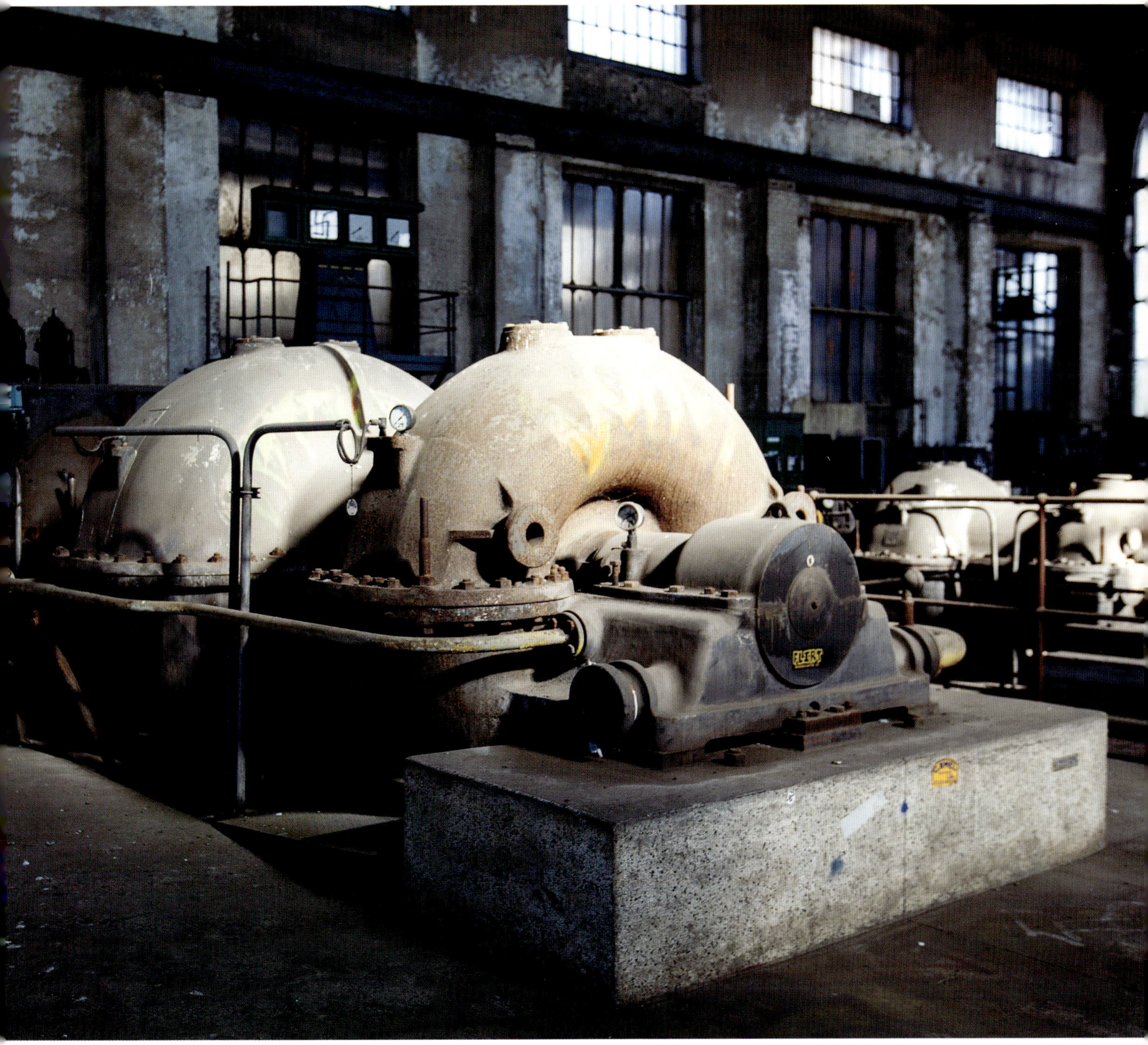

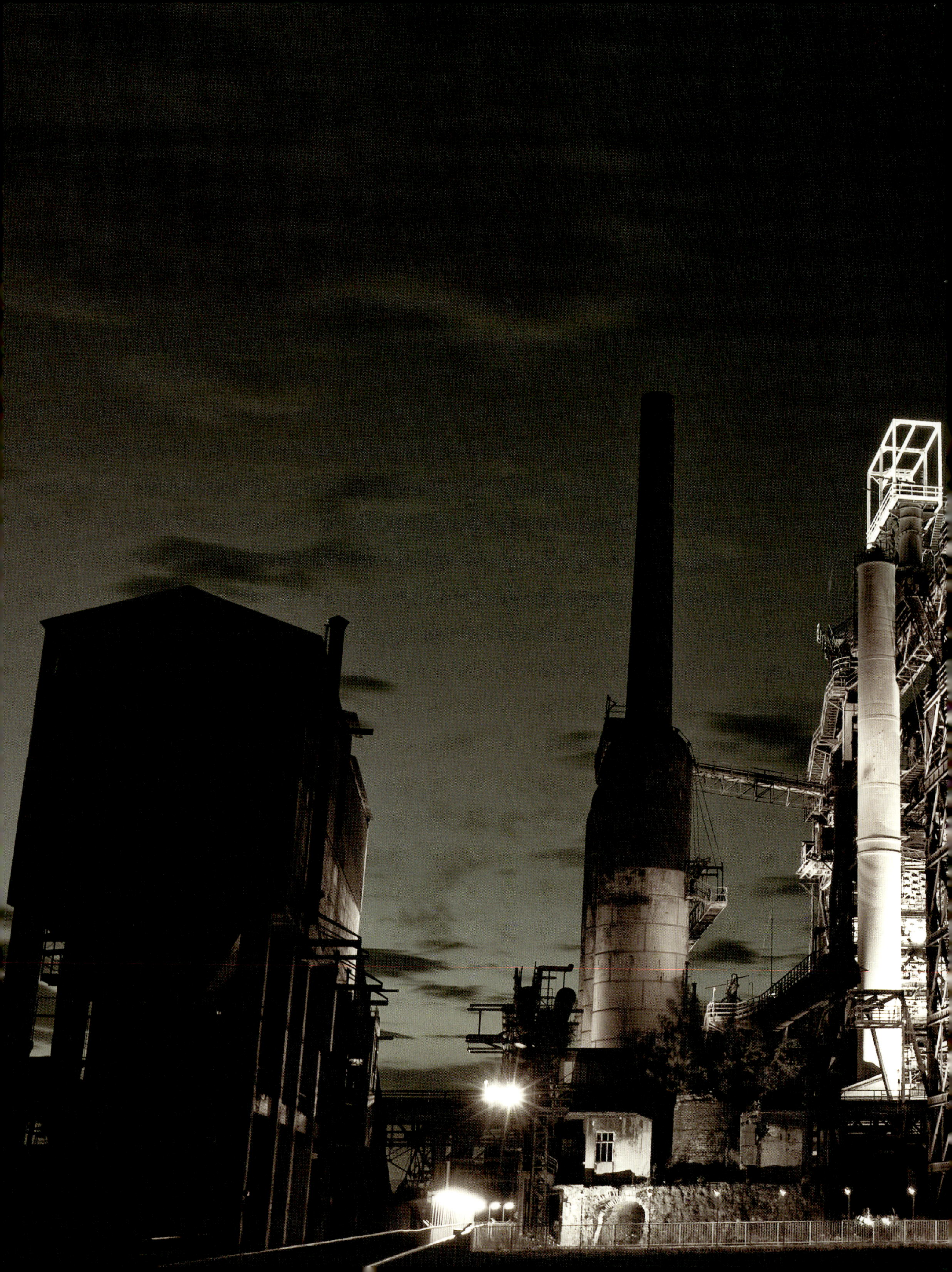

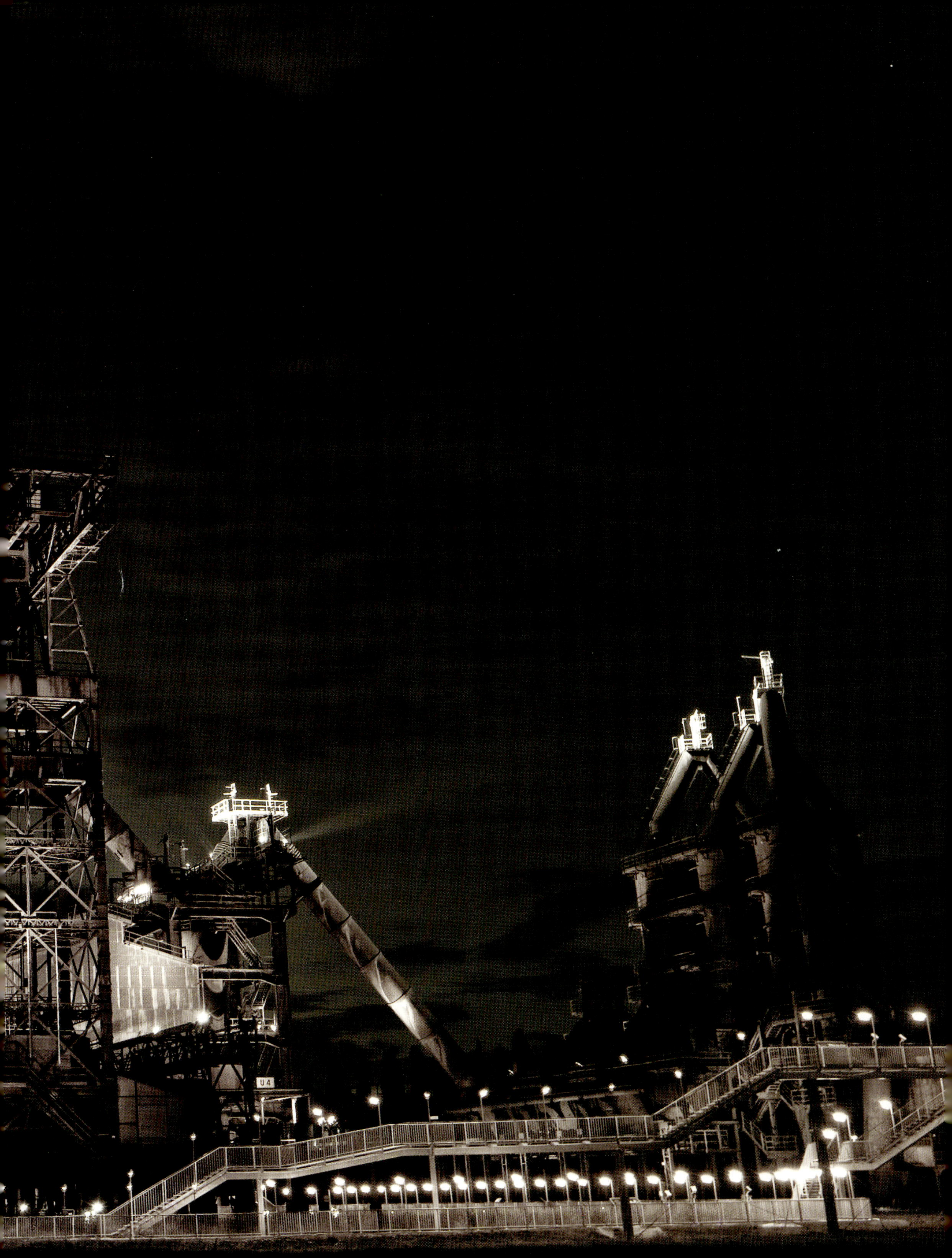
U4

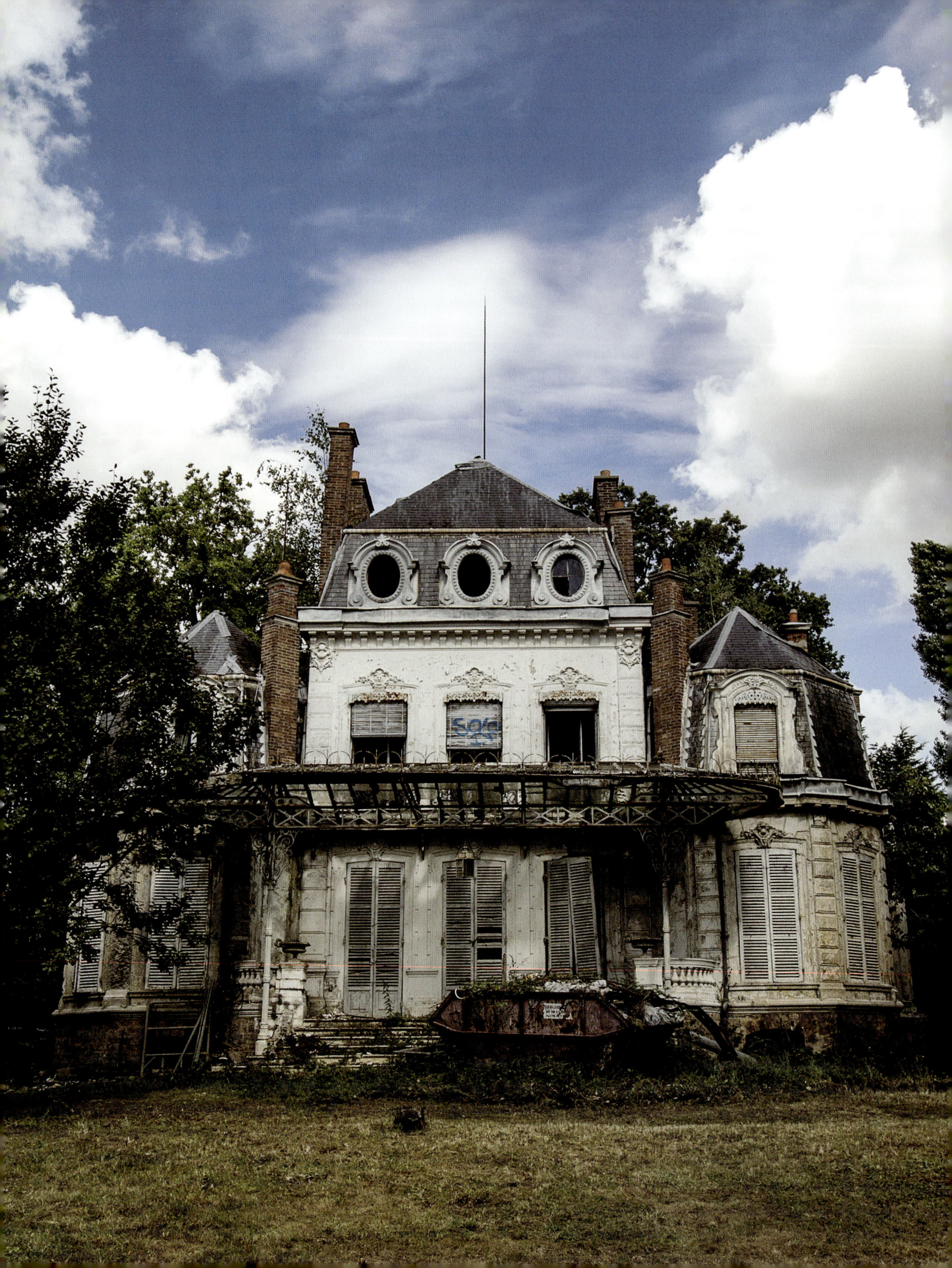

Château Verdure, Seine-et-Marne

There are still municipalities on the outskirts of Paris where green, wooded or agricultural sites prevail over urban areas. Such is the case of this small community in Seine-et-Marne, whose history seems to have evolved over the centuries in line with the rest of the country.

In the 1850s, when urbanisation was encroaching on Île-de-France, this district followed the trend. Its private forest was split up, and the owner offered it for sale as building plots, giving rise to a new type of development.

A prominent citizen bought one of these plots in 1863, and built a Louis XV-style mansion. High railings conceal the property from the outside world. Surrounded by a wooded garden, the façade is topped with a glass and steel canopy. Inset stained-glass windows illuminate the entrance.

A staircase with wrought-iron balusters leads upstairs; the ceilings and walls are ornamented with stuccowork.

Despite the promise of prosperity, the district finally saw little development due to the lack of good transport links with Paris.

Château Verdure was sold 20 years later to a rich Parisian merchant, who used it as a summer residence.

There is little reliable information on the fate of the mansion. The latest dates back to the 1950s, when another owner renovated the roof.

What then? Lack of funds for upkeep? Inheritance disputes?

There are several explanations for the current dilapidated state of Château Verdure. Its suburban neighbours have tried to protect it, with varying degrees of success.

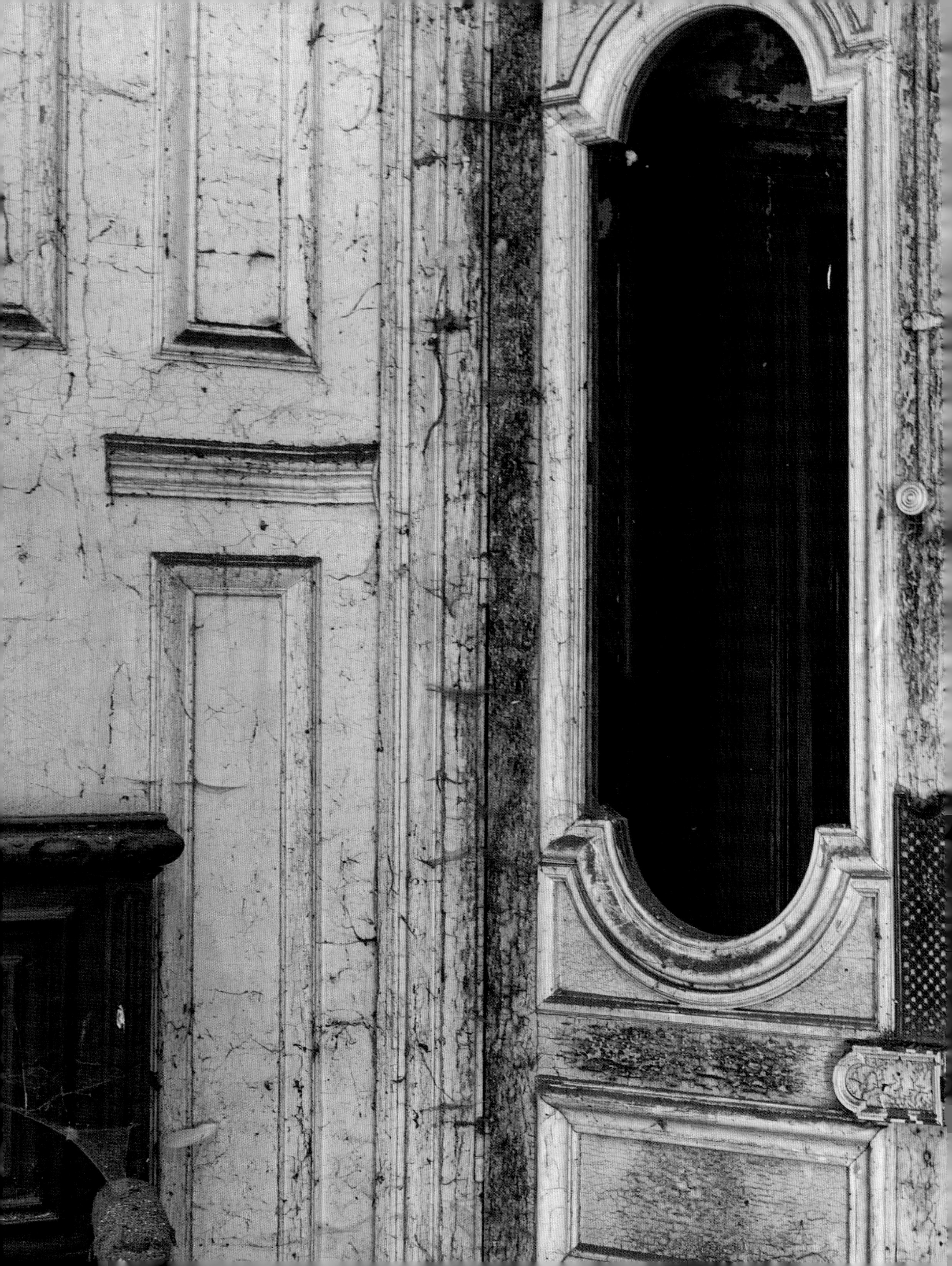

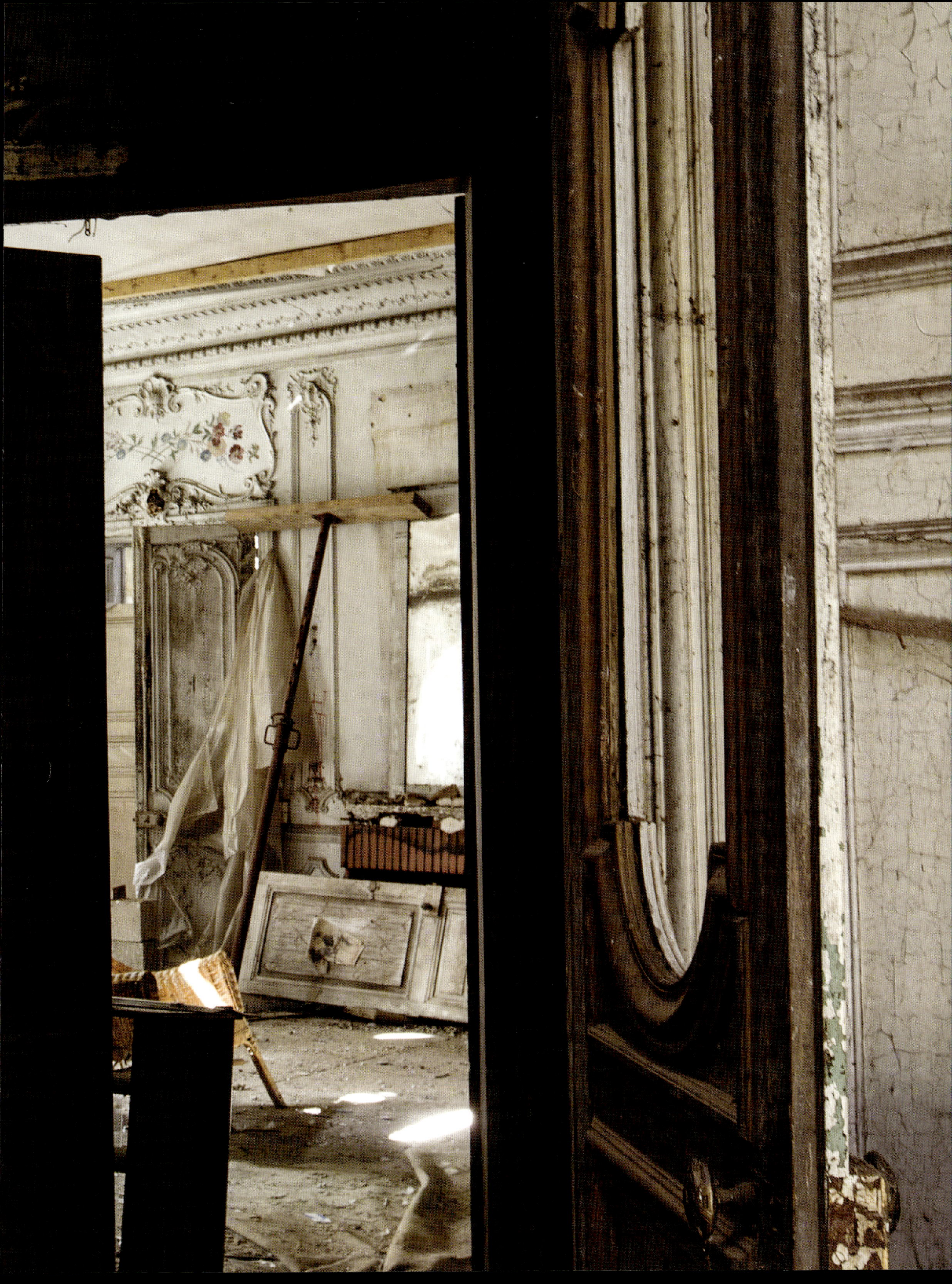

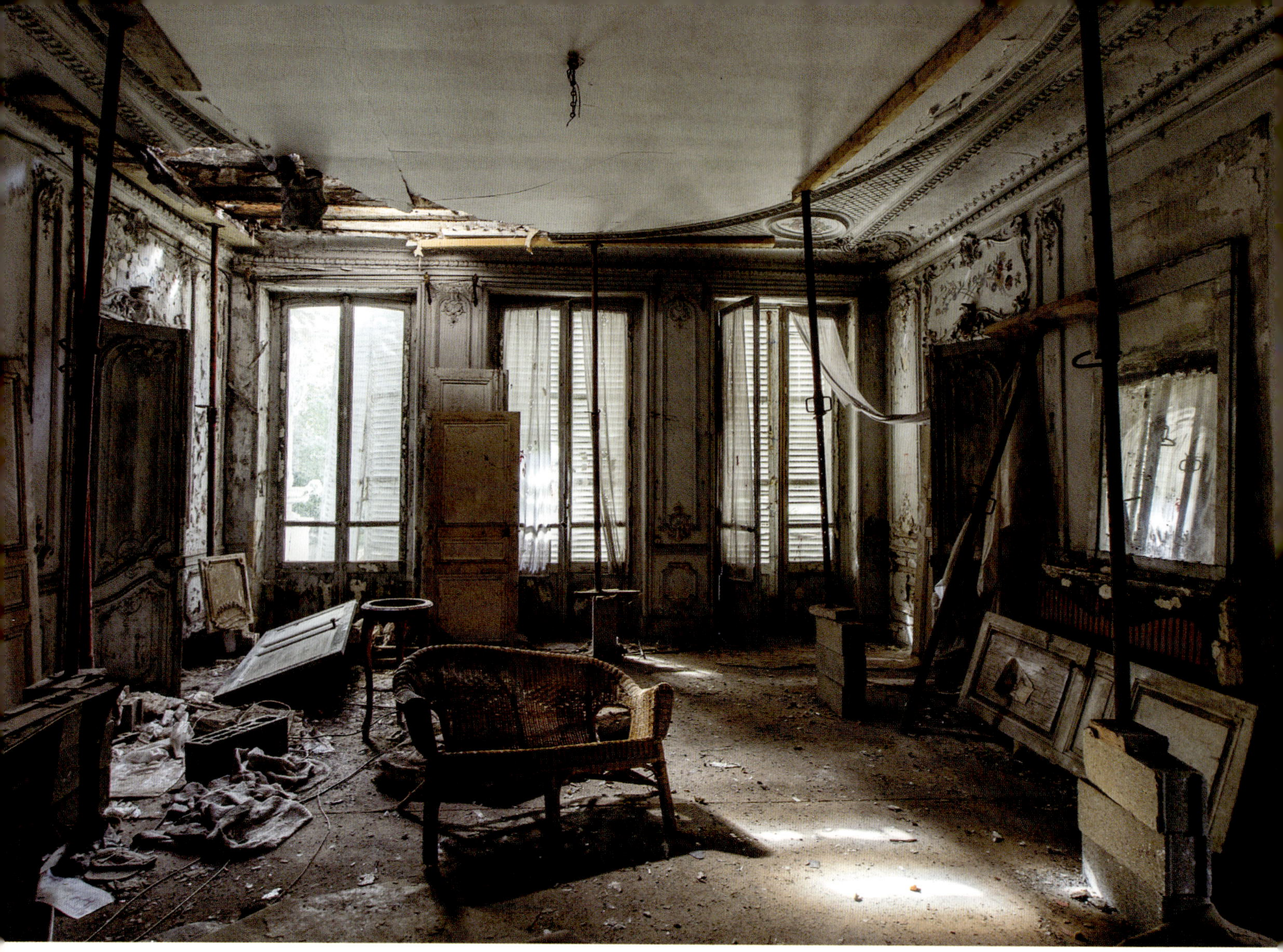

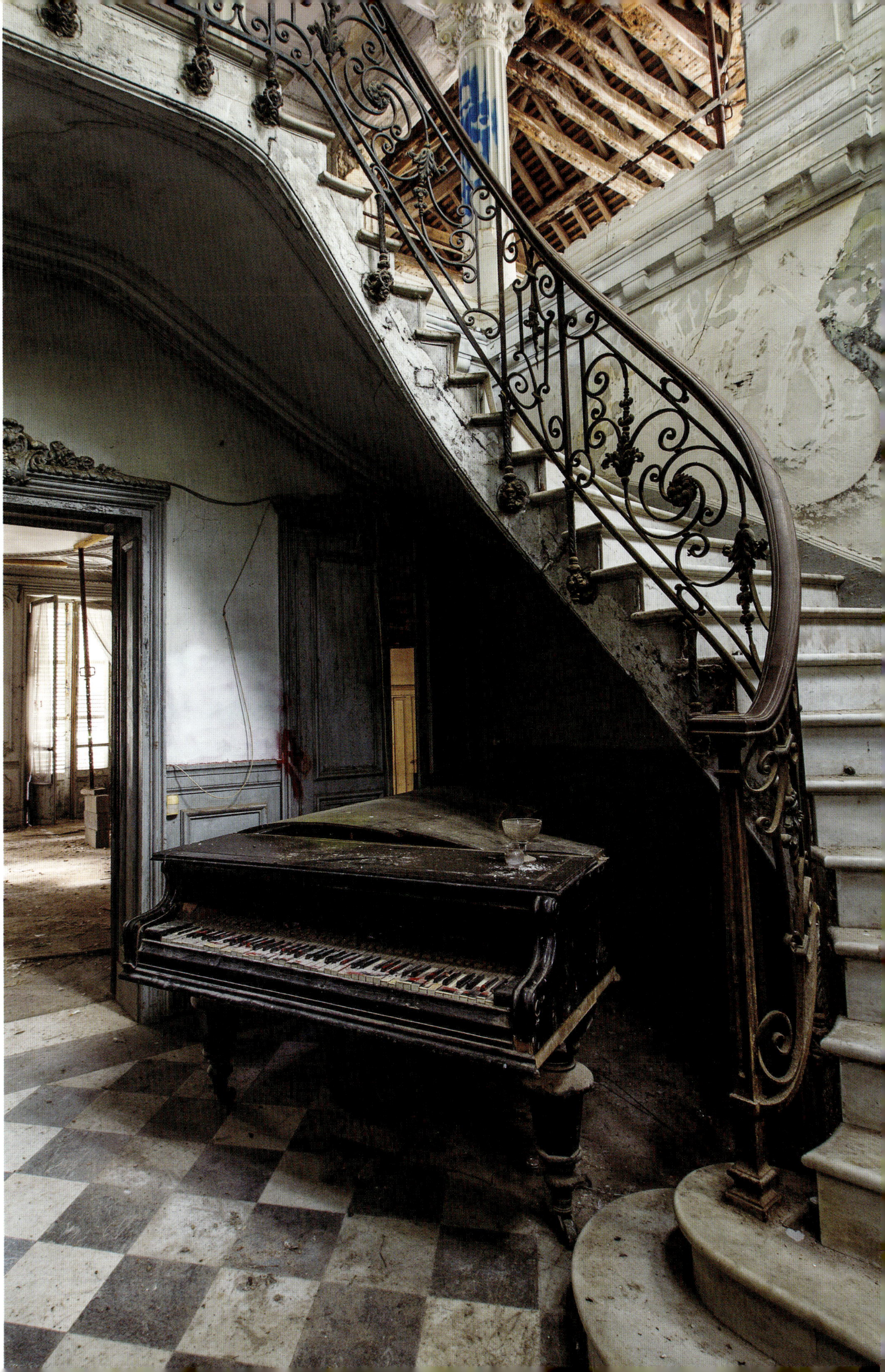

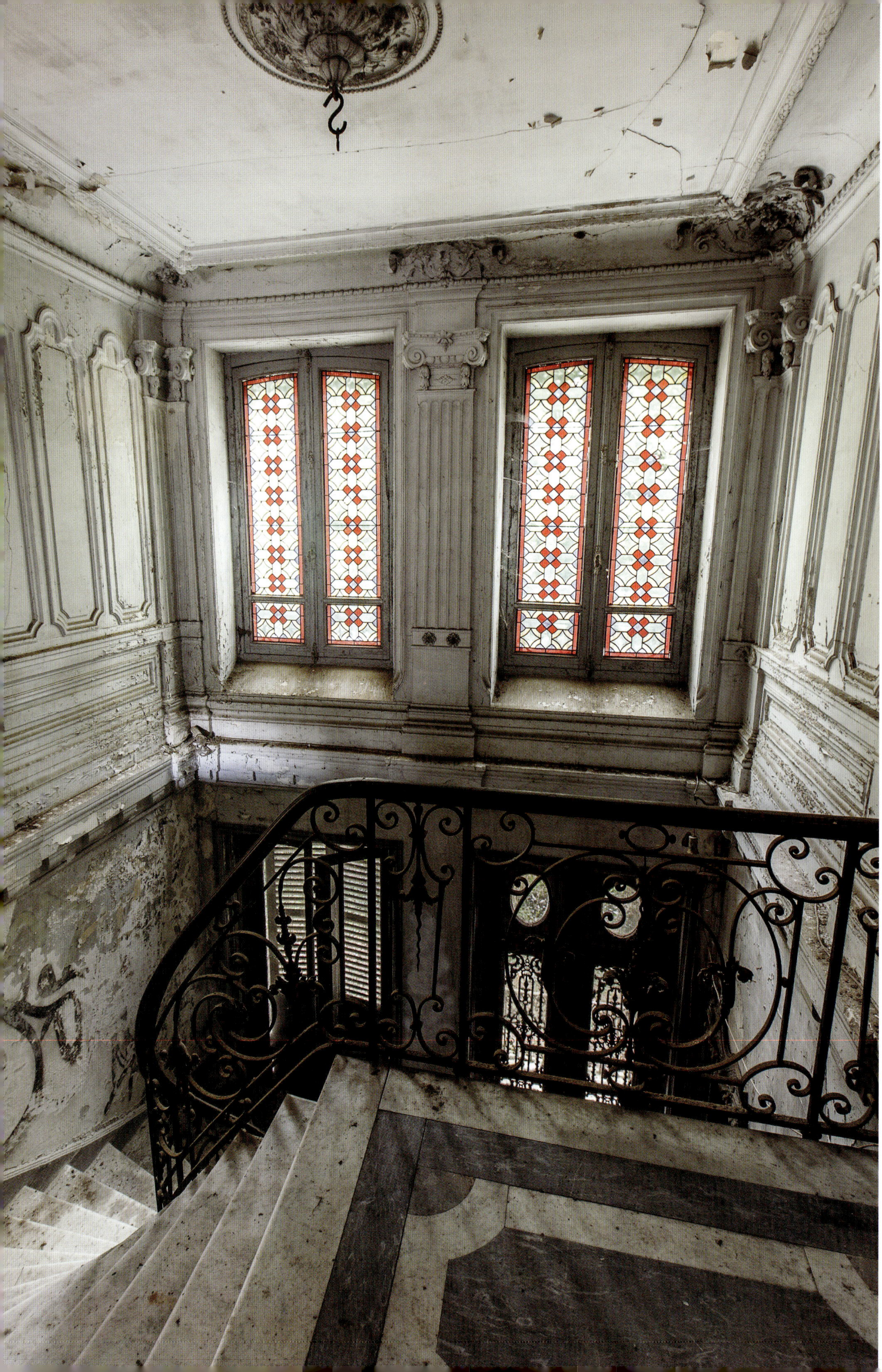

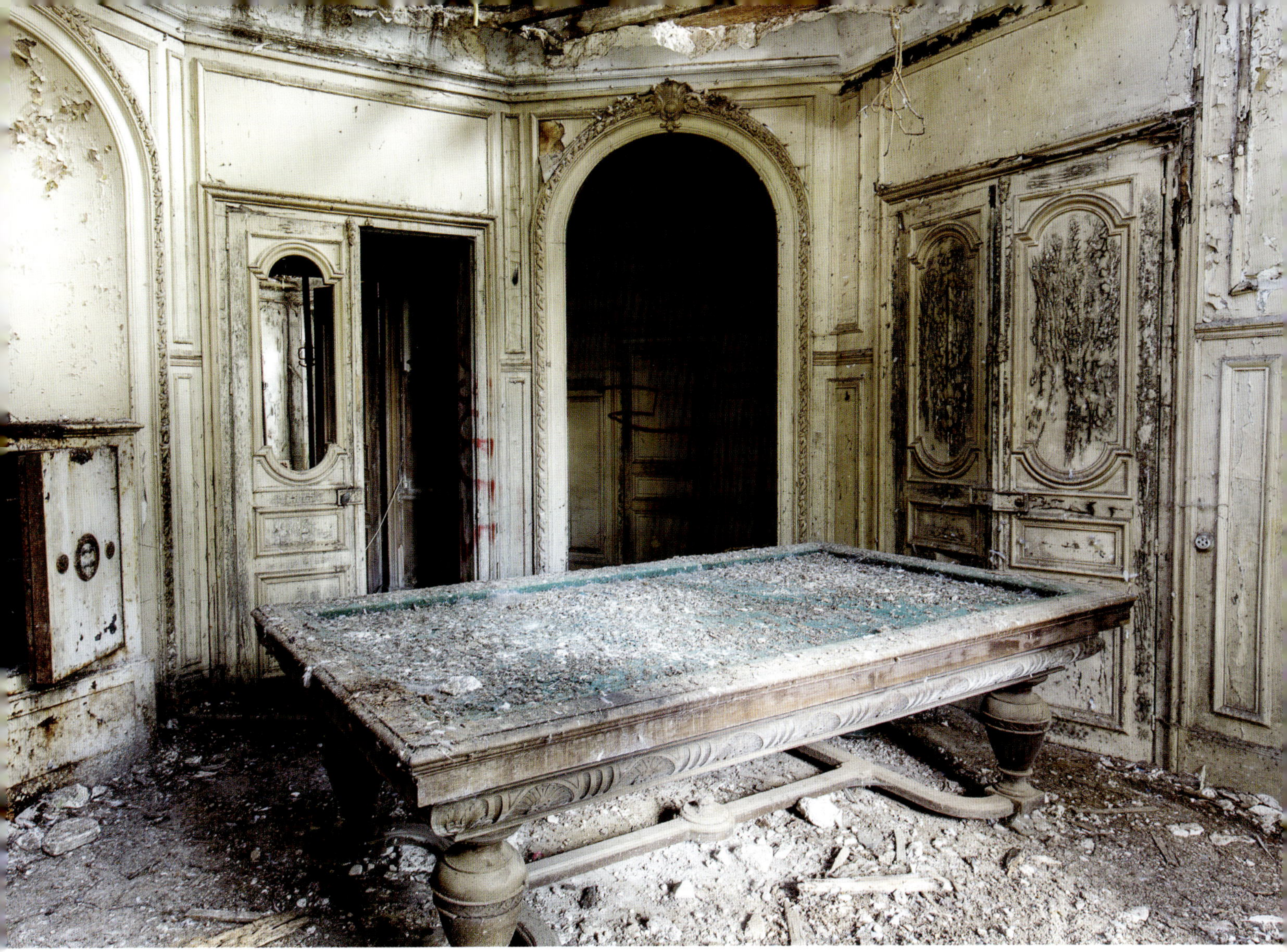

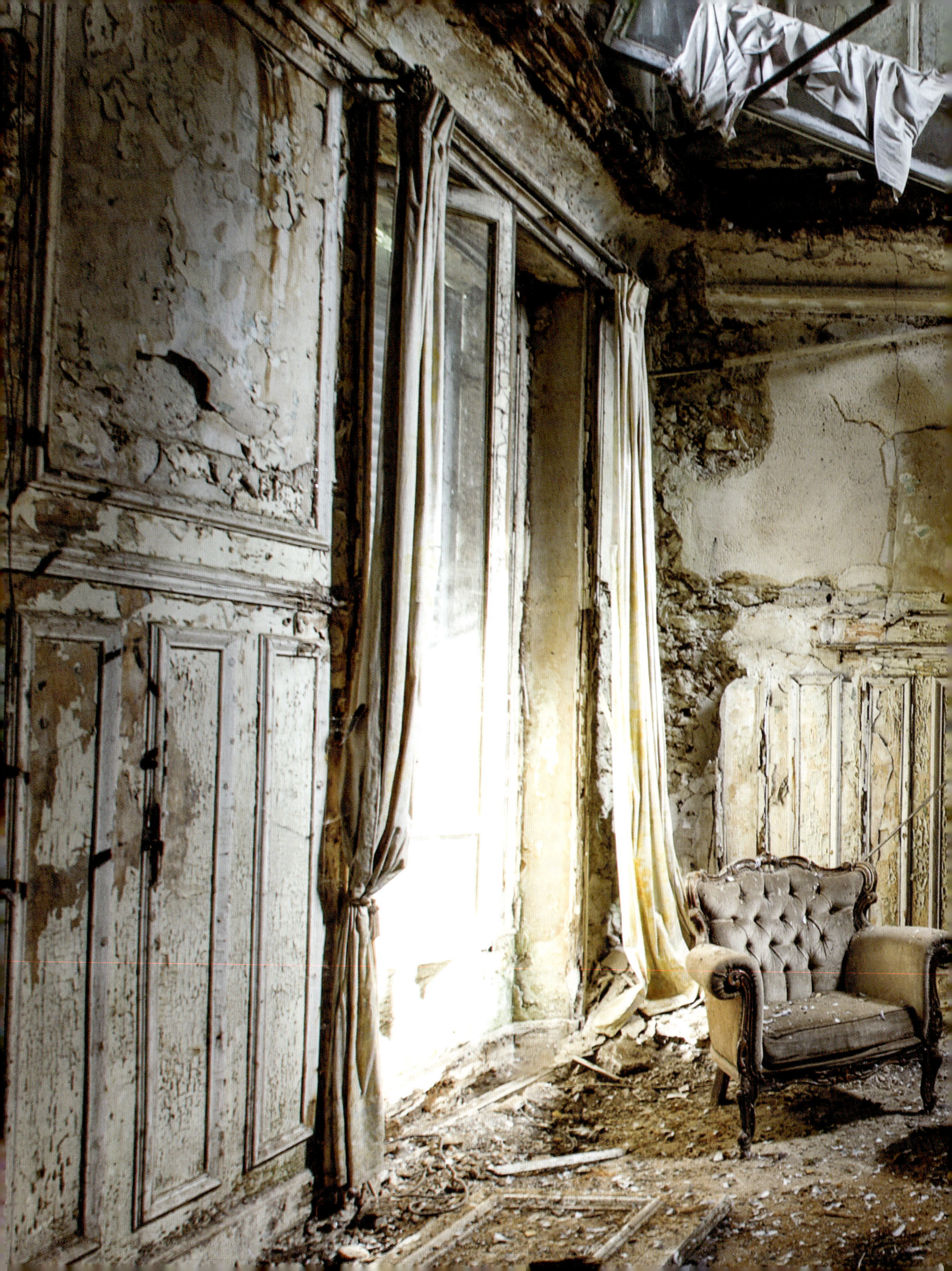

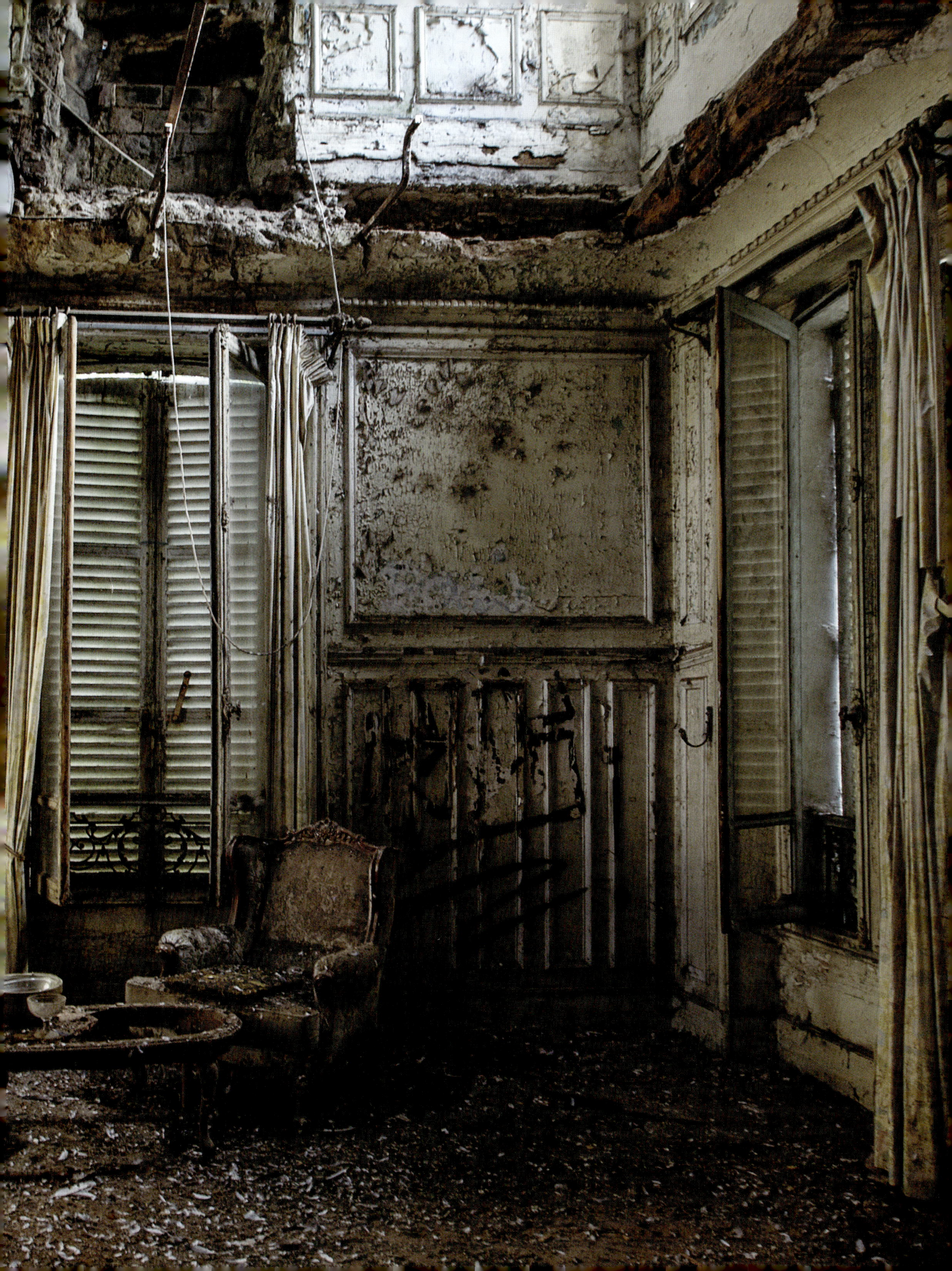

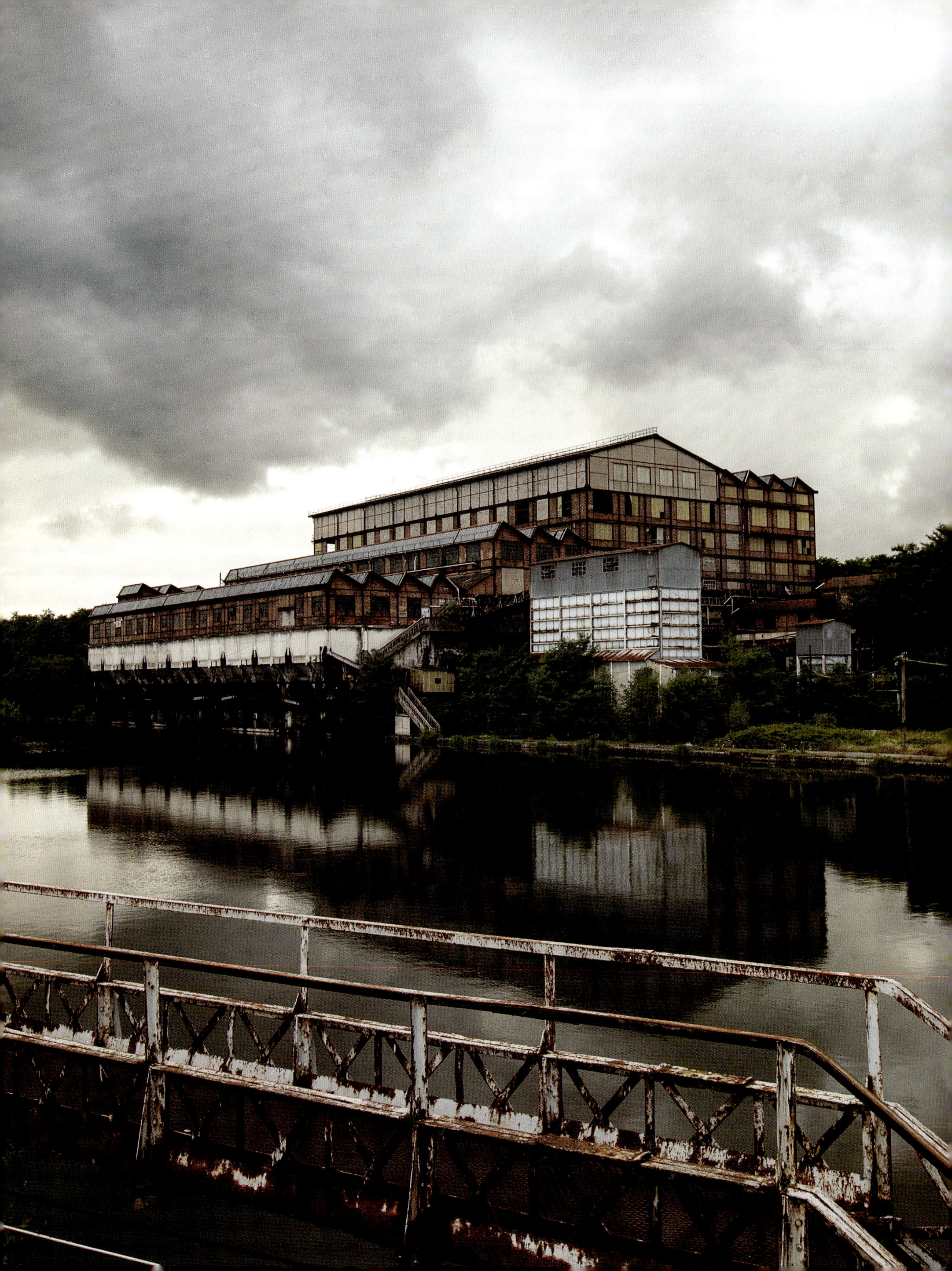

Lavoir des Chavannes, Saône-et-Loire

Freshly mined coal is an ore of varying size and quality, mixed with impurities which make it unfit for immediate use. In the mid-19th century, this raw material was sorted manually, using screens on the extraction sites, then washed. Increasing demand helped to streamline production.

The first coal preparation plants, which graded the coal and then cleaned it mechanically, soon began to appear in the European coalfields.

A limited company, Société Anonyme des Mines de Houille de Blanzy, Jules Chagot et Compagnie, owned the plant at Blanzy in Saône-et-Loire (in the Burgundy region), which had already been mined for centuries. In 1922, the company decided to set up the Lavoir des Chavannes, a veritable ore factory, in the midst of the Montceau-les-Mines coalfields.

Engineering consultants Considère, Pelnard-Caquot et Compagnie drew up the plans. The Compagnie Lyonnaise d'Entreprises et de Travaux d'Art was responsible for the masonry and Chevreau et Compagnie for the metal framework.

The two main contractors, specialists in reinforced concrete, had already been involved in the construction of the Lucy thermal power plant in Montceau-les-Mines and its adjoining housing.

The new plant was built on a 32-hectare site on the banks of a canal, near the railway station and the power station that supplied its energy. It stands 35 metres high and covers 8,000 square metres. The supporting structure, consisting of polygonal pillars and reinforced concrete beams, is on two levels, capped by a second iron-sided structure divided into four sections. The walls are built from brick. As one side of the panels is glazed, the saw-toothed roof illuminates the interior. The two lower levels were used for circulation and storage of the ore, which was processed on the upper floor. Offices and showers made from coated limestone rubble complete this immense complex.

The eight continuously rotating coal-processing lines came into service between 1927 and 1930. They supplied up to 1,000 tonnes of finished product per hour. The railway network Paris à Lyon et à la Méditerranée (PLM), which became the state-owned railway SNCF in 1938, supplied the plant with raw material extracted from the surrounding coalfields.

Once graded and cleaned, the coal was ready for shipment. It was dumped directly onto barges moored to the adjoining dock, or into one of the two hundred and sixty 20-tonne railway wagons waiting under the building. Waste material was burned in the neighbouring power station.

The plant emerged intact from the Second World War, and was soon up and running again. On 17 May 1946, legislation to nationalise mineral fuels set up Charbonnages de France, placing all the mining companies under the supervision of the Ministry of Industry.

In the following decades, the facility was constantly renovated in an attempt to remain competitive with oil. Although the mines were closing one after the other, modernisation was focused on automation: an overhead crane linking the levels, non-stop supplies of coal, and computerisation in the 1980s and 1990s, making some of the production lines completely autonomous. In spite of these improvements, exhaustion of the coal deposits led to the plant closing in November 1999.

The following year, the entire site and its facilities were registered on the supplementary inventory of historical monuments. A call for projects was then launched by the association of local authorities to find a new purpose for the site, but the allocated budget was insufficient. The abandoned buildings have been comprehensively vandalised. Their most likely fate now is demolition.

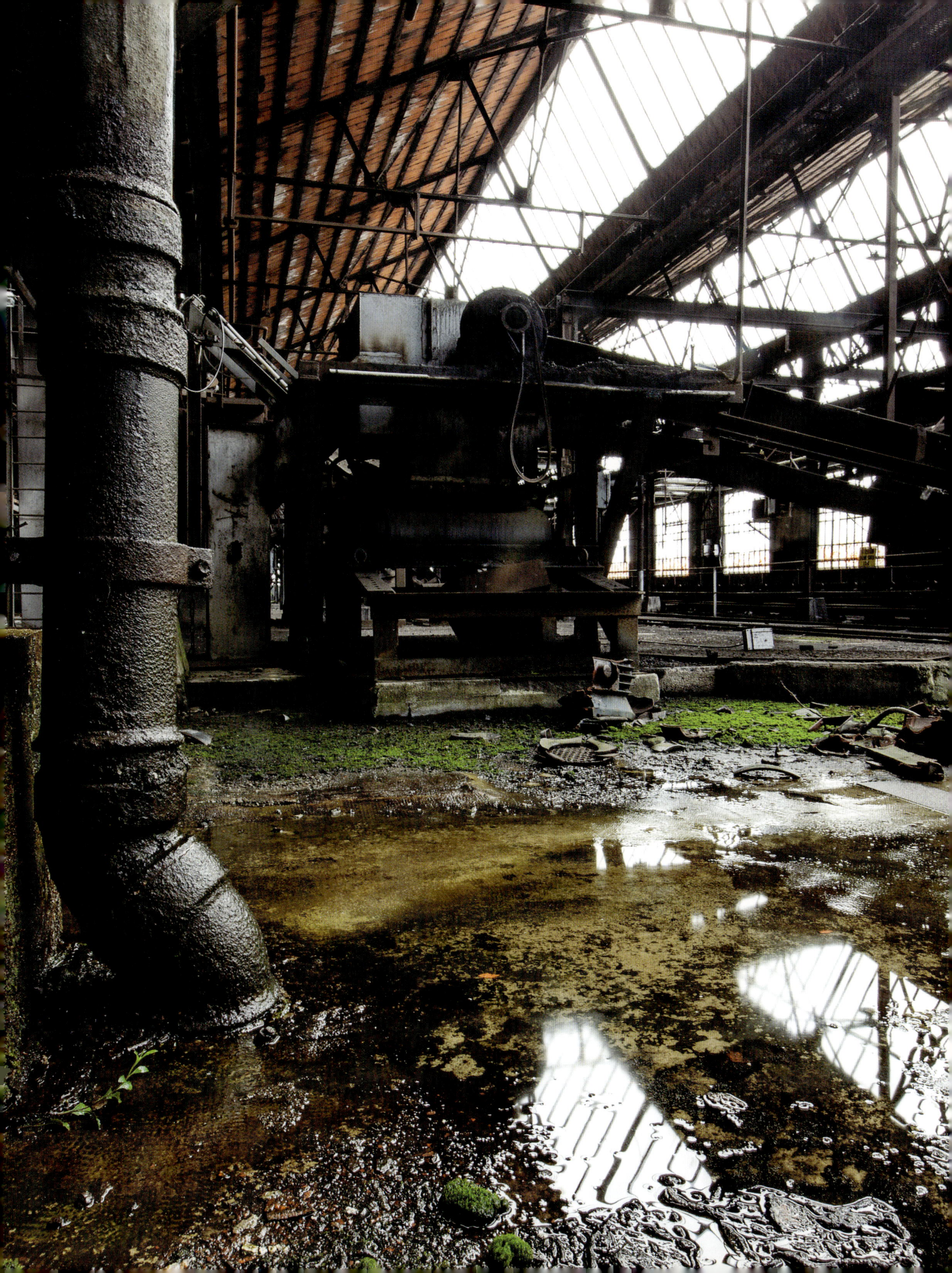

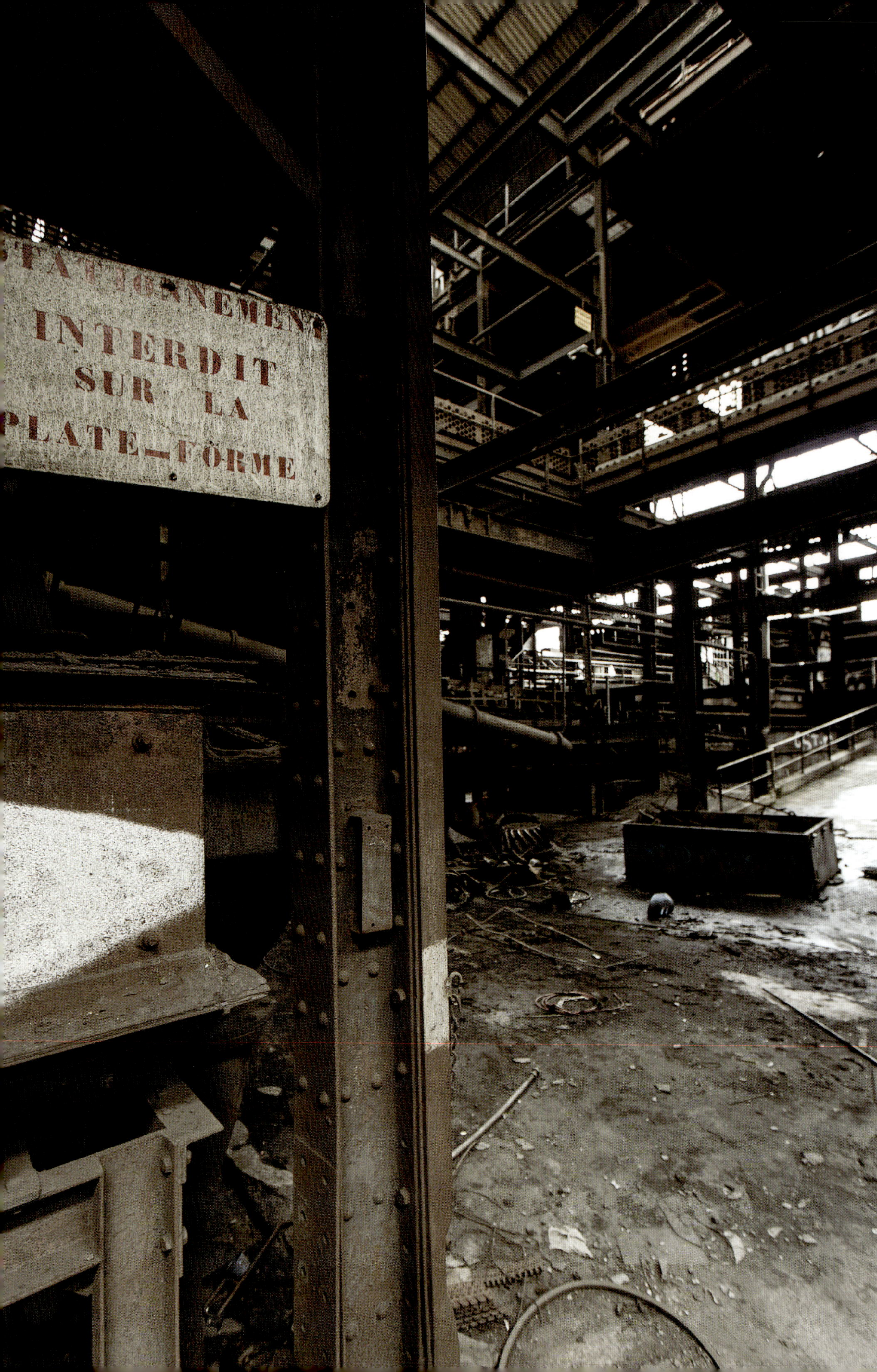
STATIONNEMENT
INTERDIT
SUR LA
PLATE-FORME

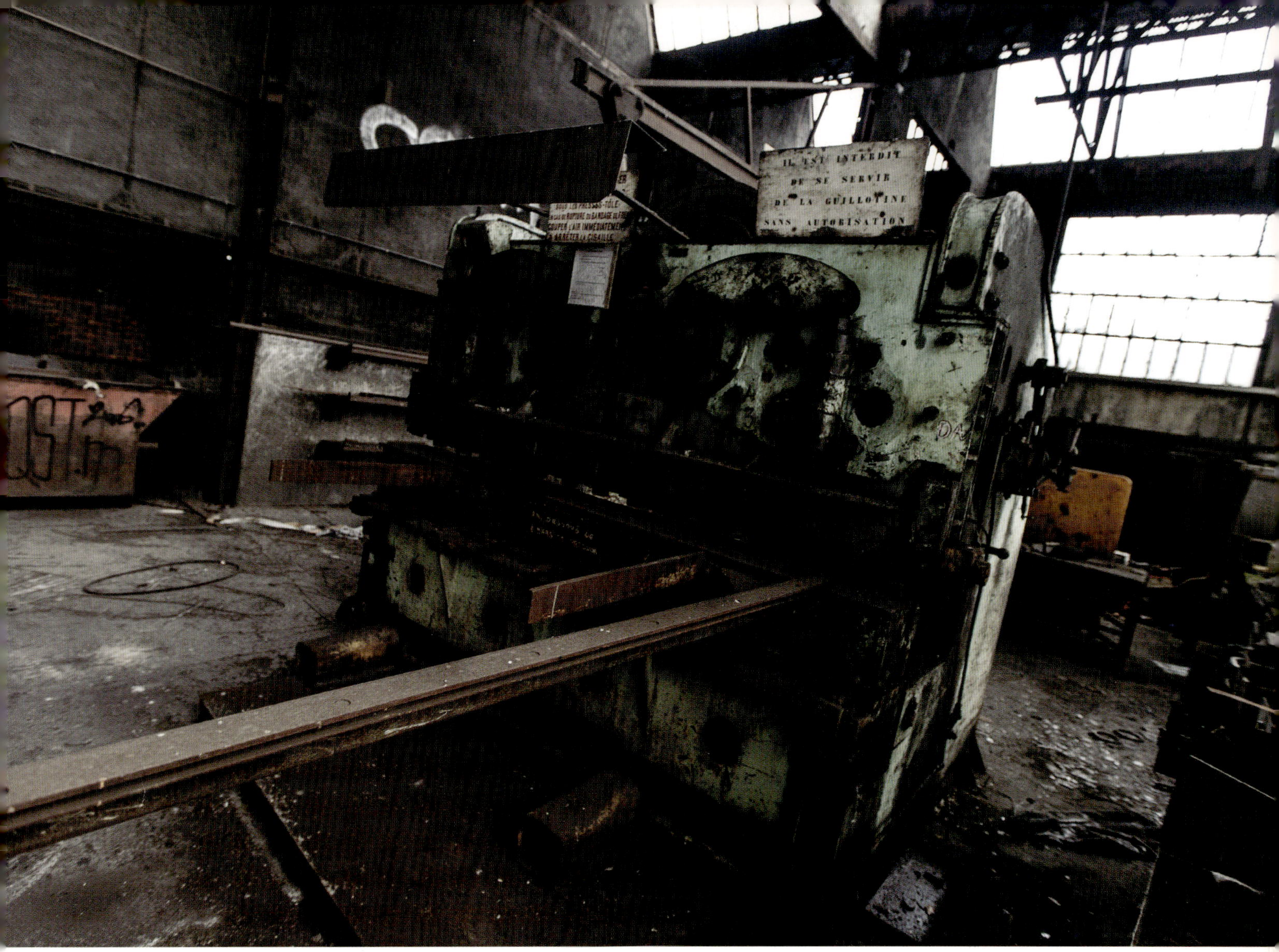
IL EST INTERDIT
DE SE SERVIR
DE LA GUILLOTINE
SANS AUTORISATION

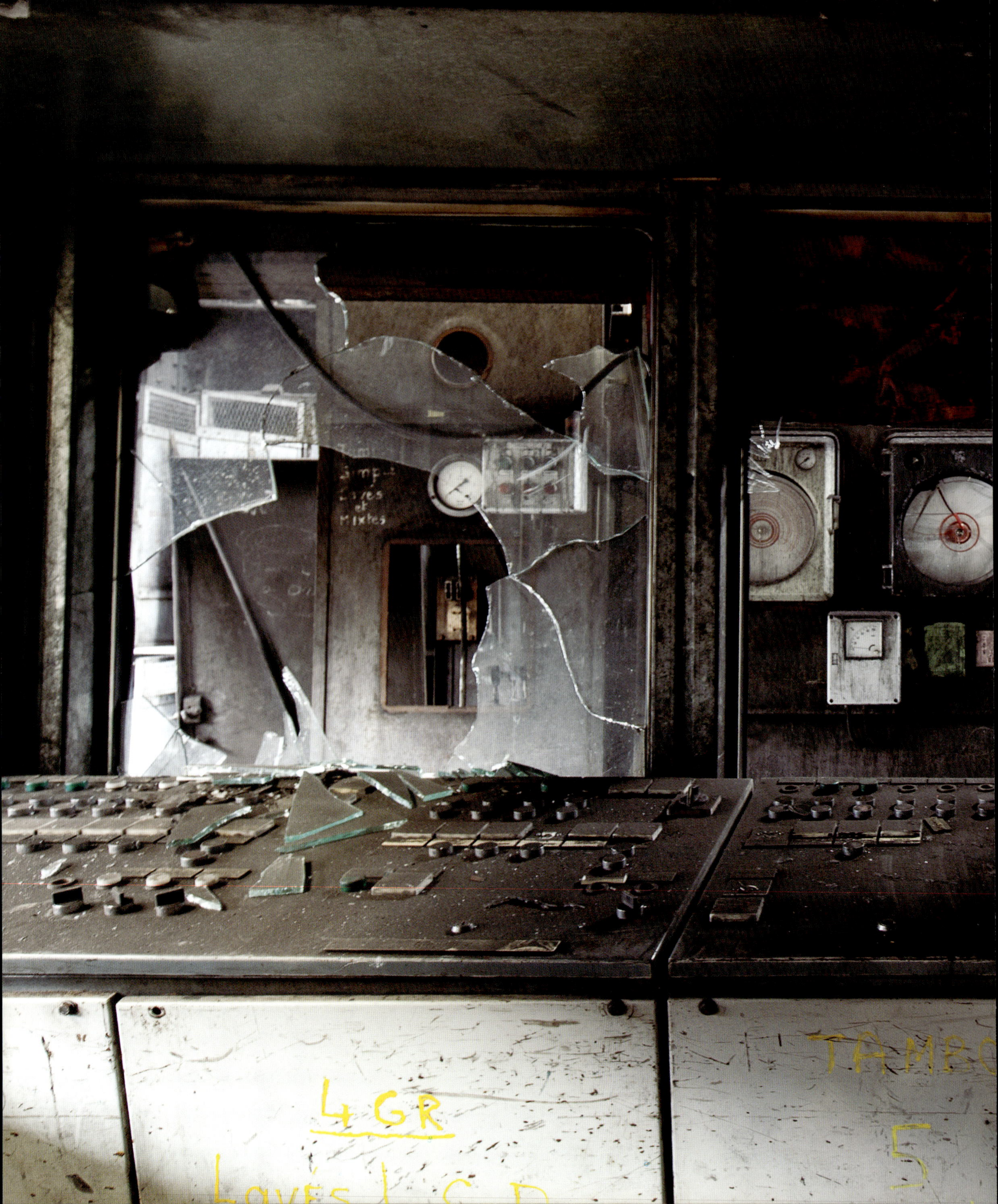
4GR
5

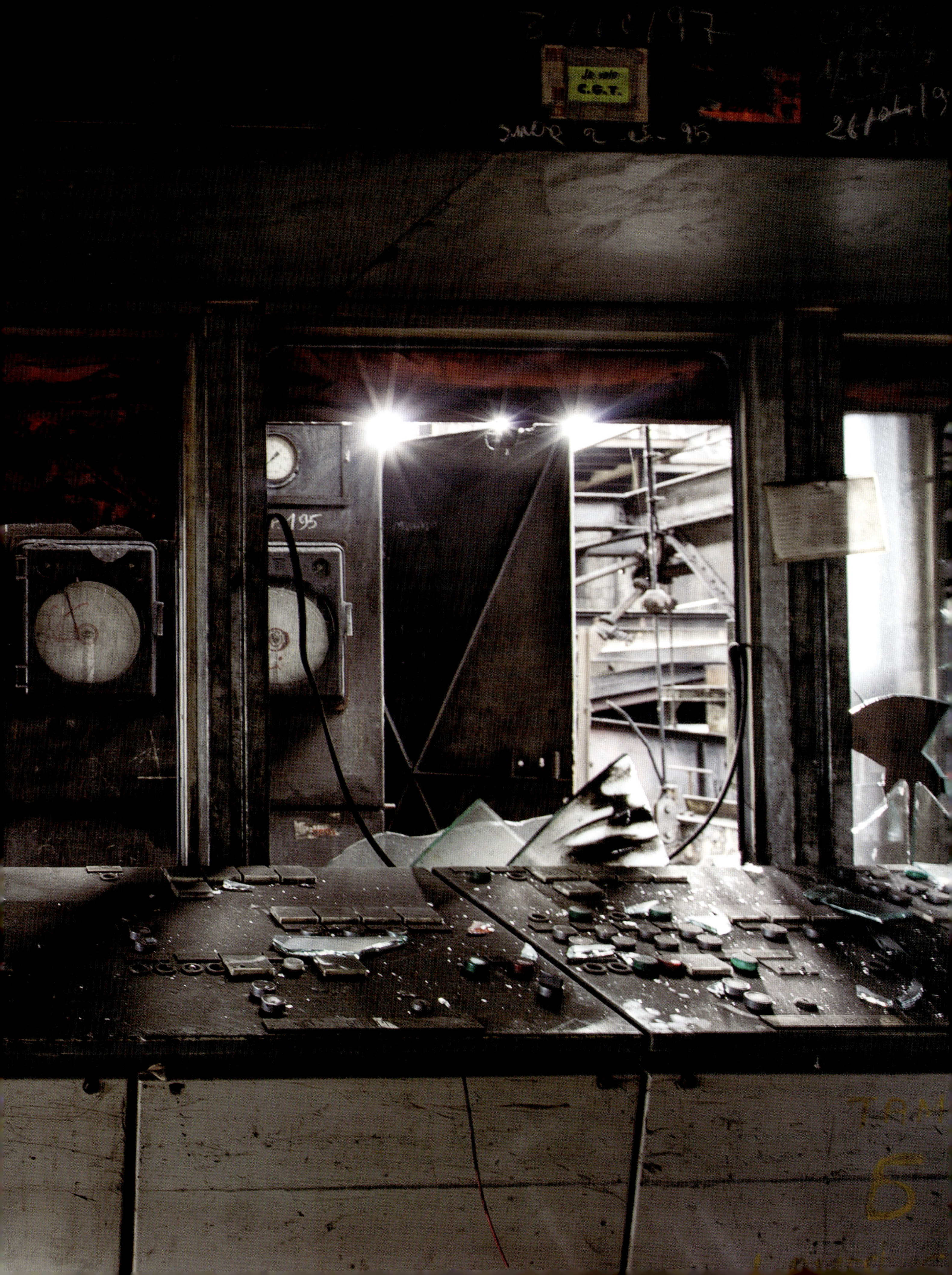
Je vote
C.G.T.

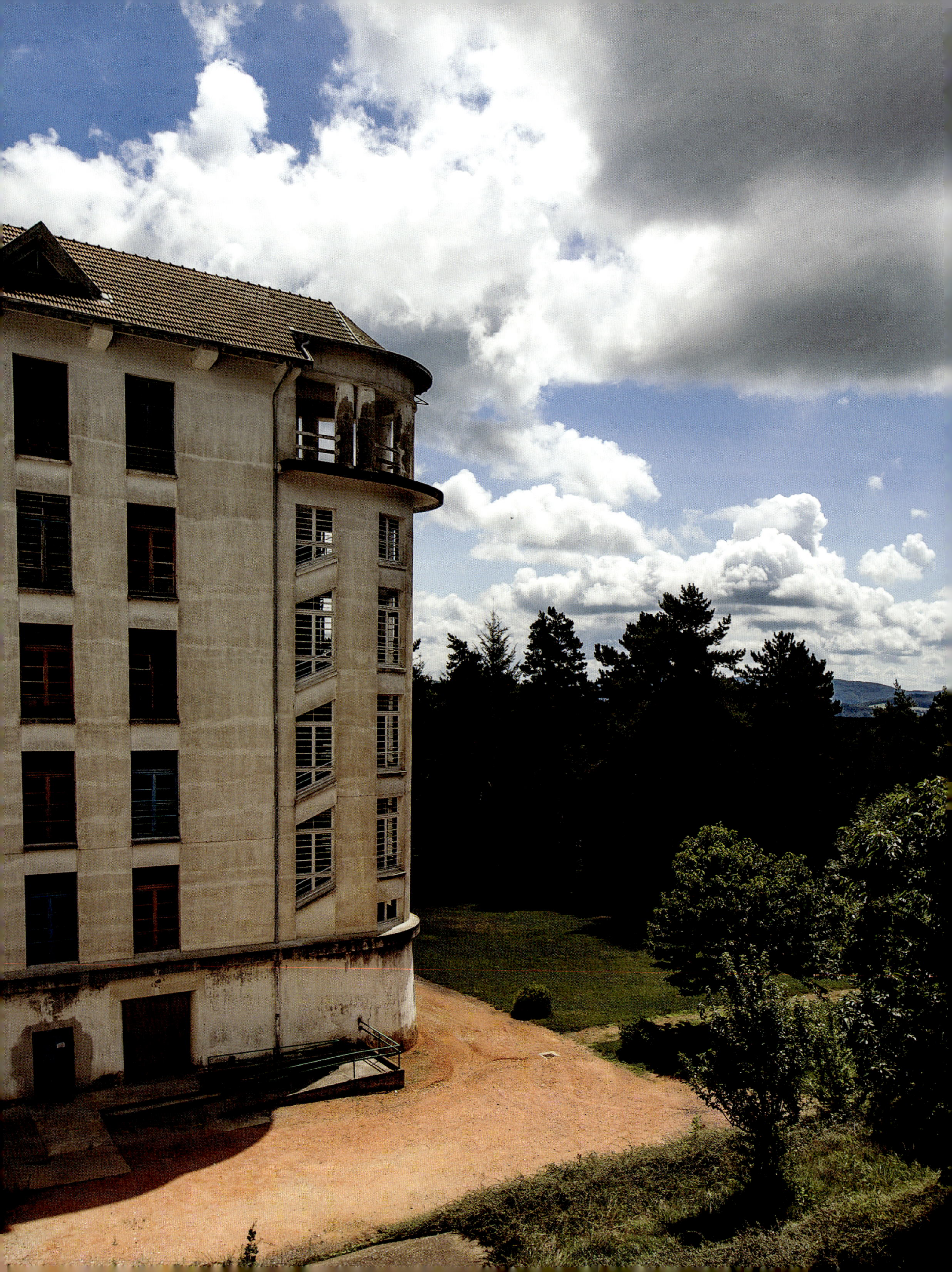

Sanatorium de Bergesserin, Saône-et-Loire

When Aube, Haute-Marne, Saône-et-Loire and Yonne agreed to build an interdepartmental sanatorium, the upsurge in new tuberculosis treatment centres had already been underway for a decade. The first stone was laid in 1932 on a hillside plot of about 10 hectares, near the small forest village of Bergesserin in eastern France.

After a number of technical and financial disruptions to the work, followed by the hardships of the Second World War, the sanatorium was finally completed in 1946.

Intended for women, it was designed by departmental architect Frédéric Bidaut along clean and uncluttered functionalist lines.

Two groups of metal-framed and painted concrete buildings are arranged at right angles around a reception hall with a semi-enclosed staircase.

The first group, a row of four rectangular buildings, was reserved for treatment and accommodation facilities for up to 210 patients. The other group includes reception areas, patients' communal areas and administrative offices. Staff lived in small houses scattered around the site.

The interiors are vibrant with light. Patients' rooms, with two to four beds, have large windows and circular balconies. The galleries are bright, the tiled roof is pierced with triangular skylights, and the staircase is illuminated by bay windows that look out over the Cluny valley.

The architect chose to blend the buildings into the landscape. They vary between three and six floors depending on the slope. Underground galleries house the equipment and boiler room.

In the 1960s, as antibiotic therapy took over the control of TB, the sanatorium was converted into an aftercare and rehabilitation service. In 1974, it was attached to Mâcon general hospital. But the ageing buildings were poorly insulated. The administration transferred the remaining patients elsewhere before deciding to close the site in 2008 and put it on the market.

Acro'Bath, an animation and games company, has acquired part of the land for a forest adventure park, but the building itself still has no takers. The cost of demolition would be exorbitant. At the time of writing, Mâcon hospital was still responsible for the deserted sanatorium, now off-limits.

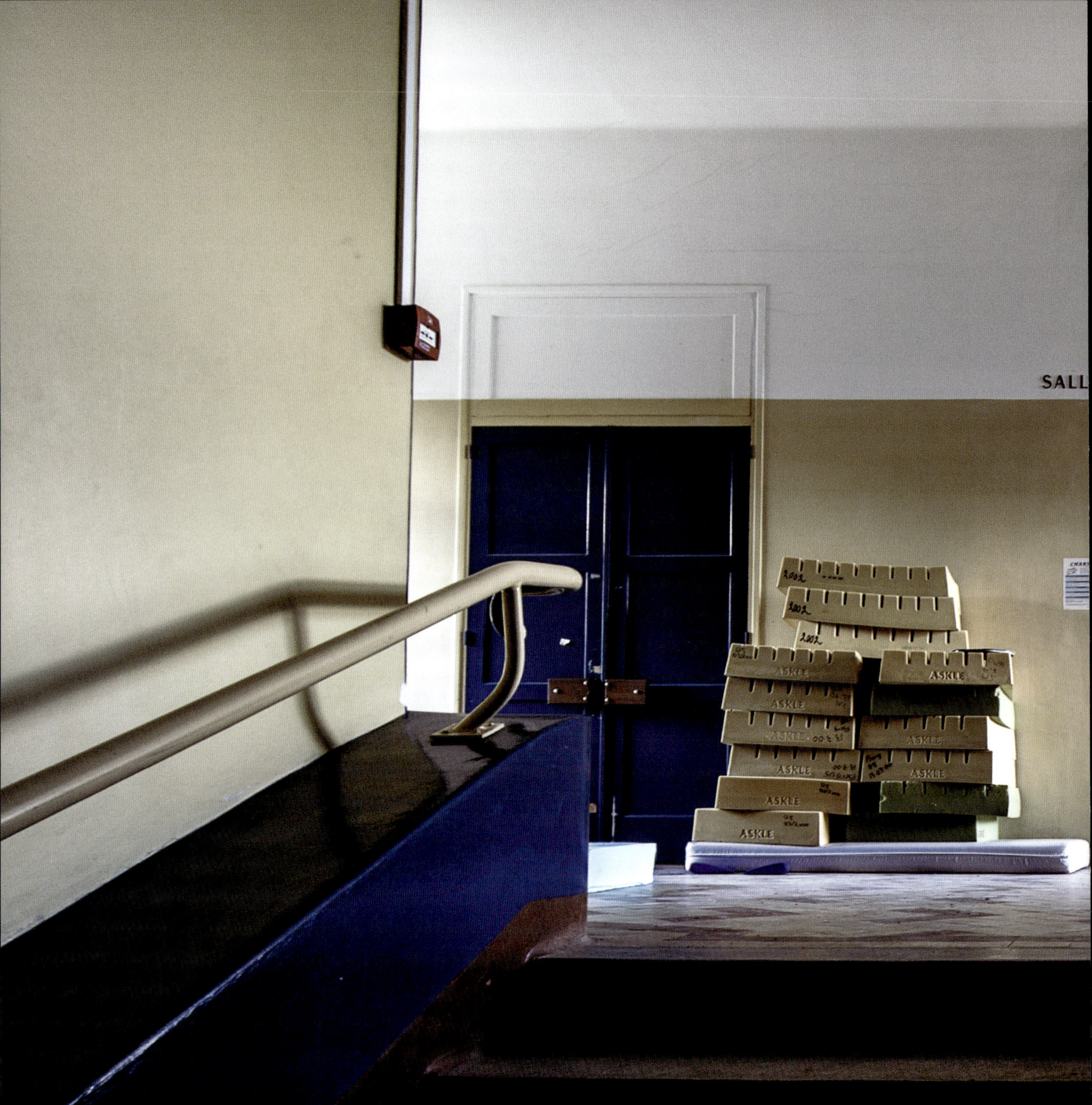
SALL
ASKLE

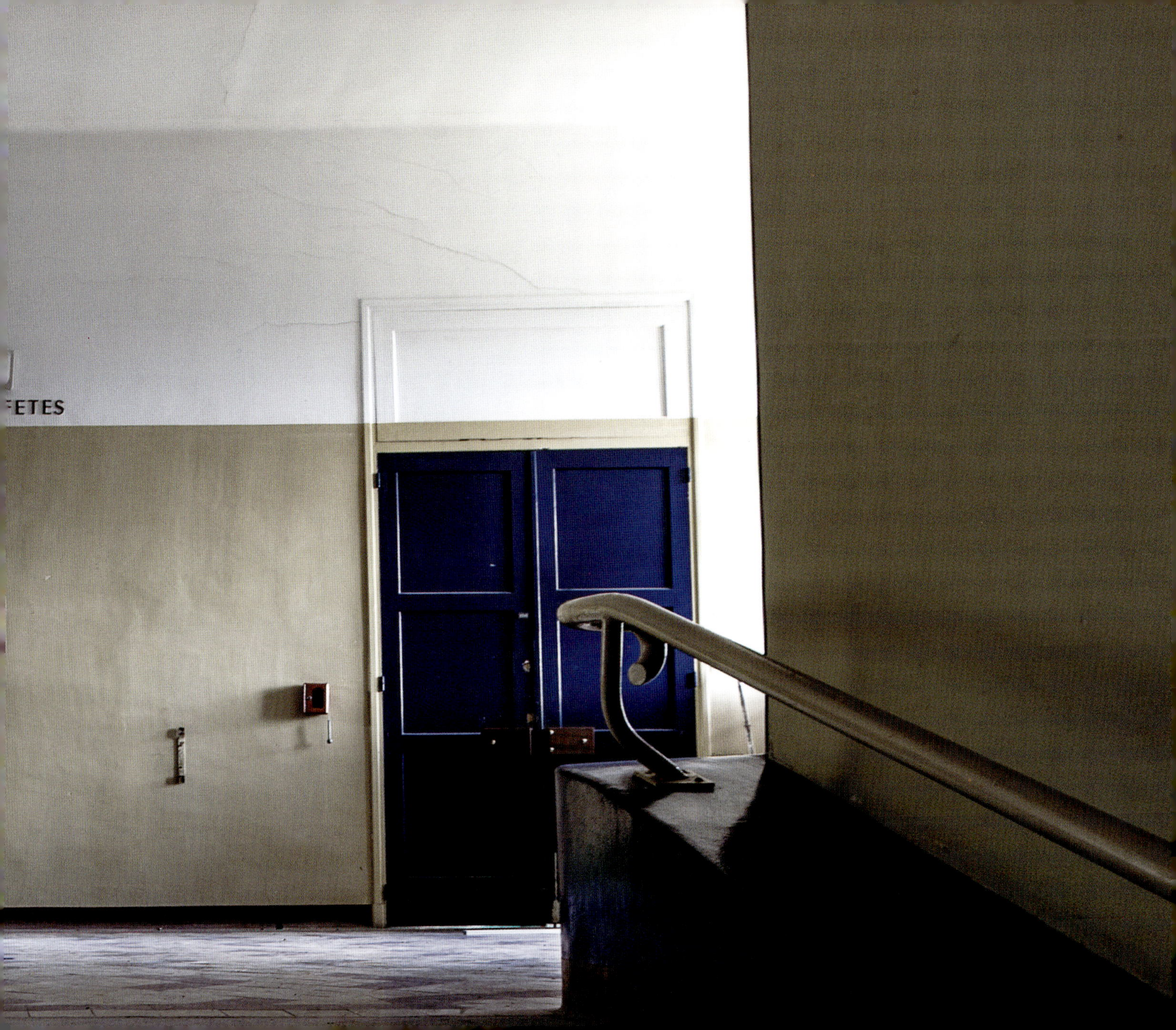
FETES

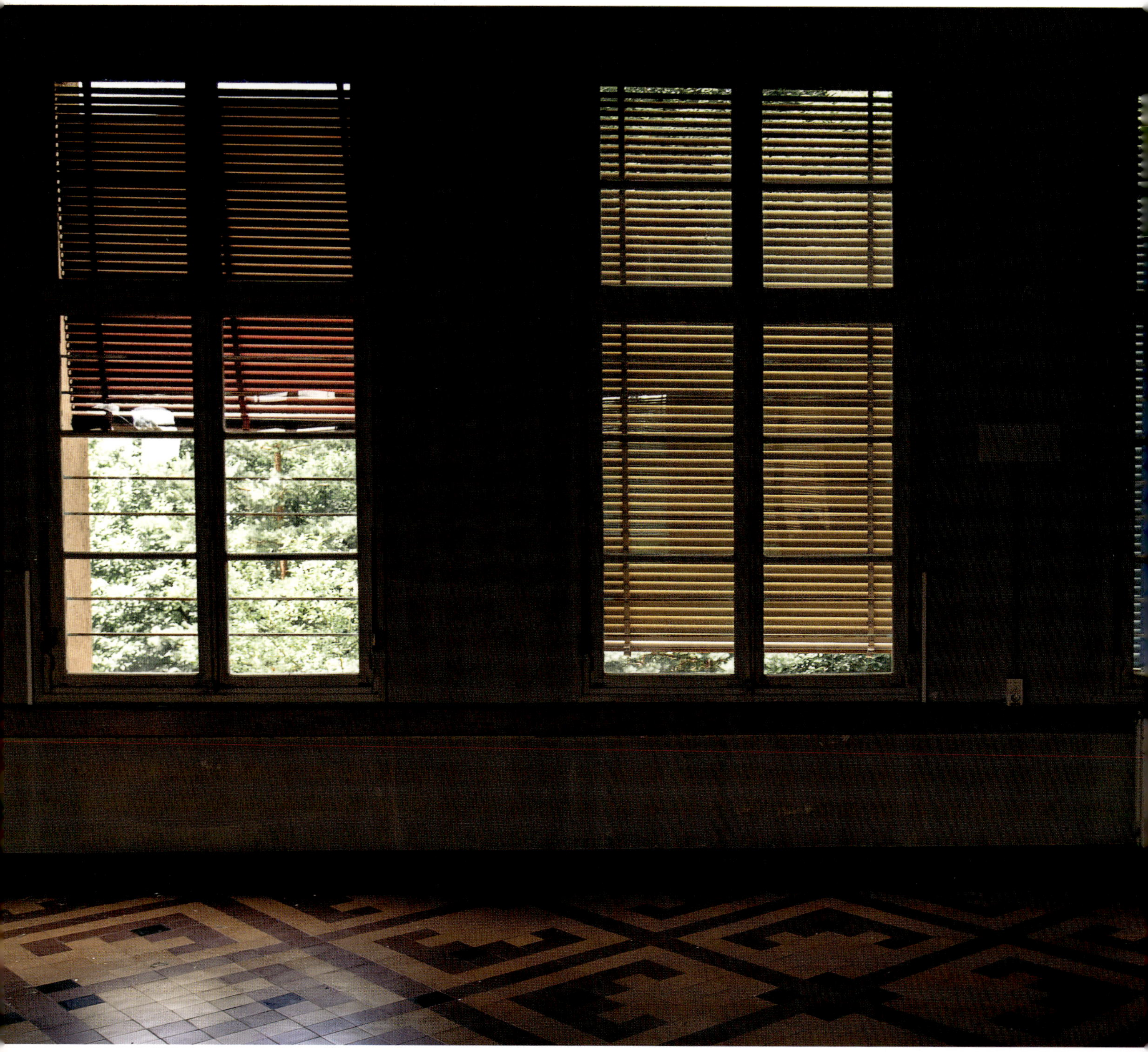

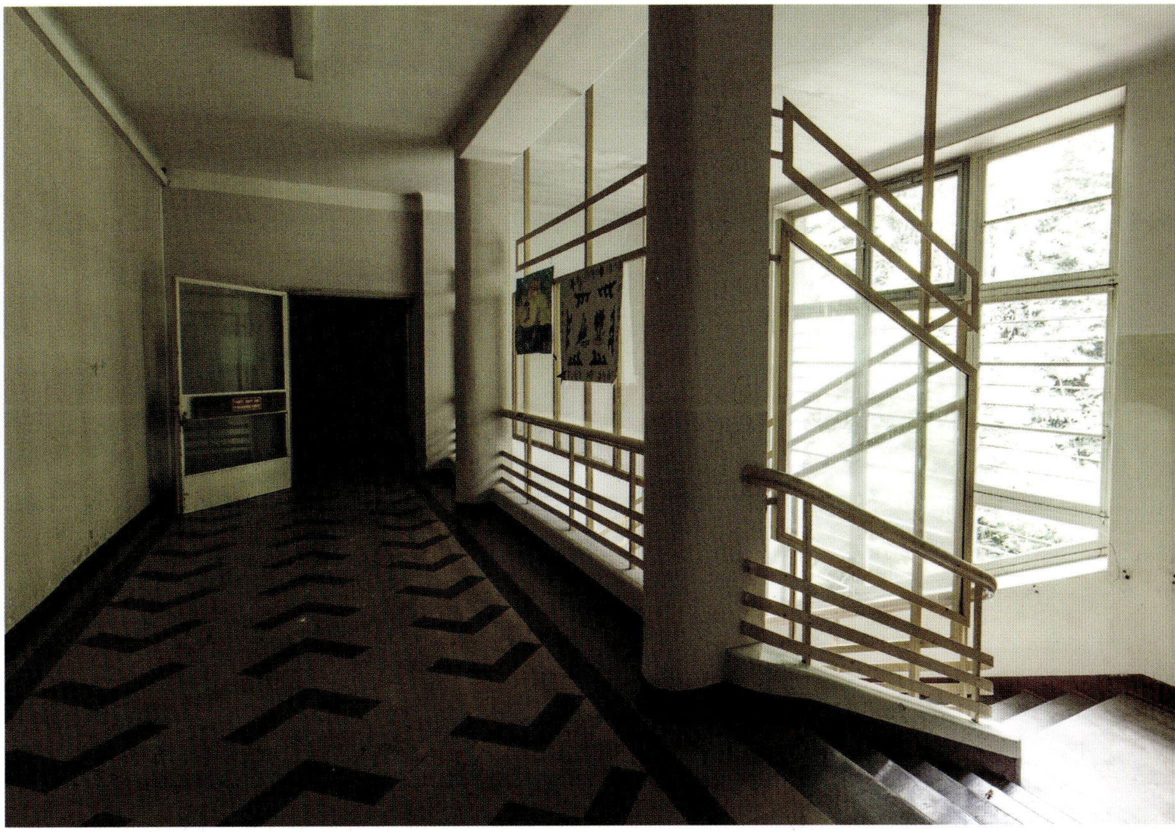

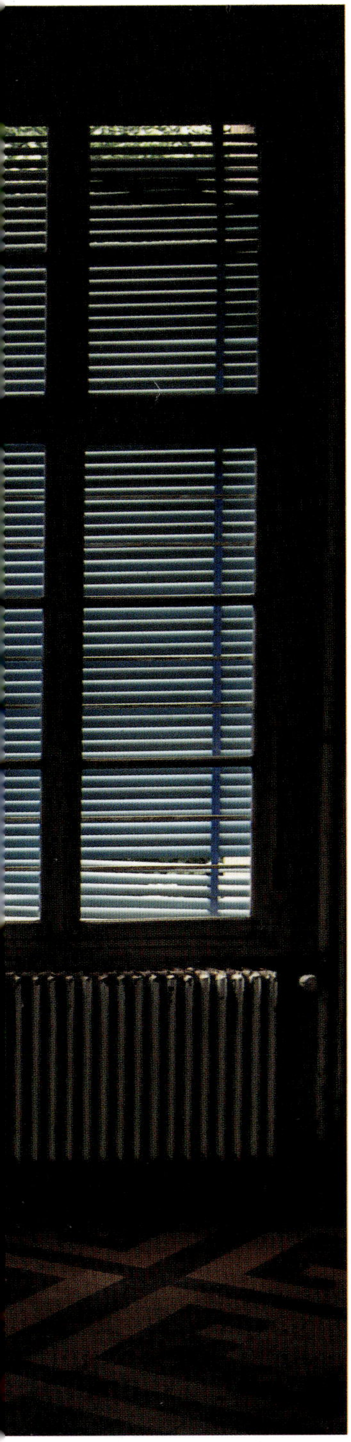

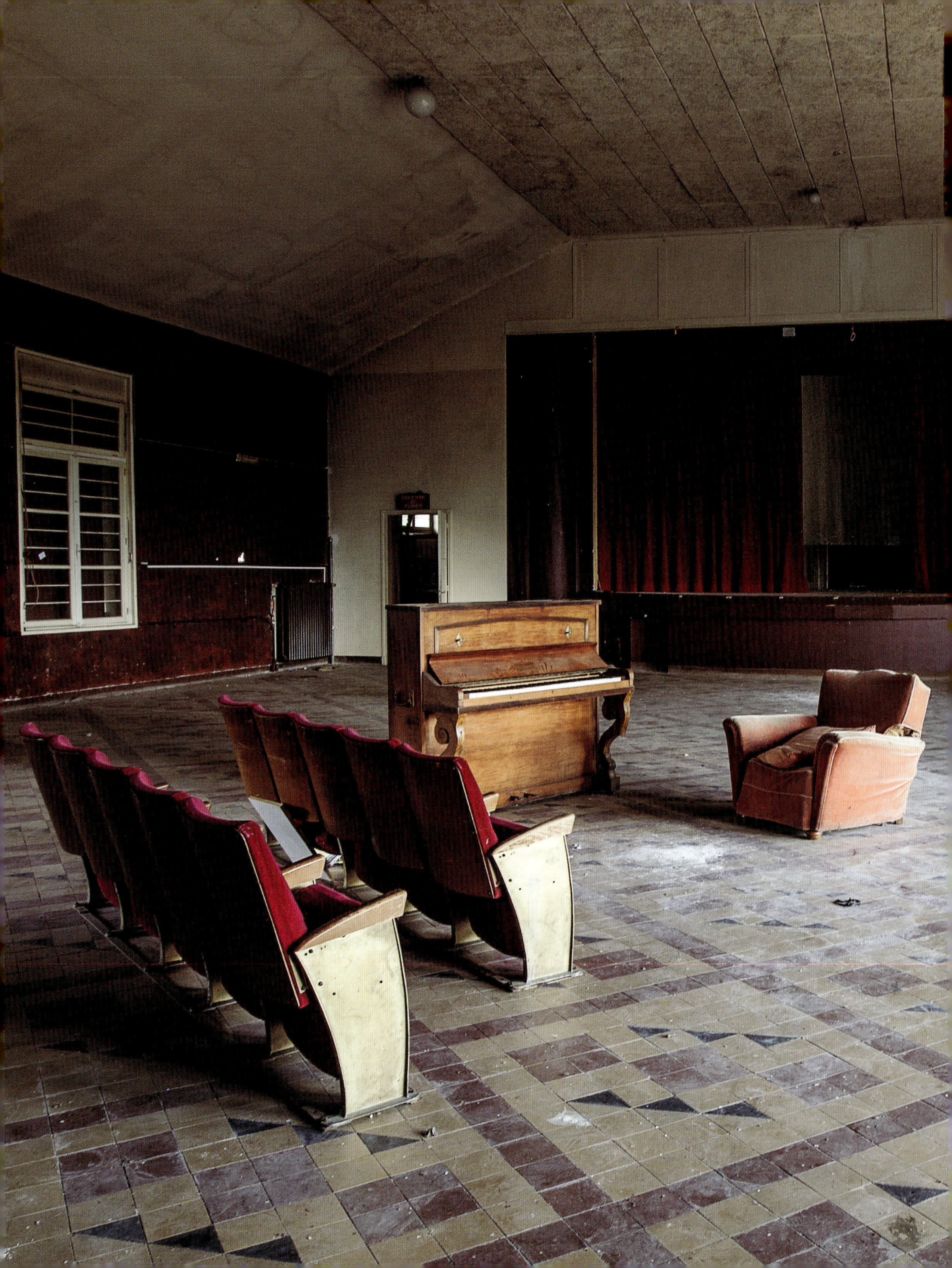

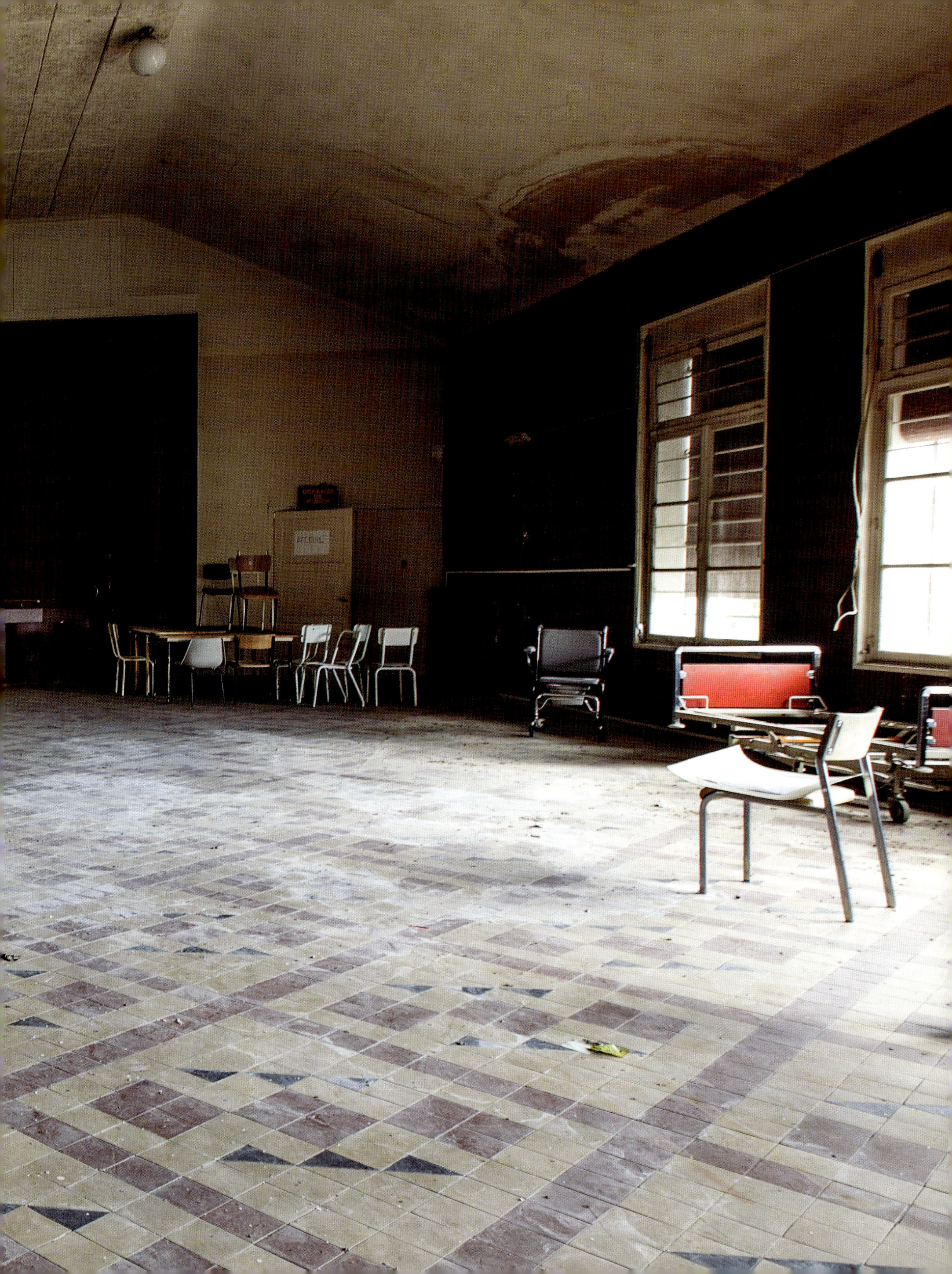

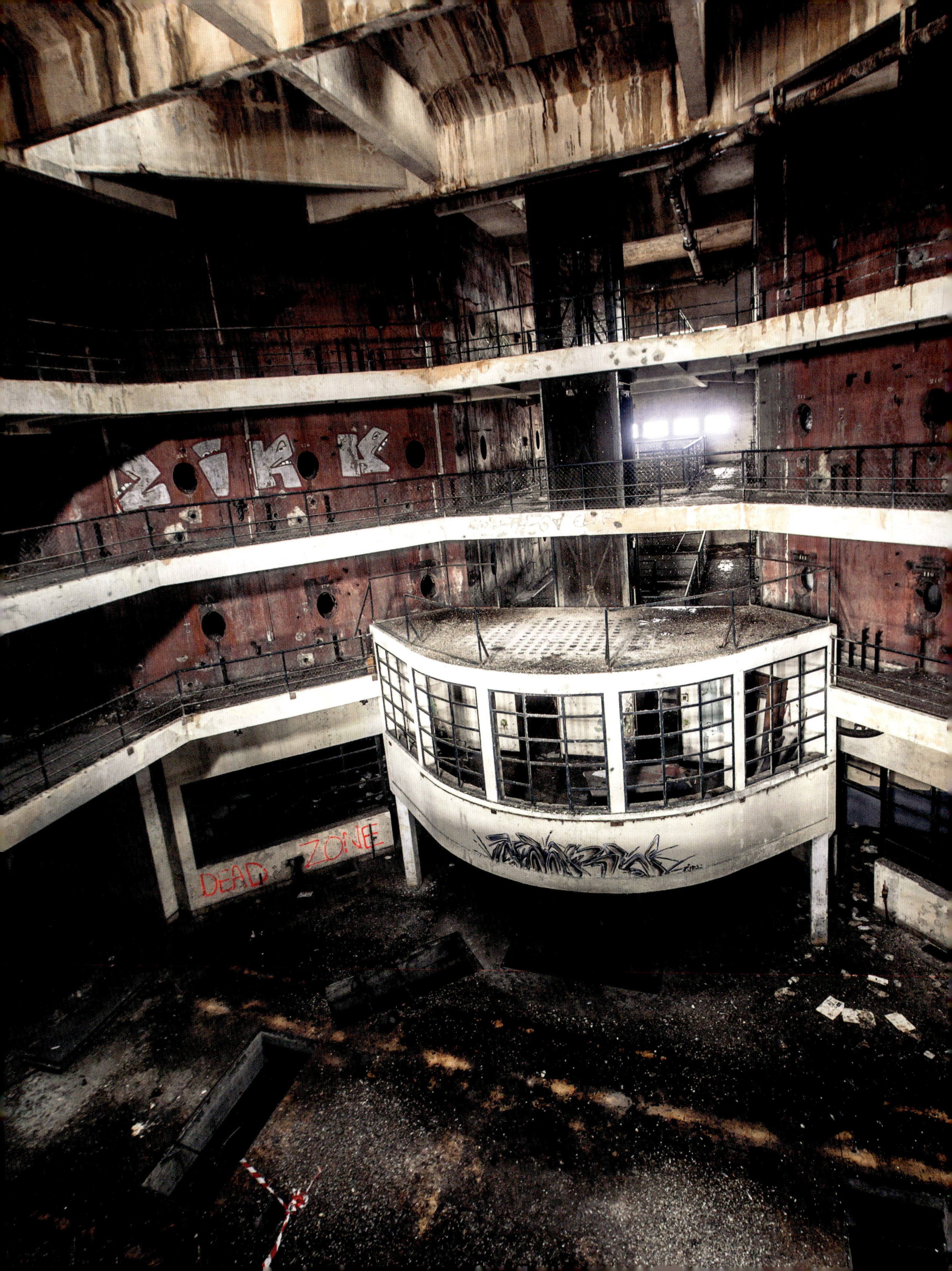
DEAD ZONE

Chai Relais, Rouen

The Normandy town of Rouen paid a heavy price in the 1939–1945 war. Among the buildings hardest hit were those of the autonomous (state-owned) port authority, whose facilities were bombed as it was liberated.

What was not destroyed was often unusable, after the neglect of the war years. The city wanted to make the best of this disaster, so embarked on a programme of reconstruction and modernisation.

The Chai Relais (wine storage cellar), built in 1950, is one of the most striking illustrations of this. Since France had experienced a shortage of wine in the 19th century, the practice had grown of importing it from the vast wine-producing areas of North Africa.

Rouen is a mecca for warehousing and for transfers between *pinardiers* (tankers full of Algerian wine; *pinard* = plonk) and the barges that deliver the cargo along the Seine. Until then, the wine had been transported in barrels that had to be loaded, unloaded and stored at the dock. These were labour-intensive operations, as were the manufacture and maintenance of the various containers.

The Rouen Chamber of Commerce commissioned architects Lefebvre et Fils to design a building to carry out all these functions. They drew up a cruciform plan on resolutely modernist lines.

Four towers in blind-fronted blocks, all of red brick, contain 250 concrete vats lined with glass for ease of cleaning, distributed over three floors. Passageways run alongside the vats, aligned on the cruciform plan, converging at the centre where the control and monitoring station is installed. On the ground floor of the south side are offices, personnel services, customs and a workshop. On the north side, a large storage room faces the transfer point for road-haulage trucks and railway wagons. The cellar, with a total capacity of 100,000 hectolitres, is strategically placed for bulk wine storage. It is built on Presqu'île Waddington, the peninsula linking the Seine to Saint-Gervais, where the Atlantic tankers dock – ideal for its role as a transit post, warehousing and strict regulation of the wine traffic. Wine arriving from North Africa was directly transferred from the tankers to vats in the basement through a network of pipelines. It was stored for administrative checks while onward transit was organised. It was then piped into storage vats on the upper floors before being loaded, still via pipelines, into truck or train containers, barrels or barges that would transport it up the Seine. Underground pipes could also deliver the wine to dealers' warehouses or to another port cellar.

To this elaborate network, capable of transferring several cargoes simultaneously, was added a drainage system and a method of evacuating the lees deposited in the vats along with the cleaning water. Twelve pumps kept the wine moving. Despite this apparent complexity, cutting-edge automation meant that the cellar could be run by a small staff. Four foremen, fourteen technicians plus an additional dozen workers controlled the outside manoeuvres. Four administrative staff completed the team. The cellar master coordinated all these operations from a central post. He supervised the flows on an illuminated panel designed by the Société du Filtre Gasquet. This company, which has subsidiaries in Bordeaux and Algeria, specialises in mechanical equipment for wine cellars. In Rouen, it was also responsible for the development of the rest of the equipment. All the details were well thought out: for example, cork tiles were fitted to the reinforced concrete walls to improve thermal insulation.

The building was opened on 15 December 1950 in the presence of several government ministers. The chamber of commerce retroceded it to the autonomous port 18 years later. The customs offices were retained on the ground floor until they relocated in 1993.

The previous year, the cellar had hosted the Octobre en Normandie association for a cultural event that turned out to be a one-off. The building was subsequently abandoned. Despite attempts by the port of Rouen to keep people out, 100 tonnes of red copper pipes quickly disappeared. The ransacked building, flooded by high tides, inevitably deteriorated.

A first tender was launched in 2014, without success. At issue was the vast restoration cost of 15 million euros. In 2016, Paris, the Métropole Rouen Normandie, Le Havre and their port authorities united around a new call for projects entitled "Reinventing the Seine", aimed at the innovative conversion of forty riverside sites. As part of this initiative, the cellar has attracted four proposals scheduled for consideration in 2017.

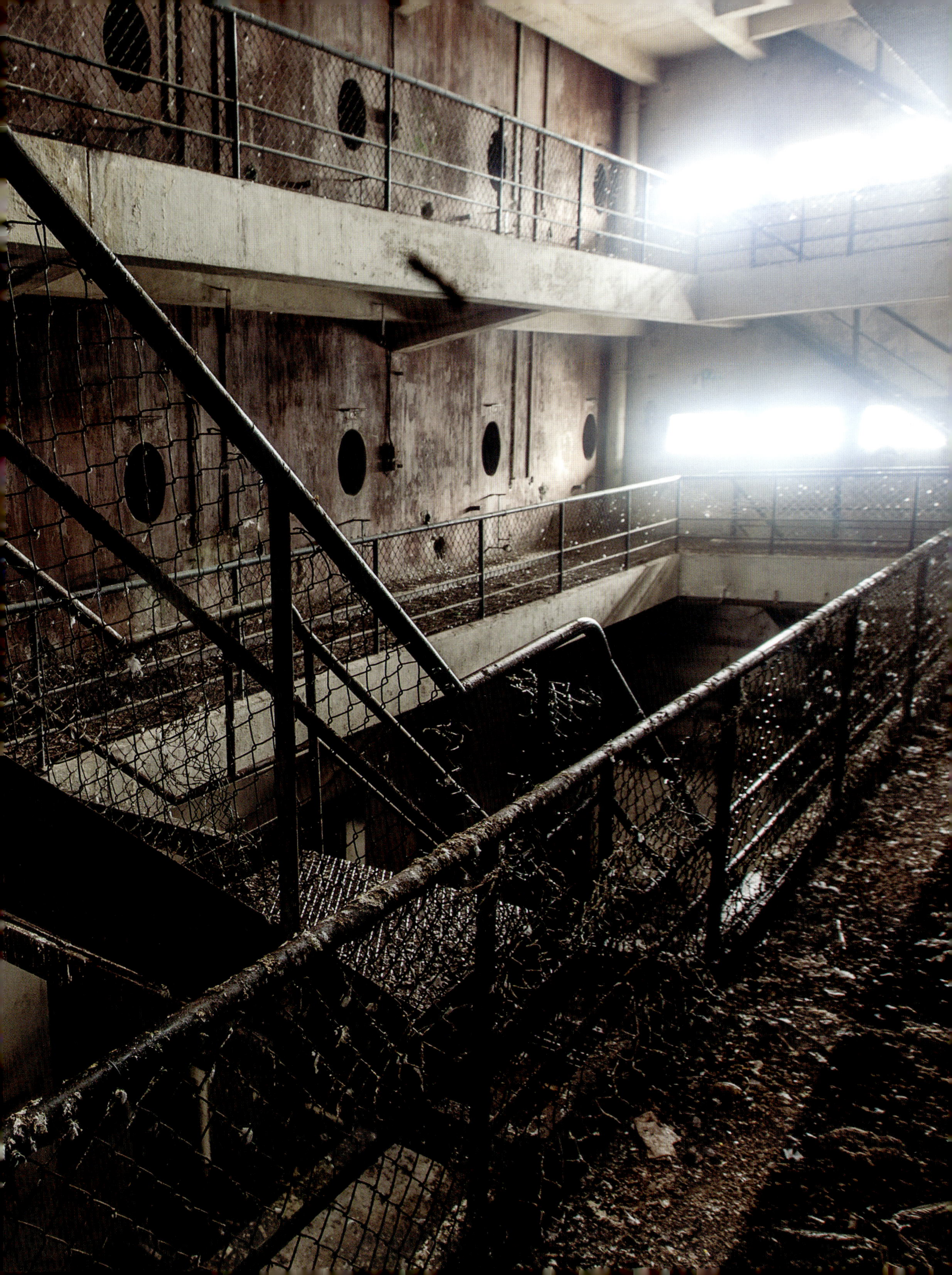

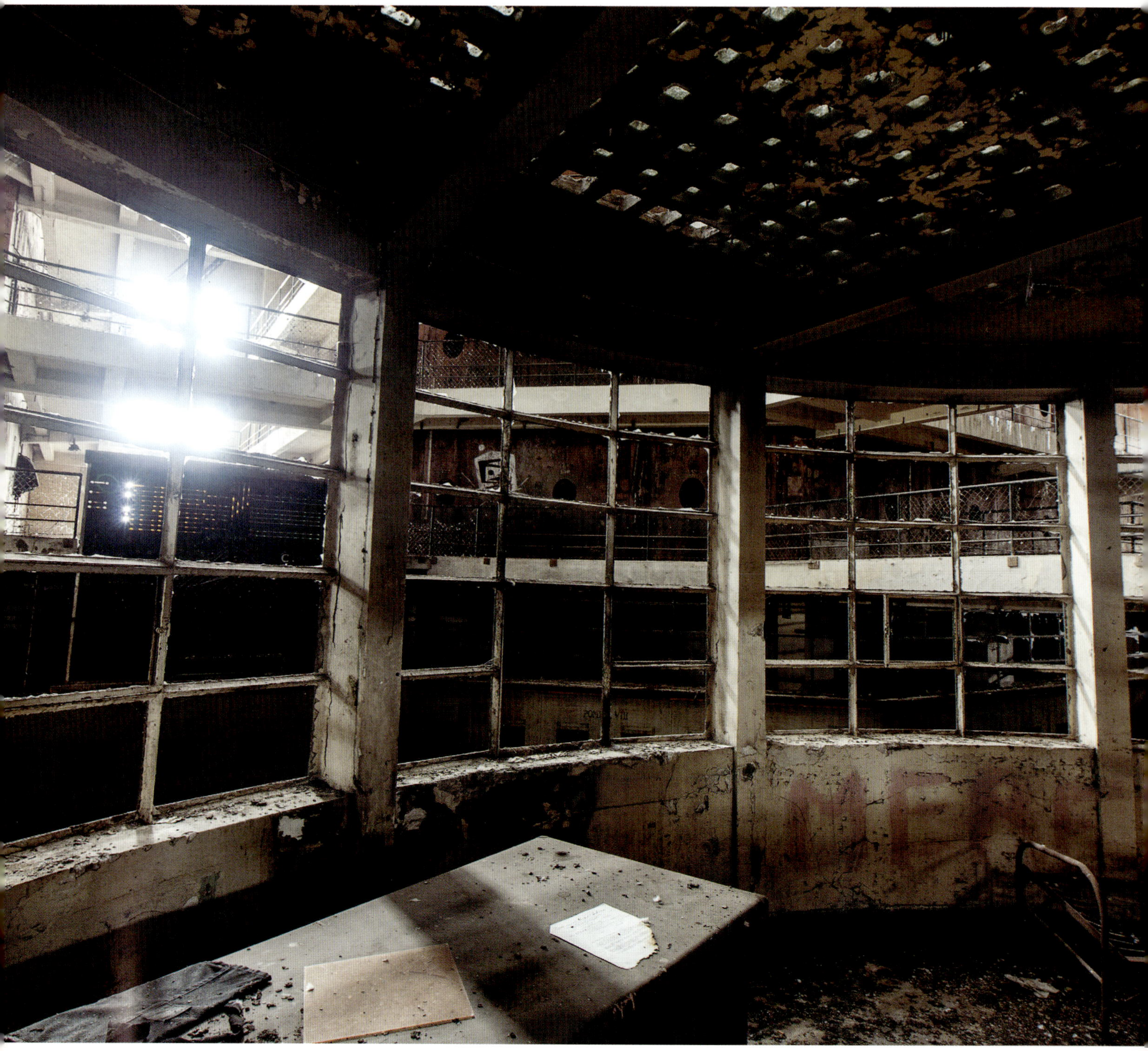

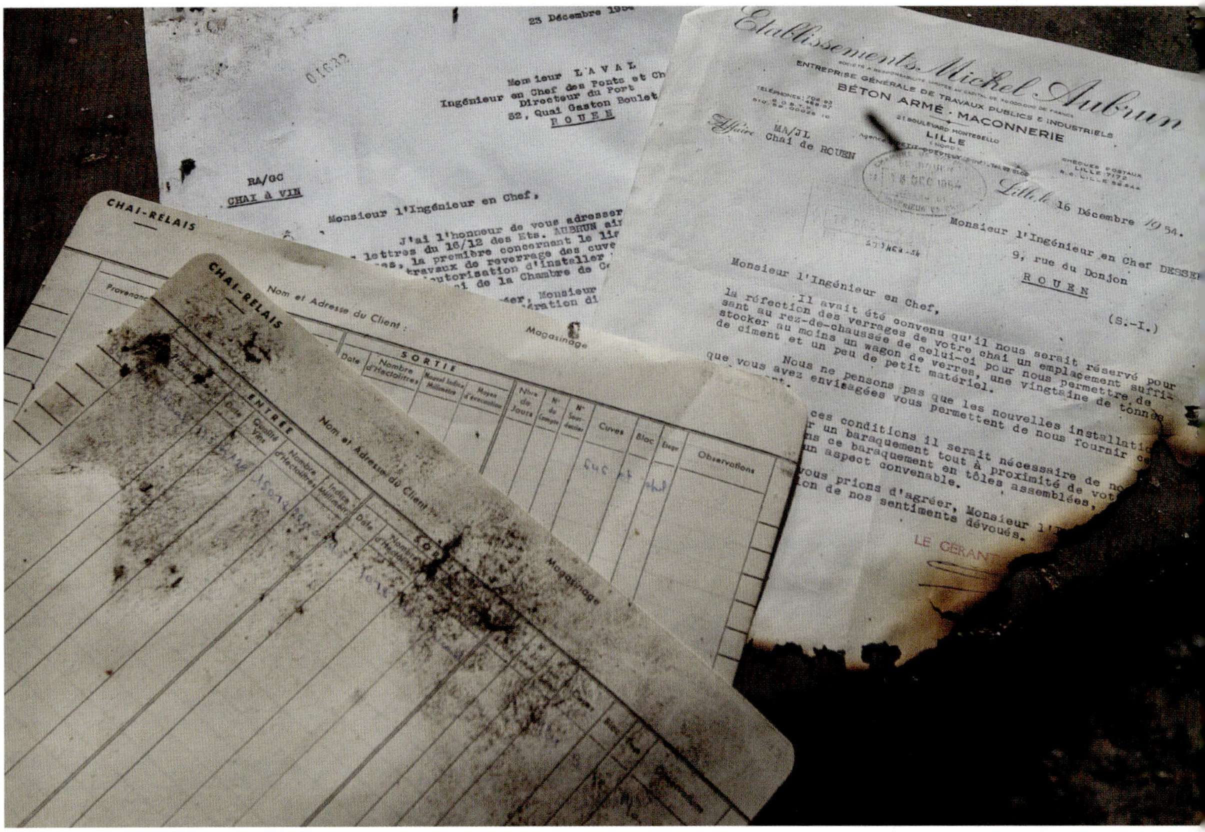

Etablissements Michel Aubrun
ENTREPRISE GÉNÉRALE DE TRAVAUX PUBLICS & INDUSTRIELS
BÉTON ARMÉ . MAÇONNERIE
LILLE
Affaire Chai de ROUEN
Lille, le 16 Décembre 1954.
Monsieur l'Ingénieur en Chef
9, rue du Donjon
ROUEN
Monsieur l'Ingénieur en Chef,
LE GÉRANT
23 Décembre 1954
Monsieur LAVAL
Ingénieur en Chef des Ponts et Ch
Directeur du Port
52, Quai Gaston Boulet
ROUEN
RA/GC
CHAI À VIN
Monsieur l'Ingénieur en Chef,
CHAI-RELAIS
Nom et Adresse du Client :
Magasinage
SORTIE
ENTRÉE
Cuves
Observations

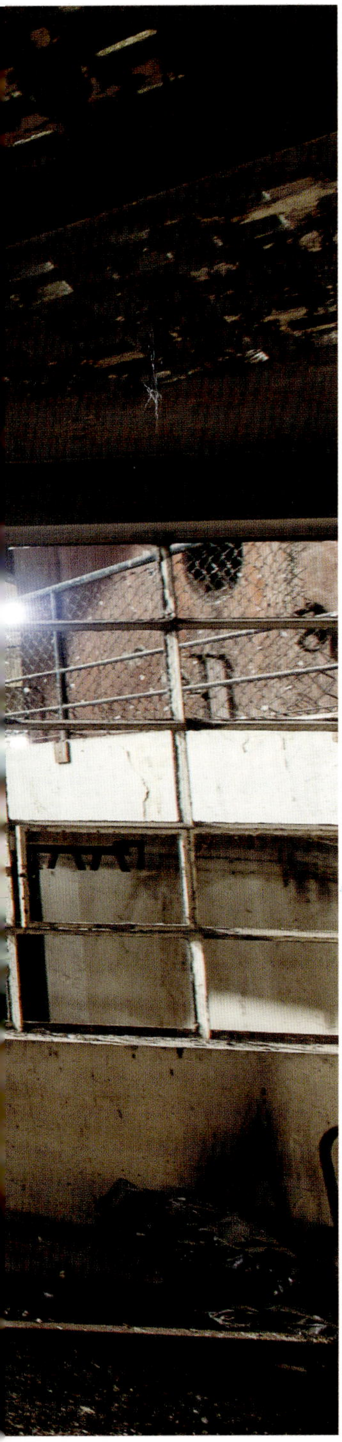

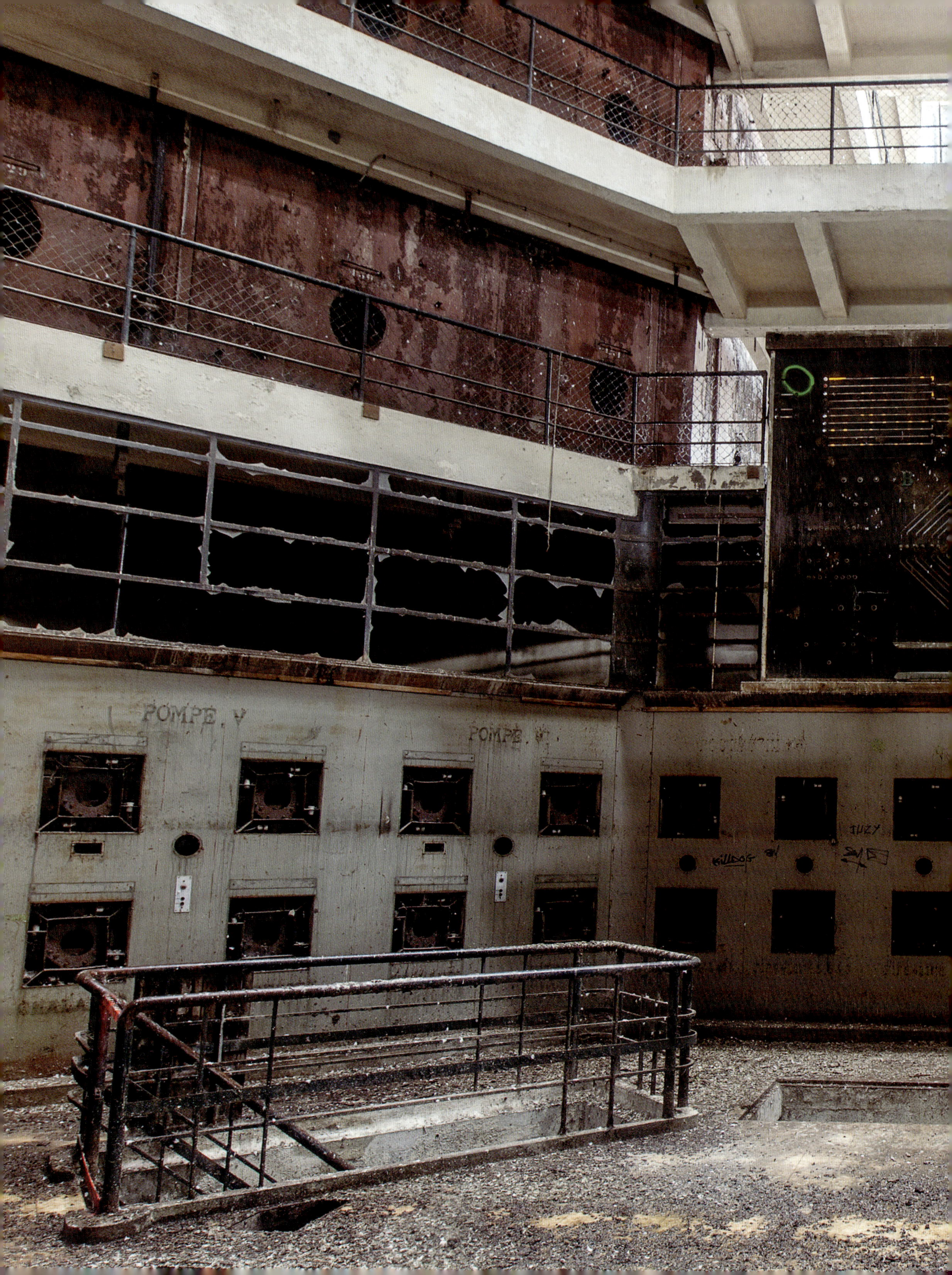
POMPE . V
POMPE V

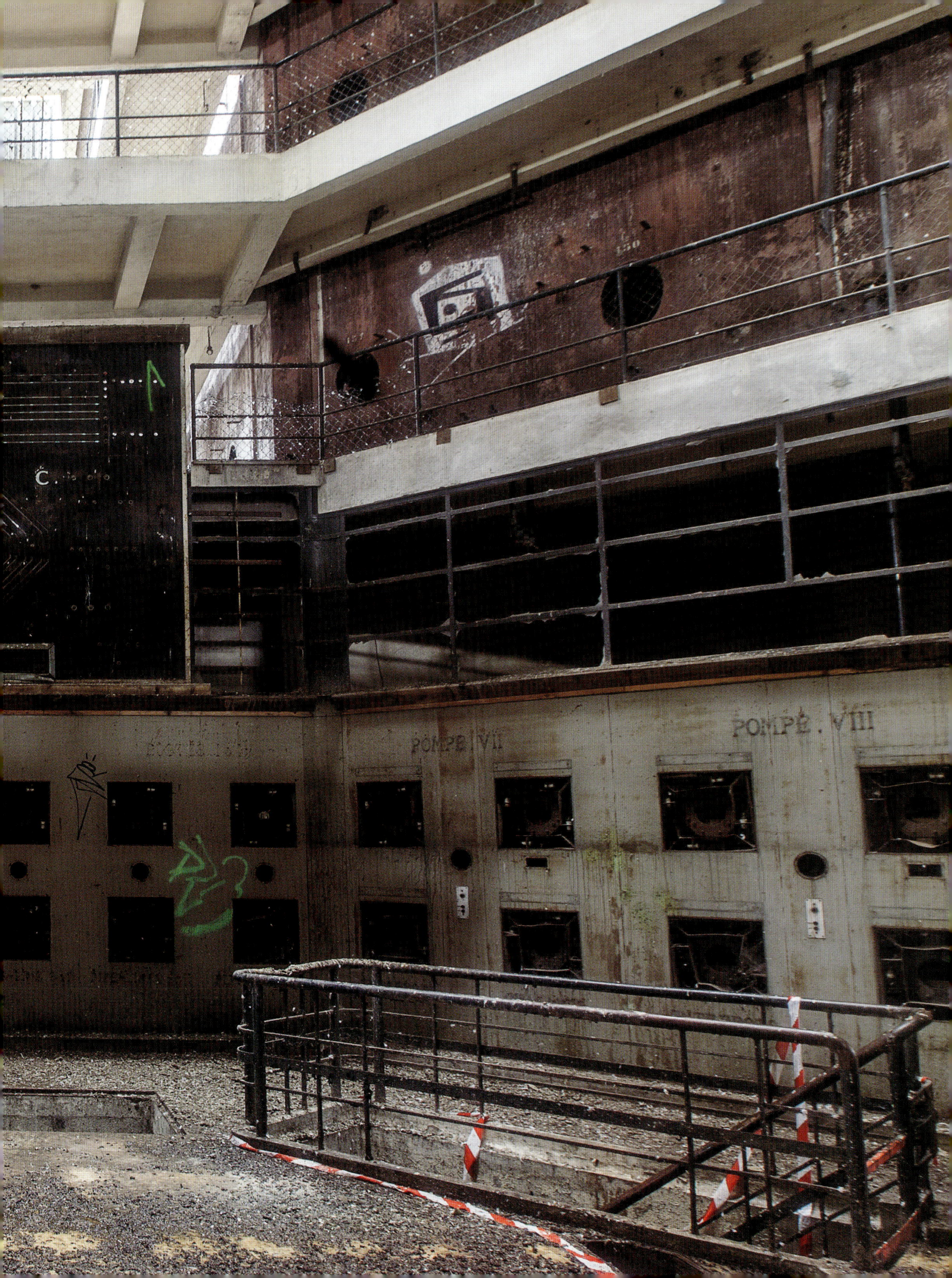
POMPE VII
POMPE . VIII

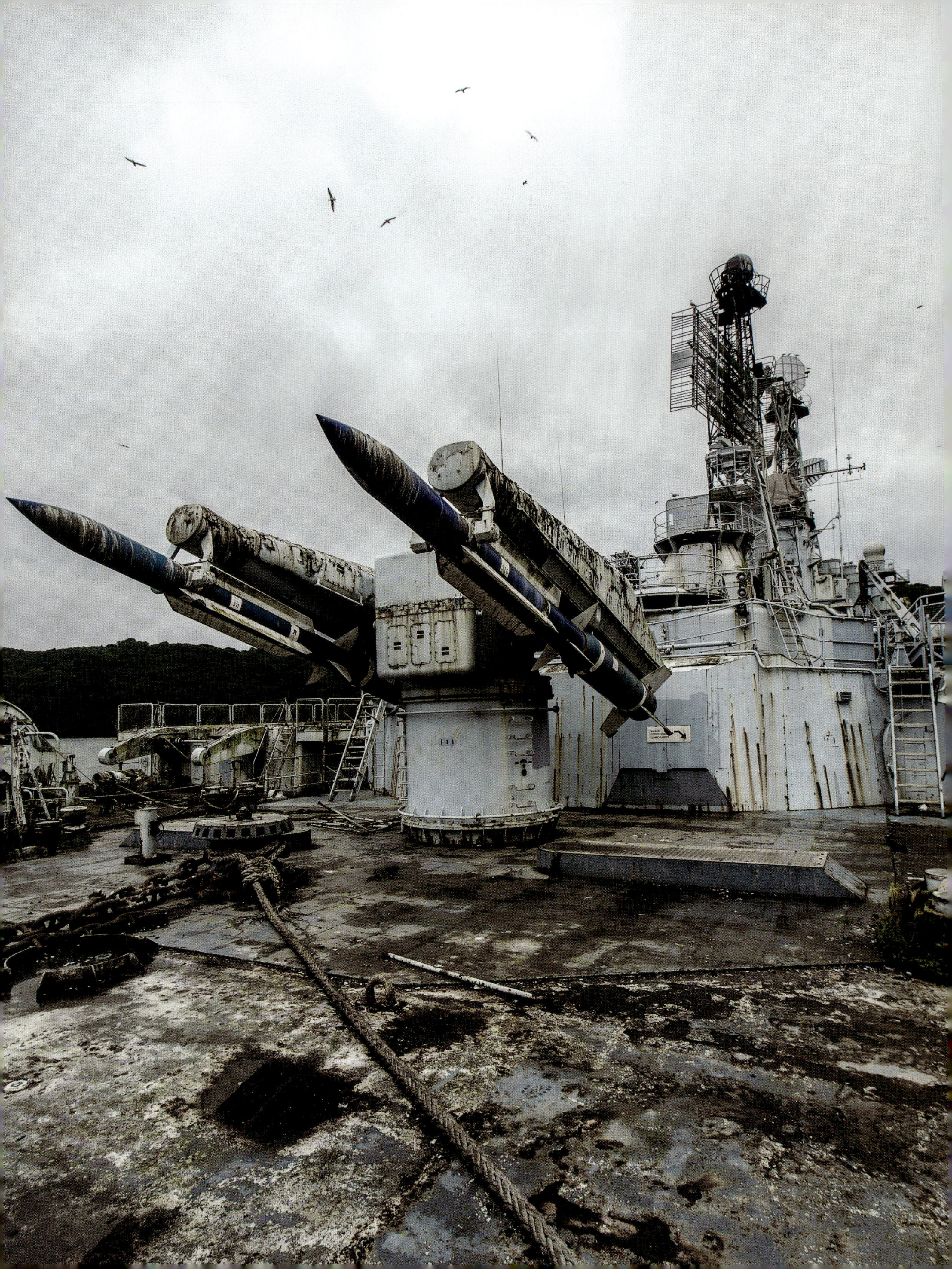

Marine graveyard, Landévennec, Finistère

The seven communes of the Crozon peninsula occupy a narrow outcrop of land in westernmost Brittany. Nestled in the bay of Brest, Landévennec, the smallest of them, enjoys a more congenial climate than its neighbours. It is also sheltered by a bend in the Aulne, the coastal river of Finistère, which flows into the ocean after a last meander where the waters are deep enough to accommodate larger vessels.

The idea of berthing ships there was first mooted in the 17th century, but no action was taken until 1858, when Napoleon III opened a naval base. In the mid-20th century, the naval reserve ships gave way to those awaiting decommissioning. Tighter environmental legislation now obliges shipowners to respect certain regulations for vessels at the end of their working life.

Before mooring, they must first be decontaminated. They are then coated with a layer of antifouling paint to preserve them while in storage. This stage is indispensable as the bay is classified as a Natura 2000 EU nature protection zone. All these operations are banned during the bird-nesting season.

The hulls are moored in the bay until being towed to a ship-breaking yard.

While the ships' graveyard at Landévennec has acquired a certain notoriety – an observation viewpoint has even been set up at the entrance to the village – the approach to this military site (which is under surveillance by the navy) remains off limits.

In early 2017, two frigates and an Antarctic patrol boat were waiting to be stripped down at Landévennec. Others will soon be joining them.

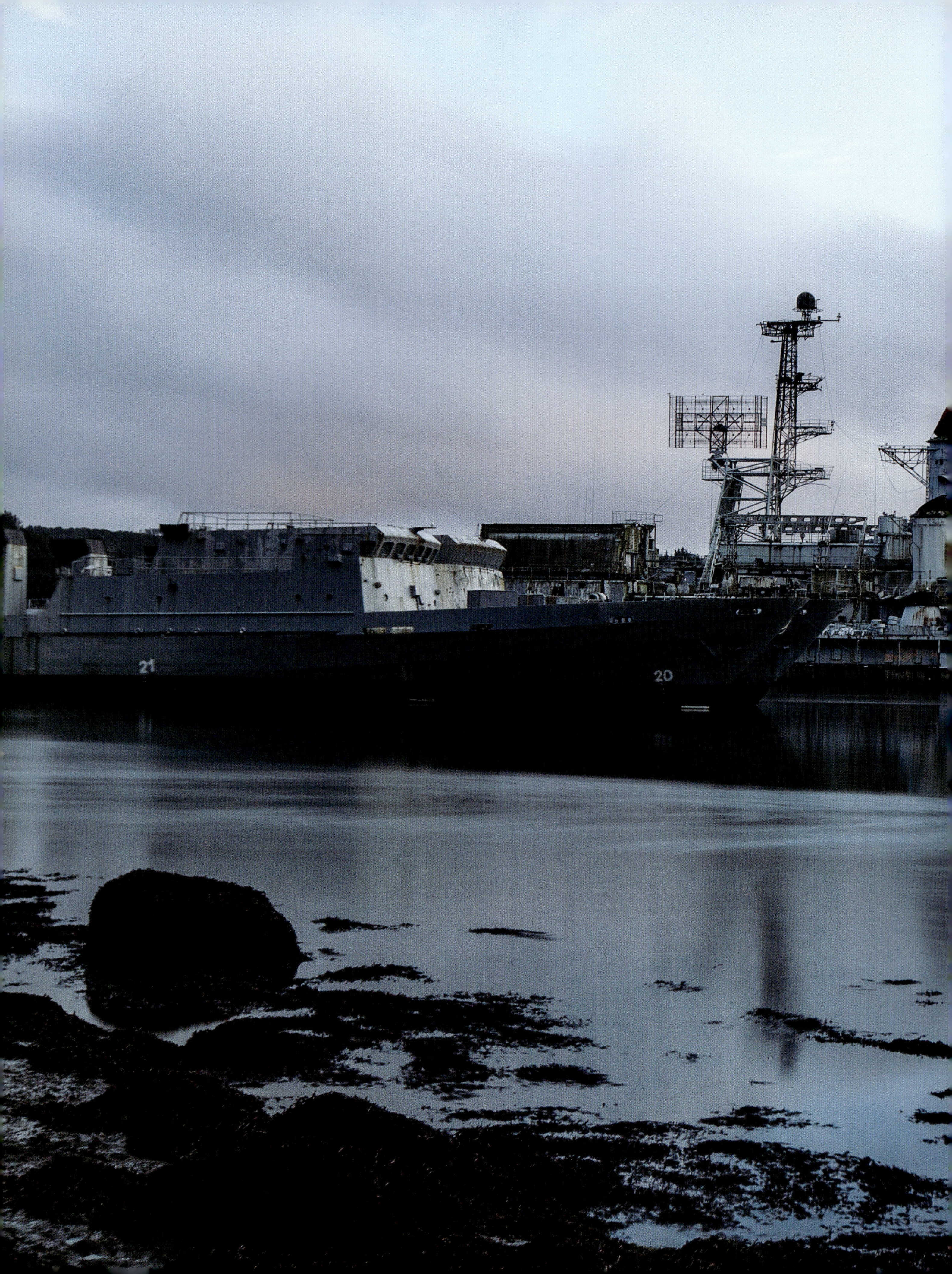
21
20

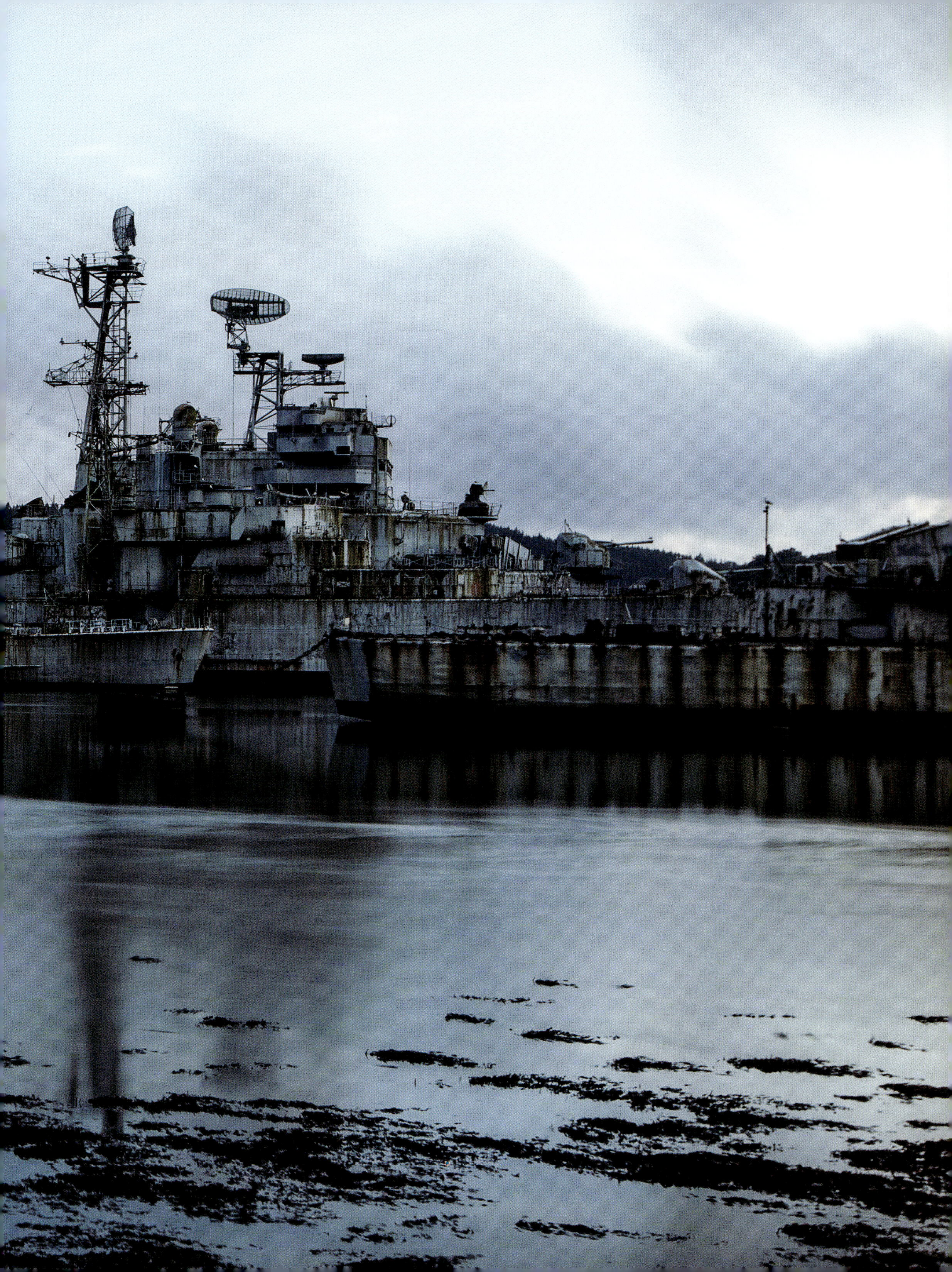

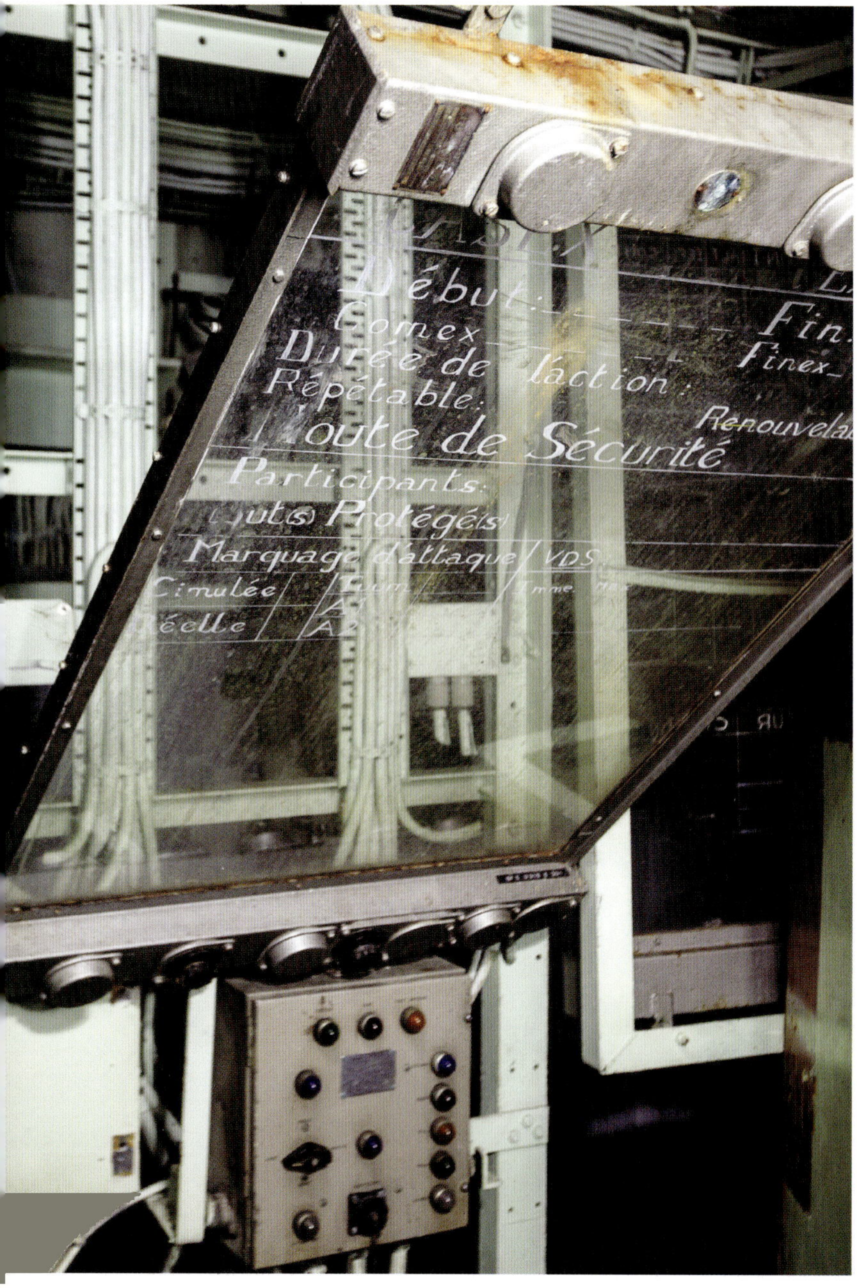
Début
Comex
Finex
Durée de l'action :
Participants :
Marquage d'attaque
VDS

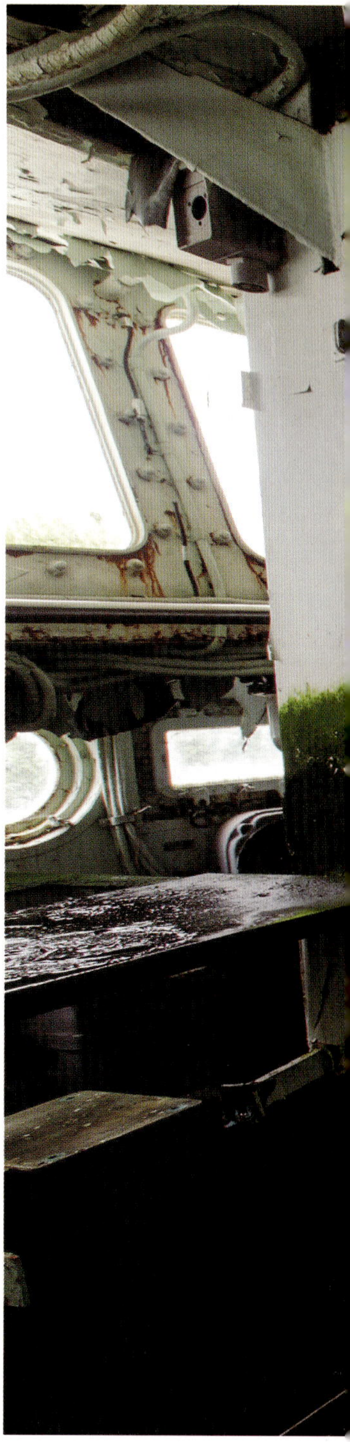

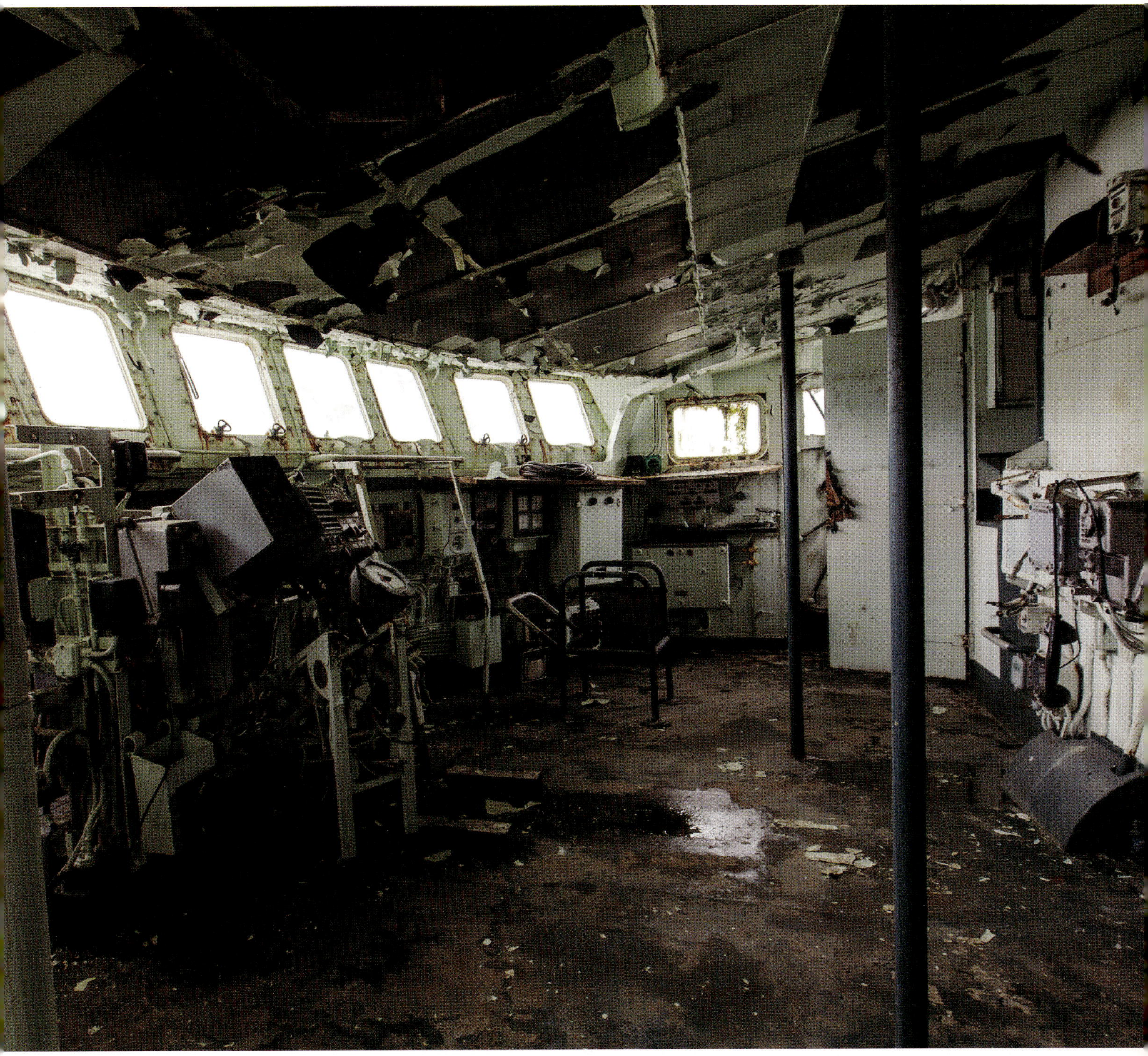

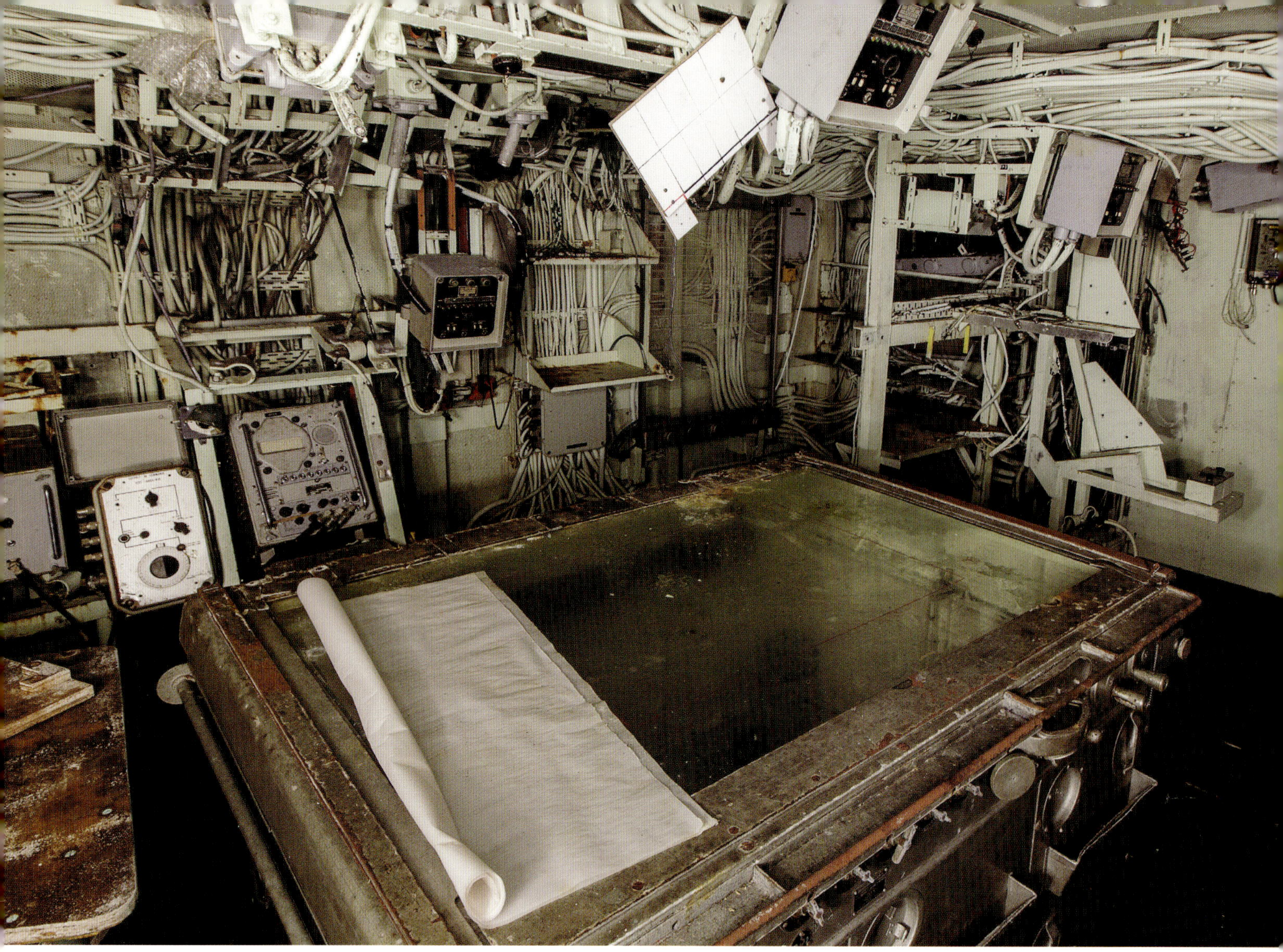

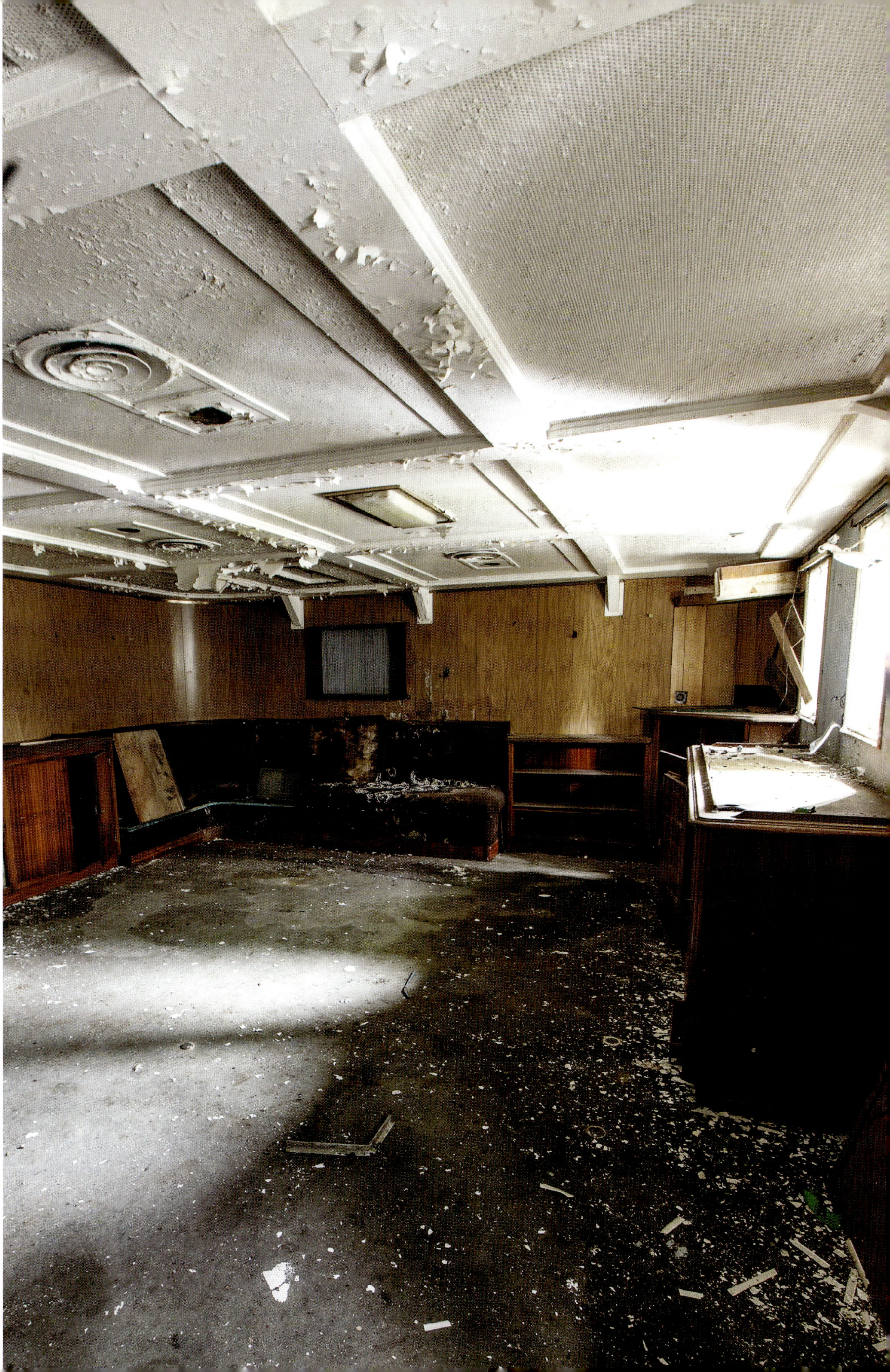

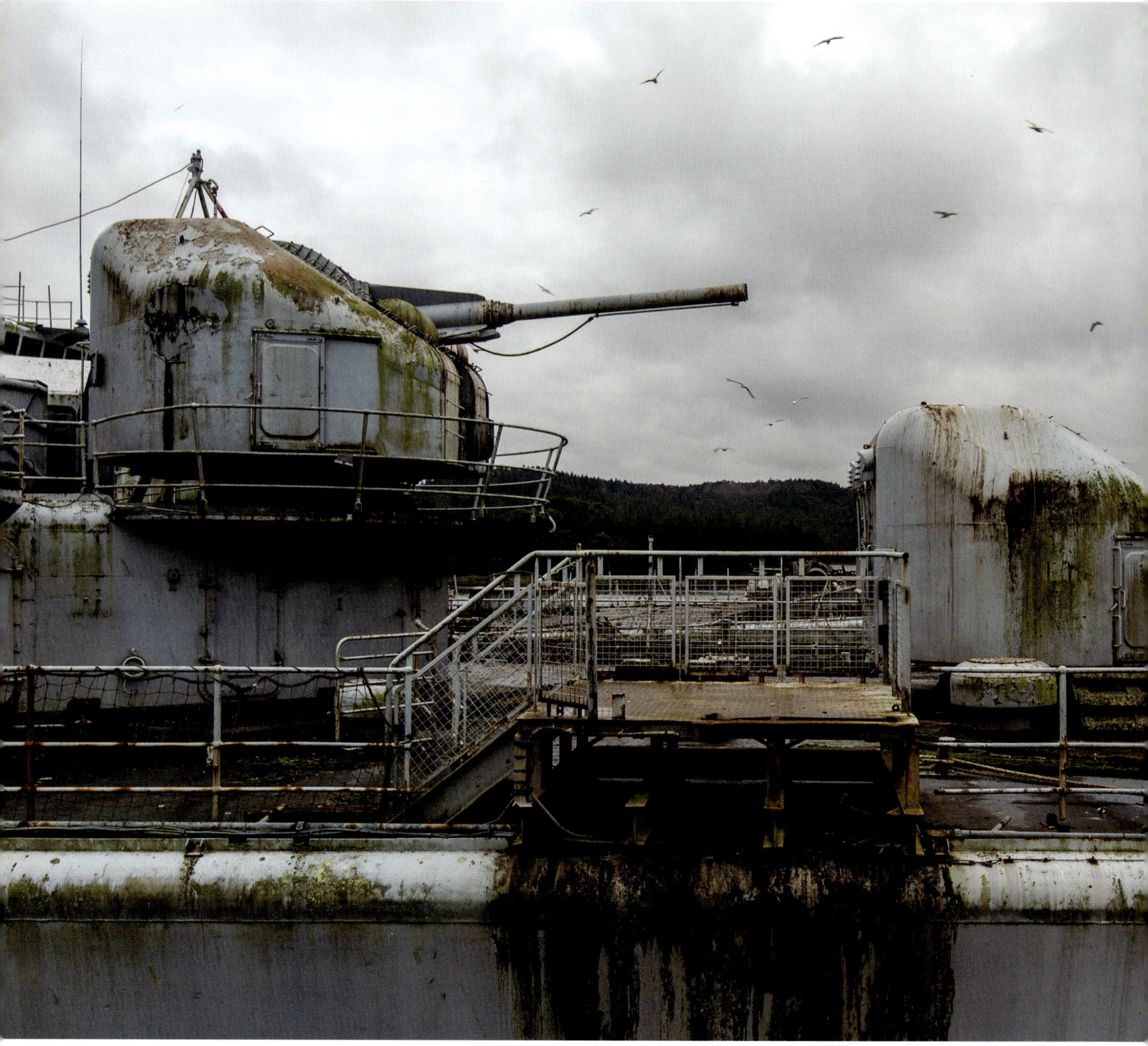

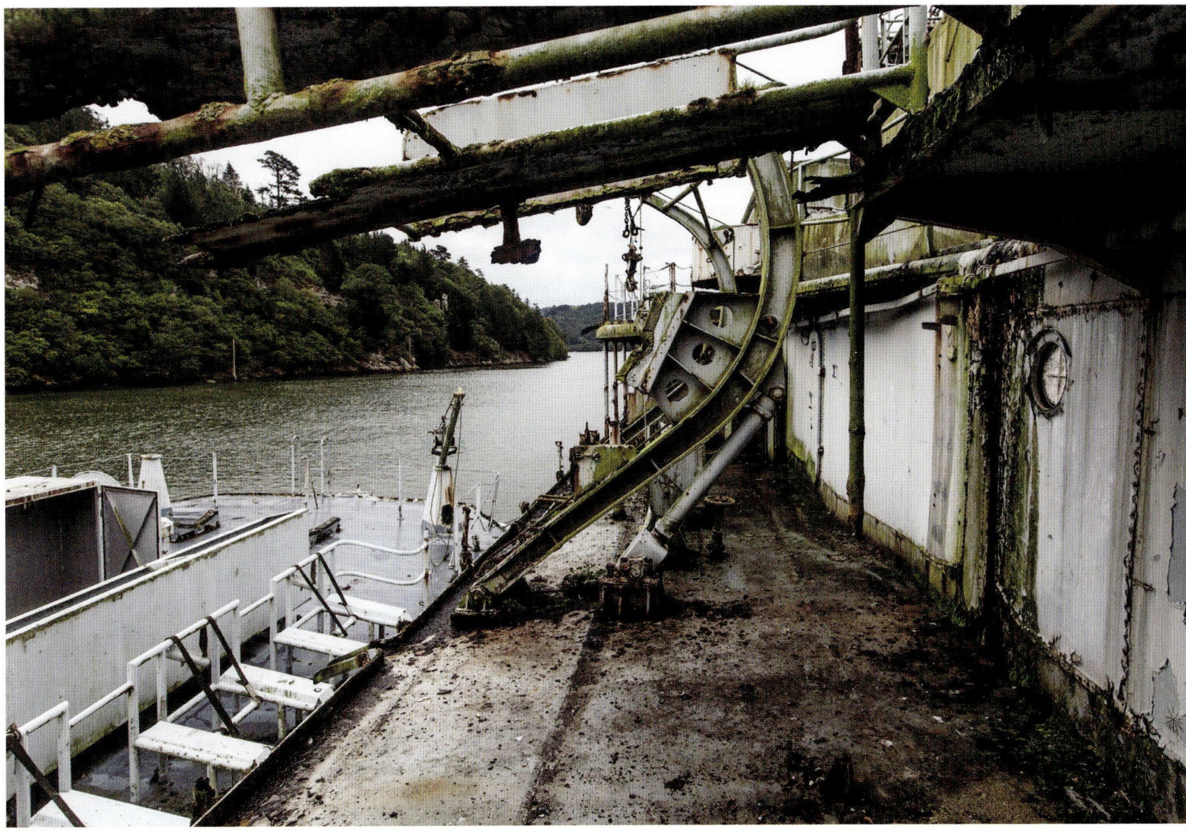

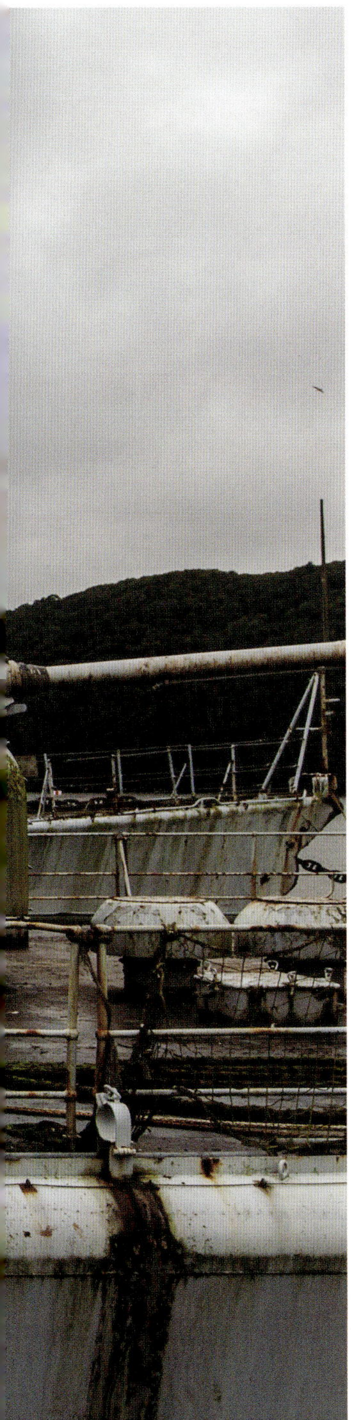

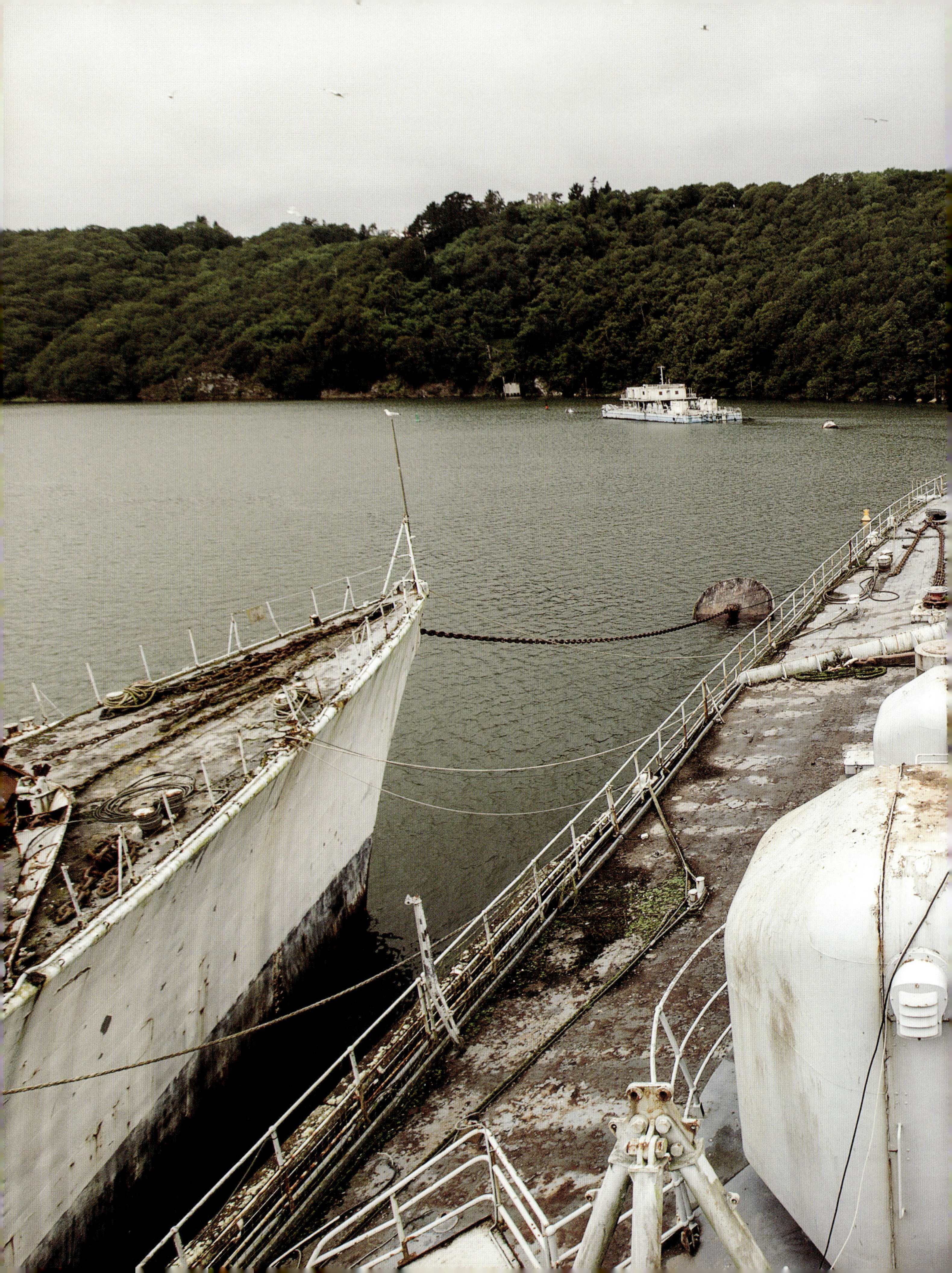

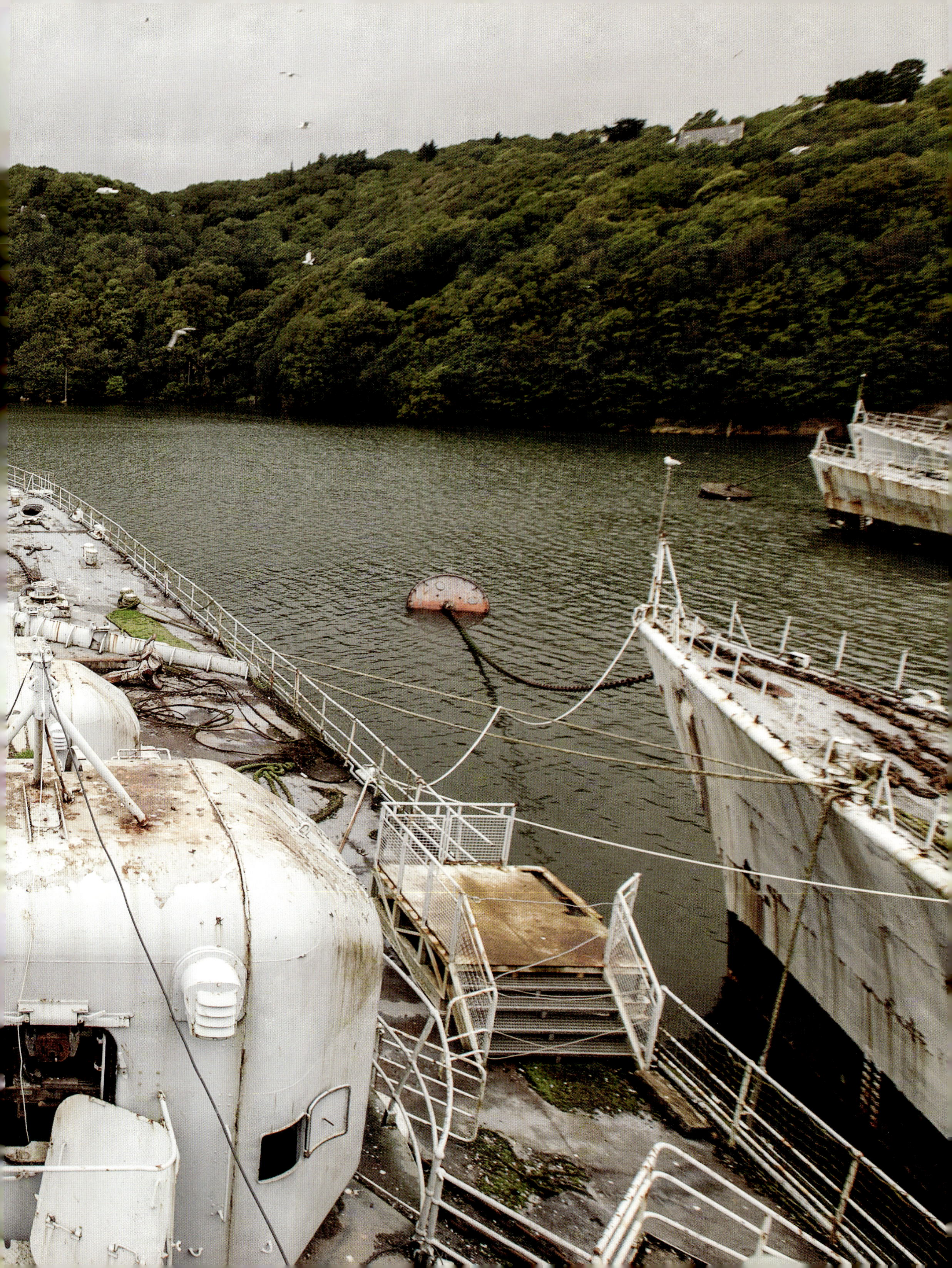

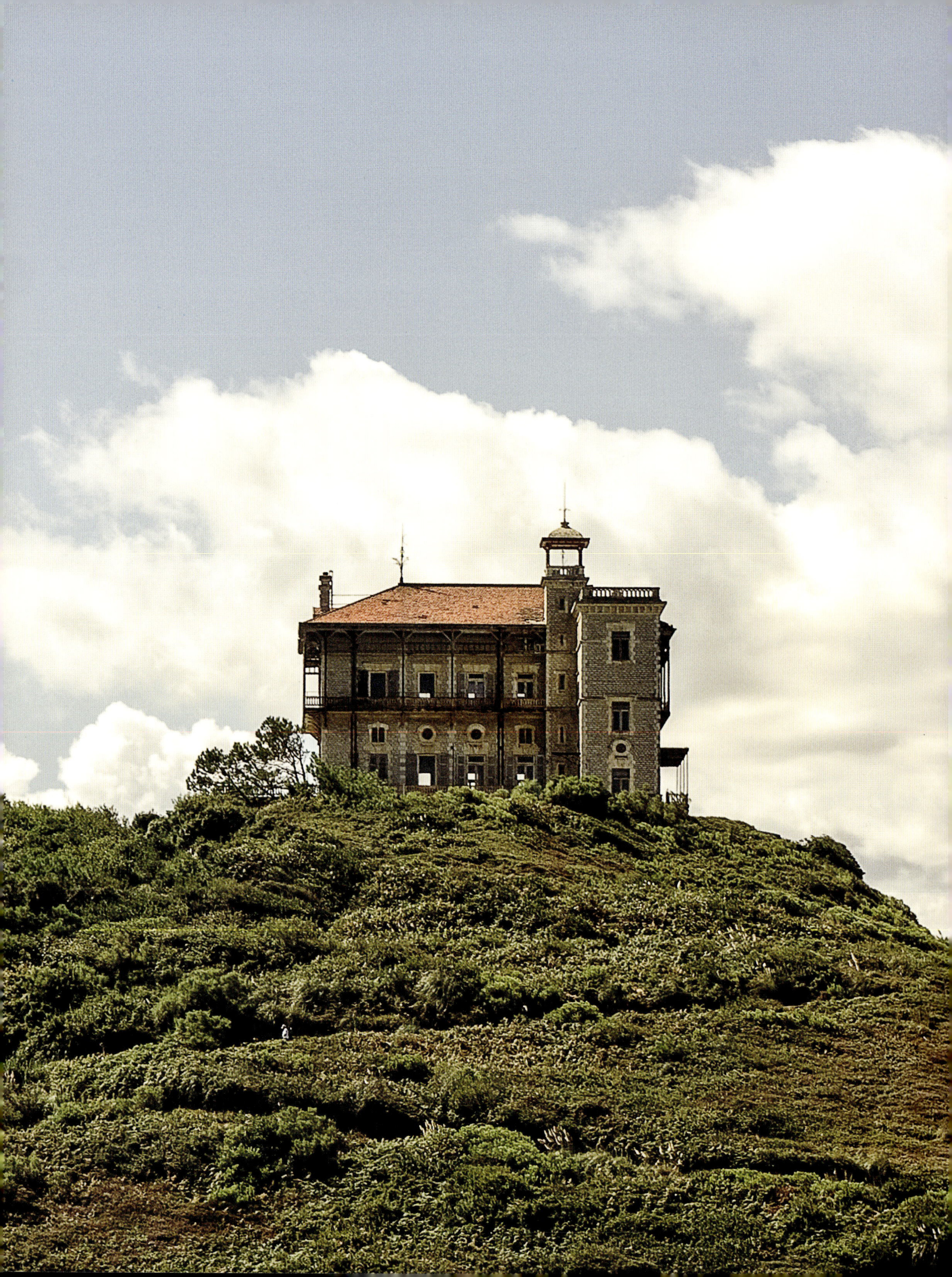

Château d'Ilbarritz, Hayange

Baron Albert de l'Epée, born on 17 September 1852, was a Wendel, the dynasty of forge owners from Hayange in north-eastern France over six generations. The advent of the industrial era had greatly enriched the family at the head of one of the country's largest iron and steel empires.

Albert suffered from chronic bronchitis that undermined his health, so he was unable to undertake any serious studies or follow a career. As a shareholder in the family group, however, he could live on his dividends.

He was an eccentric – passionate about music, new ideas and hunting. He travelled in pursuit of his passions, but with the constant obsessive fear of aggravating his medical condition. Jura, Brittany, Alpes-Maritimes ... whenever a destination attracted him, he built a beautiful residence for occasional visits.

One of his trips took him to the Basque coast, its climate reputedly beneficial for respiratory troubles. He was captivated by the region and bought 60 hectares of land south of Biarritz on the hill of Handia, a remote promontory overlooking the Atlantic. Then he commissioned Gustave Huguenin, a local architect responsible for several eclectic buildings, to design a chateau.

Construction began in 1894. For four years, forty men worked secretly behind high barriers to create a residence with a personality as idiosyncratic as that of its owner.

The first requirement was to install a monumental organ designed by the Parisian organ-maker, Aristide Cavaillé-Coll. This two-storey instrument, the largest ever owned by a private individual, and a galleried organ room was built with a 12-metre ceiling.

One of the baron's residences had lost its roof, carried away by a gust of wind. To avoid a similar incident at Ilbarritz, he and Huguenin planned an incredible roof composed of five superimposed layers. They stacked oak, welded zinc sheets, vitrified and sealed sandstone plates, asbestos and flat tiles – all riveted to an iron frame that was securely fastened to the balconies and bristling with lightning rods. The balconies and terraces are all tarred and covered with a lead screed and then ceramic tiles.

The hypochondriac baron, who was obsessed with hygiene, paid particular attention to health and safety: the solid oak doors are double thickness, the windows have double or triple glazing. Rainwater was collected and filtered for distribution to all floors via a sophisticated system of electric pumps. It ran from silver-plated taps. The heating was by electric lamps and radiators. The basements were paved with stone. All curtains, carpets and other textiles likely to attract dust were banned. Interior decoration was reduced to large mirrors and features made from precious wood or marble.

The exterior appearance of this 3,000-square-metre building is an incarnation of this quest for sobriety. Huguenin borrowed from the "hygienist" architecture of a sanatorium to conceive the chateau, which is designed over three floors in the form of a T. The longest bar is the main building housing the organ room. Two towers of unequal height are linked at right angles.

Some fifteen buildings connected by 4 kilometres of covered galleries make up this enormous property. There are numerous kitchens, a bakery, a hydroelectric plant, a bathing hut, several heated swimming pools, a medieval castle, a Chinese-style kennel and a look-out tower 40 metres in height.

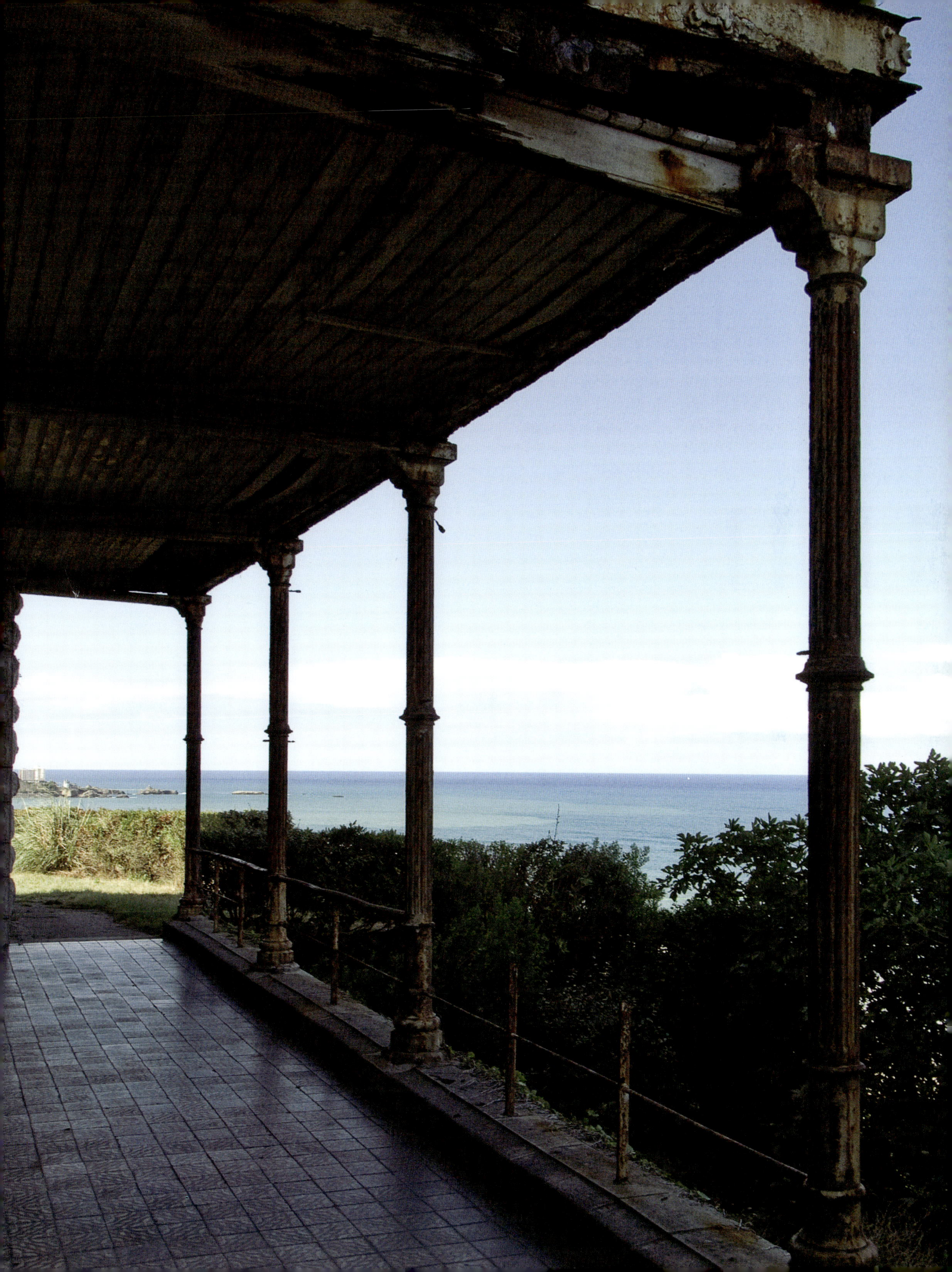

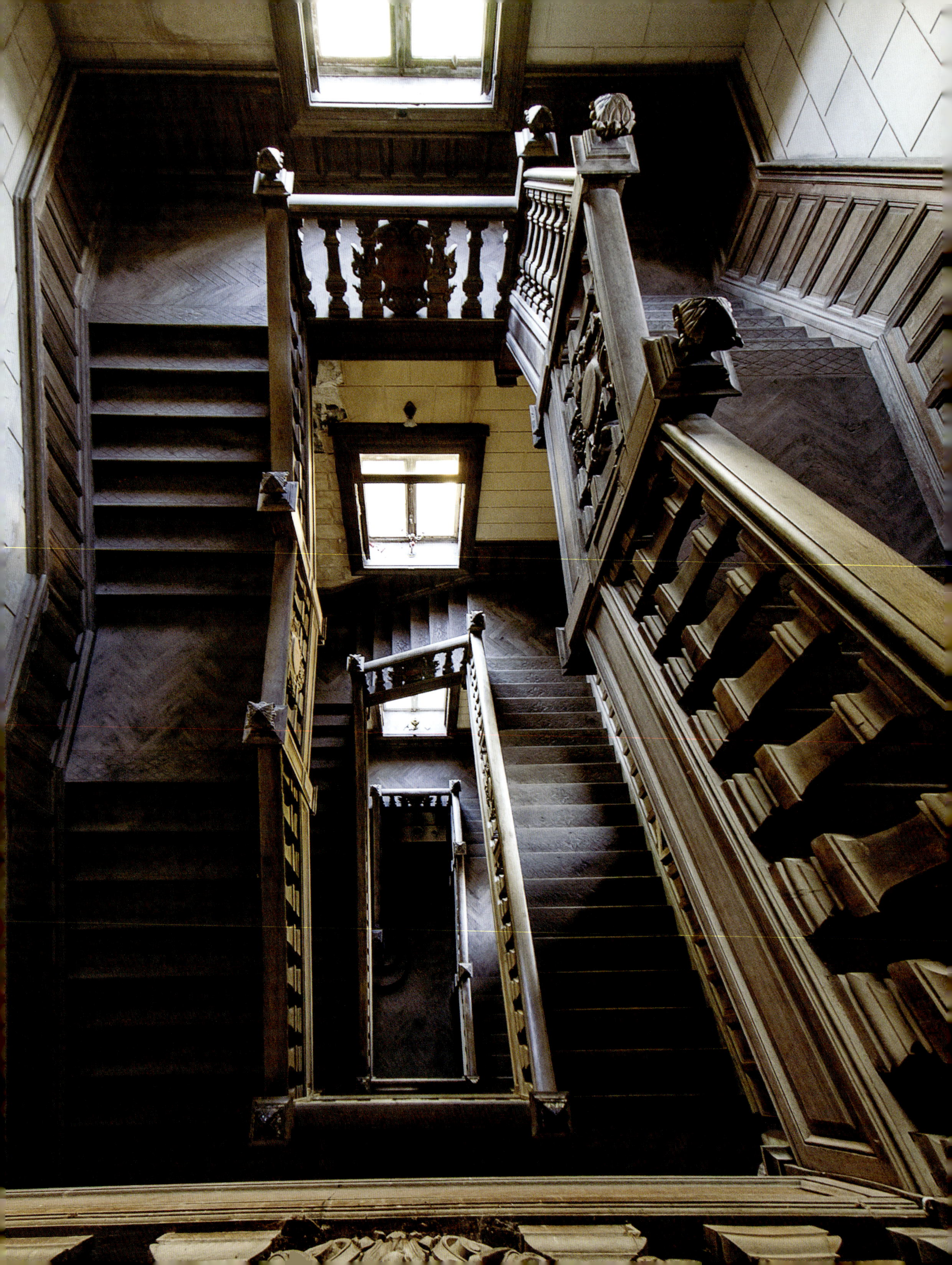

In 1897, Albert de l'Epée finally settled in his Biarritz domain with his mistress and her mother. Both were accommodated in the luxury villa the baron had built by the sands at the foot of Handia hill. A year later the idyll ended, along with their affair, and he abandoned Ilbarritz.

The organ was dismantled in 1903 and eventually relocated to the Basilica of the Sacred Heart in Montmartre.

Two years later, the baron reinvested in his chateau. A smaller organ was commissioned from Cavaillé-Coll's successor for the main hall. This new craze was to be of short duration, however, as the chateau was sold on 24 December 1911. It was acquired by Pierre-Barthélemy Gheusi, director of the Parisian Opéra Comique, who wanted to turn it into a theatre. War broke out and Ilbarritz was used as a hospital.

After the Armistice, the estate was broken up and the ancillary buildings demolished. The chateau was converted into a sanctuary for refugees from the Spanish Civil War before being requisitioned by the German army. After years of postwar neglect and vandalism the building was in a derelict state, but it was finally renovated in 1958 as an up-market hotel. Further modifications were then made, with the addition of a chapel. In April 1960, it hosted the first French tests for colour television broadcasts to the general public. Registration as a historical monument on 30 May 1990 put an end to the conversion projects. In 2014, abandoned, Ilbarritz was bought by businessman Bruno Ledoux, who plans to invest the 12 million euros needed for its restoration. The new project: another luxury hotel following the plans of French designer Ora-ïto. By 2017, negotiations between the architects and Bâtiments de France were under way.

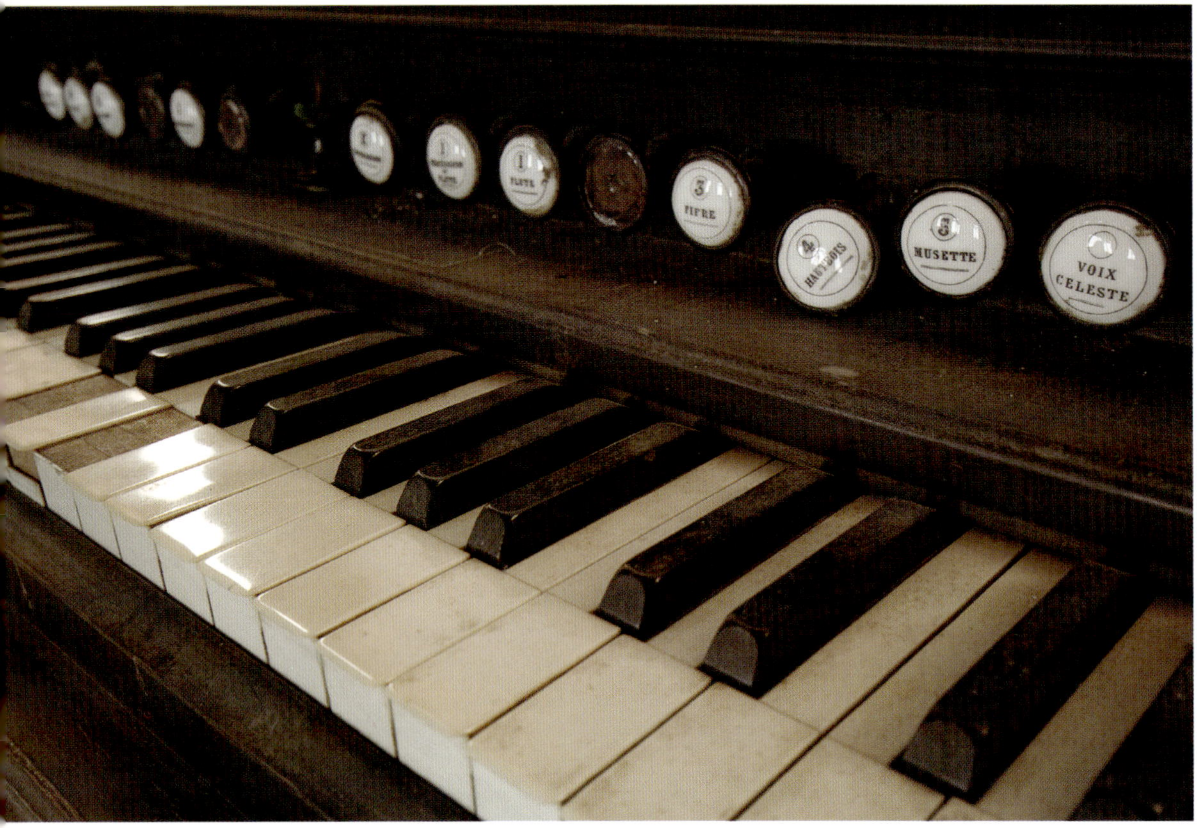
FIFRE
MUSETTE
VOIX CELESTE

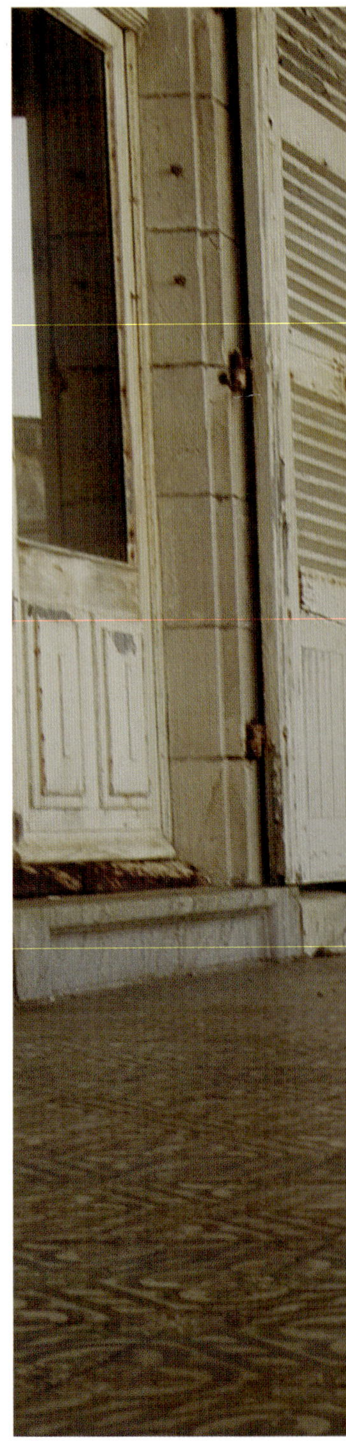

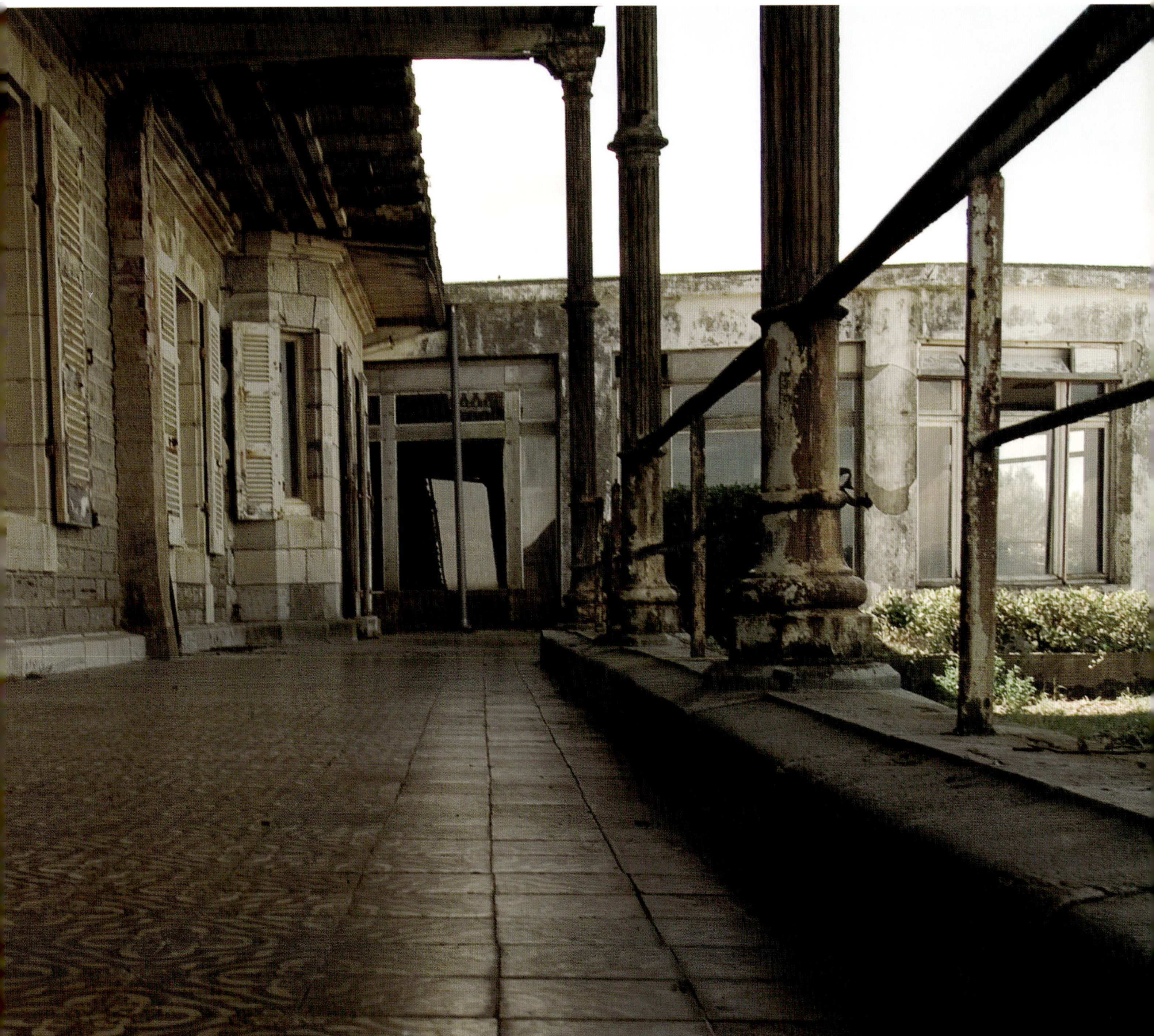

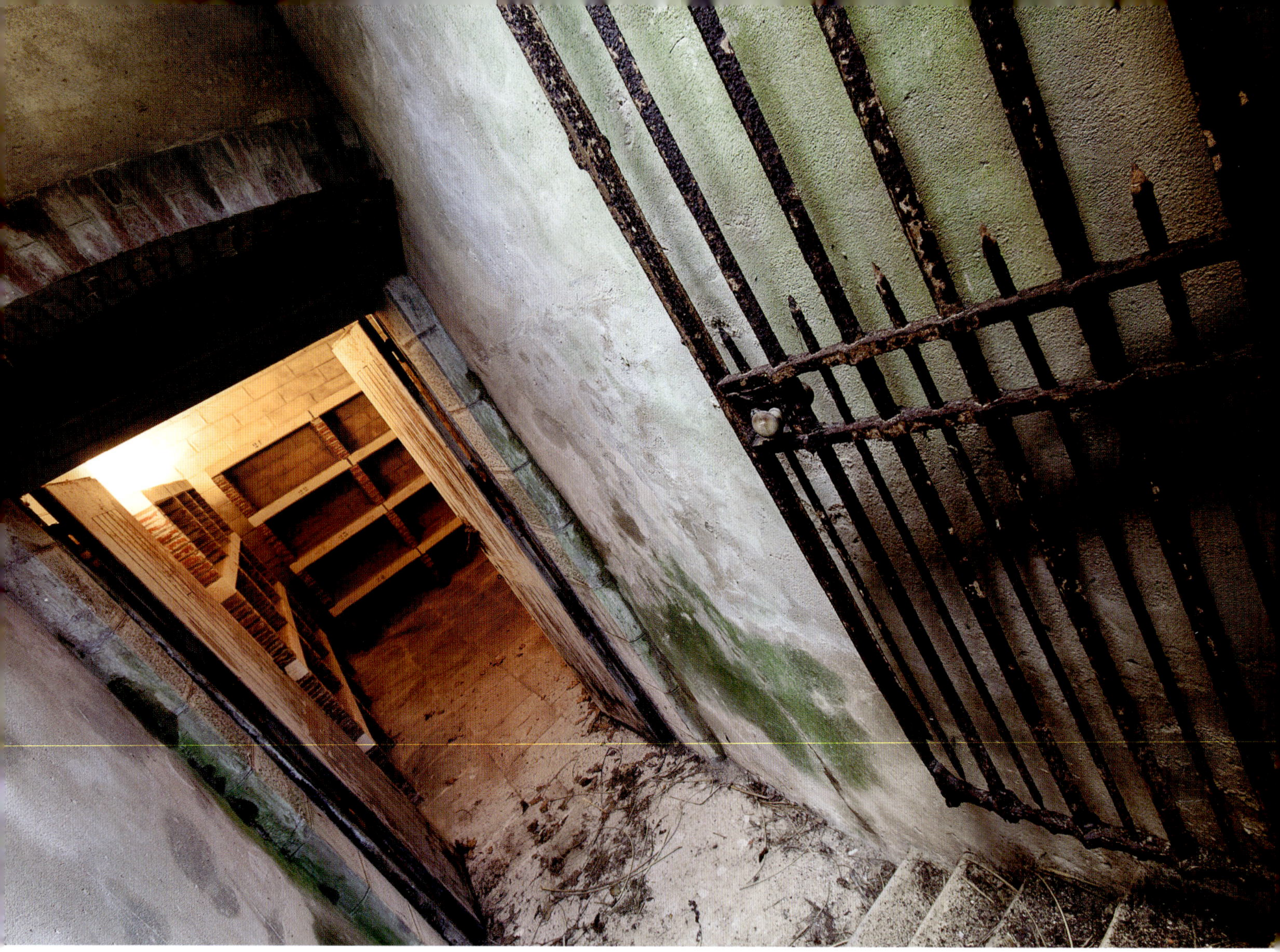

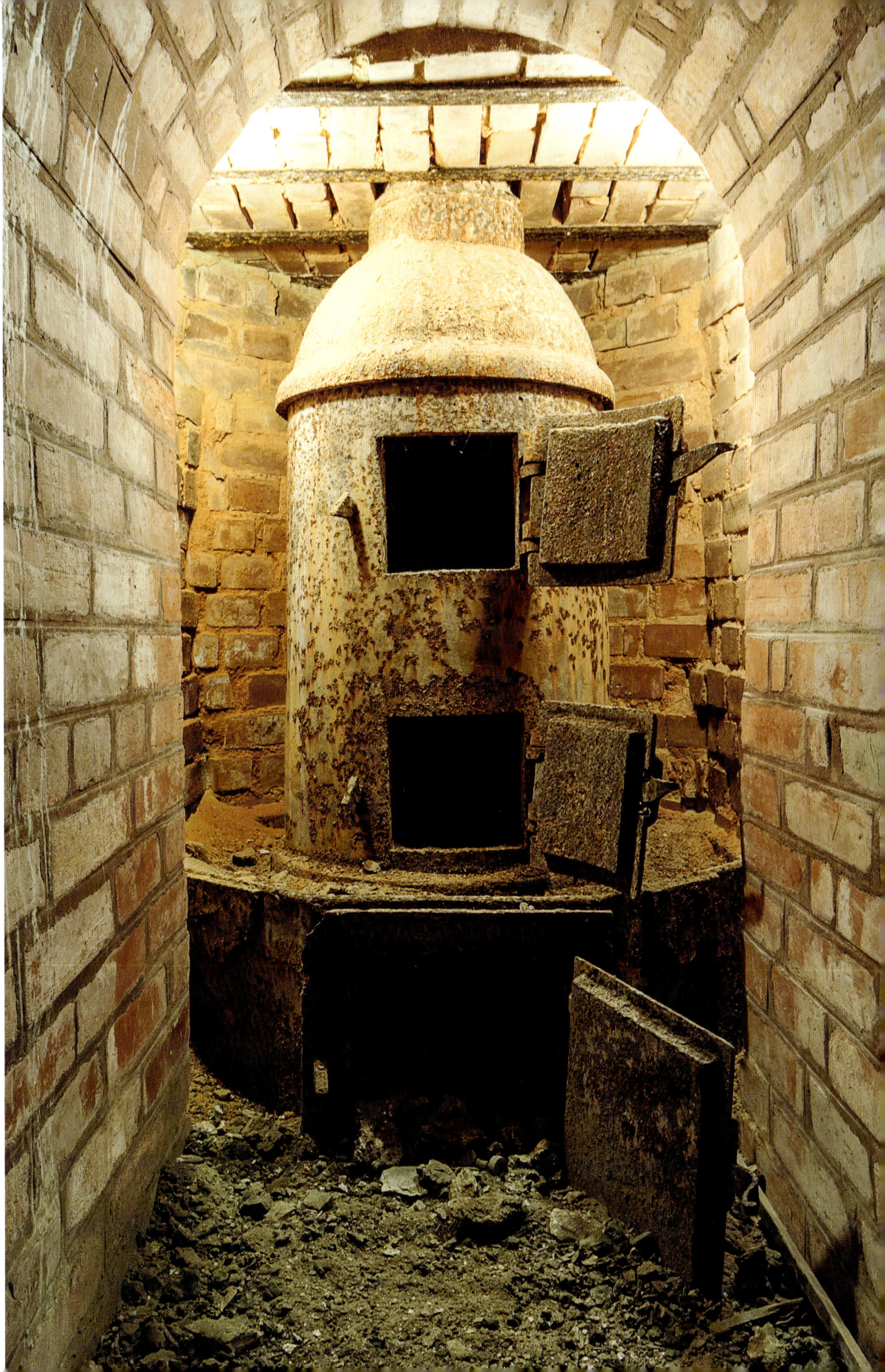

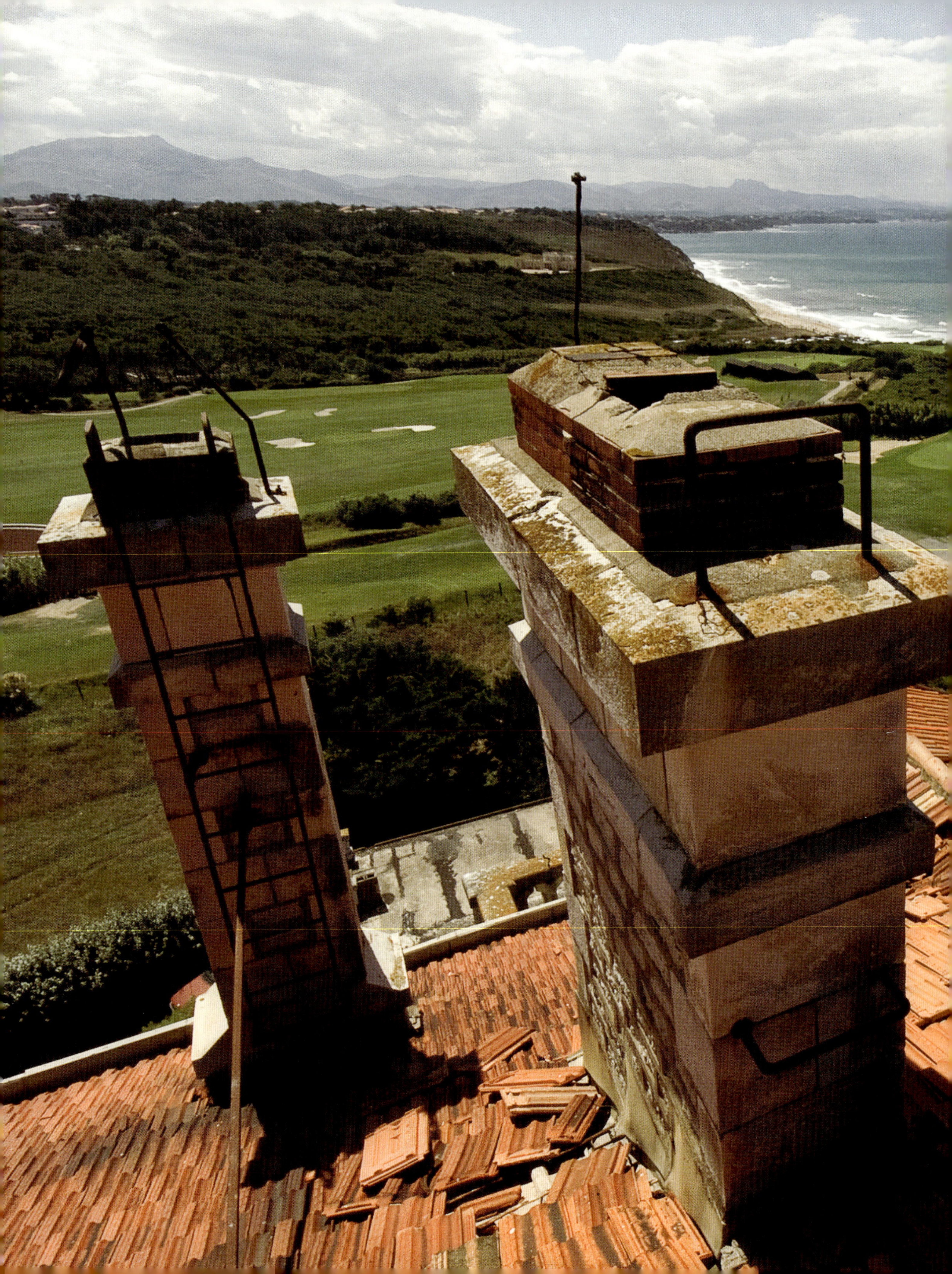

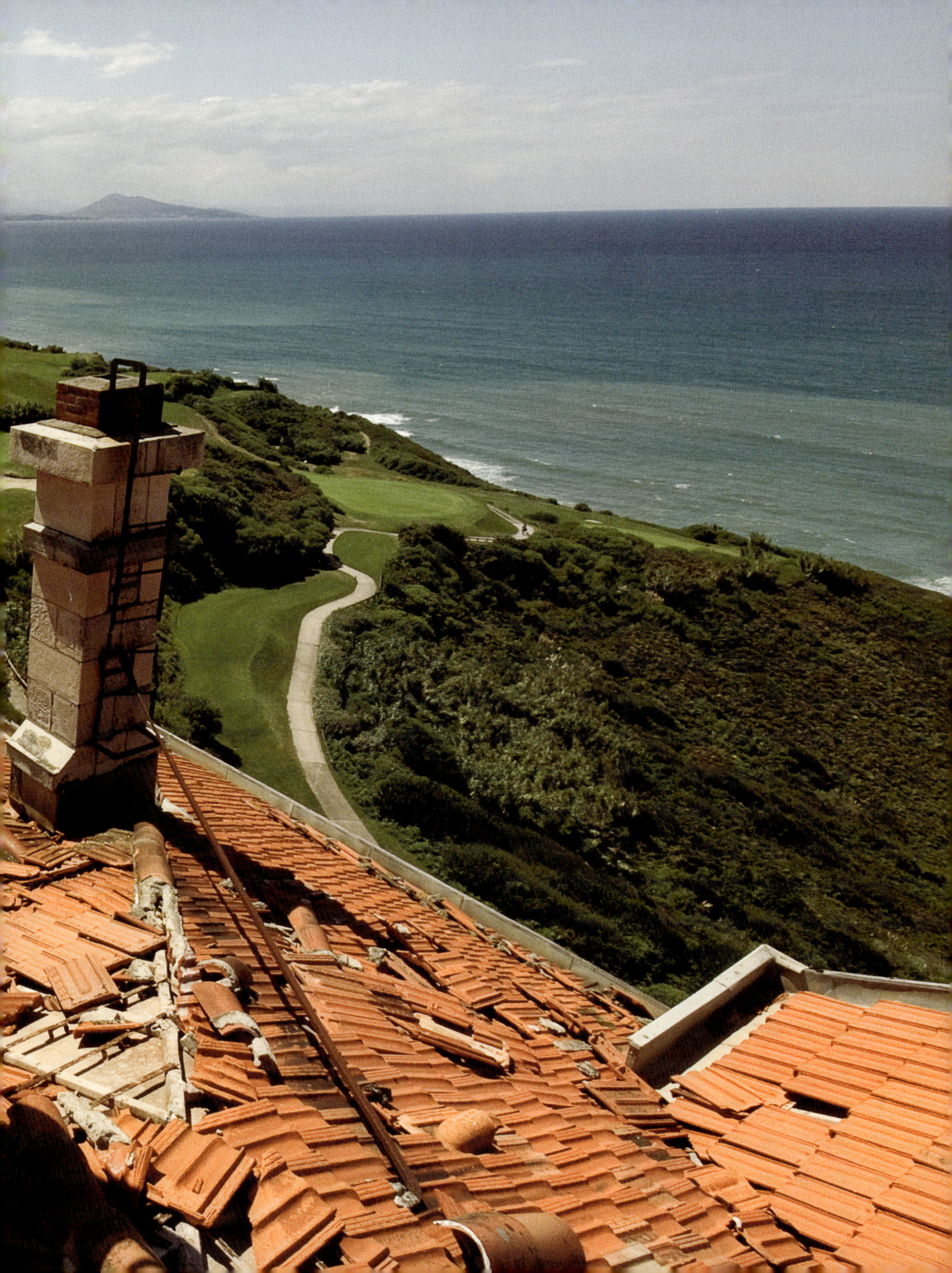

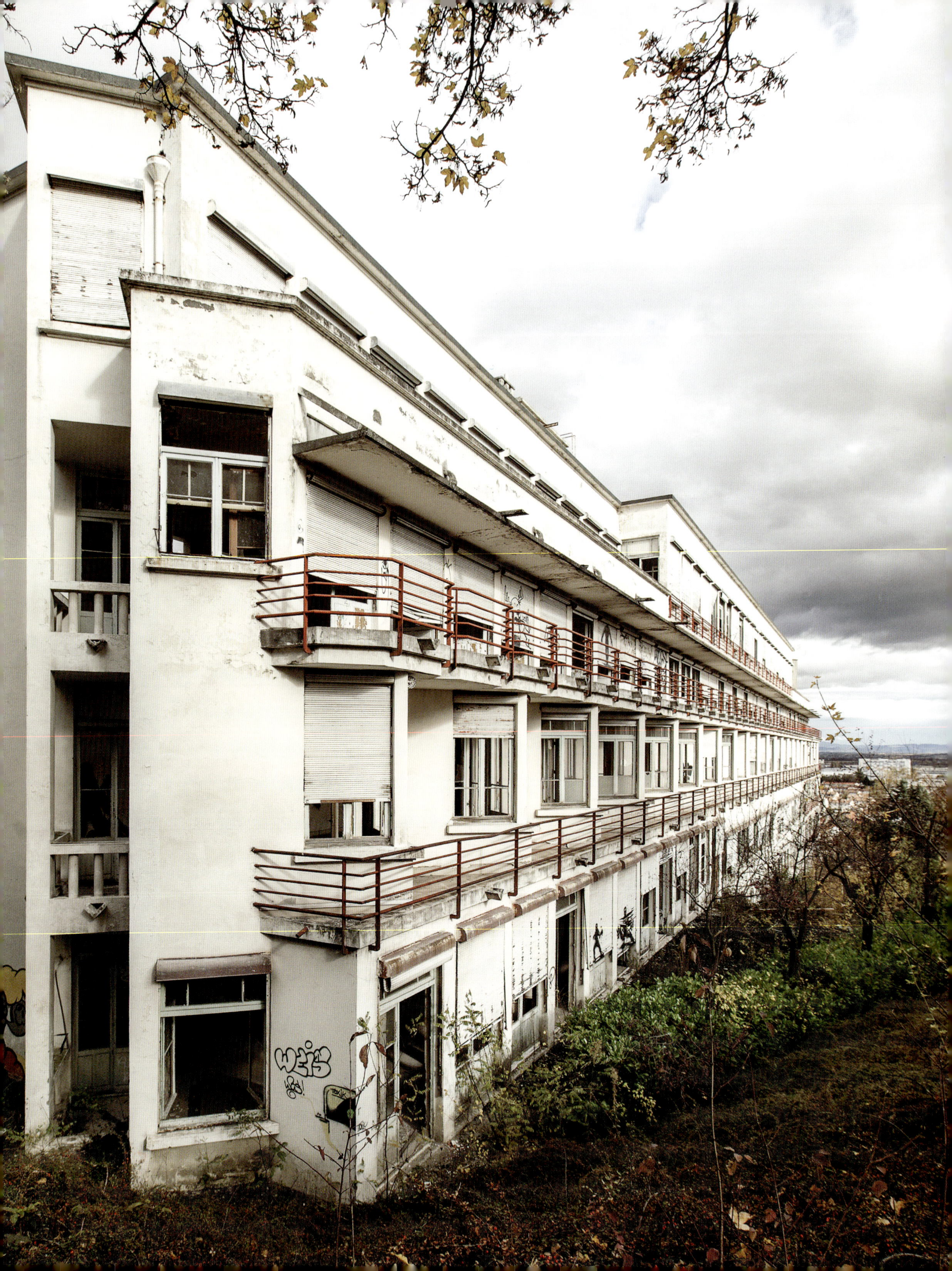

Hôpital-Sanatorium Charles Sabourin, Clermont-Ferrand

Although there are no accurate figures for the number of tuberculosis-related deaths in France in 1900, the contagious nature of the disease and the flood of patients into the hospital services forced the state to take action. Among the legislation adopted was the Honnorat law (named for its sponsor, deputy André Honnorat), passed in 1919, which obliged each department to provide a sanatorium to treat tuberculosis patients while isolating them from the rest of the population.

In Clermont-Ferrand in central France, however, these patients were still sent to the Hôtel-Dieu in the city, until in 1935 the urban district was equipped with a sanatorium designed by the architect of the city hospices, Albéric Aubert. He was inspired by the modernist theories of Corbusier and Bauhaus founder Walter Gropius. This building, with its radically different lines, stands on the side of a hill to the north-east of the city. It describes a long T-shape with the crossbar stretching on both sides for some hundred metres, and scarcely 10 metres wide. The metal-framed concrete structure was designed to resist the frequent tremors in this earthquake-prone region.

The clean, uncluttered layout is based on the principles of the functionalist movement. The medical unit is located in the north wing, while rooms for 200 patients face south to make the most of the sunlight. Large bay windows break up the façades. On the second floor, a partly translucent concrete dome further brightens the interior with its omnipresent whiteness.

Particular attention was paid to thermal and acoustic insulation, heating, and the circulation of air and water. The innovations even included the distribution to all services of hot water, a rare commodity at the time.

In addition to the rooms on three floors and the inevitable general services, the facilities included a chapel, places to live and relax, even a solarium on the roof terrace that patients could reach with the aid of a bed-lift. Staff were housed in a separate building. The complex was named Hôpital-Sanatorium Charles Sabourin, in memory of a doctor who was famous for his work on pulmonary conditions.

The sanatorium, damaged during the Second World War, was under repair until 1950 and underwent several modifications. During this period, antibiotics were beginning to prove themselves in the fight against tuberculosis and the isolation of patients was no longer deemed necessary, freeing up space for the treatment of other lung problems and the study of allergies. Sabourin was decommissioned in 1997 after the reorganisation of Clermont-Ferrand medical services. A permit for its demolition was signed the following year, provoking a strong reaction from associations and professionals involved in the preservation of the architectural heritage. Their mobilisation led to the complex of buildings and gardens being registered as a historical monument on 24 March 2000.

The state acquired the property in 2002 to house the École Nationale Supérieure d'Architecture de Clermont-Ferrand (ENSACF), which had been in the cramped premises of the former school of chemistry in the city centre.

A tender for projects was launched in 2007 by the Établissement Public de Maitrise d'Ouvrage des Travaux Culturels. The Parisian urban architectural firm of Besset-Lyon won. It favoured the preservation of typical features, especially the building's roots in the landscape and its relationship to the light, while adapting it to modern standards.

An extension has been added to the formerly less-developed north façade.

The project, completed in time for the start of the 2015 academic year, was rewarded with the ArchiDesignClub 2016 prize.

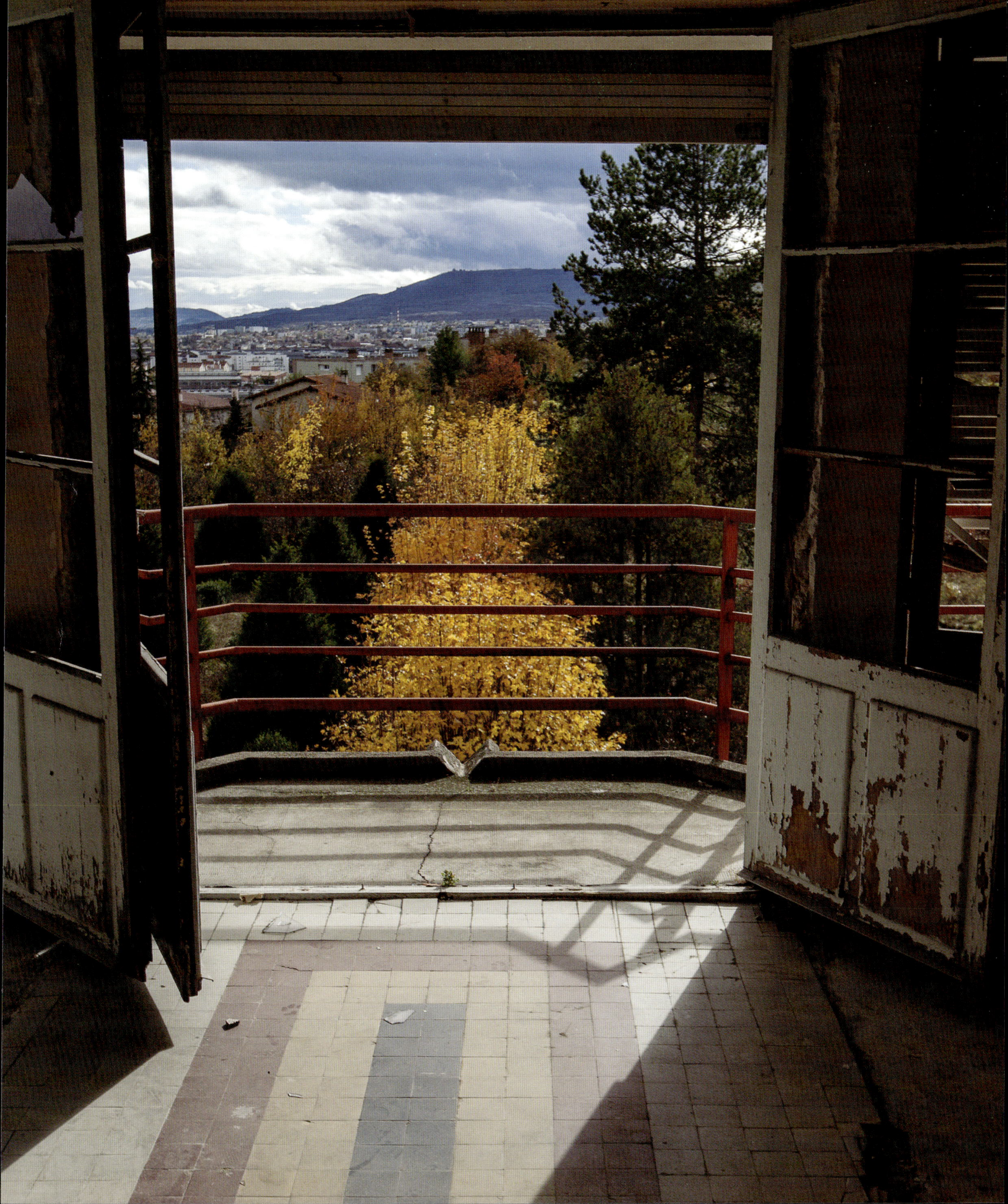

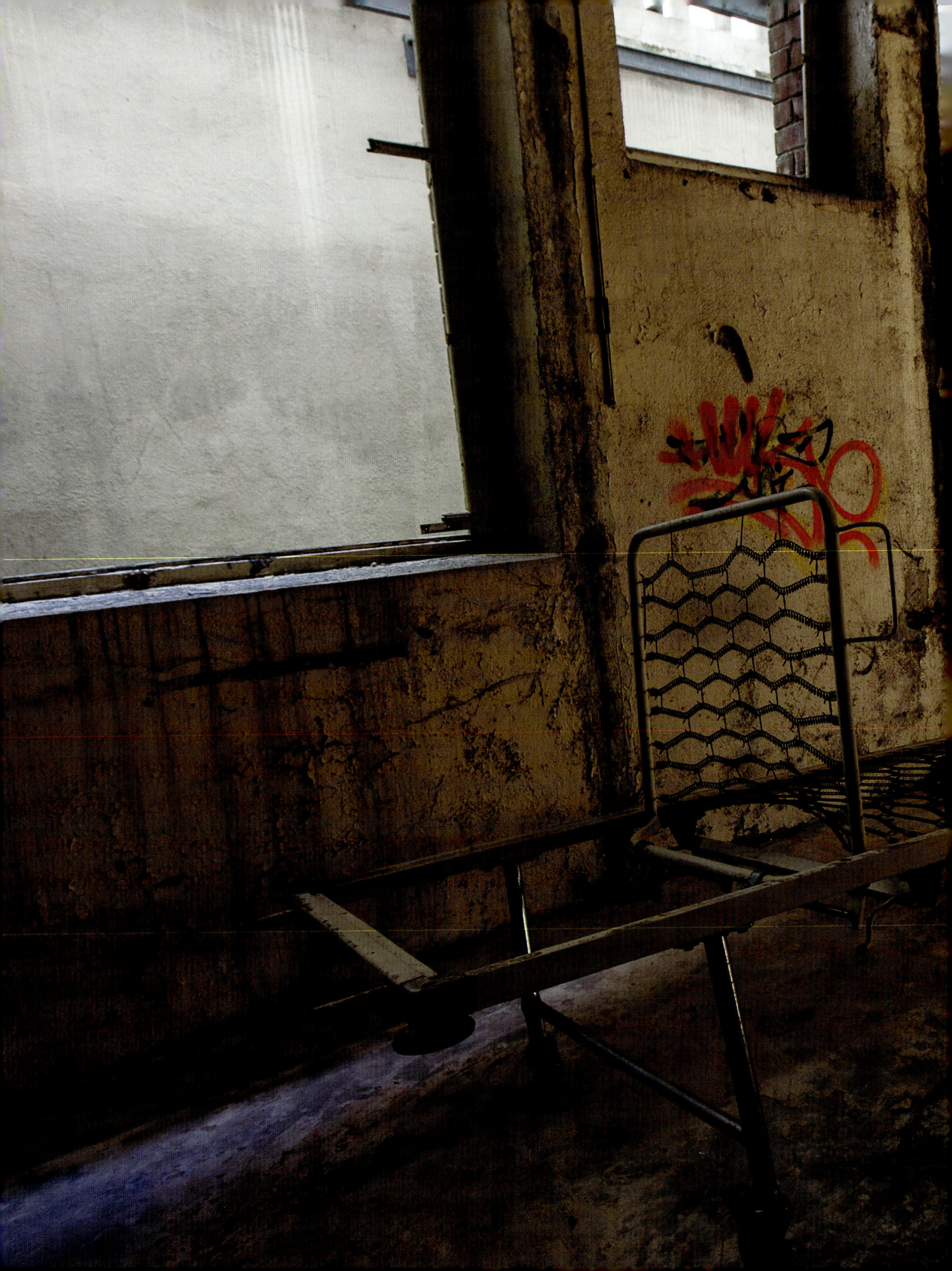

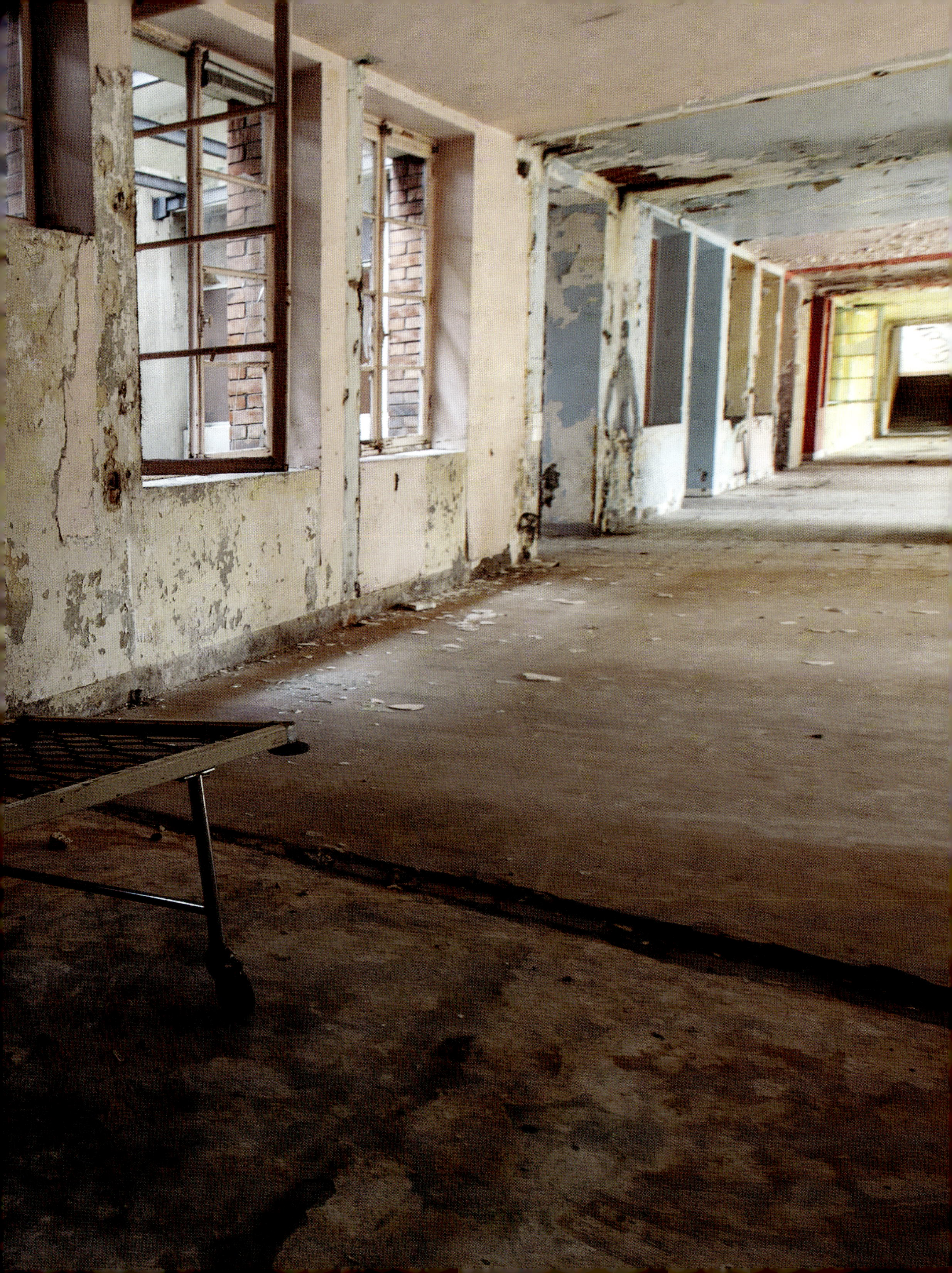

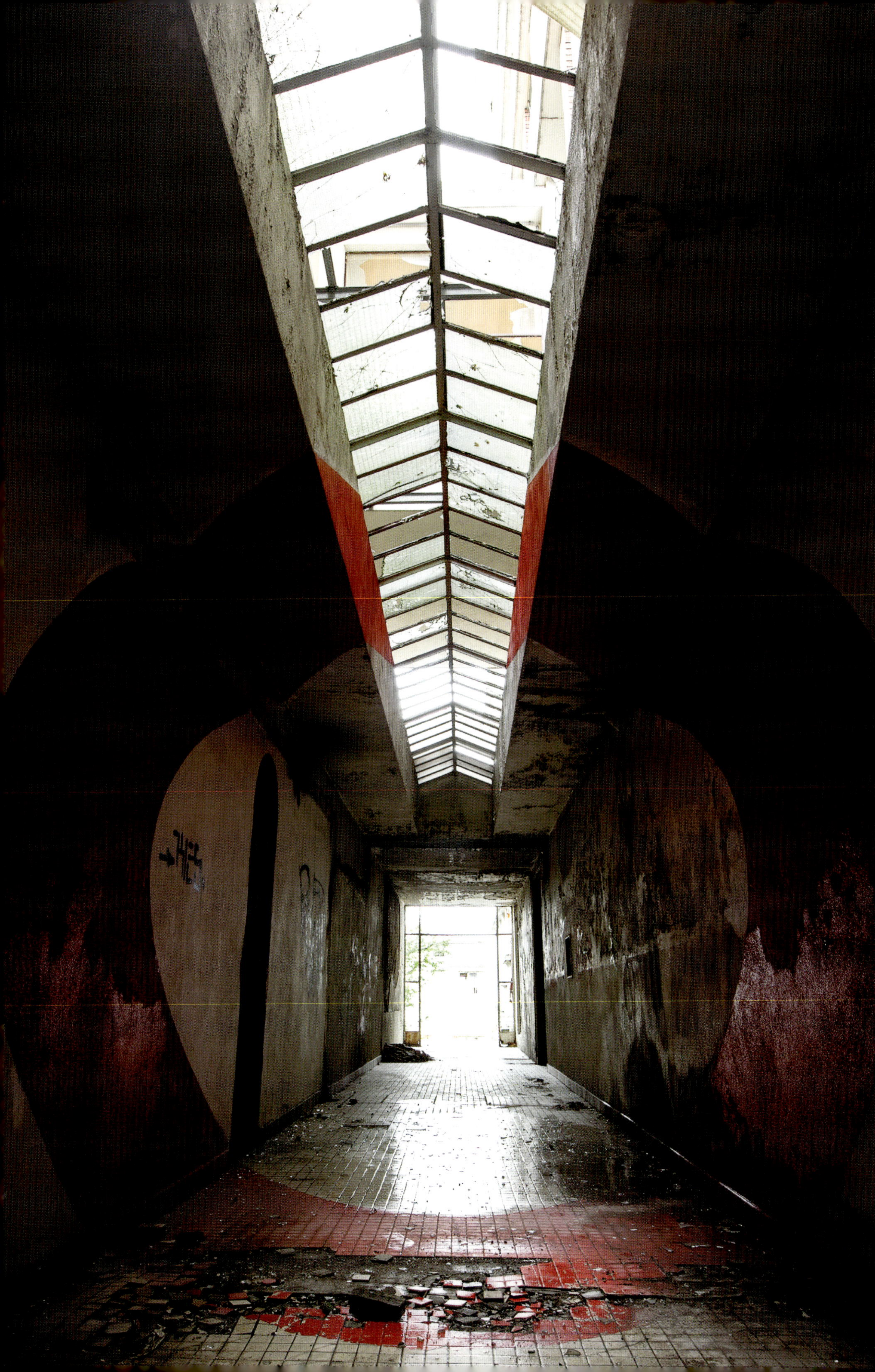

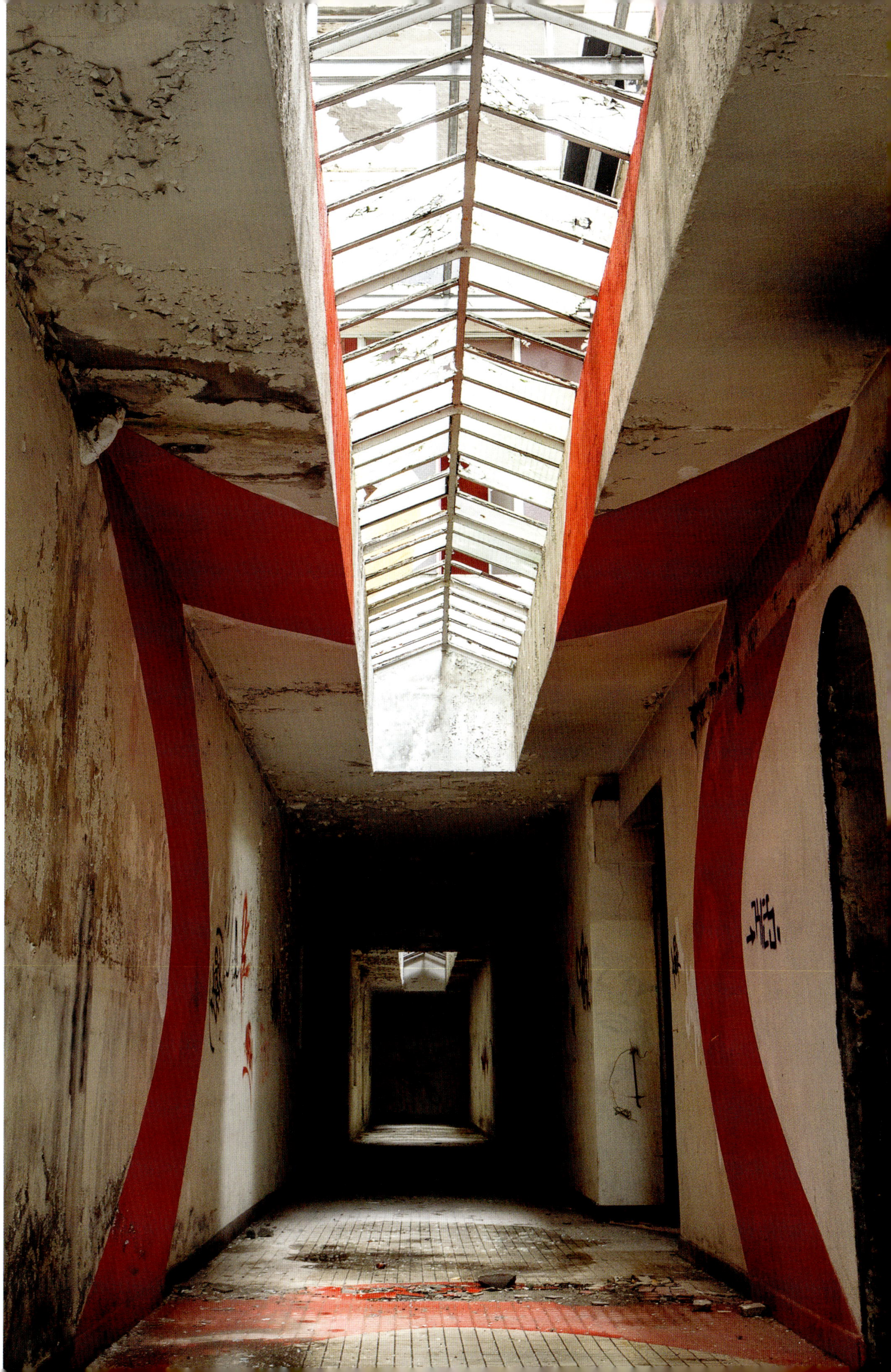

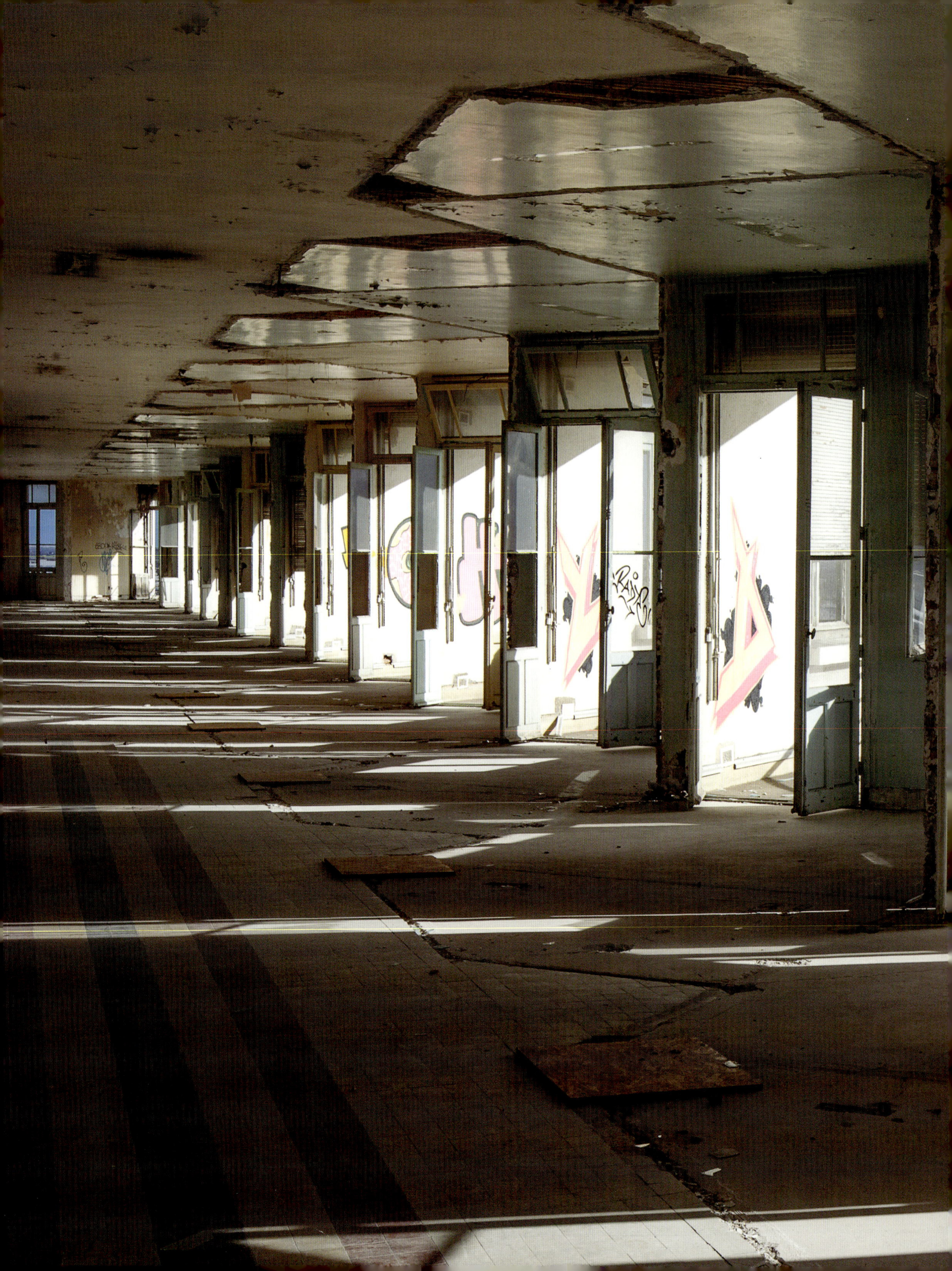

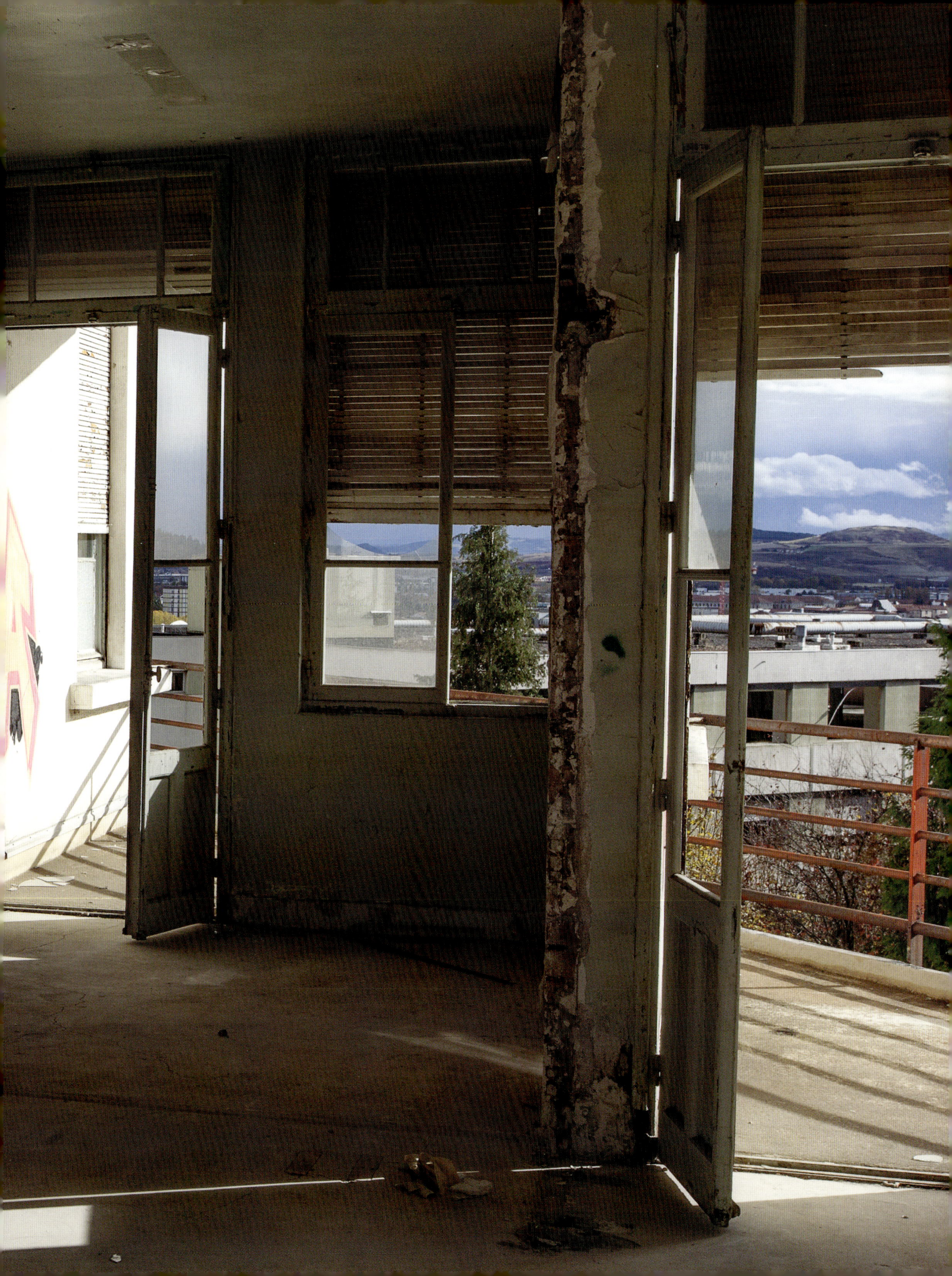

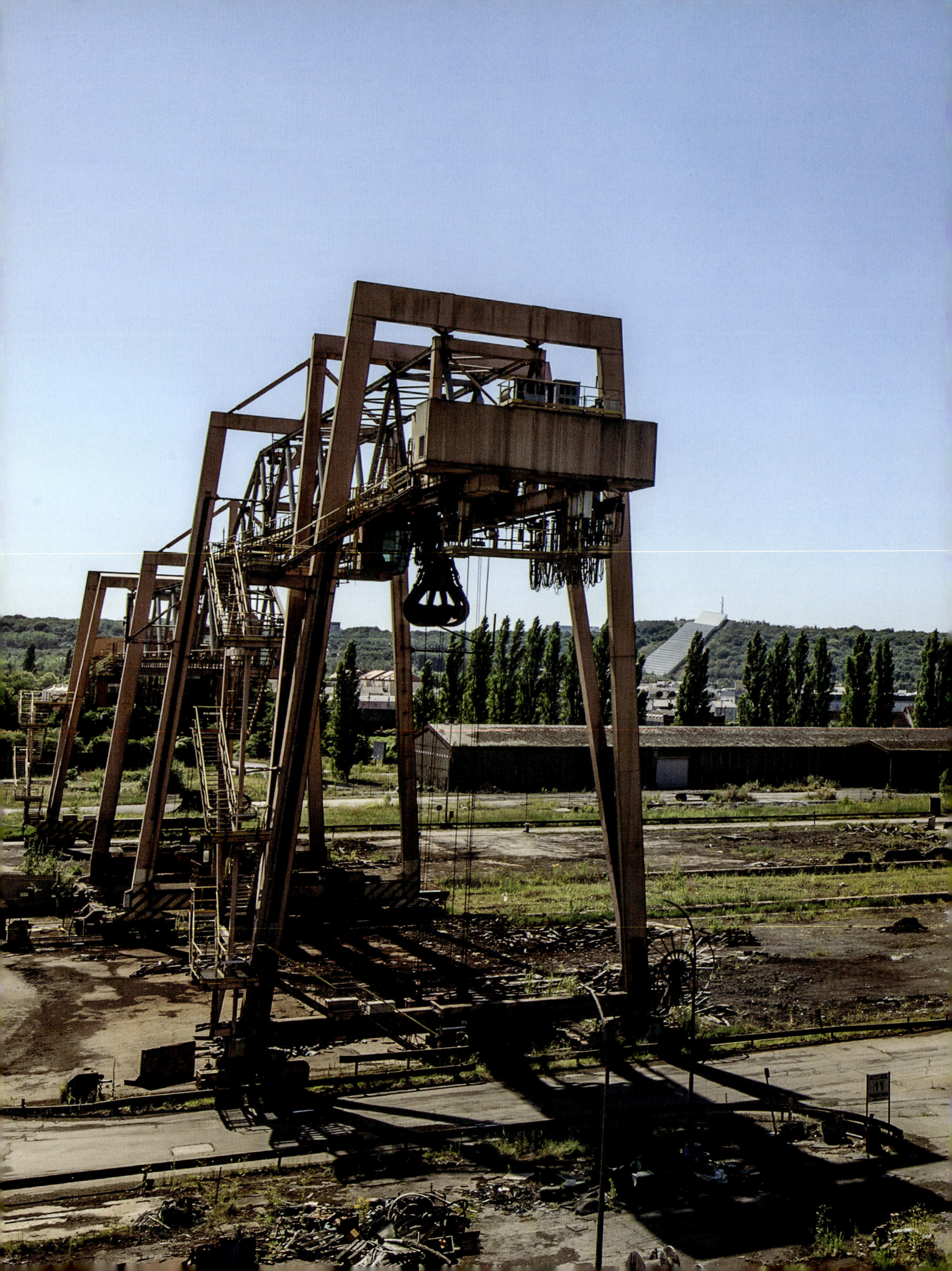

Gandrage, Lorraine

When Kaiser Wilhelm I proclaimed the German Empire on 18 January 1871, Alsace-Lorraine became German territory. Ten years later, a German built the first iron and steel plant in the Moselle commune of Gandrage (German Gandringen). In 1918, when Lorraine was returned to France, the steel industry was taken over by French companies.

The sector experienced uninterrupted growth for fifty years. At the turn of the 1970s, three-quarters of French tin and more than a quarter of the Common Market's production came from Lorraine.

Yet the golden age of the Lorraine steel industry was already over.

The major reconstruction projects launched after the Second World War was drawing to a close and the demand for steel was falling.

On the other hand, the increasing globalisation of trade favoured maritime over land transport routes. Finally, surface mines were becoming more competitive than their underground counterparts. All these parameters stacked up against the Lorraine production.

Despite this uncertain context, the Société des Aciéries de Lorraine, founded by the SIDELOR group and Wendel, built a new oxygen-based steel manufacturing plant in Gandrange between 1964 and 1969. The integration of this steelworks, then the most modern in Europe, on the same site as the blast furnaces, was meant to streamline the production line. Although the idea seemed good, success was less certain. Due to the choice of technology and the over-sized complex of 40,000 tonnes of steel and concrete over 500 hectares, the Gandrange steelworks struggled to turn a profit against a background of worsening crisis in the industry.

Modernisation, successive plans for state aid, the nationalisation of the sector in the early 1980s and its reprivatisation in the 1990s – everything was tried, unsuccessfully, to preserve the Lorraine coalfields. The sites closed one after the other. On 31 March 2009, it was the turn of the Gandrange steelworks. So decided the group owner ArcelorMittal, number one in the steel industry resulting from the merger between the European Arcelor and the Indian Mittal Steel.

The steelworks became a gigantic industrial wasteland except for a fully modernised rolling mill and a research centre. By 2016, only the activity of these two sectors seemed to be sustainable.

Dismantling the huge steelworks and converting the land into new housing, green spaces and activities is under negotiation – an operation that could take another twenty years.

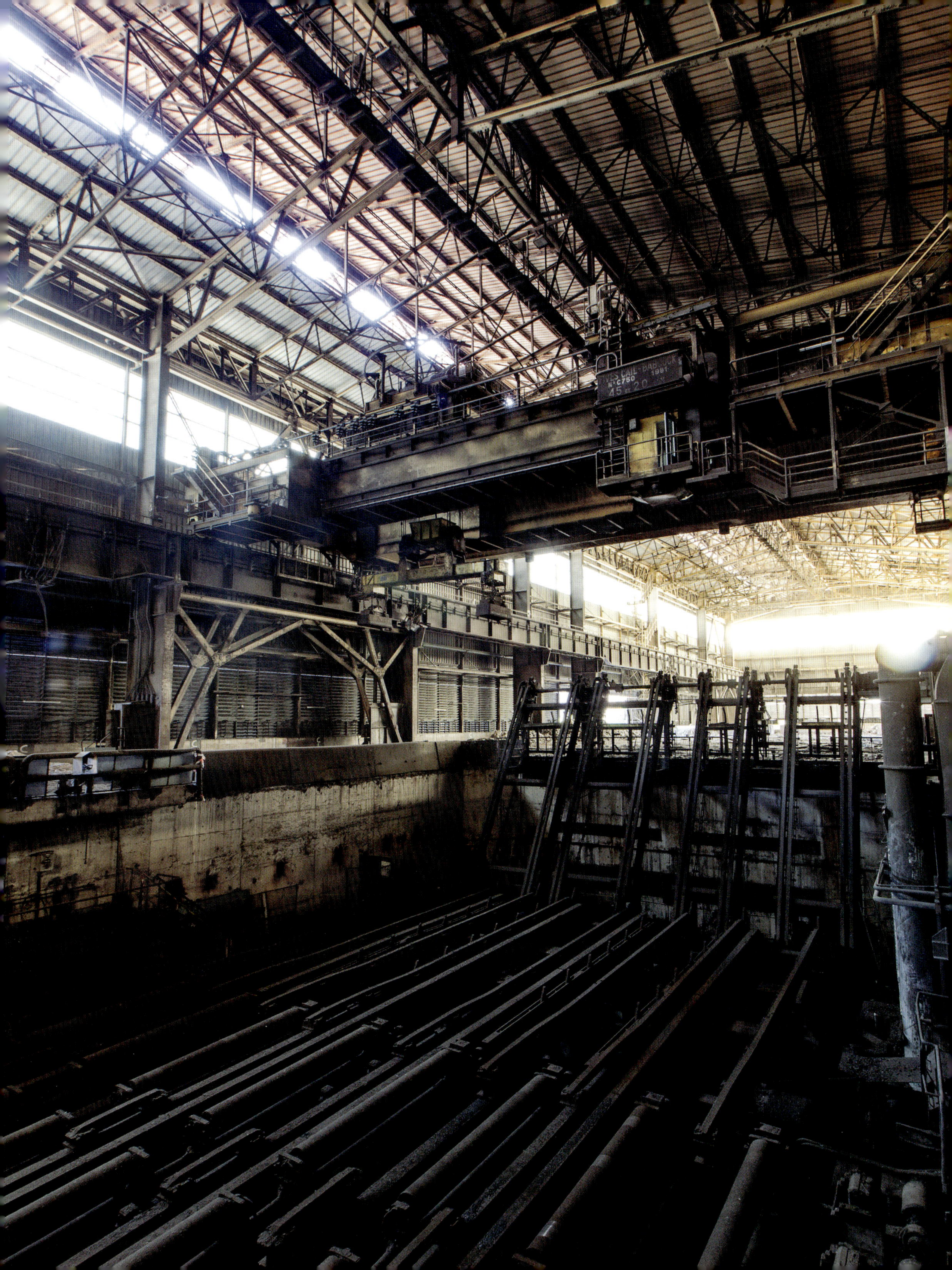
C750

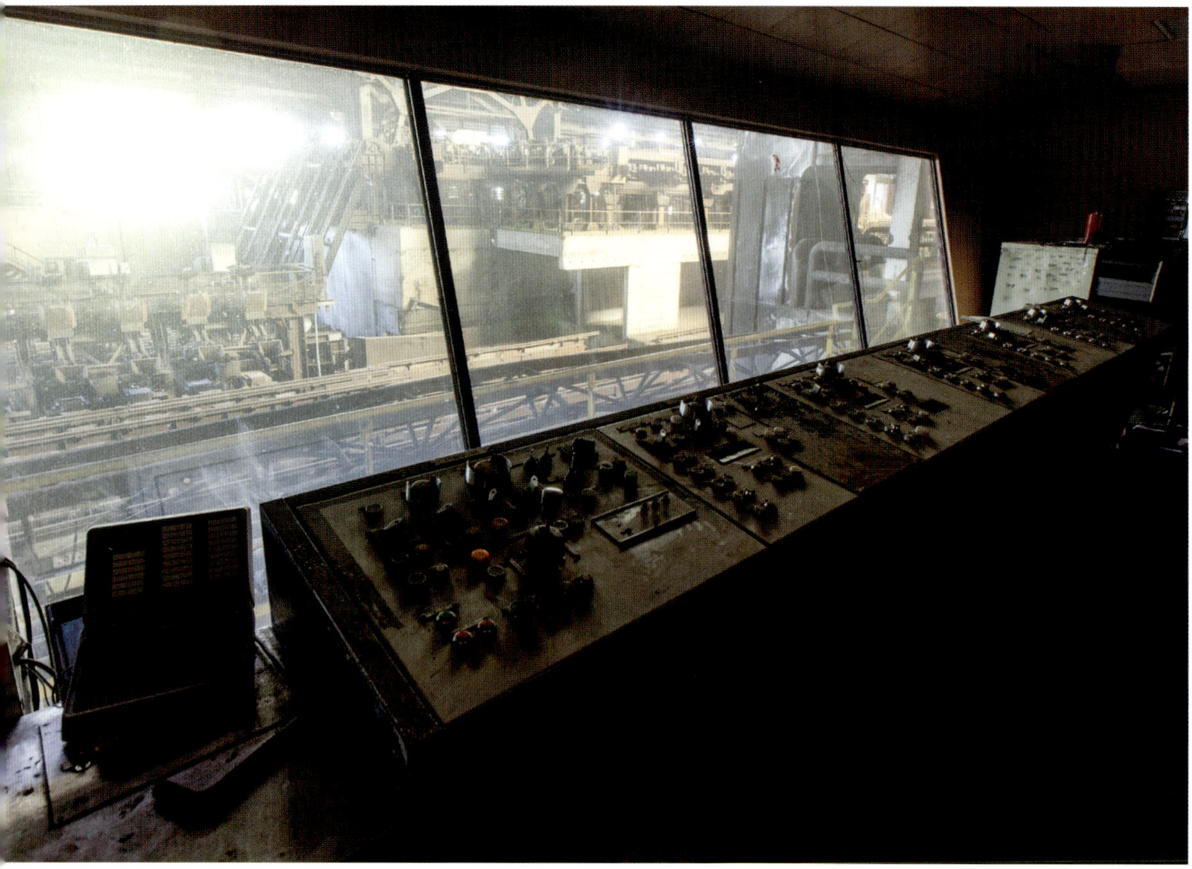

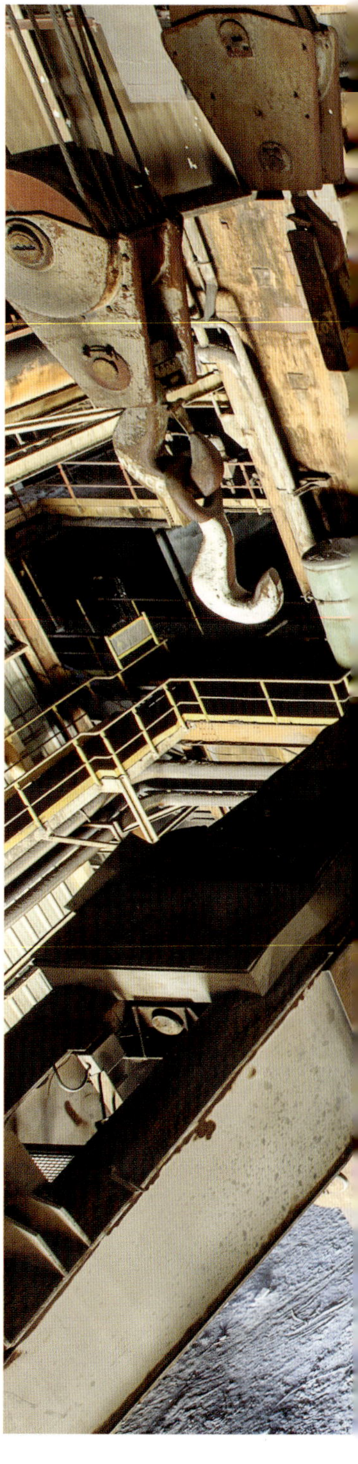

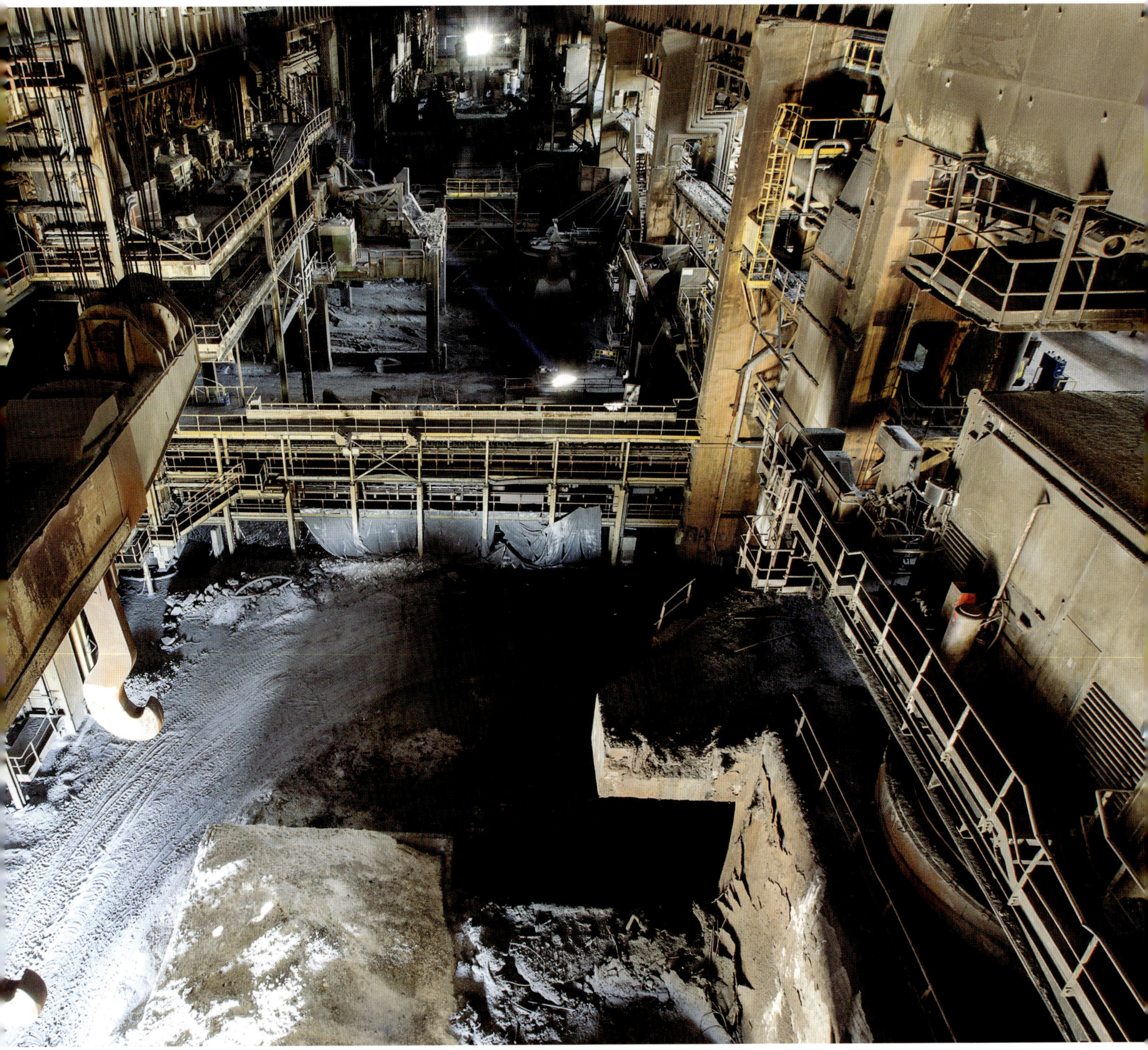

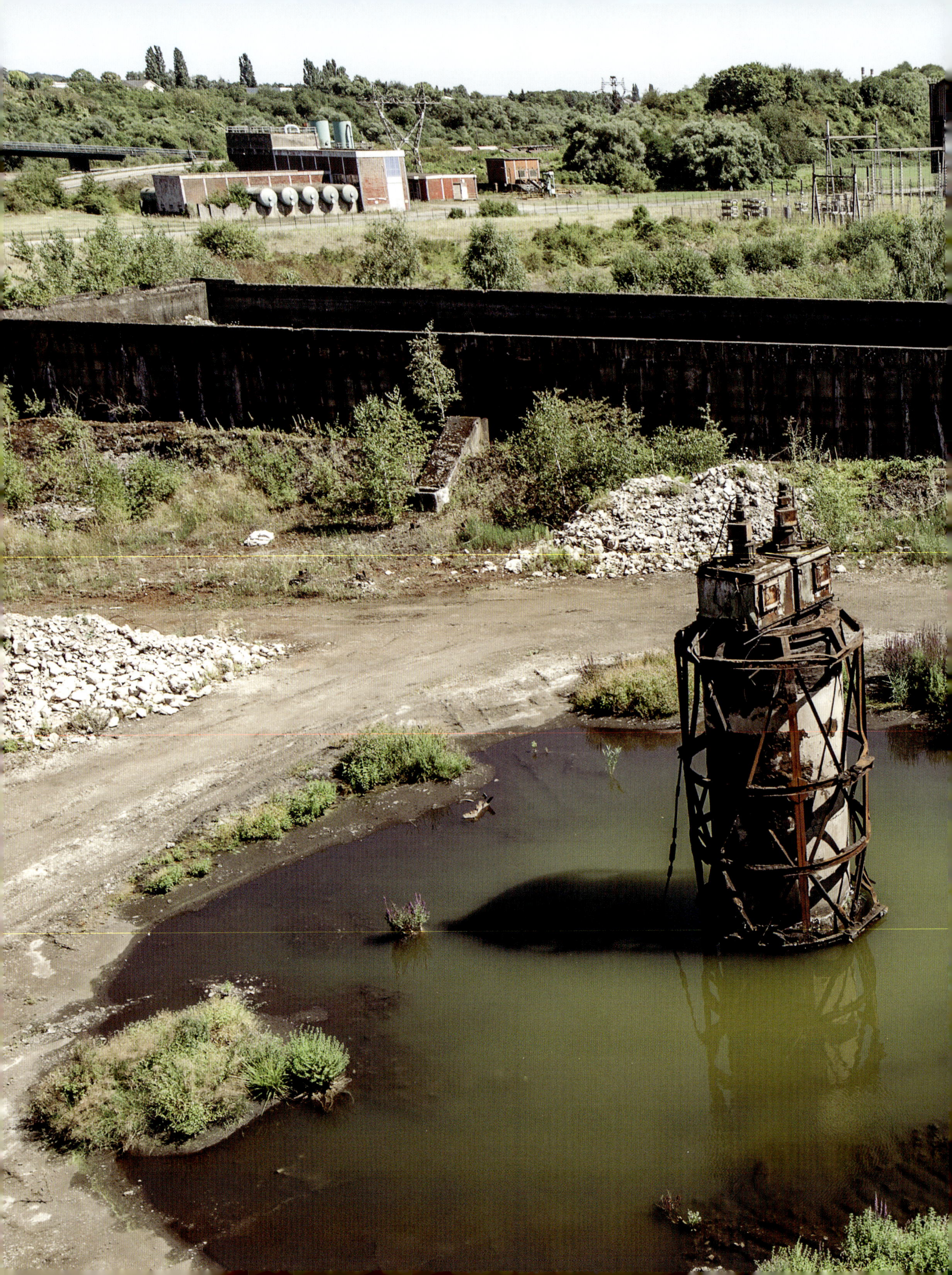

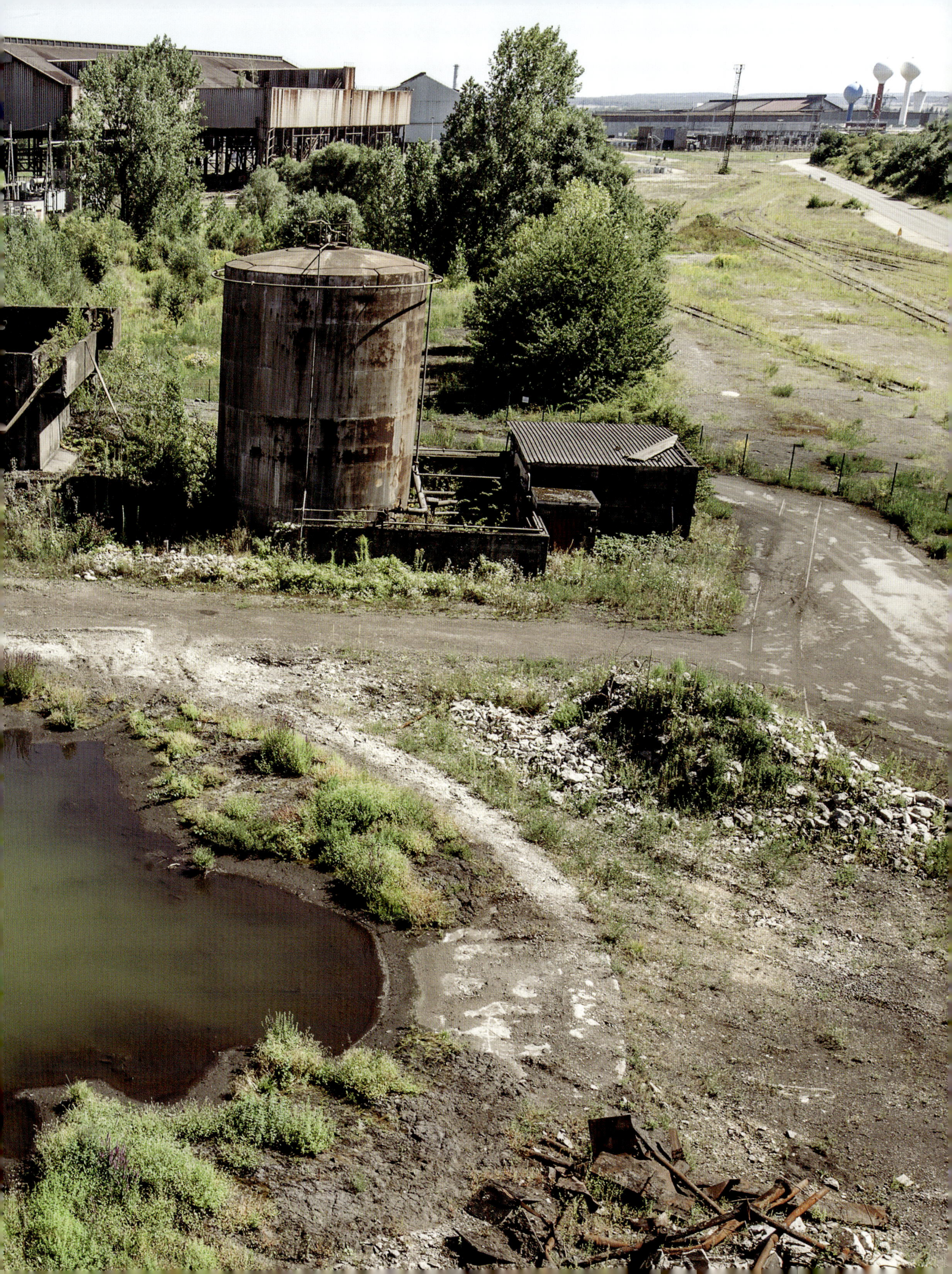

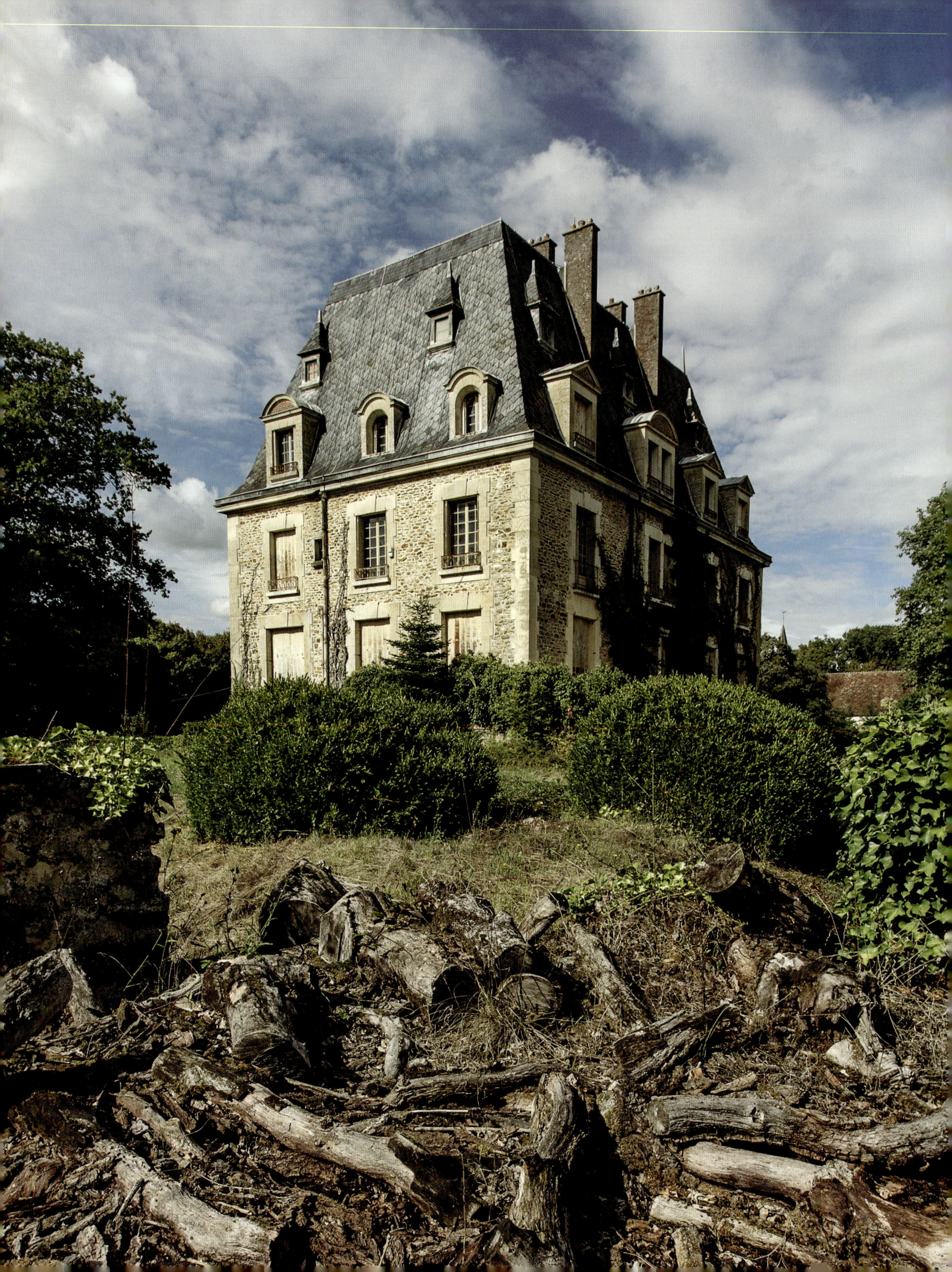

Château des Faisans, Île-de-France

In the 12th century, France was divided into numerous duchies and counties.

The royal domain surrounding Paris was a strip of territory with borders guarded by small fortified castles. Taking advantage of this protection, people's homes were built nearby. The addition of a chapel or church ultimately conferred village status on these settlements.

The small Île-de-France town where Château des Faisans is located probably had the same origins.

The original fortress, a one-time royal residence, was destroyed in the wars and its ruins scattered or recycled.

In its place stands the chateau, which can still be seen today. It was built at the close of the 19th century for a rich banking family.

Standing in the middle of a park bordering the neighbouring estate forest, it sidelines local building regulations by its choice of materials: stone and brick for the main house, slate for the hipped roof. Its dimensions and the corner tower contribute to the manor-house look.

The interior is built around a solid wooden staircase overlooked by a shimmering glass dome. A small elevator cage gives access to the upper storeys.

Large mirrors, marble fireplaces, wall mouldings, wood panelling or stretched fabric, mosaic, tiled or carpeted wooden floors – the property is richly furnished and there is even a trio of semicircular arches dividing the main salon.

After the site was abandoned, water infiltrating through the dome seriously damaged the upstairs rooms.

The chateau remains under close guard, however, and all points of entry are blocked.

Since 1996, the garden has been listed as "remarkable" in the French general inventory of cultural heritage.

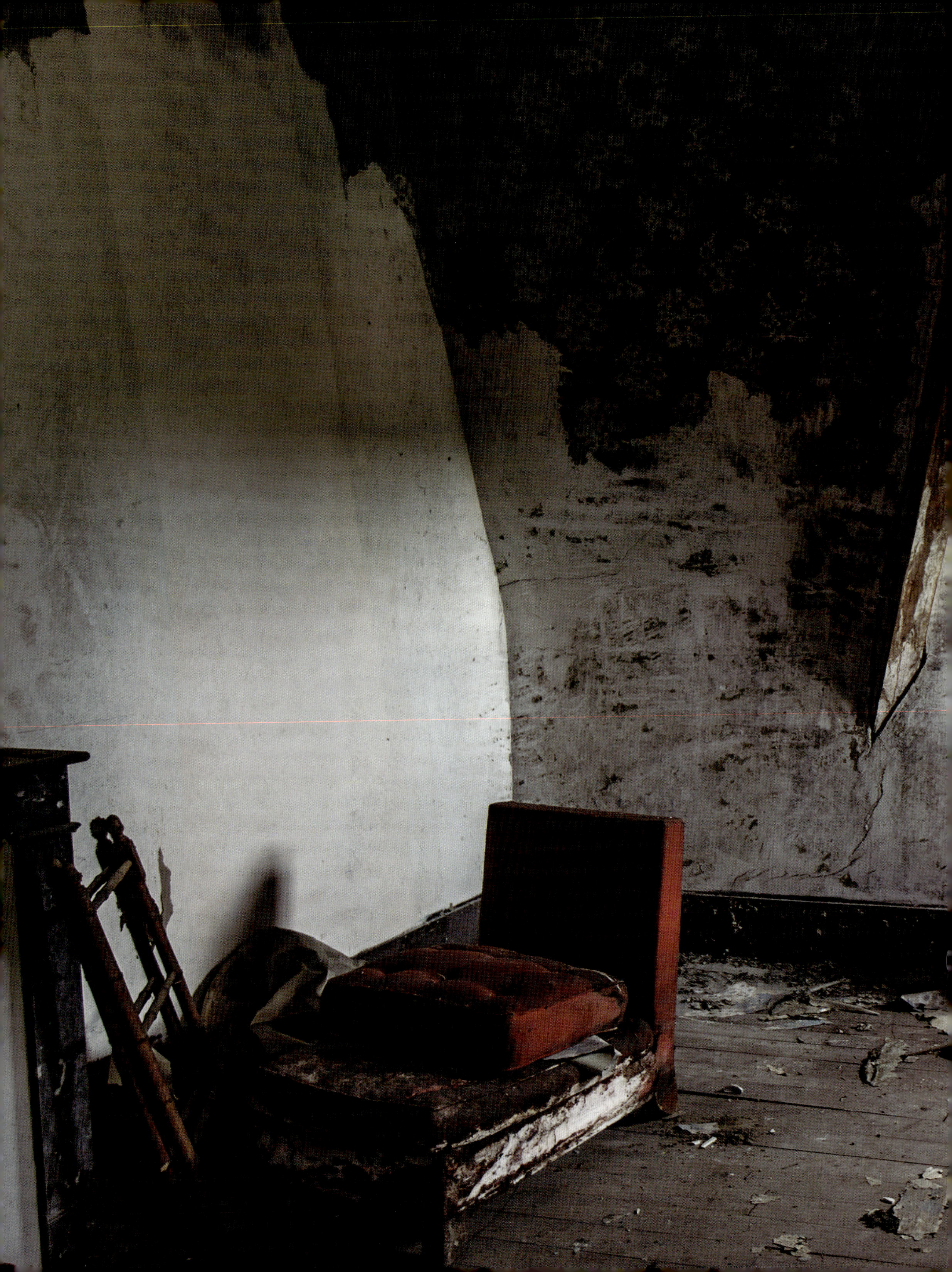

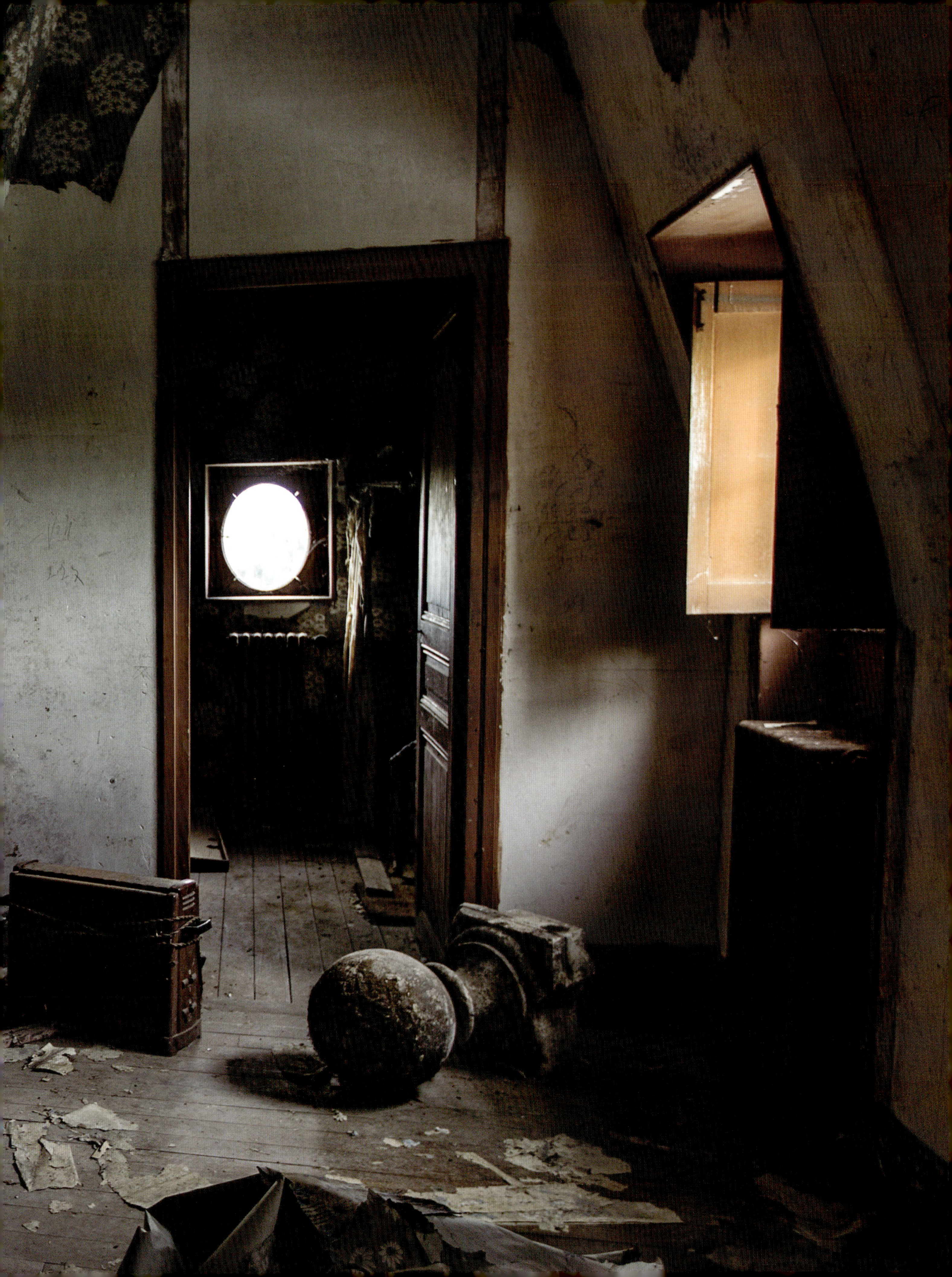

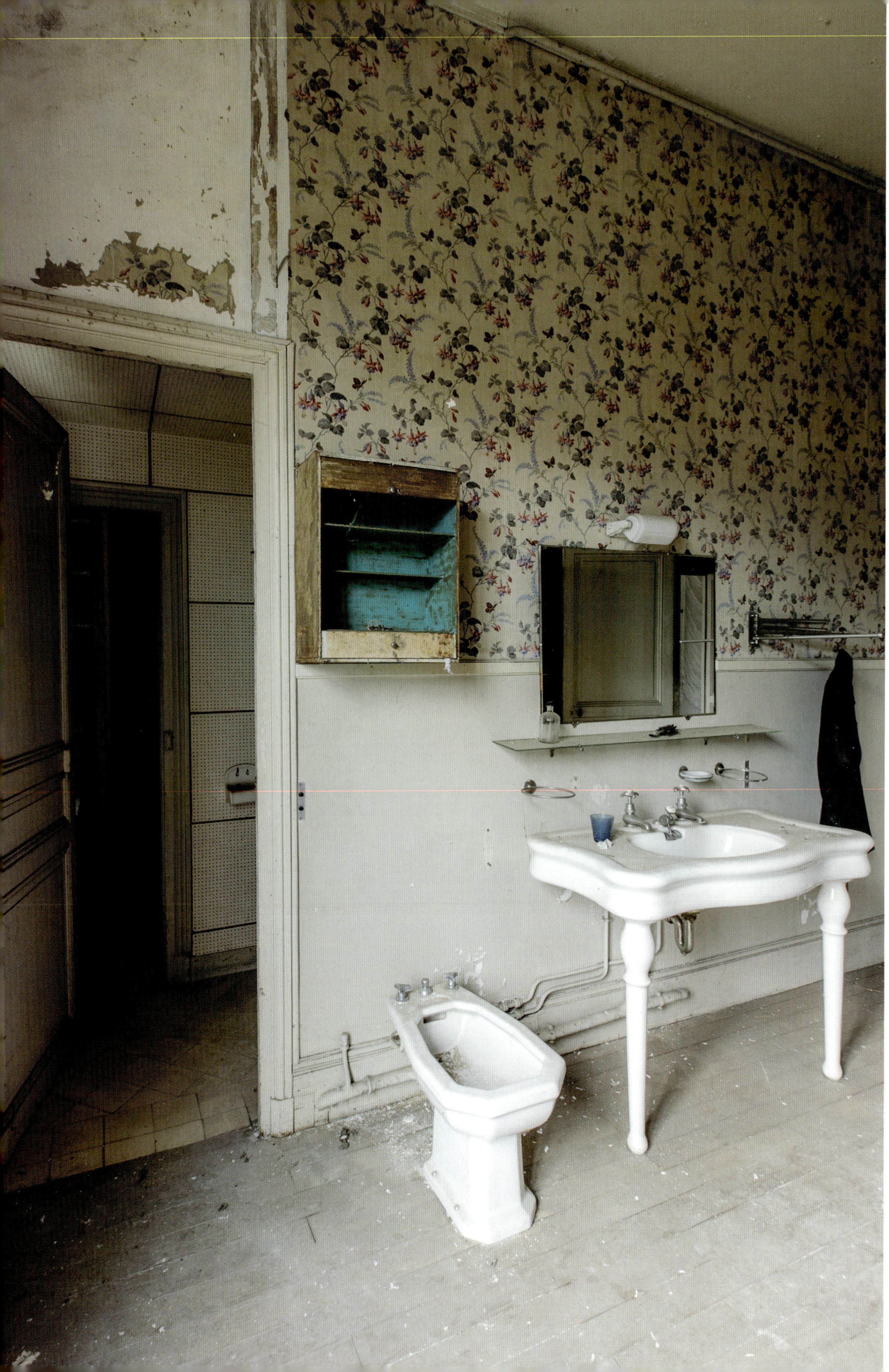

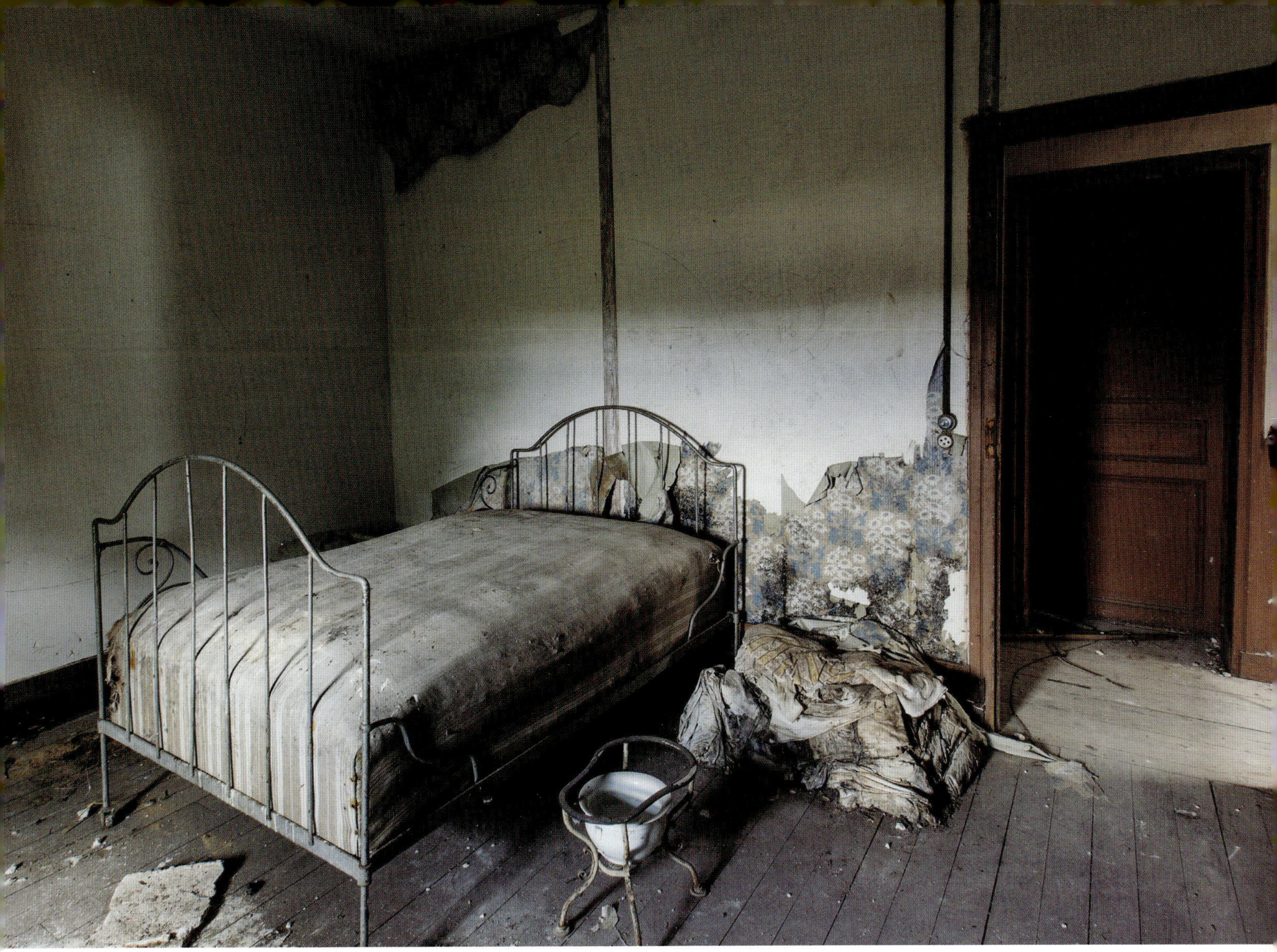

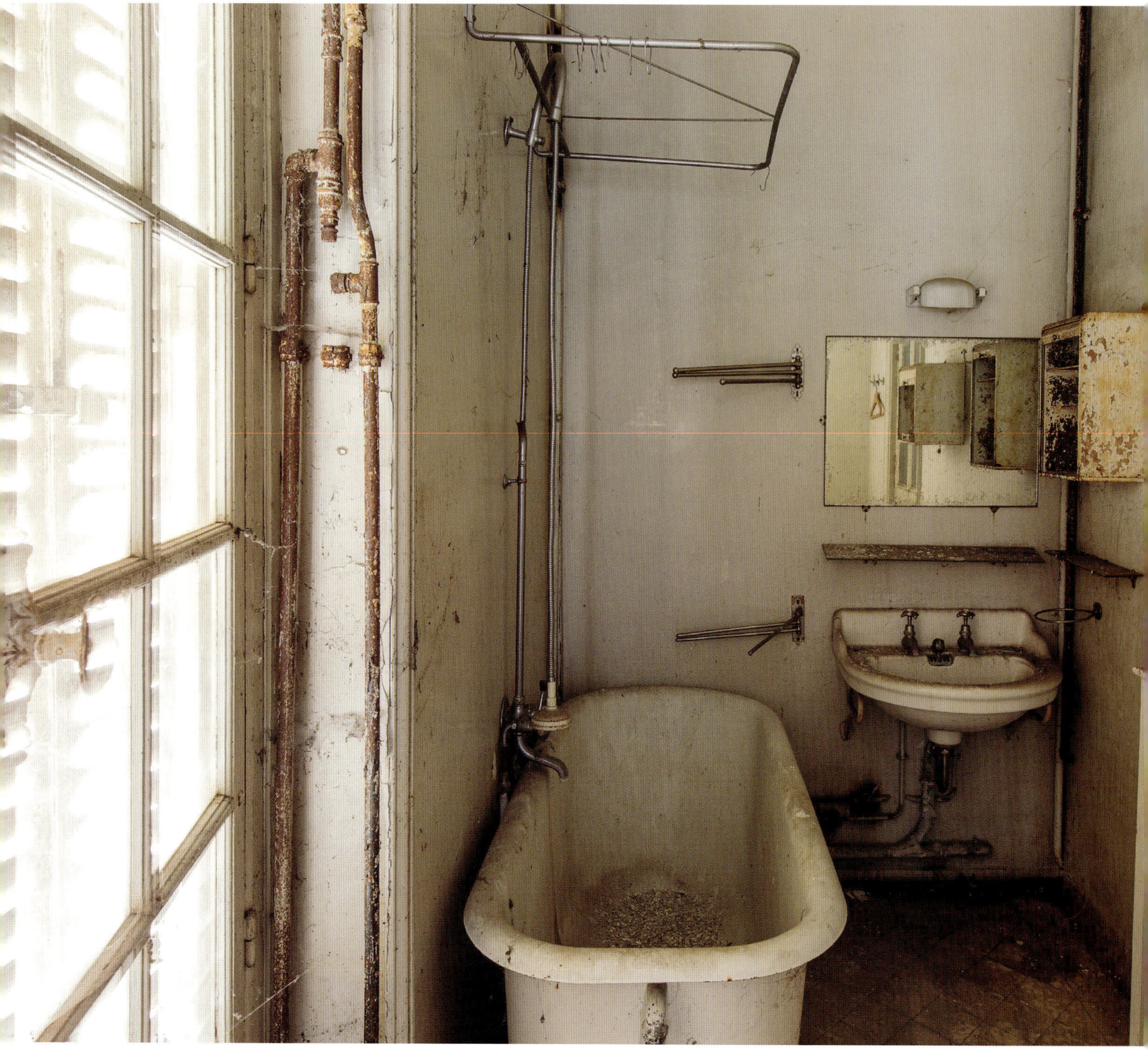

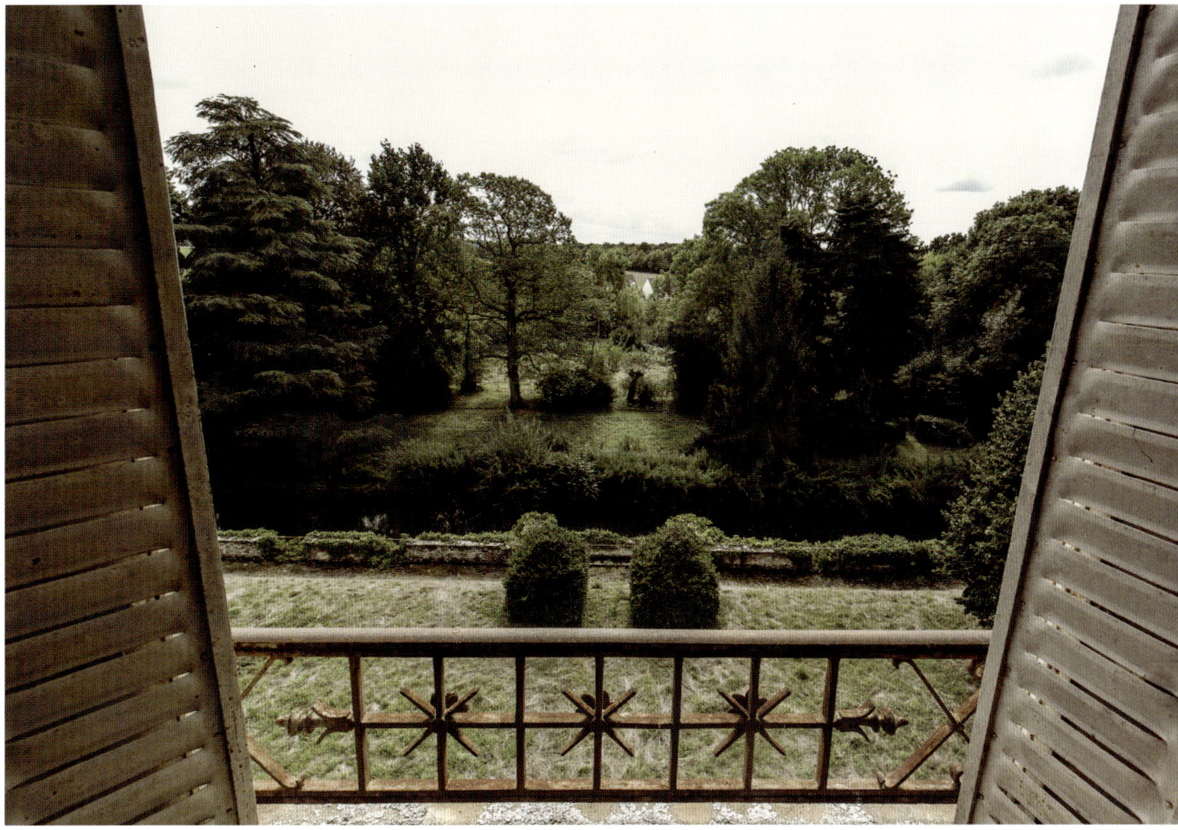

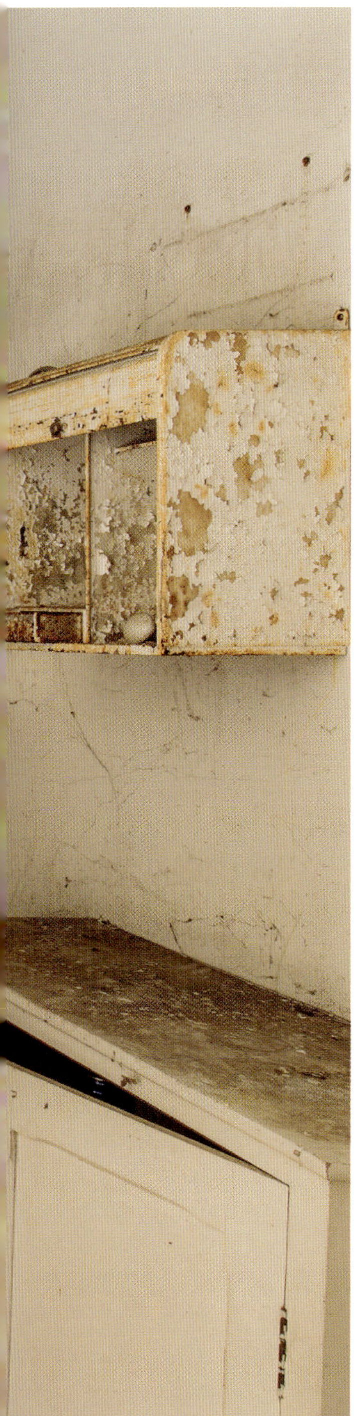

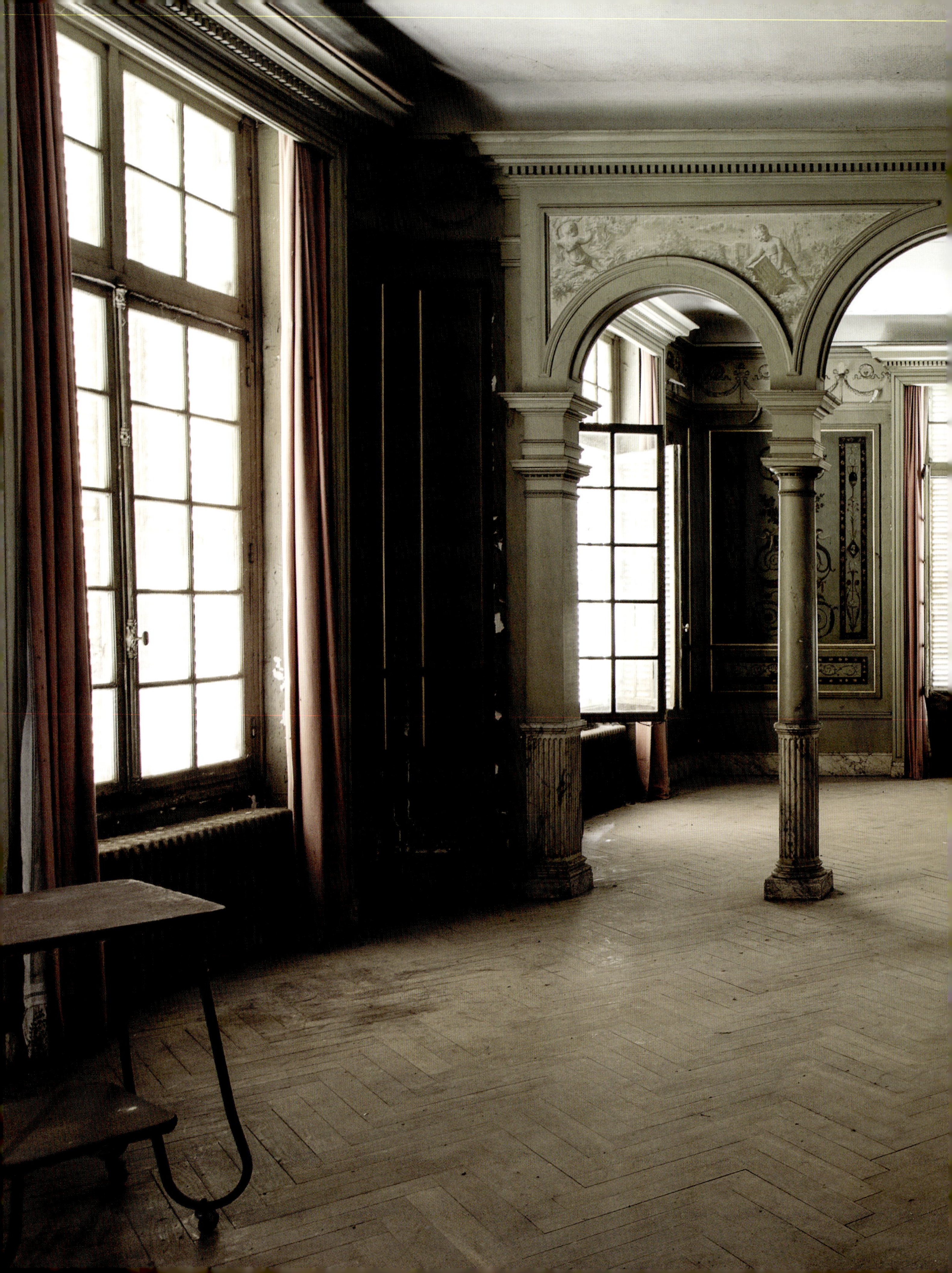

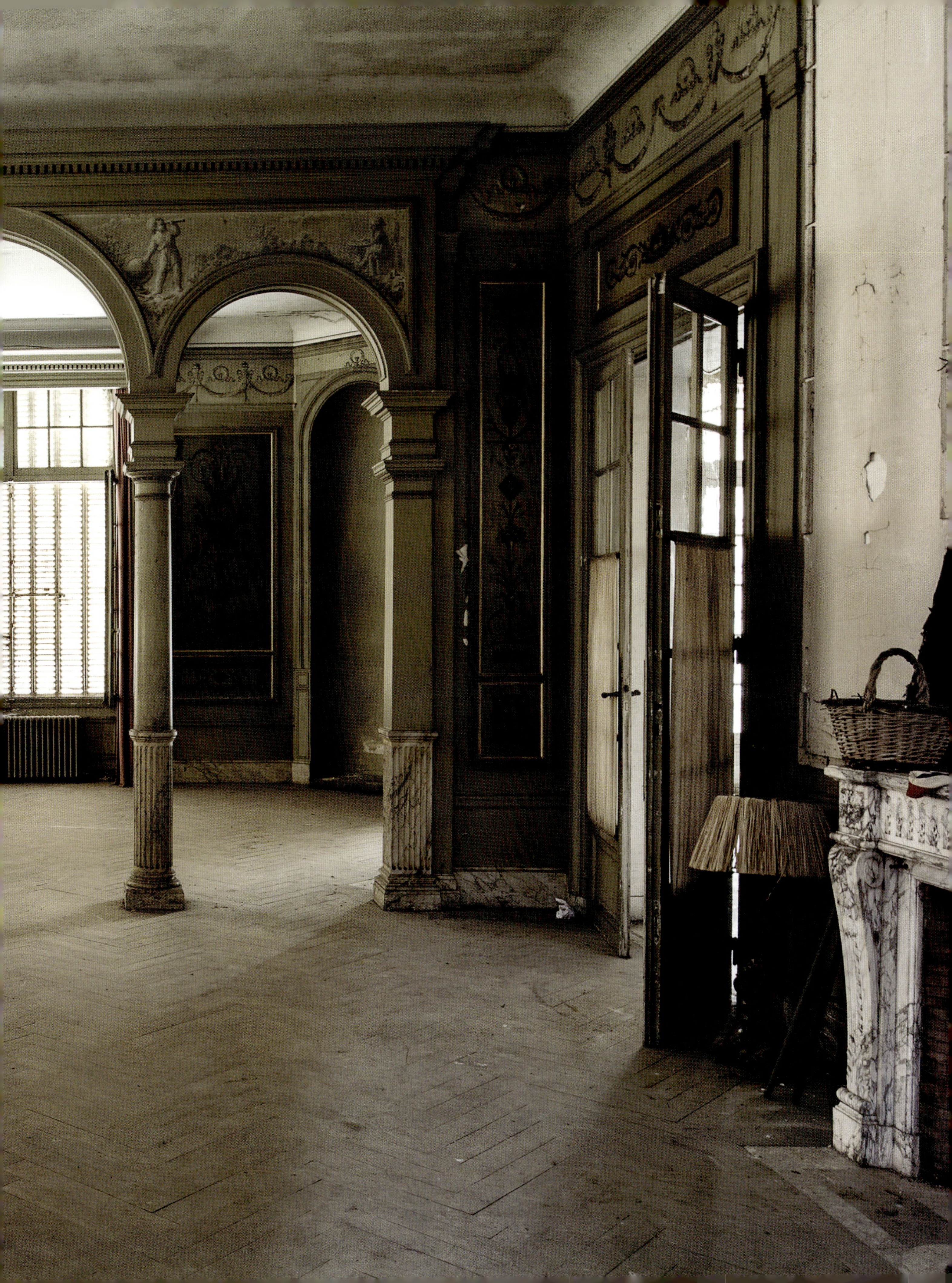

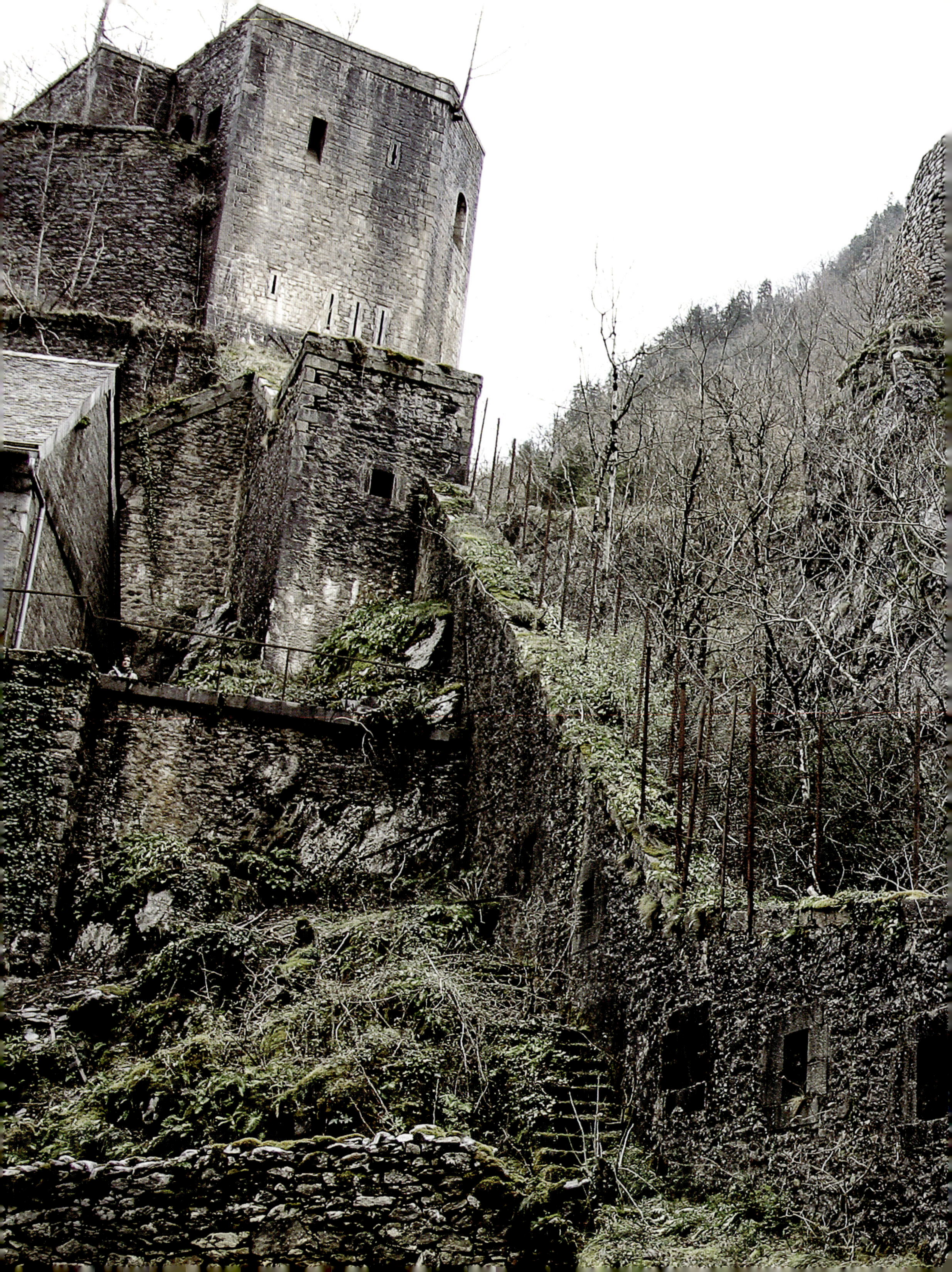

Portalet, Col du Somport, Pyrénées-Atlantiques

The Aspe valley forms a strategic axis between France and Spain. Over the centuries, it has been a Roman road linking Bordeaux to Zaragoza, part of Via Tolosana, one of the roads to Santiago de Compostela, and a busy commercial and military road. A toll station, Poutou fort, was built at one of its narrow passes in the 15th century. The right of passage was lifted in 1789. The post then became a military fort, part of the French strategy to deter the threat of a Spanish invasion. Then at the beginning of the 19th century, it contributed to the cordon sanitaire set up during the yellow fever epidemic on the other side of the Pyrenees.

In 1842, Louis Philippe I decided to build a new fort called Portalet (little gateway) a few hundred metres higher than the old fort, which was abandoned.

A massive structure was erected on the flanks of the rock, at an altitude of 765 metres and over 150 metres of uneven ground. It rises at the summit of a precipice known as the Gorge d'Enfer, at the bottom of which flows the torrential stream of Gave d'Aspe. This challenging site, echoing the stormy relations of the communes whose land surrounds the fort, delayed the work, which was finally completed in 1870.

Accommodation for 400 servicemen over 2,300 square metres was planned. In reality, there would be only a few dozen of them – soldiers detached from the 18th infantry regiment of Pau.

The layout of Portalet follows the constraints of the site. A two-arched stone bridge connects the road to a winding track. This climbs up to a second bridge leading to the front terrace. Above was the powder magazine. Inside, a guardroom, barracks and officers' mess spread over two levels. An upper blockhouse with bell-shaped sentry boxes, fitted with a dozen cannon and three mortars, defended the fortress. The guard patrolled around a walkway and through galleries dug into the mountainside.

Although it was designed to repel a possible Spanish offensive, the fort only had to deal with sporadic incursions, breakaways from the third Carlist civil war that divided Spain in the 19th century.

In 1914, war finally arrived from the east. The Pau regiment was called to the front and left the fort guarded by territorials. In 1927, Portalet was finally disarmed.

Then the state leased the fort as a mountain holiday camp for the cadets of the Bordeaux diocese until 1939, when it was again taken over by the army.

The Vichy regime incarcerated Léon Blum, Edouard Daladier, Maurice Gamelin, Georges Mandel and Paul Reynaud there, all judged responsible for the defeat of France. At the end of the war, Marshal Pétain spent a few months in its cells before ending his days in detention on Ile d'Yeu. The 18th regiment then took over the site.

The fort was decommissioned in 1962 and sold by auction four years later to Jacqueline Fraiman, a valley resident, who for a while envisaged a hotel conversion but finally abandoned the property. The tangled undergrowth and harsh local climate led to its rapid deterioration, not helped by passing vandals.

The fortified complex and its access roads were registered for the first time as a historical monument in July 1992. In 1999, as Portalet was really becoming derelict, a group of villages – the Communauté des Communes de la Vallée d'Aspe – purchased it.

The first refurbishments only began in 2004. The following year, two new decrees allowed the entire Portalet fort, the now-ruined Poutou and the roads leading to them, to be listed.

Successive tranches of restoration, combining work placements for prisoners and research in partnership with the regional office of cultural affairs, have opened up part of the site to small groups of tourists. In 2016, there were some 4,000 visitors to the fort and its annexes.

A "mountain plan", co-financed by the EU to make the valley more attractive, intends to increase this figure tenfold, notably by suspending a footbridge above the Gorge d'Enfer, which would allow easier access. Completion is expected in 2020.

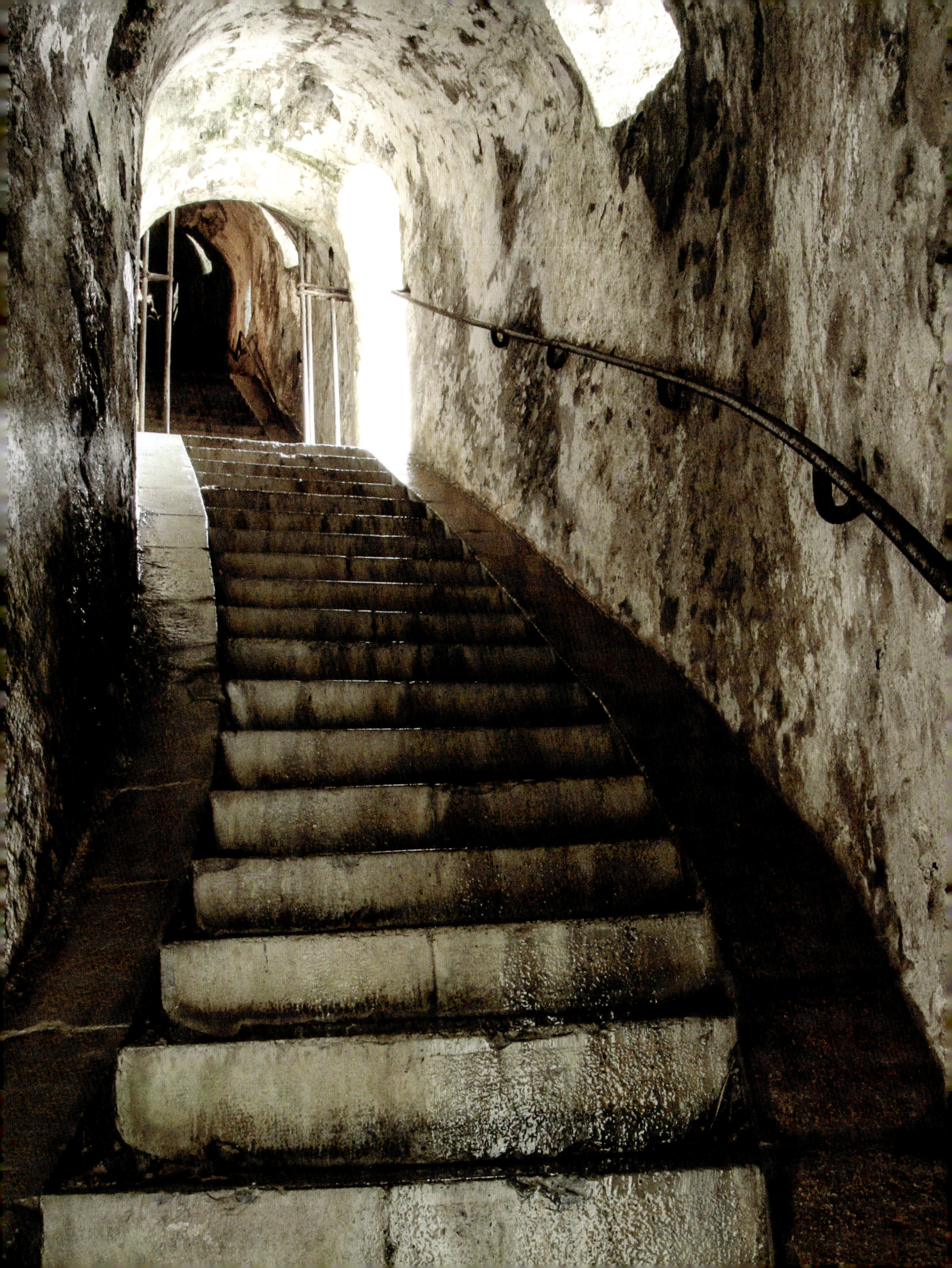

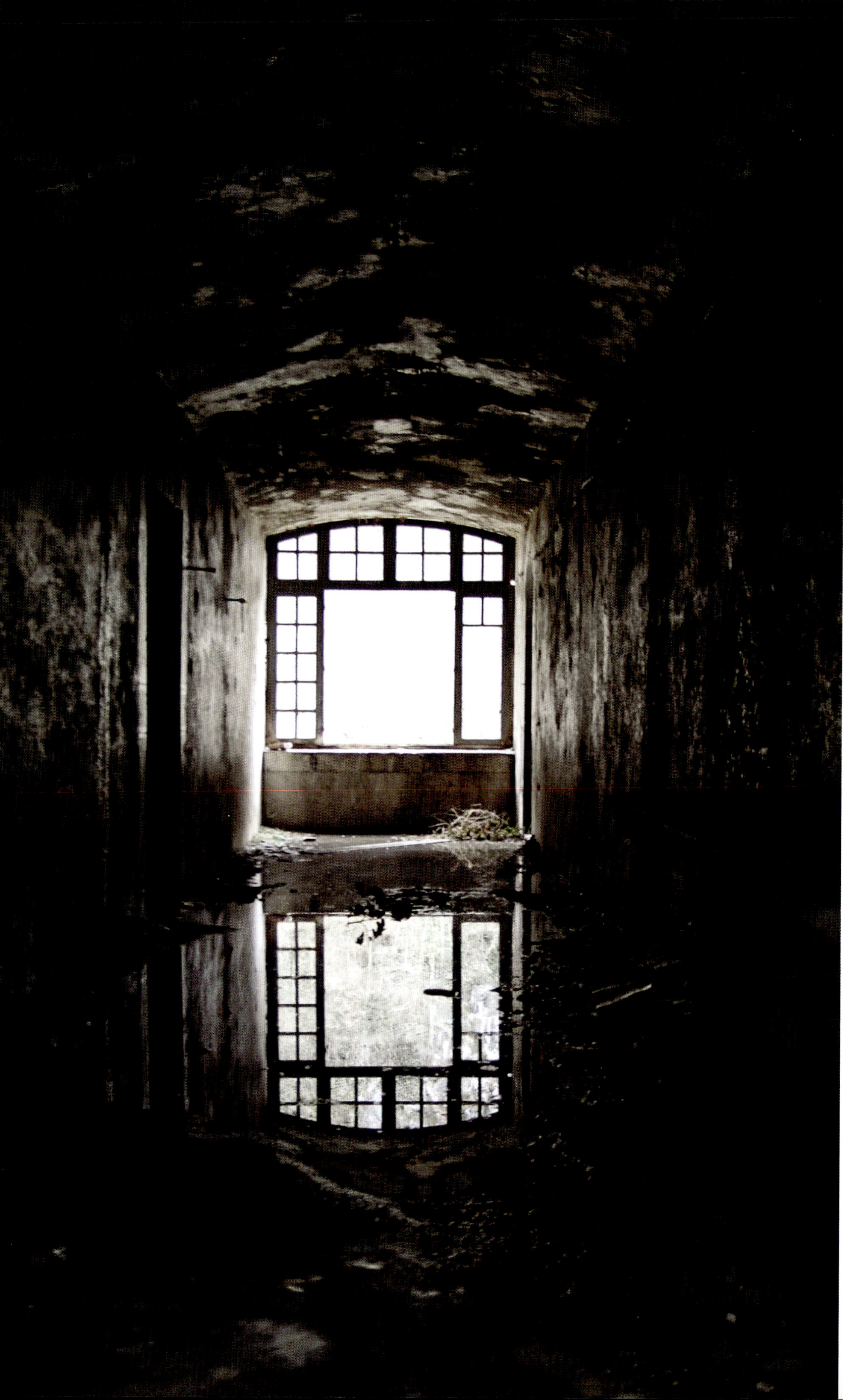

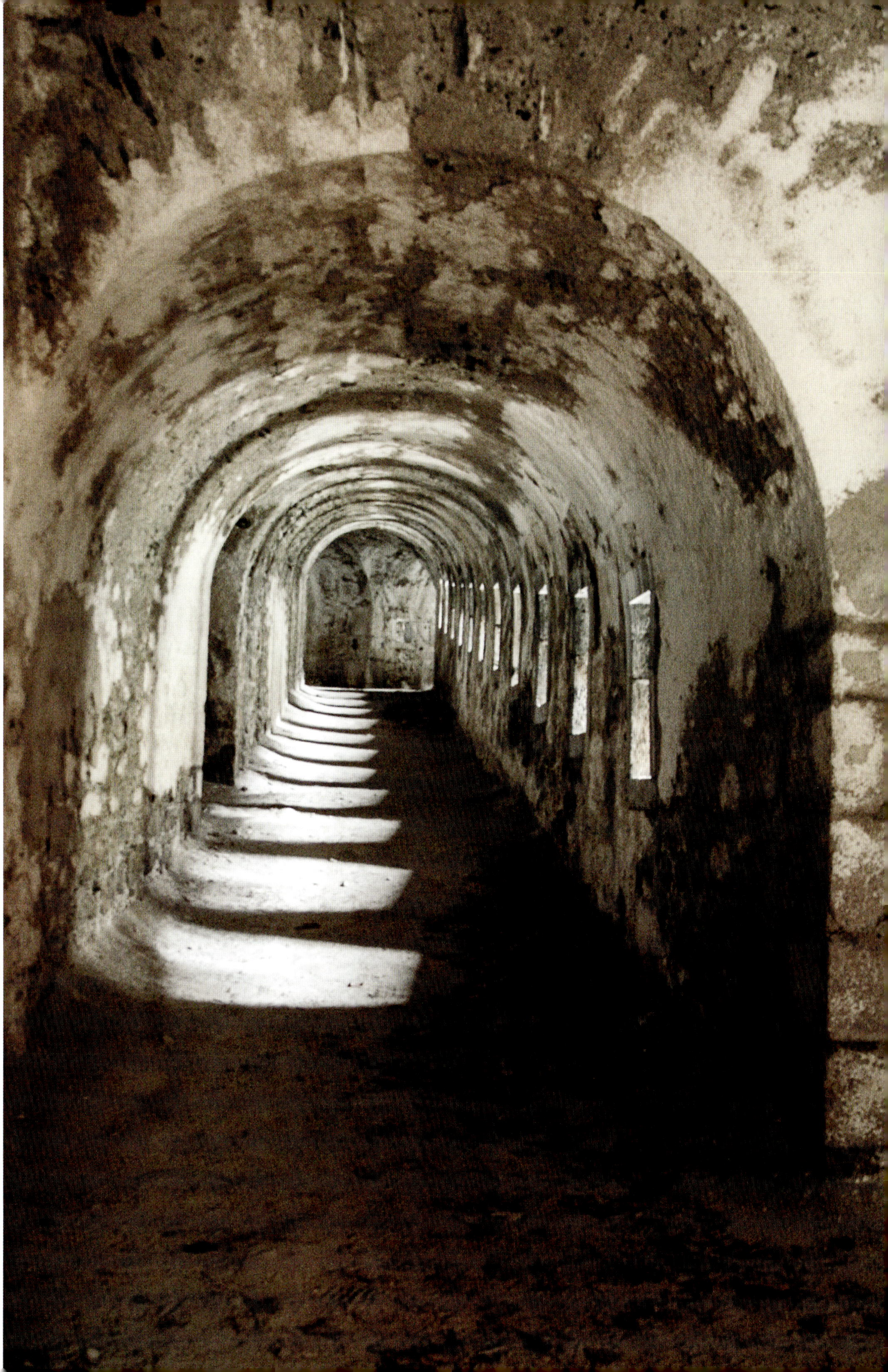

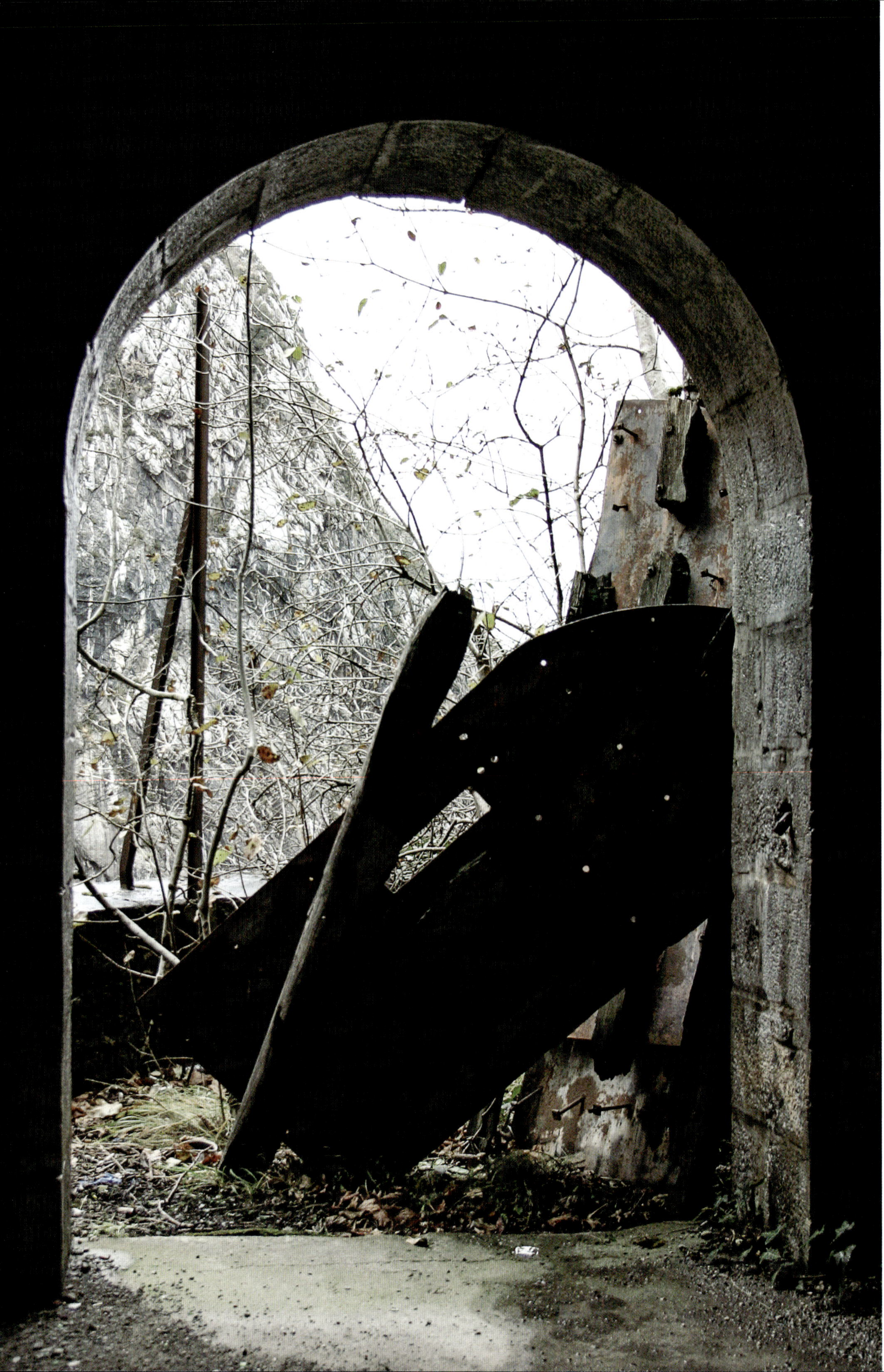

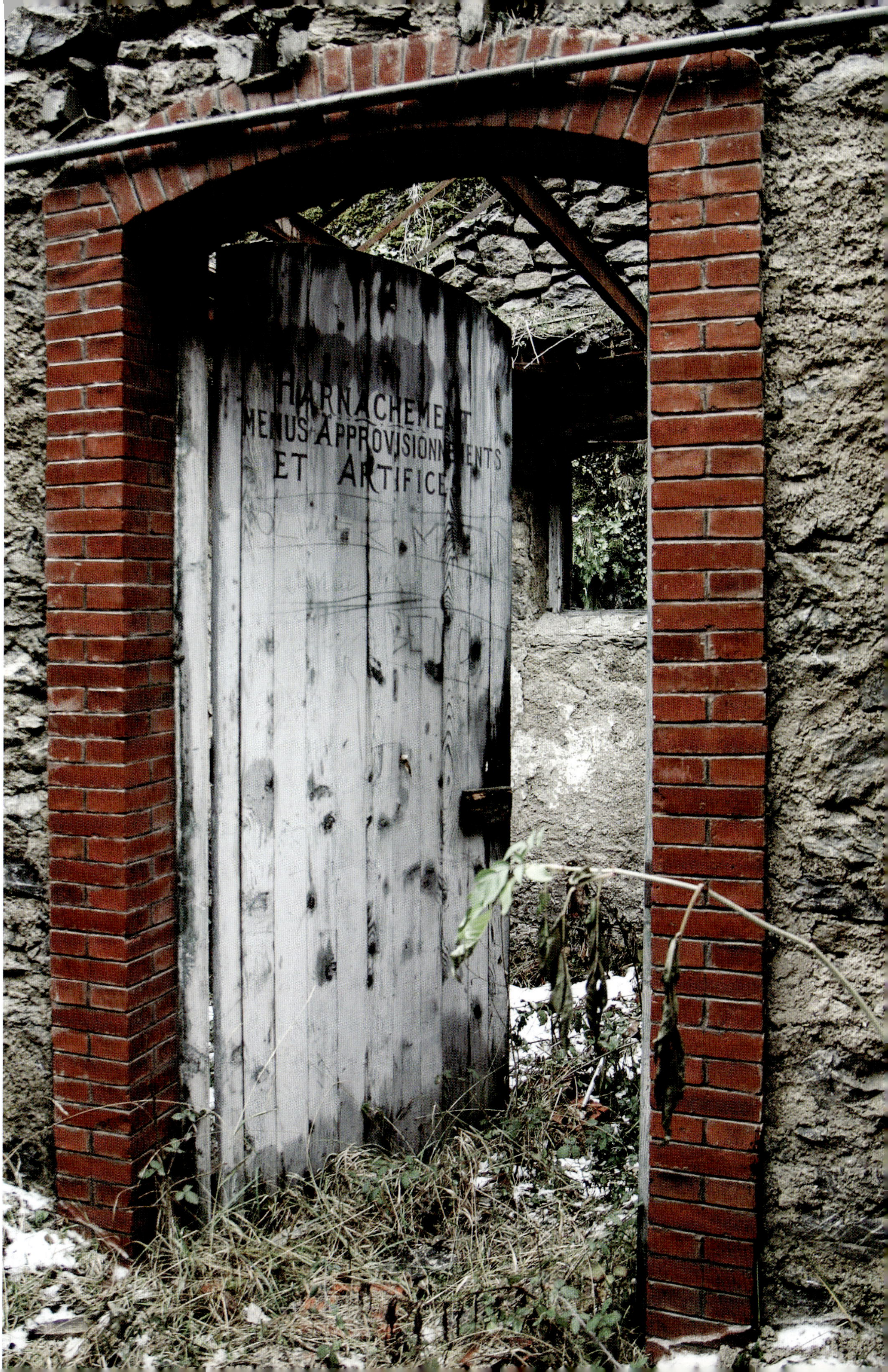
HARNACHEMENT
MENUS APPROVISIONNEMENTS
ET ARTIFICES

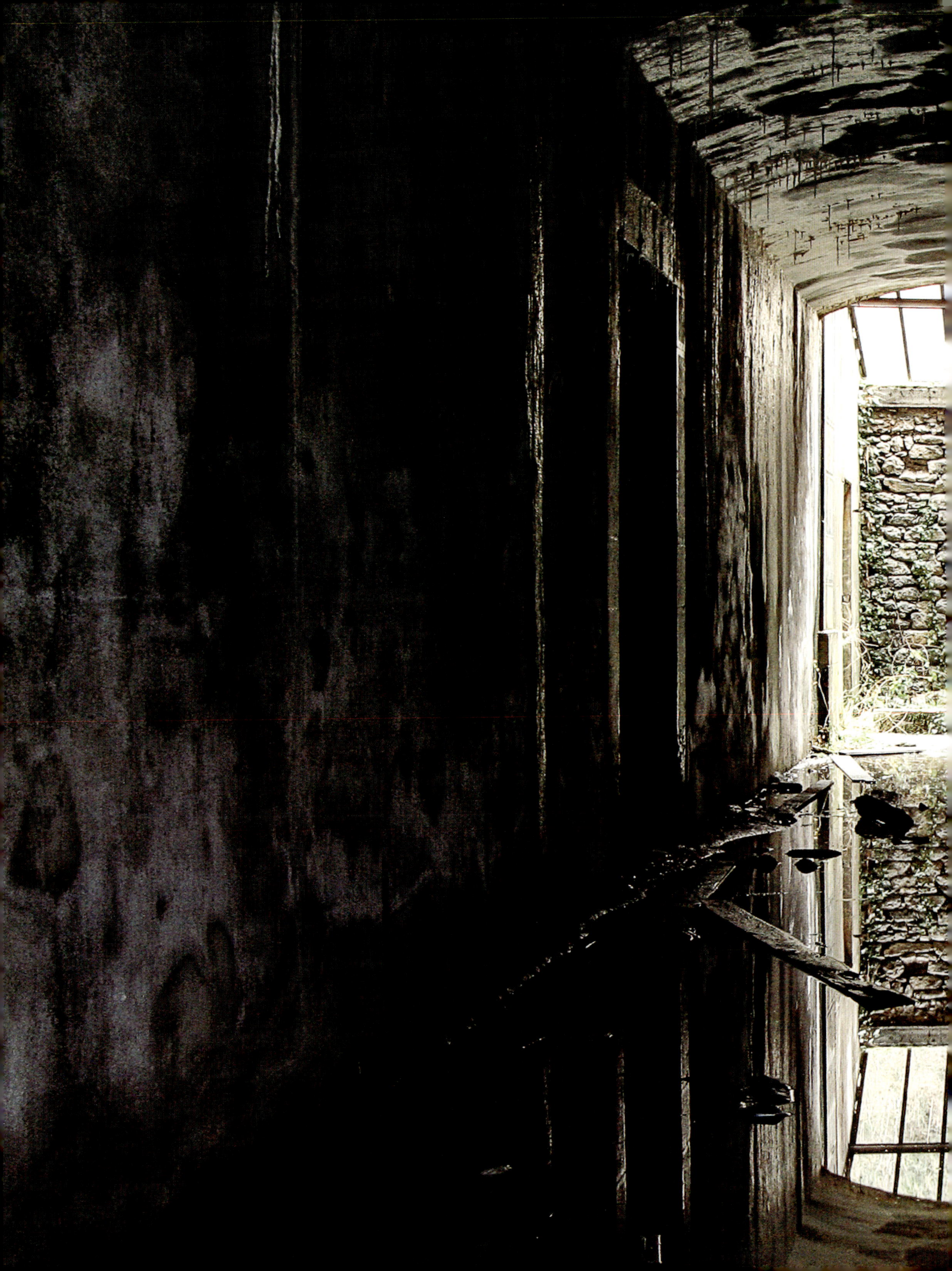

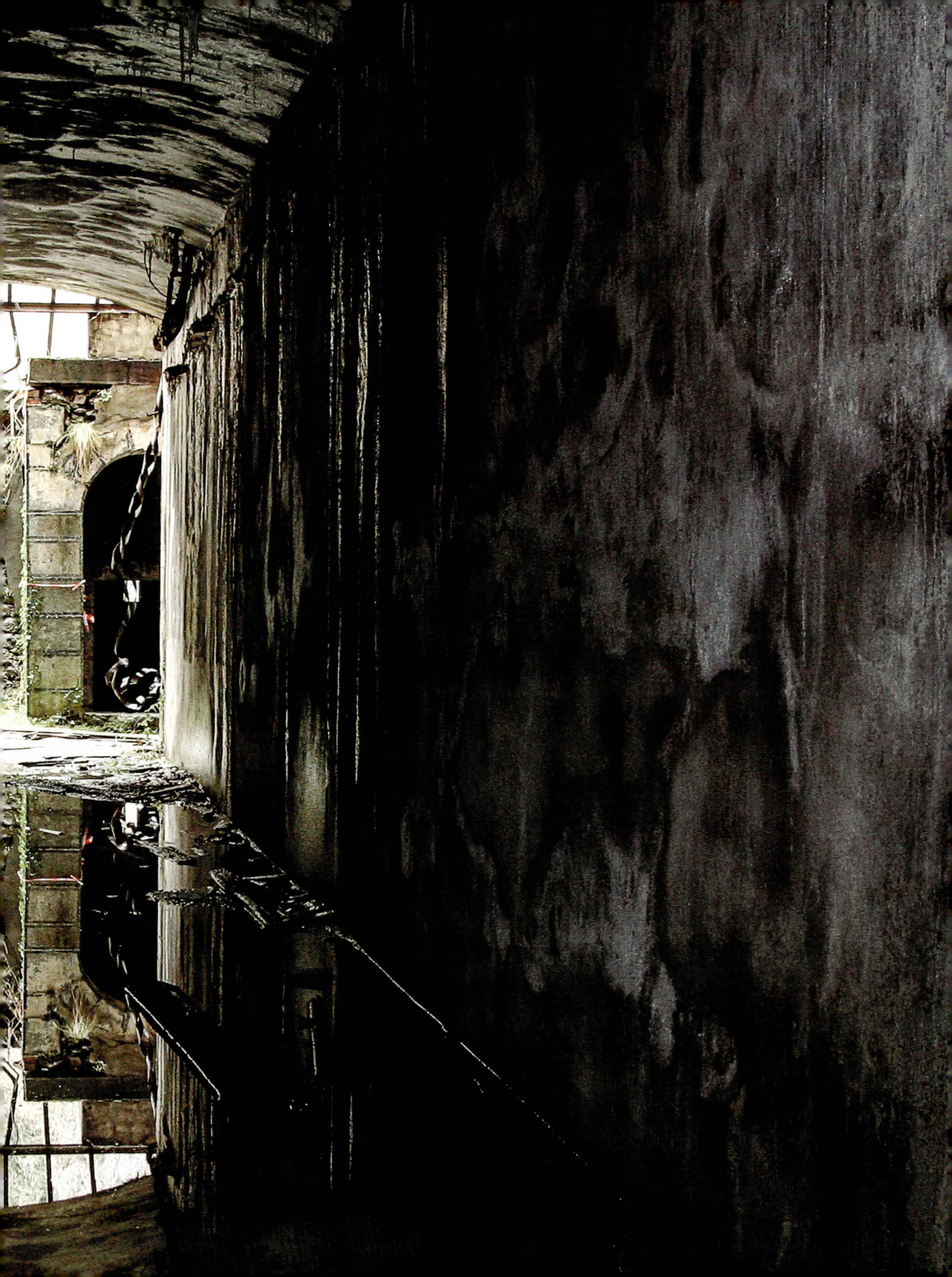

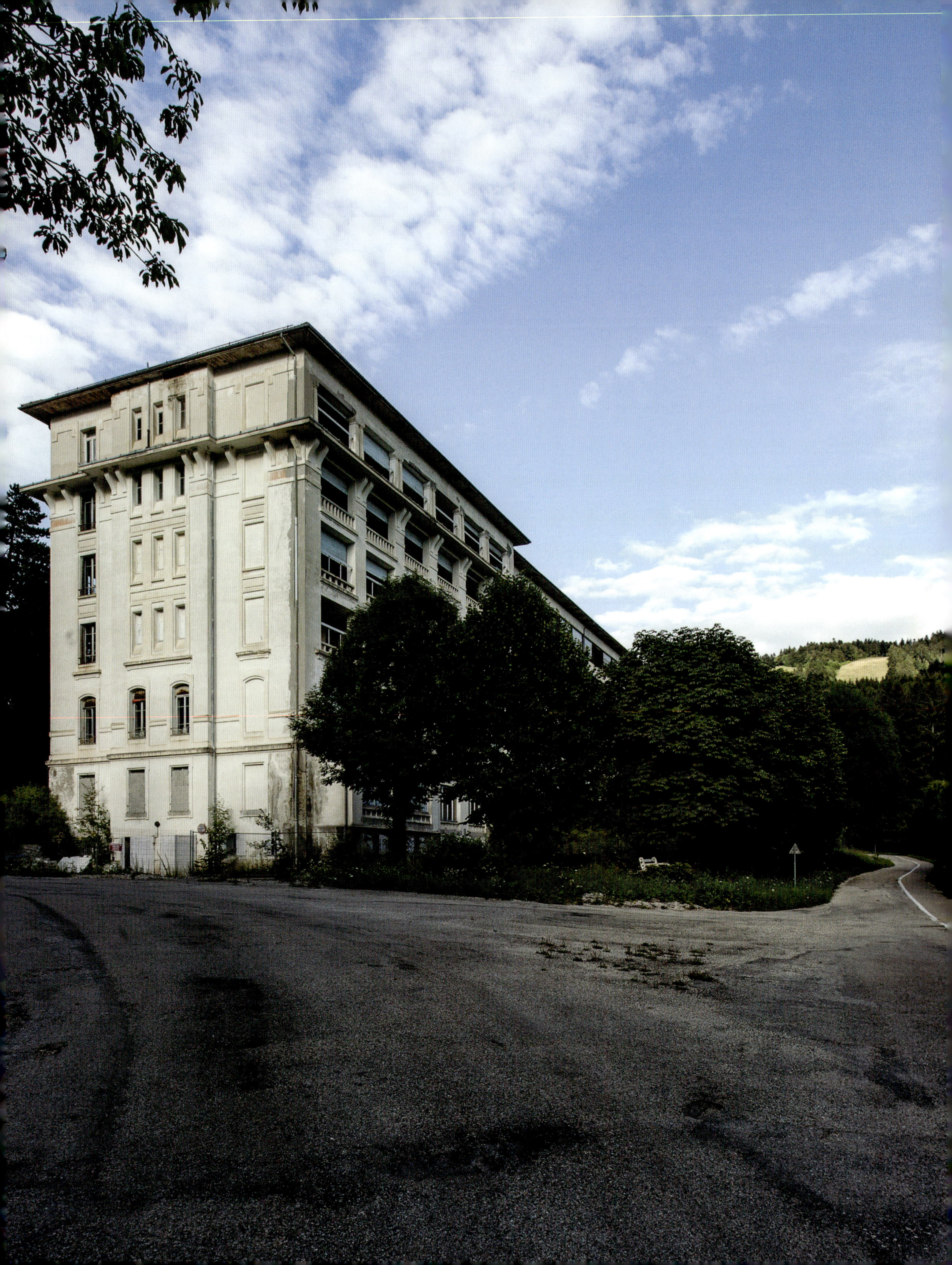

Hauteville, Savoie

The large number of sanatoriums built in France in the first half of the 20th century gave an unexpected boost to many villages whose scattered population had often relied on agriculture as their only means of subsistence.

This is particularly true of Hauteville, set on a mountain plateau halfway between Annecy and Bourg-en-Bresse. It became a genuine mountain resort by specialising in the treatment of tuberculosis patients and providing accommodation for their families.

At the time, several factors were taken into consideration to increase patients' chances of recovery.

First requirement: a remote town at an altitude free from the stale urban air, which incidentally reduced the risk of infection by removing those who were ill from population centres. Not too high, though, as patients could suffer altitude sickness.

Similarly, fresh air was desirable but could also be harmful. The site had to be protected from excessive draughts. Finally, the proximity of coniferous woods with their beneficial essences was a plus, so long as the patients were not deprived of sunlight.

Hauteville, 900 metres above sea level on the Bugey plateau and in the shelter of the wooded foothills of the Jura, had everything necessary for a model spa town. The first plan to set up a sanatorium in the commune was put forward by Dr Frédéric Dumarest, son of a local physician. Over a two-year period, under the patronage of the Œuvre Lyonnaise des Tuberculeux Indigents (a Lyonnaise charity for destitute consumptives) and its founder, the engineer and philanthropist Felix Mangini, Dumarest built a 120-bed sanatorium for low-income citizens.

The facility, opened on 23 August 1900, followed the models Dumarest had studied during his travels in Germany, pioneer in the hospitalisation of TB patients. It consisted of a main block connecting two sloping wings, one for men and the other for women. The wings faced south and enjoyed maximum sunshine.

The prognosis was generally good as Dr Dumarest selected so-called sanatoriable patients. They were young, had recently contracted the disease, had limited lesions that were developing favourably, and had no medical or social contra-indications. These criteria were sometimes relaxed when beds were standing vacant.

Five years later, not far from this first sanatorium which was attached to Lyon's state hospitals, a private institution of more modest size opened – Bellecombe. This time, treatment was aimed at a wealthier category of patient. There were only a few places on the plateau that could accommodate the relatives of TB patients, who were sometimes under treatment for several years. A mass of hotels, guesthouses and B&Bs sprang up, soon followed by shops to supply the needs of patients and their companions. This new economic windfall transformed the initial local reticence into a shared enthusiasm. In 1912, when Dumarest introduced the mechanical respirator or artificial lung to France – the first really effective treatment for tuberculosis – the Belligneux sanatorium, also reserved for a wealthy clientele, opened.

Two years later, war broke out. More than 16,000 soldiers would be treated on the plateau. The Red Cross, which moved in during the hostilities, in turn set up a sanatorium for women. While Hauteville's international reputation was growing, a tourist association was vainly trying to organise the life of the resort. However, the uncoordinated construction of health facilities and hotels of various sizes continued until 1939. Many Jewish families took refuge in the city's institutions and lodging houses during the Occupation.

The introduction of social security after Liberation brought new patients to Hauteville, until tuberculosis was finally eradicated by antibiotics.

Geriatrics, addiction treatment, pulmonary medicine, follow-up care or training centres – the sanatoriums were constantly seeking new vocations to survive the changing times.

Conversion into a multidisciplinary health centre could not prevent the closure of dozens of facilities. Hauteville, which has become an industrial wasteland, is now attempting to develop its heritage properties along new lines. The mayor plans to convert the finest buildings into second homes, while a drilling survey is scheduled for early 2018 to try and locate a thermal spring.

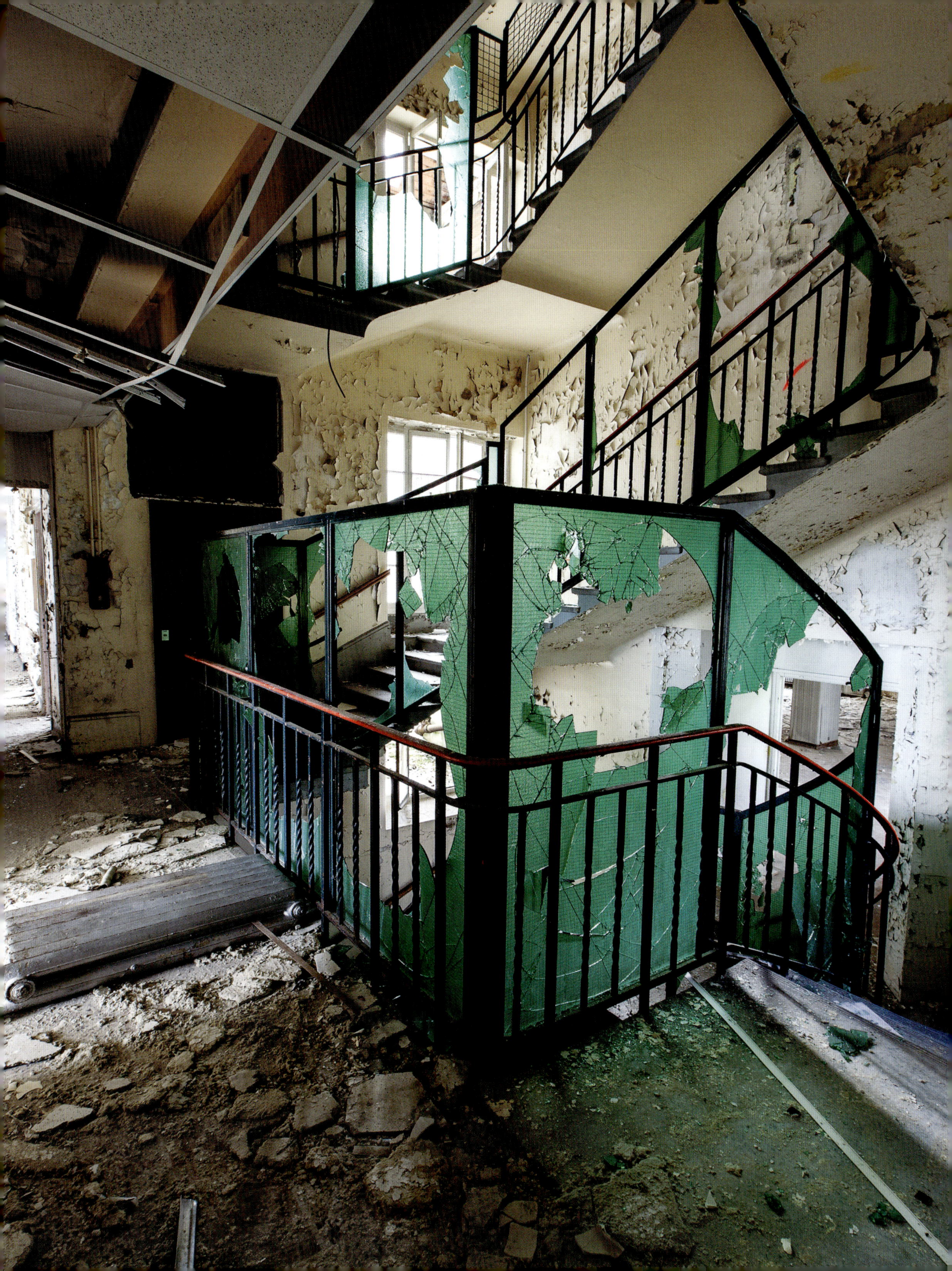

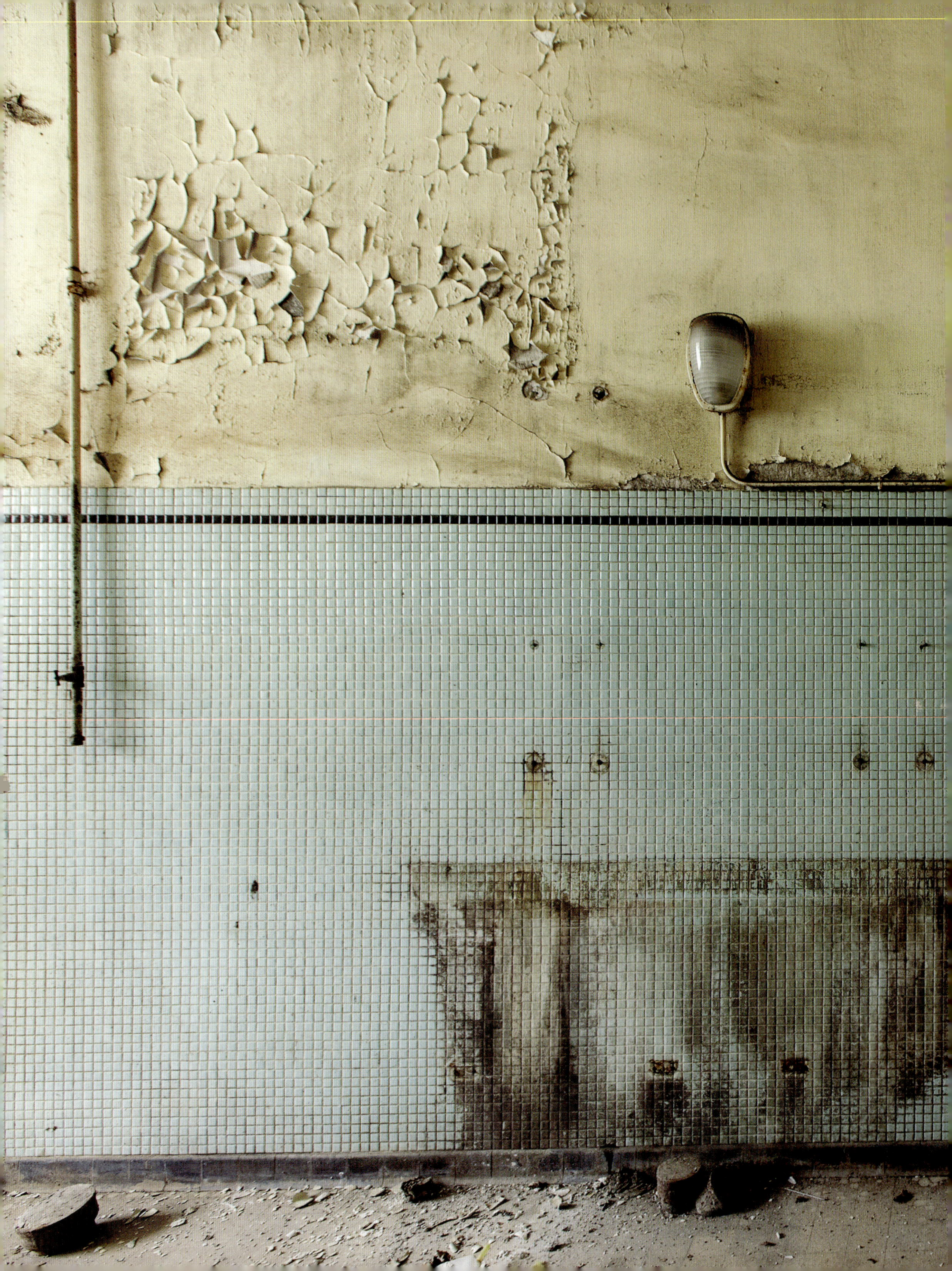

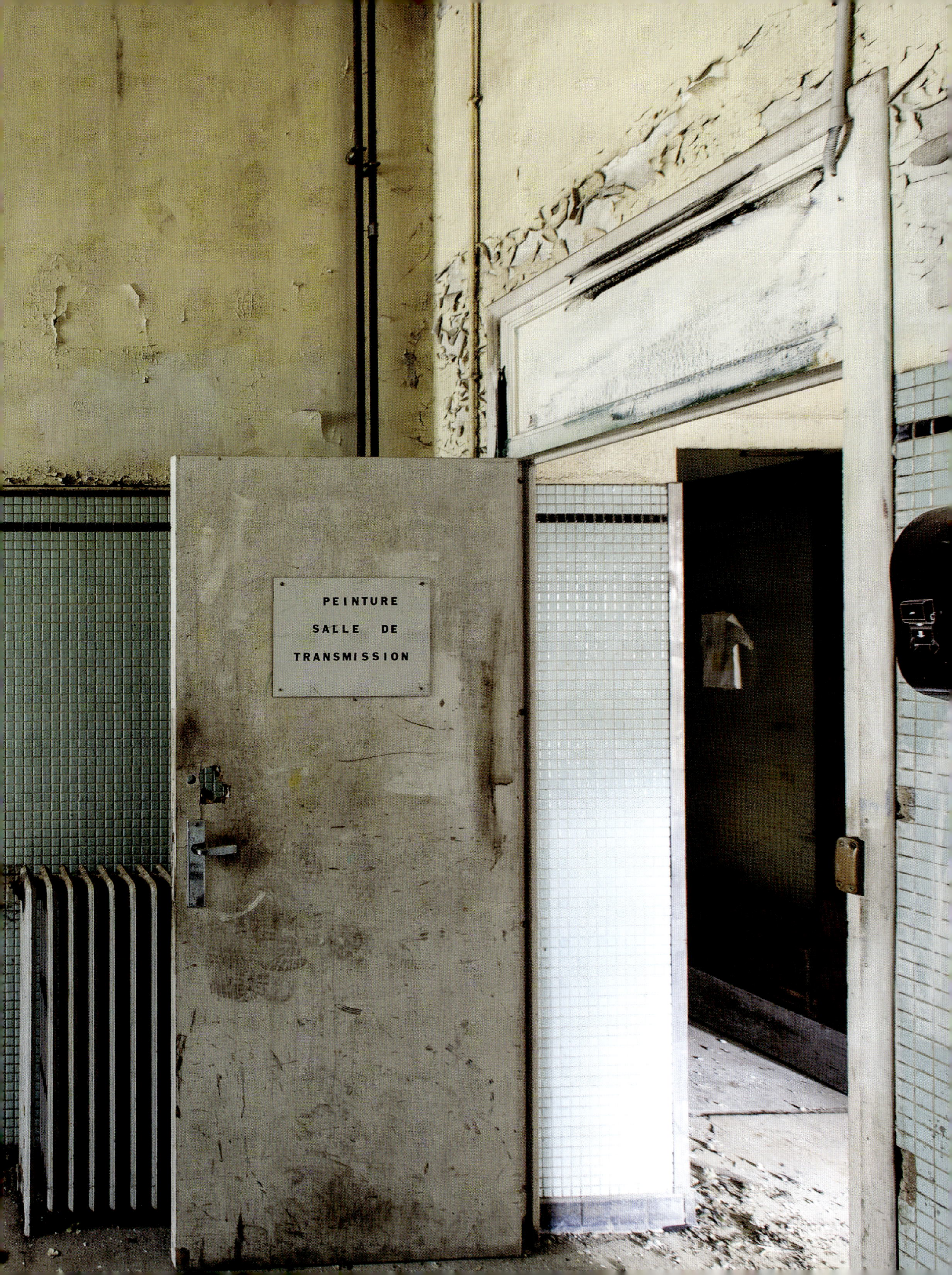
PEINTURE
SALLE DE
TRANSMISSION

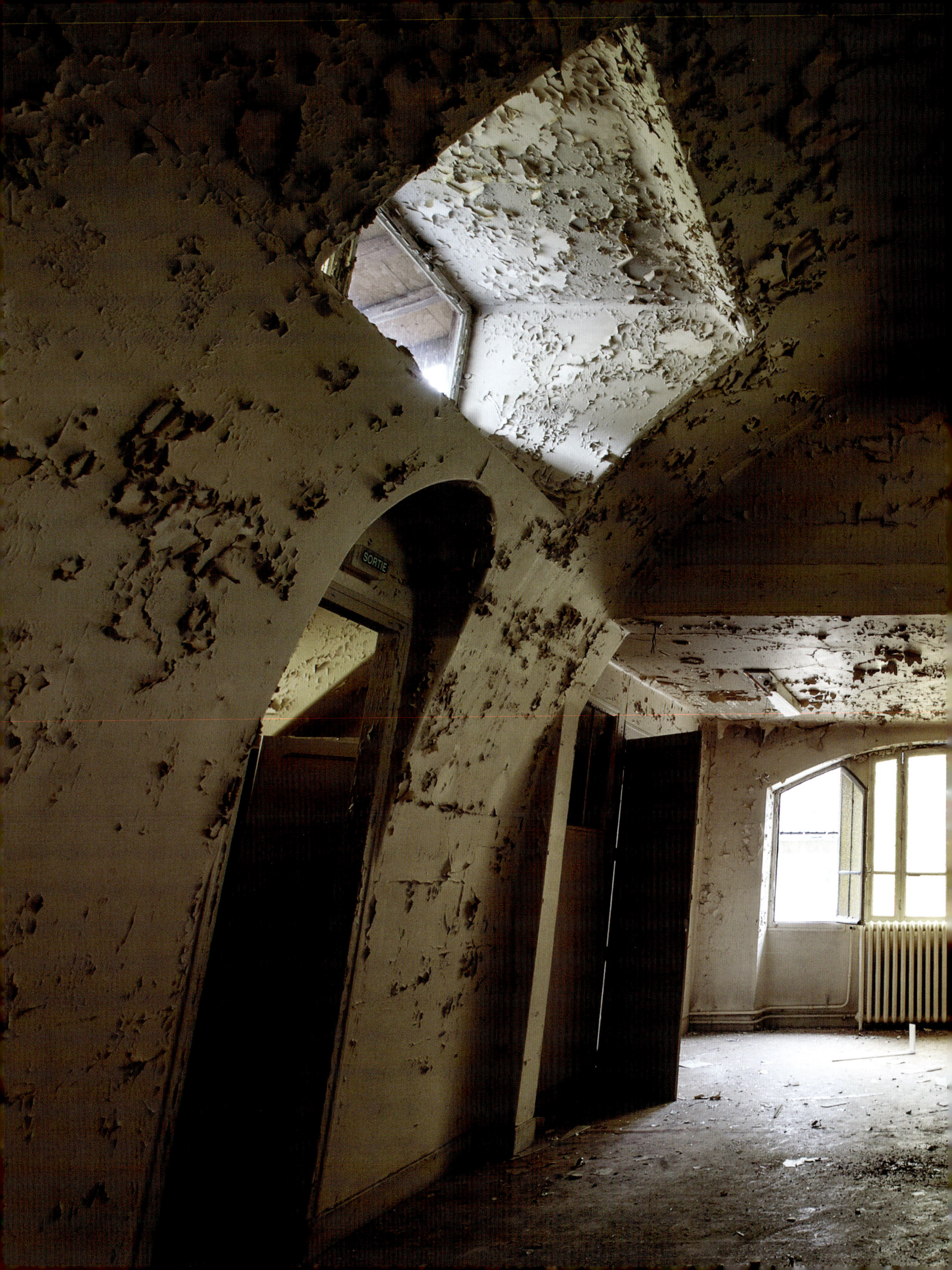
SORTIE

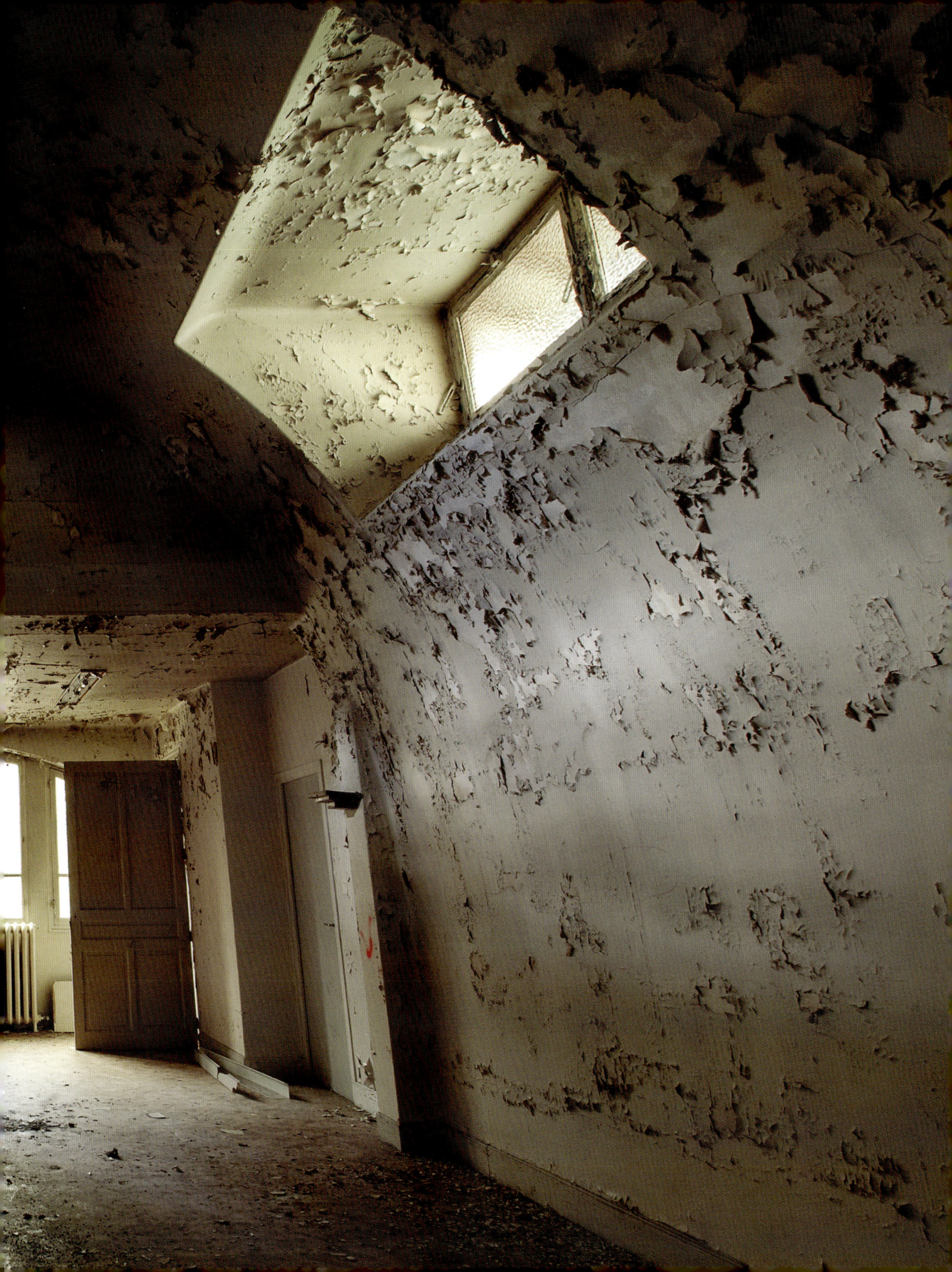

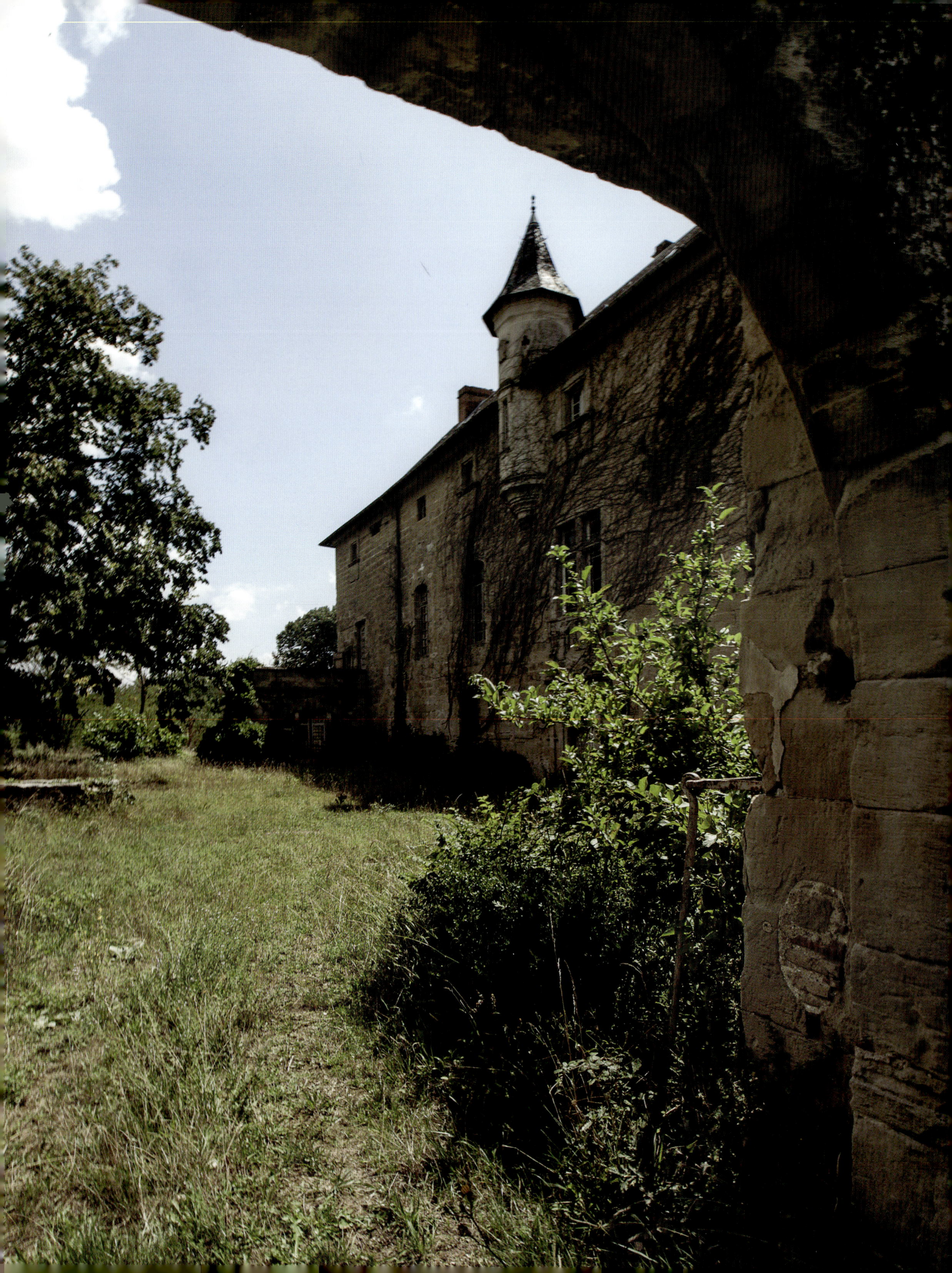

Château de Lézignac, Graulhet

The name of Graulhet is thought to derive from the word *grenouille* (frog) in the Occitan dialect of the south of France, recalling the streams and marshes surrounding the ancient city perched on its rocky peak.

The site, which had been inhabited since prehistoric times, had its own chateau in the Middle Ages. When the 12th-century crusade against the Cathar heretics prevailed, the Roman Catholic majority in Graulhet prospered and settled down to work in textiles and leather. Later, a new source of wealth was added: the cultivation of woad (plant that gives a blue dye). The Cistercian monks of neighbouring Candeil abbey contributed to the region's economic development.

The count who ruled over these lands handed the estate over to the monks. It included Château de Lézignac and a mill fed by the Dadou, the river that supplies Graulhet with water. The successive abbots made Lézignac their summer residence. Only the foundations remain from this period.

The existing building dates almost entirely from the 15th and 16th centuries, as indicated by "1561" carved on the pediment of the Renaissance-style door. Access is through a stone gateway and across a courtyard that also serves the farm buildings.

An entrance hall, kitchens, a large dining room with ornate chimney and a room of more modest dimensions make up the ground floor.

A grand staircase with a stone balustrade leads to a spacious reception room, which has another finely carved 16th-century fireplace. At this level the windows are arched, whereas on the lower floor they are mullioned. The chateau also has a brick dungeon. The rest of the building is local dressed sandstone.

When the estate was sold as a national asset by the Revolutionaries of 1789, it comprised a chapel, dovecote, stables, barn, wooded park and cultivated land, in addition to the chateau and mill. A grain trader bought it.

Following renovations in the 19th century, the chateau lost its defensive fortifications and a number of its annexes.

On 1 March 1977, the façades, the slate roofs of the chateau and the dovecote, the staircase with its balustrade, and the fireplaces in the main room on the ground floor and on the first floor were registered as historical monuments.

In 1983, a businessman opened a hotel-restaurant that is now closed. He is currently setting up a conservation association to raise funds and recruit volunteers to help restore Lézignac.

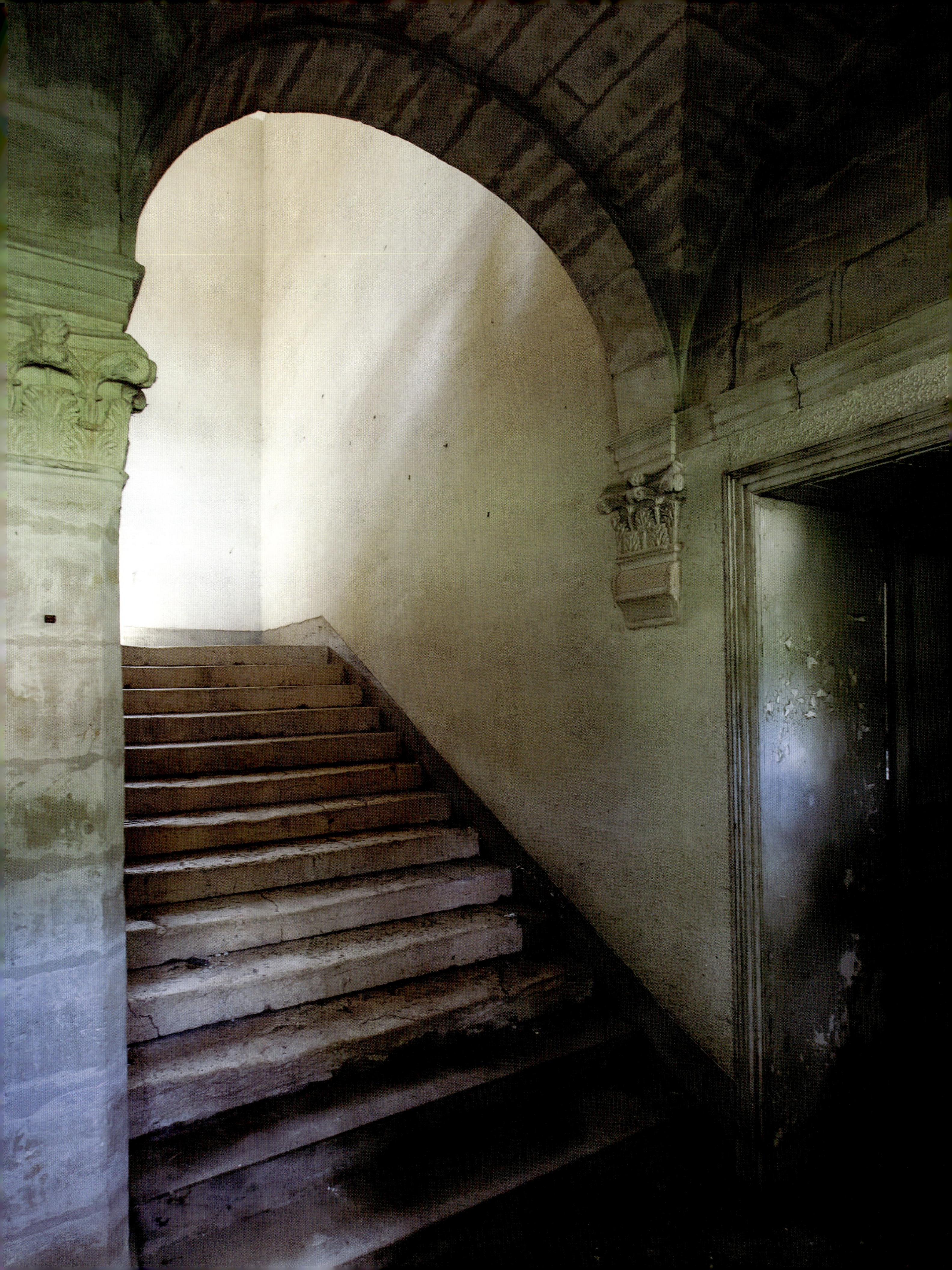

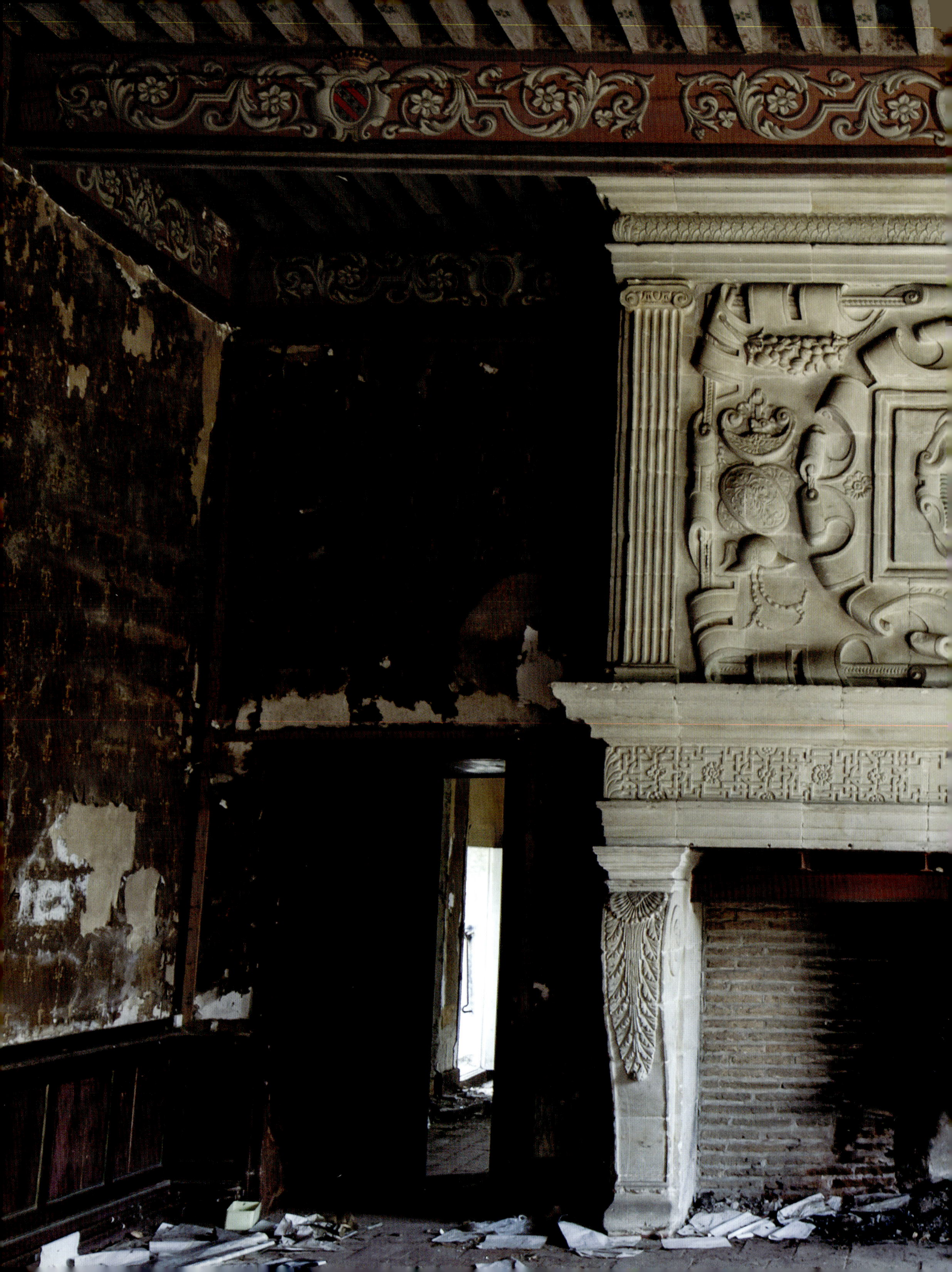

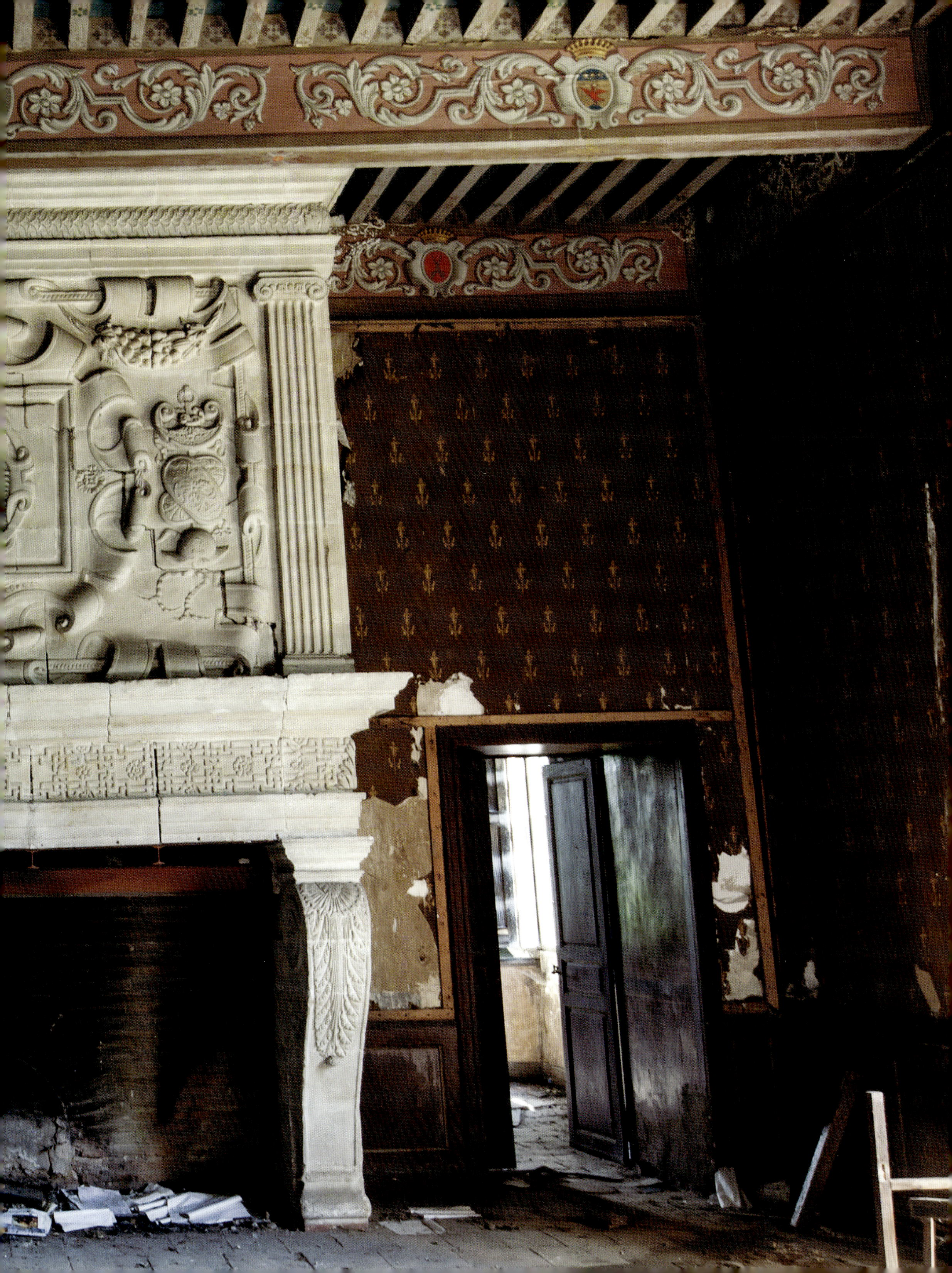

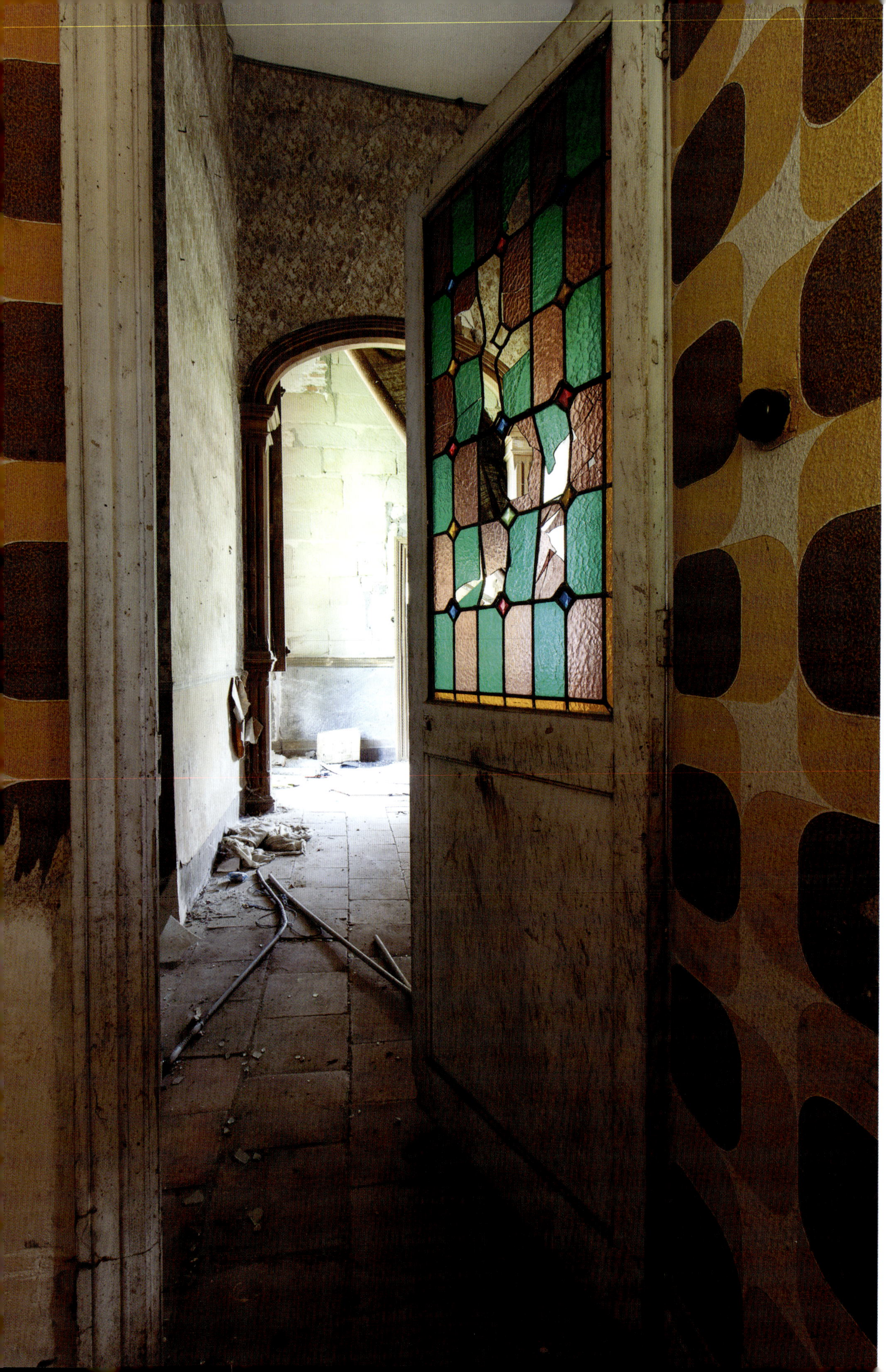

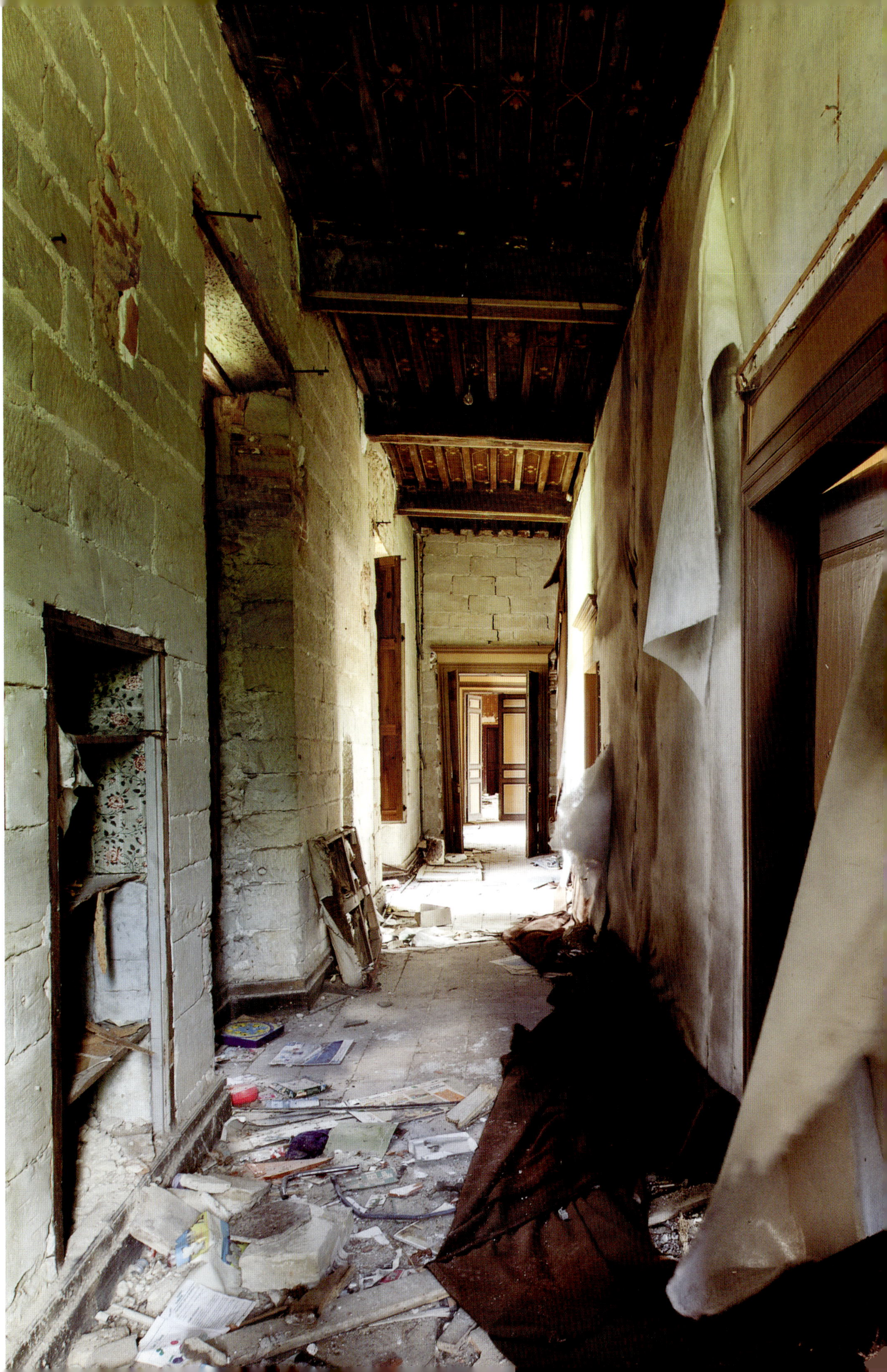

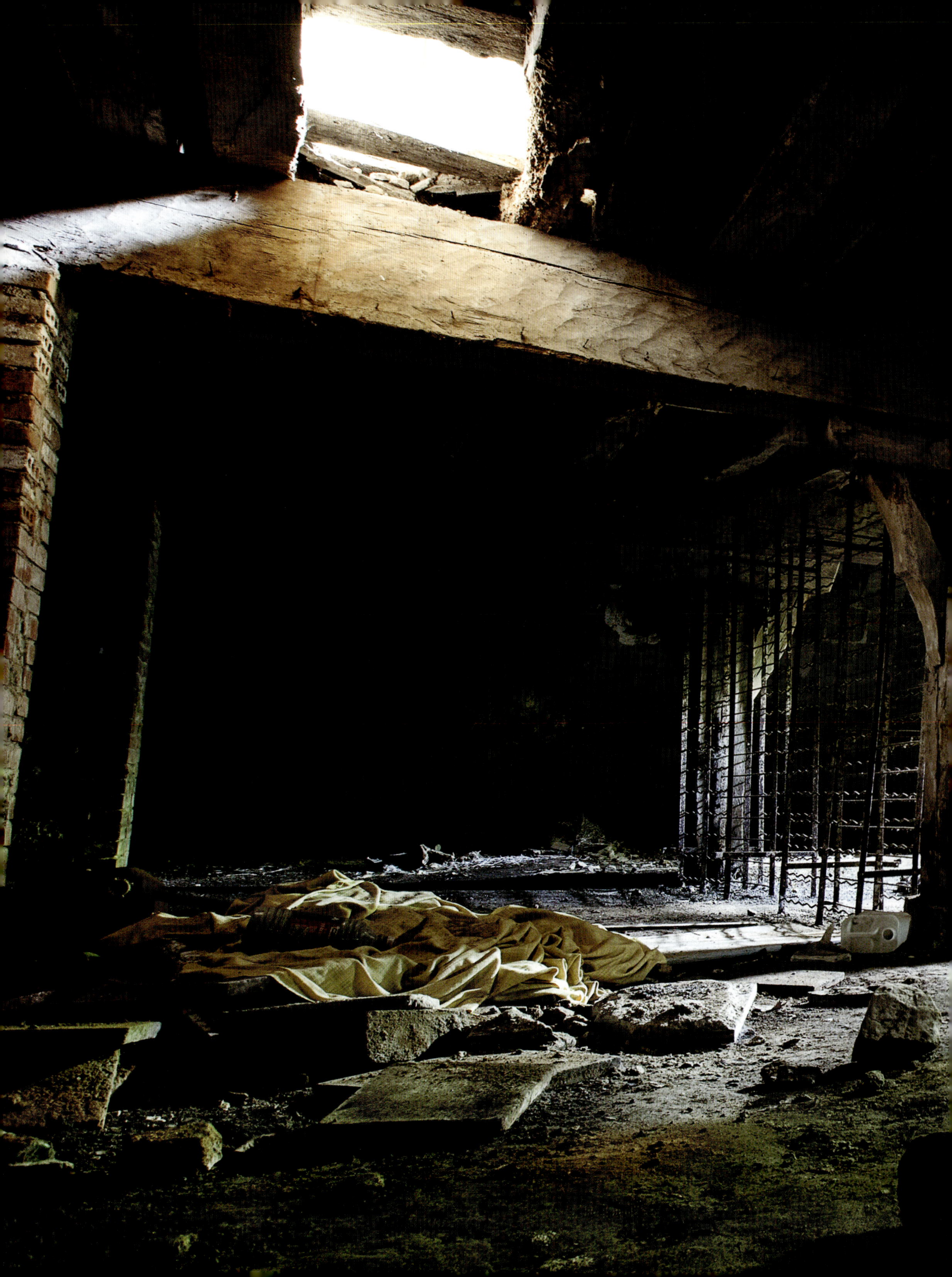

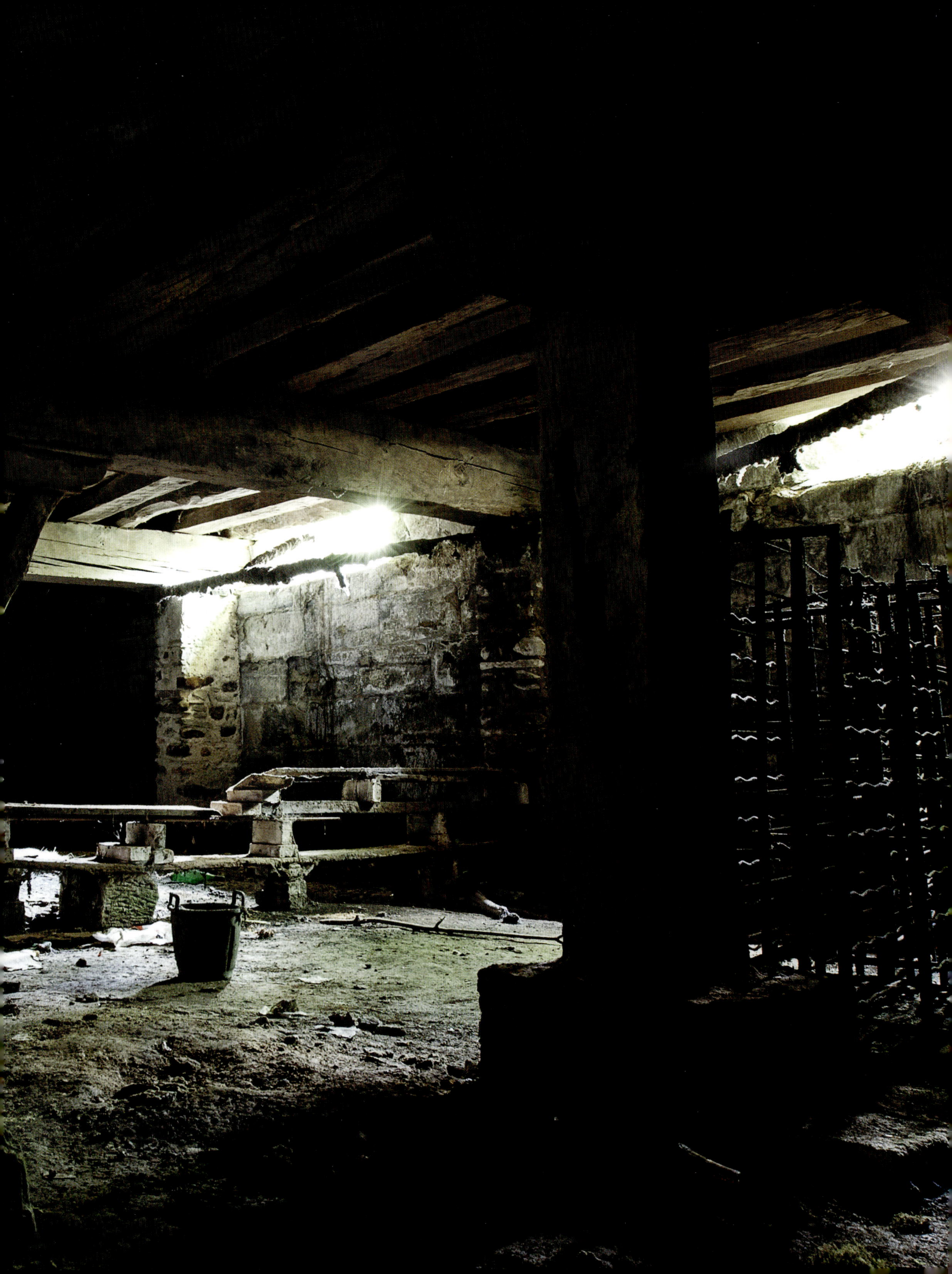

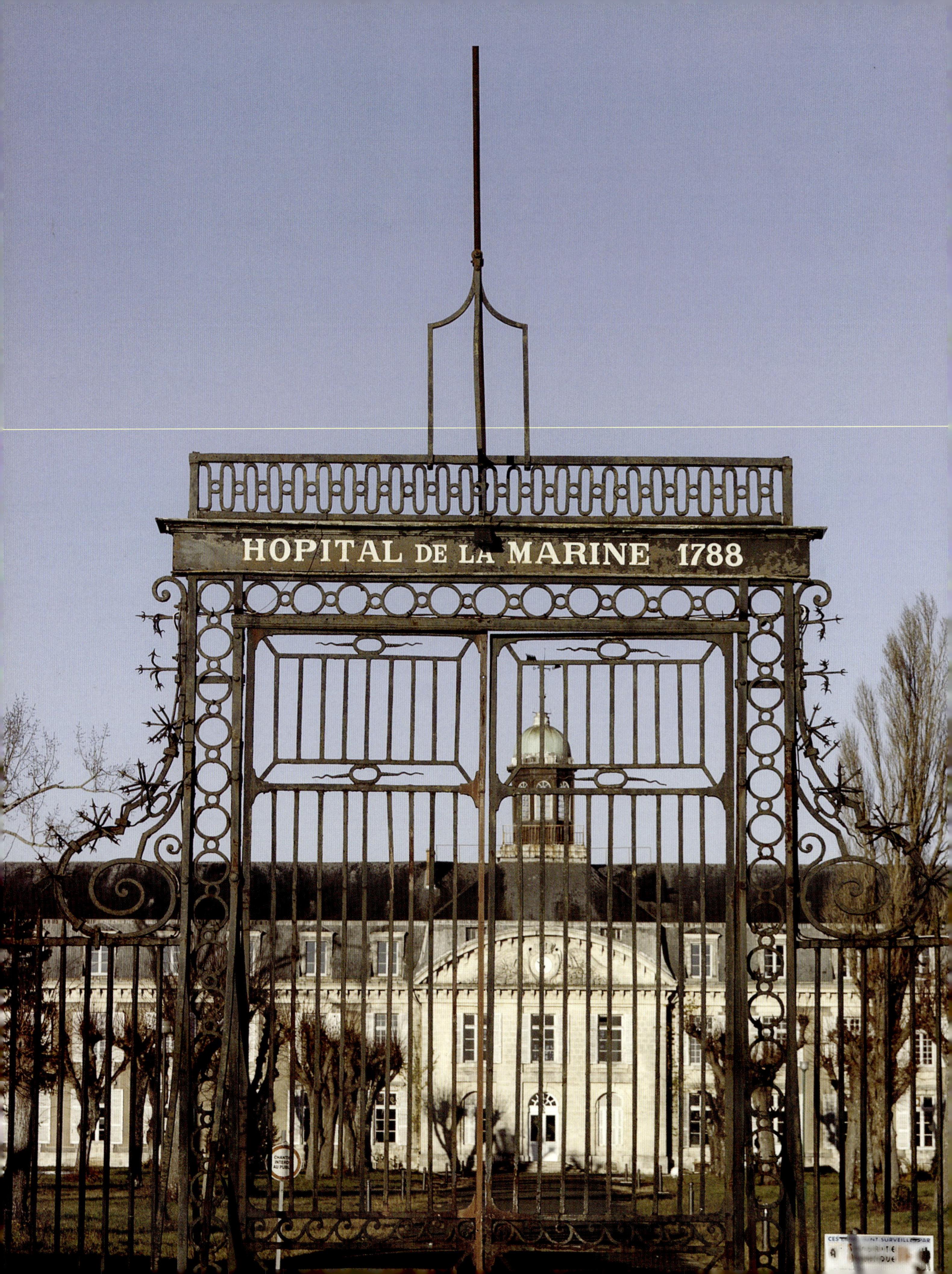
HOPITAL DE LA MARINE 1788

Hôpital de la Marine, Rochefort, Charente-Maritime

In 1666, Jean-Baptiste Colbert, controller-general of finance and secretary of state for the French navy under King Louis XIV, chose the port of Rochefort to install a military arsenal for the navy. The city is both open to the Atlantic and protected by the neighbouring islands of Aix, Ré and Oléron. The rapid development of the arsenal, and the regular disembarkation of war wounded, led to the neighbouring commune of Tonnay-Charente's hospital being transferred there. When this became too overcrowded, the hospital was forced to move again. Pierre Toufaire, chief engineer of the navy's civilian buildings, was in charge of the project. The fire of 1772, which destroyed a large part of the Hôtel-Dieu district of Paris, drove him to seek a location beyond the city walls. Toufaire opted for the nearby headland known as "la Butte".

The Hôpital de la Marine was opened in 1788 after five years of building work. It had a capacity of 800 beds but could accommodate up to 1,200 if necessary. It was reserved for military personnel, sailors and shipyard workers.

Structurally, the building was inspired by the bungalow-style architecture of the British Royal Naval Hospital at Stonehouse, Plymouth. The H-shaped construction, which connects a main body with four wings designed to group patients according to their condition, was in use until the early 20th century. Wide openings in the frontages allowed fresh air and sunlight to penetrate and purify the atmosphere.

A round chapel with an octagonal dome overlooks the central entrance hall. The more mobile patients could celebrate Mass from a gallery on the second floor. Four other pavilions in the lateral wings, isolated from the rest, were reserved for contagious cases.

The world's first naval school of medicine, opened in 1722 in Rochefort, was later housed in one of these pavilions. At first it specialised in anatomy and surgery, but in 1890 it was turned into a medical college, a role that lasted until it closed down in 1964. The students had access to a vast library and a botanical garden planted in the 13,000 square metres of tree-lined courtyard surrounding the buildings.

Two other chapels, together with technical and administrative services, completed the property. Wells were bored on site, as the city depended on them for its supply of drinking water. Although no fresh water was found, the boreholes did reveal a thermal spring which is still flowing today.

A civilian hospital was built next door during the 19th century. The military hospital was in use until 1983; in 1965, its entrance and the main chapel, façades, pavilions and various other features were awarded protection under the historical monuments designation.

In 1989, a real-estate company acquired the property but left it standing empty except for the school, which was converted into a national museum for the former naval school of medicine, and another pavilion that was used for accommodation.

The following decade saw several rehabilitation proposals, but they all came to nothing. After endless complications, the city administration took over in 2015. Restoration is now on the cards, while preserving the historic character of the site. A spa complex including accommodation and a park, and offering a wide range of treatments, is scheduled to open around 2021.

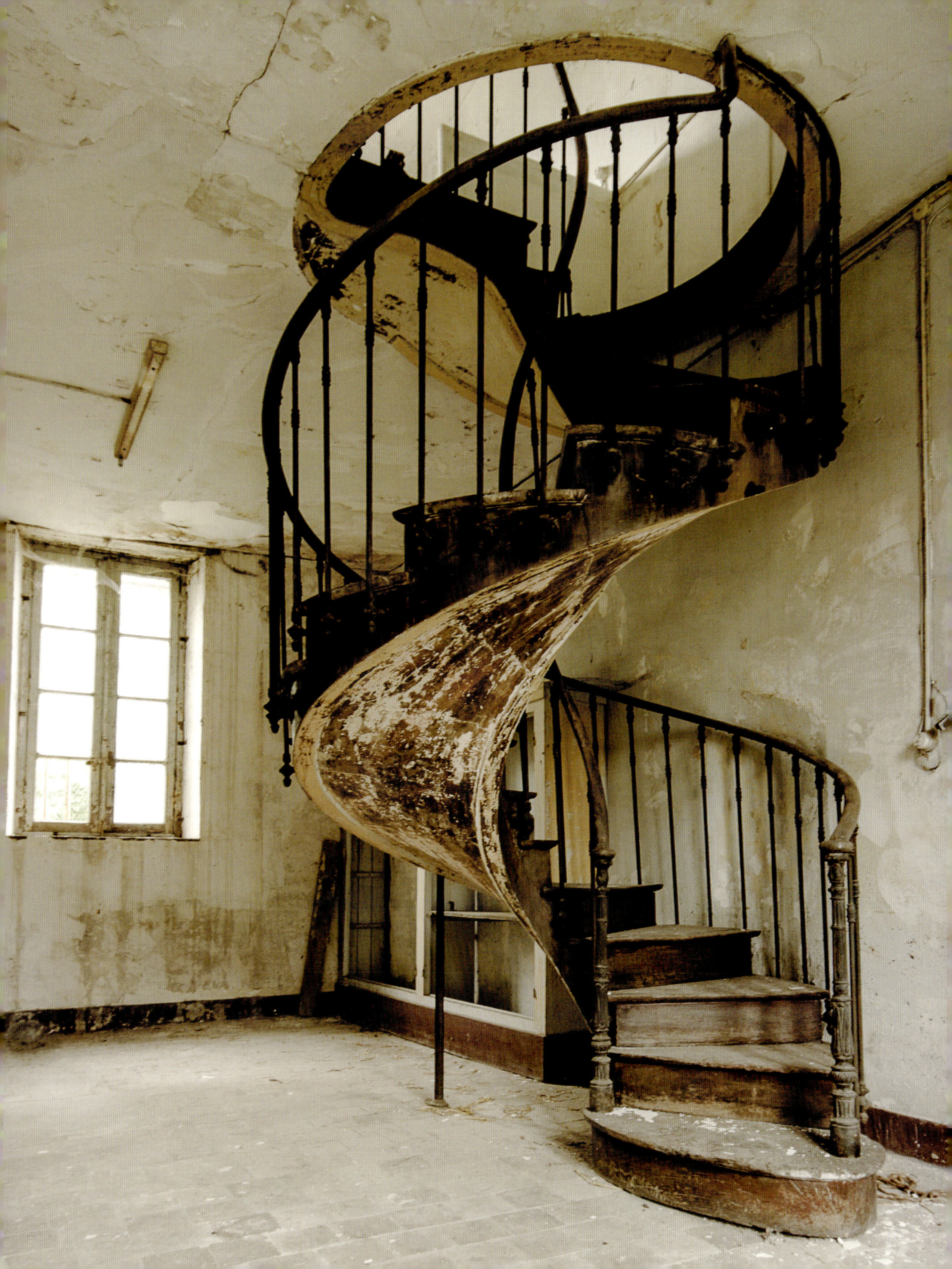

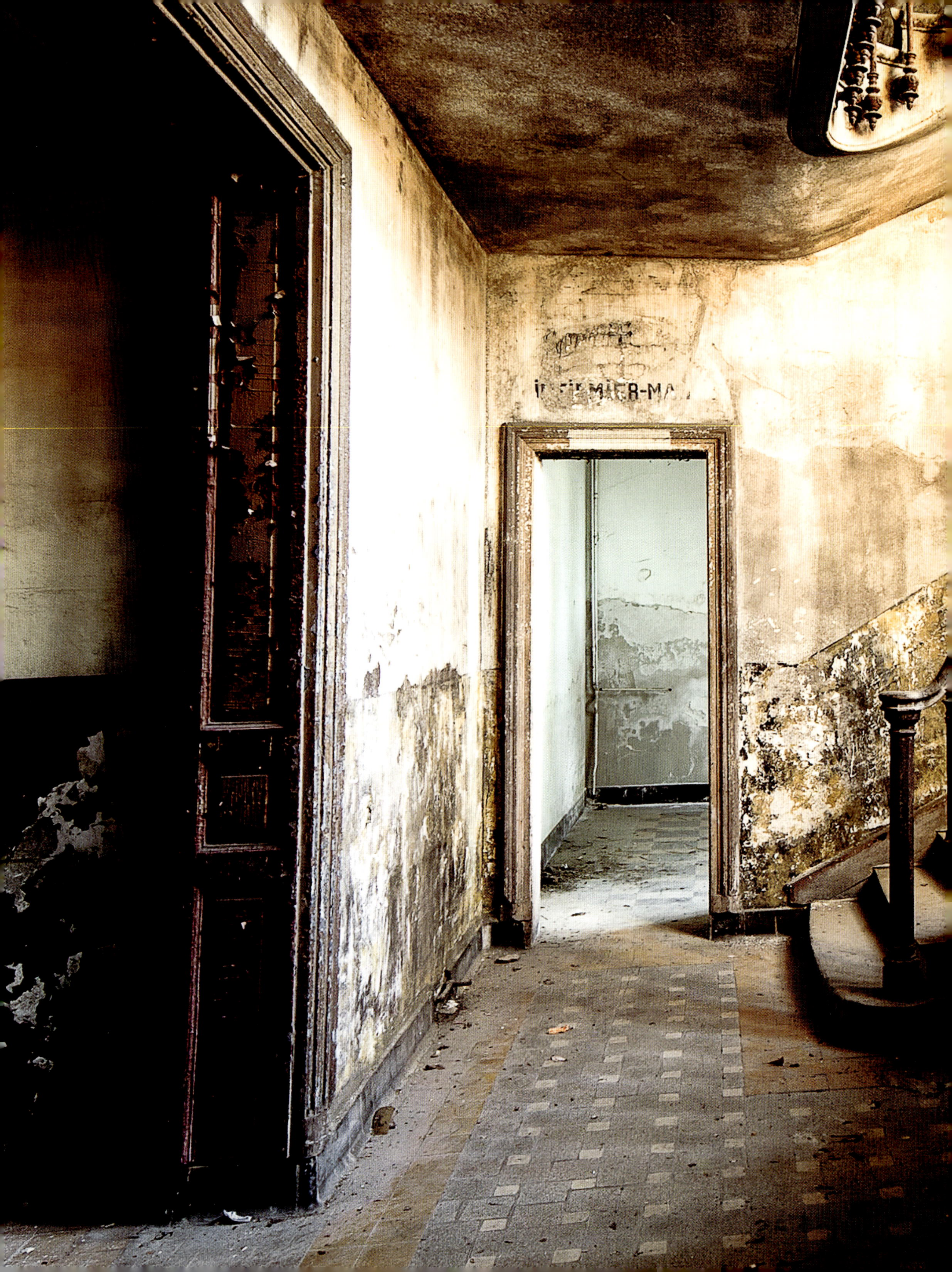

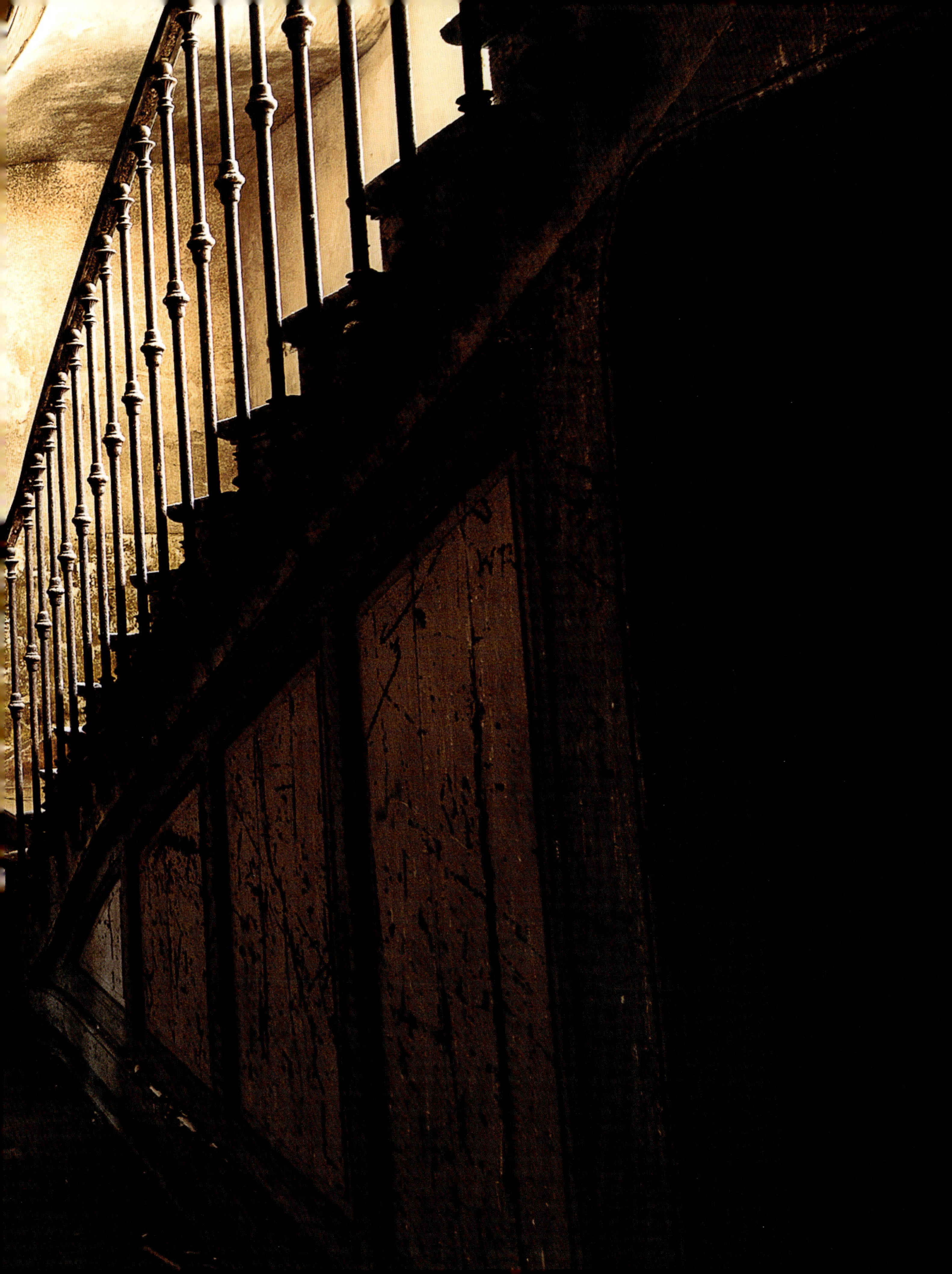

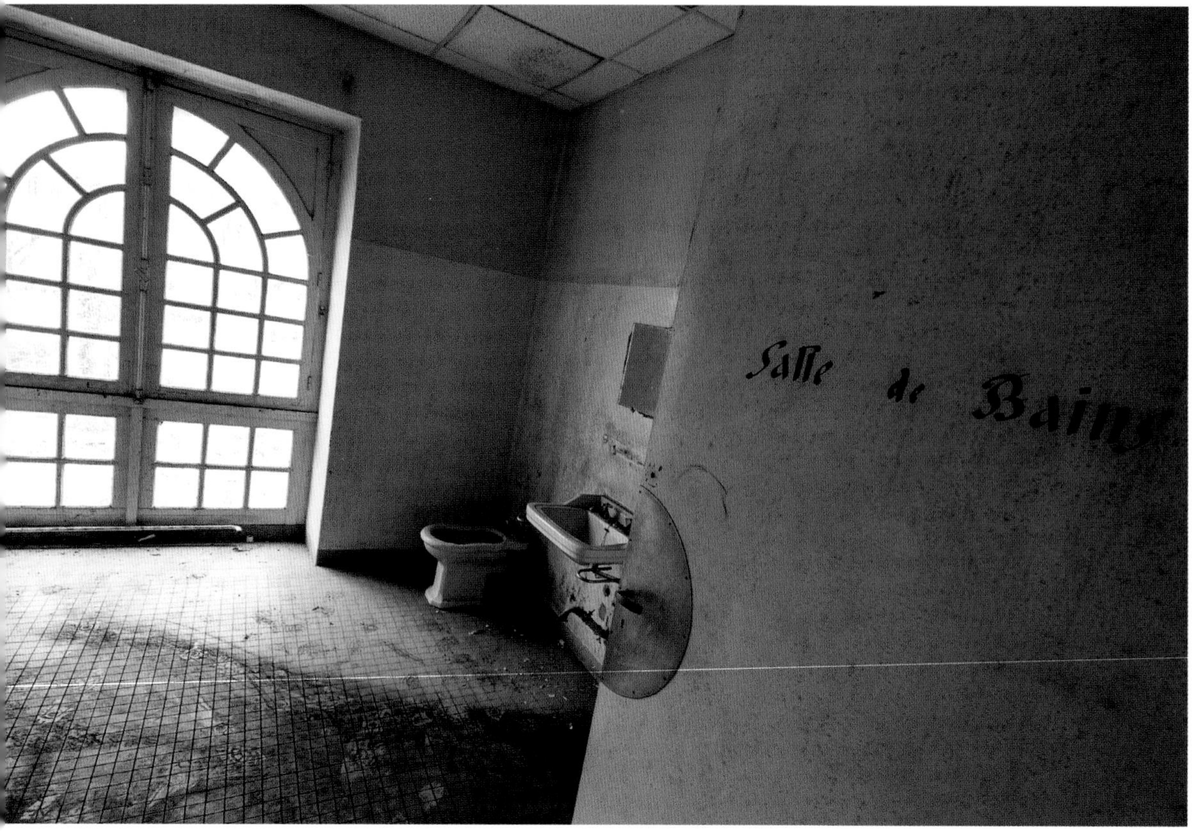
Salle de Bain

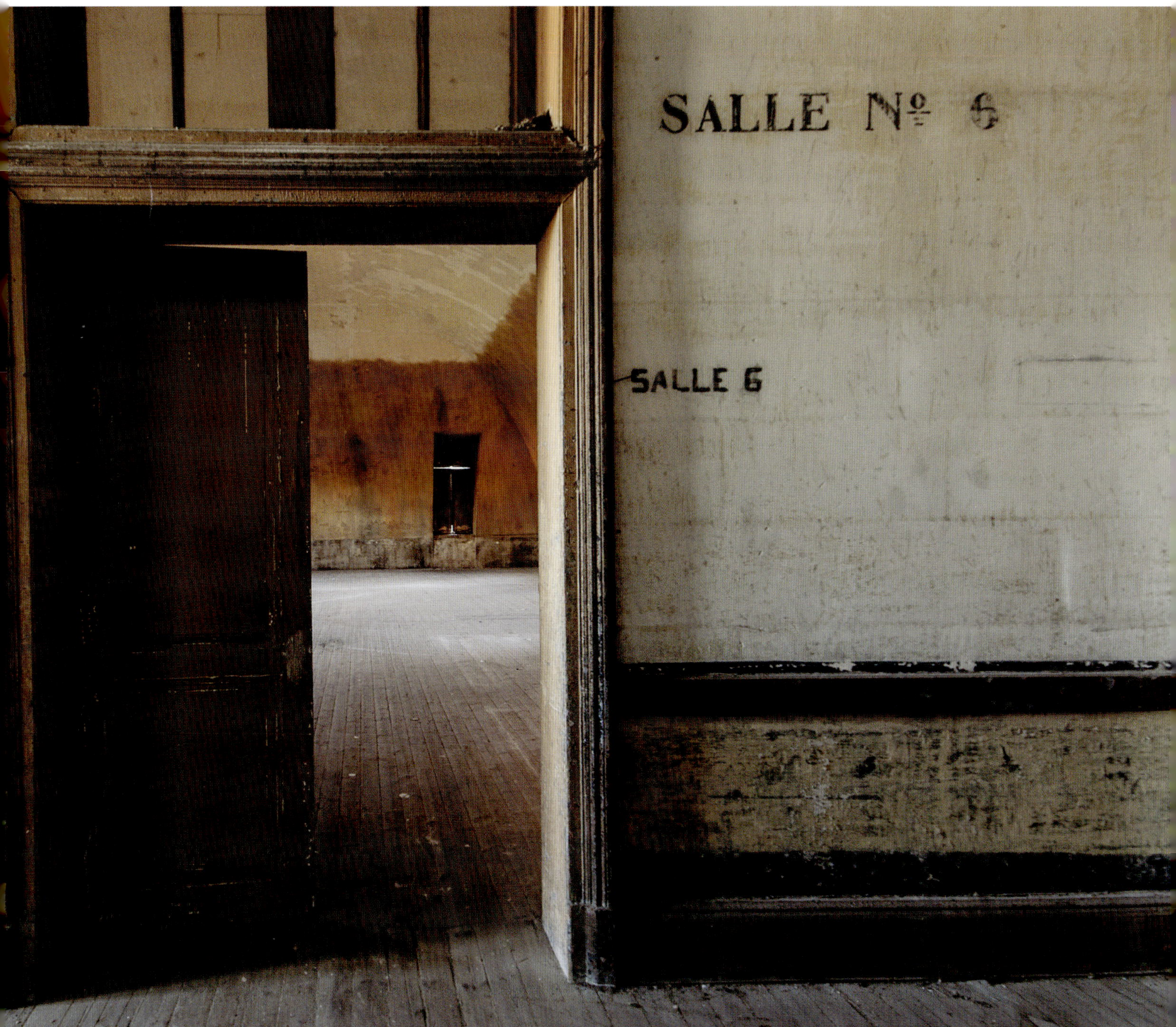
SALLE N° 6
SALLE 6

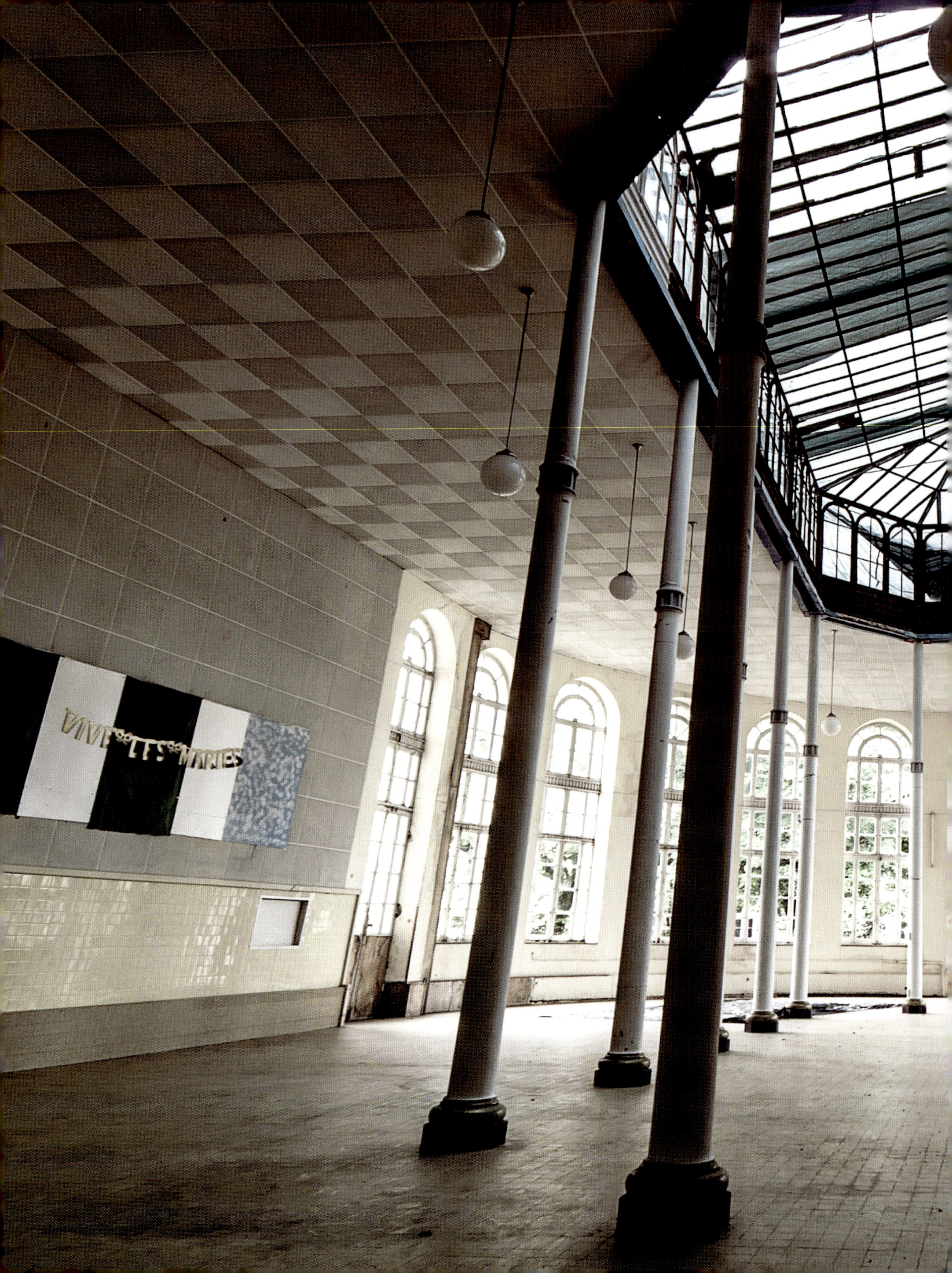
VIVE LES MARIES

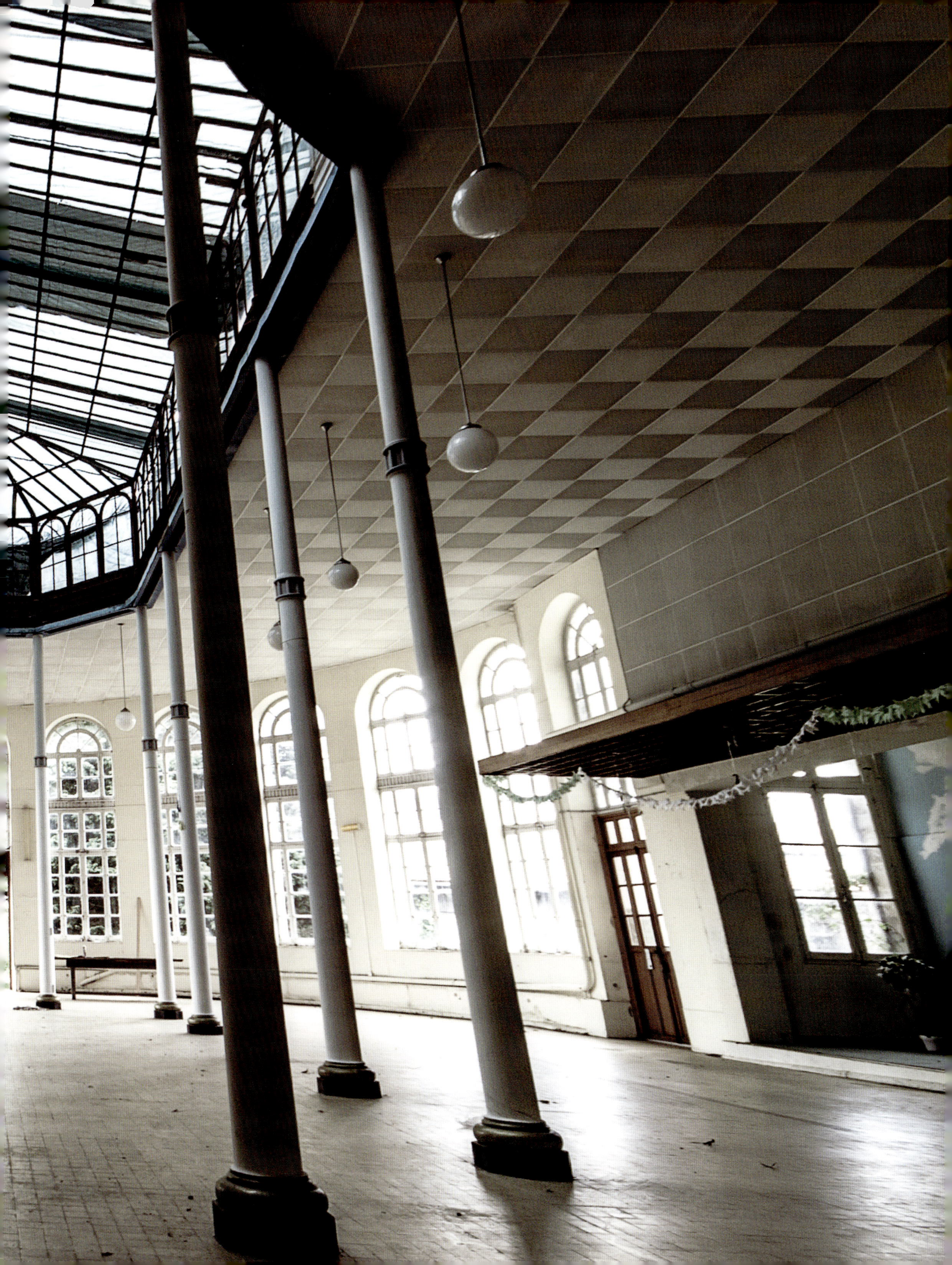

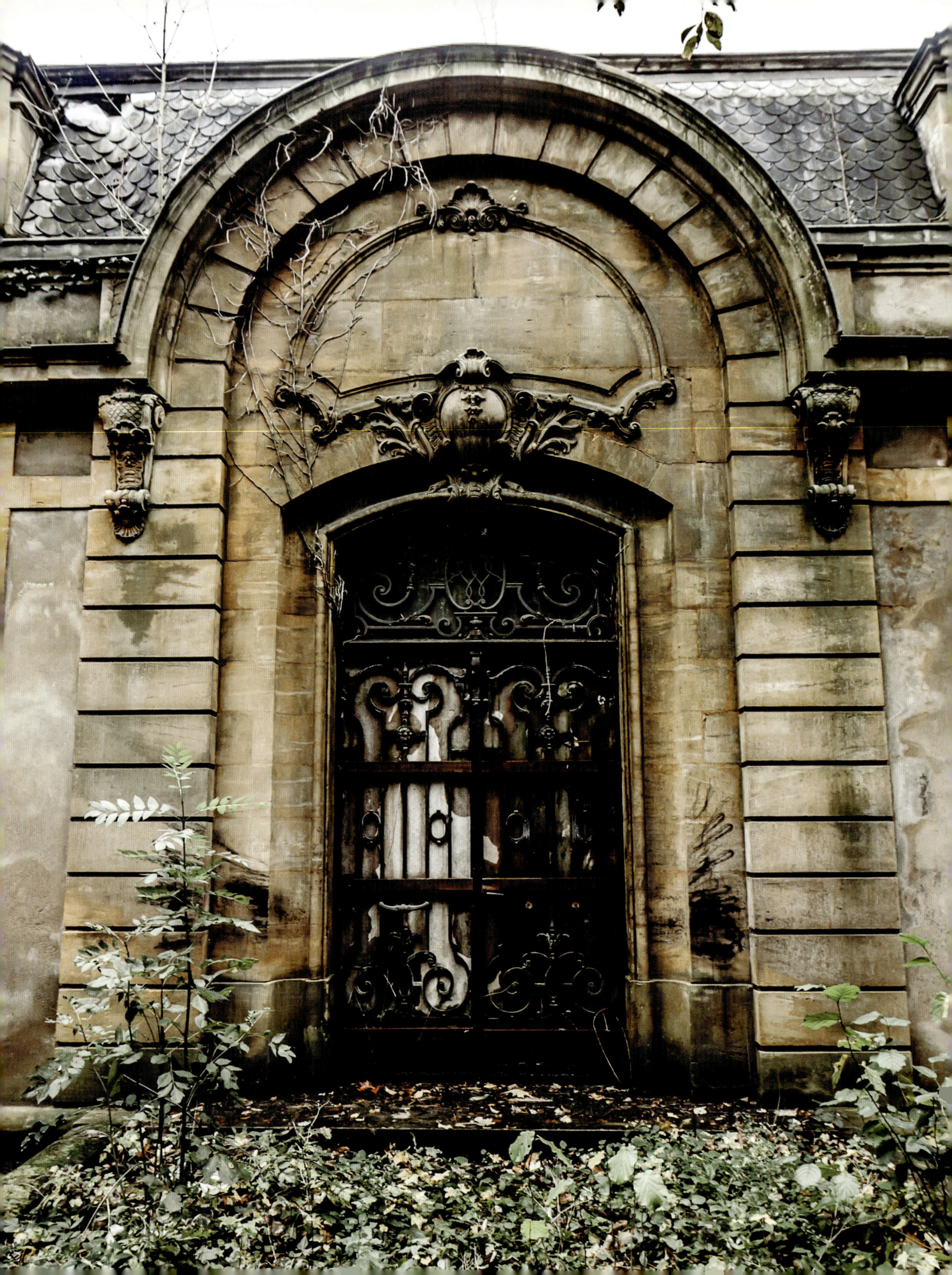

Grands Bureaux Wendel, Hayange

The Val de Fensch iron and steel industry is inextricably linked to the history of Lorraine. The Hayange archives record forges dating as far back as the beginning of the 15th century.

Nevertheless, when on 1 April 1704, Jean-Martin de Wendel bought the Rodolphe forges from a landowner who could not afford to maintain them, the region was still largely rural.

Its industrialisation was mainly associated with the descendants of the new forge owner. The Wendel empire grew over the generations, and throughout the vagaries of history, to become one of the great names of the French iron and steel industry. The epicentre was always Hayange, where Jean-Martin had built the family chateau.

By the end of the 19th century – Lorraine had been annexed by Germany – the seventh generation of Wendels was in charge. The youngest of three brothers, Jean-Marie Humbert, was the group's co-manager and he embarked on modernising the company. He restored the chateau and in 1892 built the Grands Bureaux Wendel, an imposing Louis XV-style building, next door.

The wrought-iron balustrades and the vast central light well shape the interior of the grand office space. But the company grew rapidly and needed an extension to its premises: this was built in 1826 for the eighth and last generation of Wendel steelmakers.

Their steel mills were nationalised in the early 1980s, and the heirs turned to business and investment.

On 24 July 1987, the offices were registered as a historical monument. The site was abandoned twenty years later by the family, who were scattered around the four corners of the earth, and is still awaiting restoration.

The chateau, on the other hand, is now a restaurant.

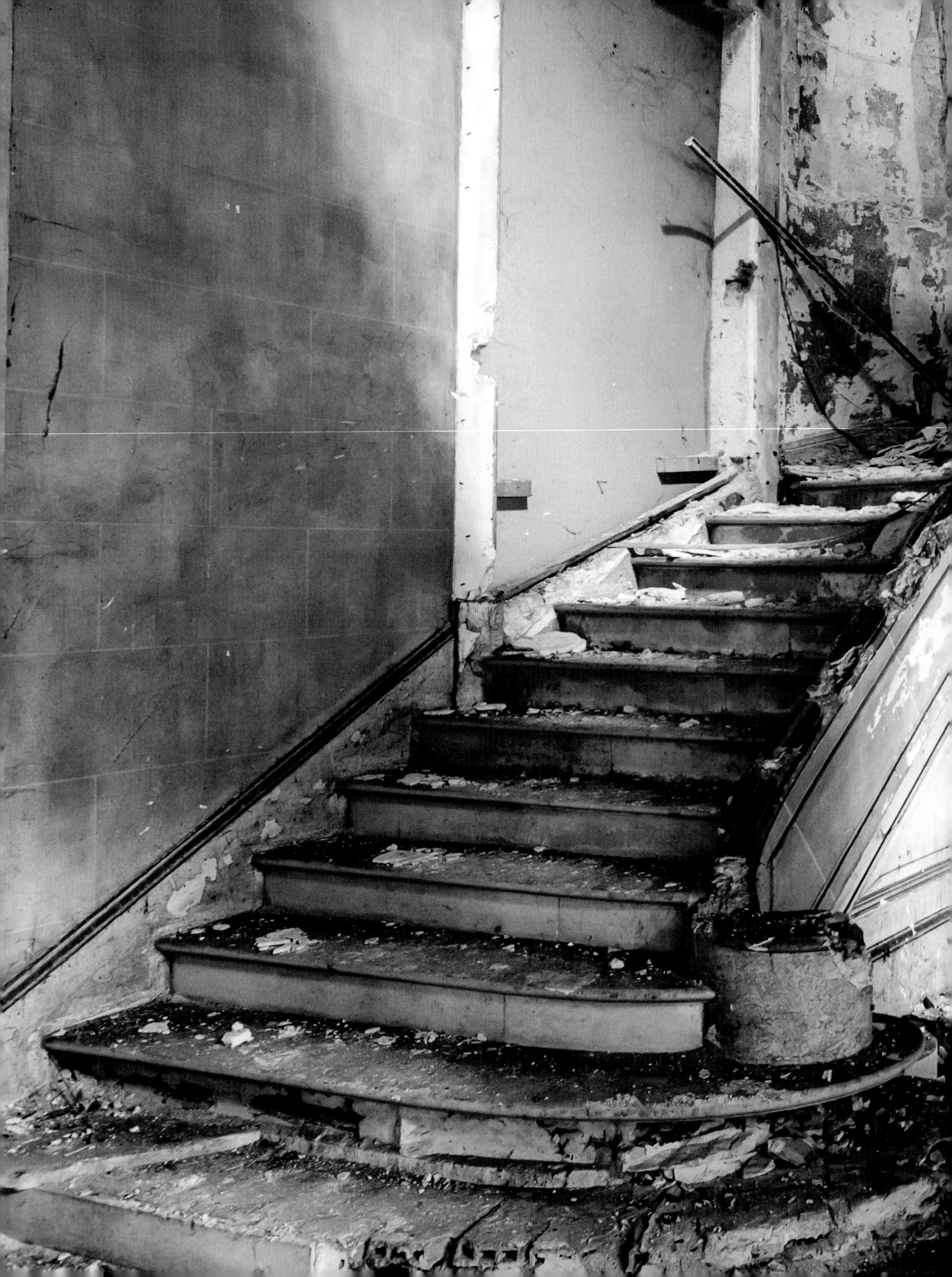

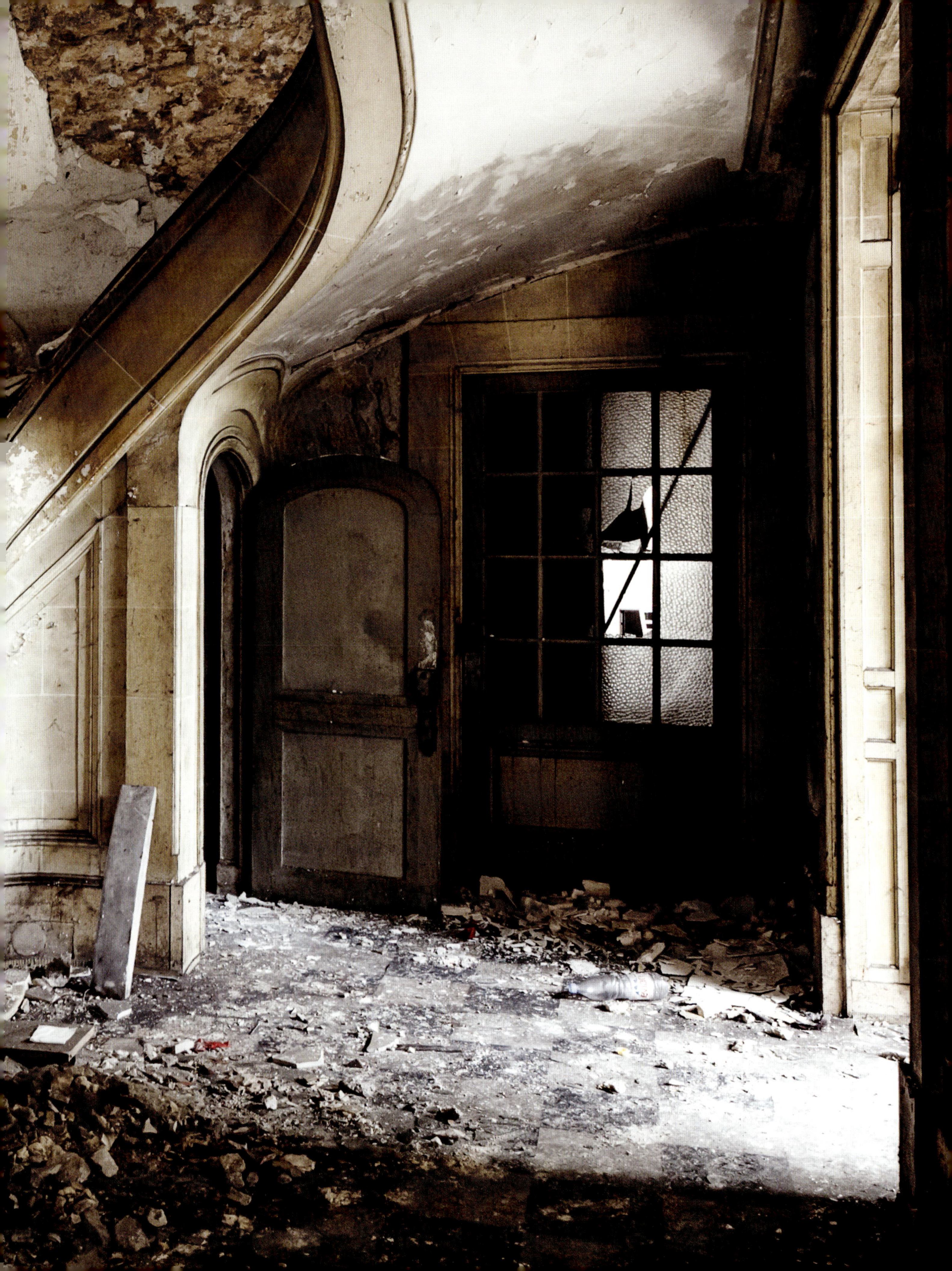

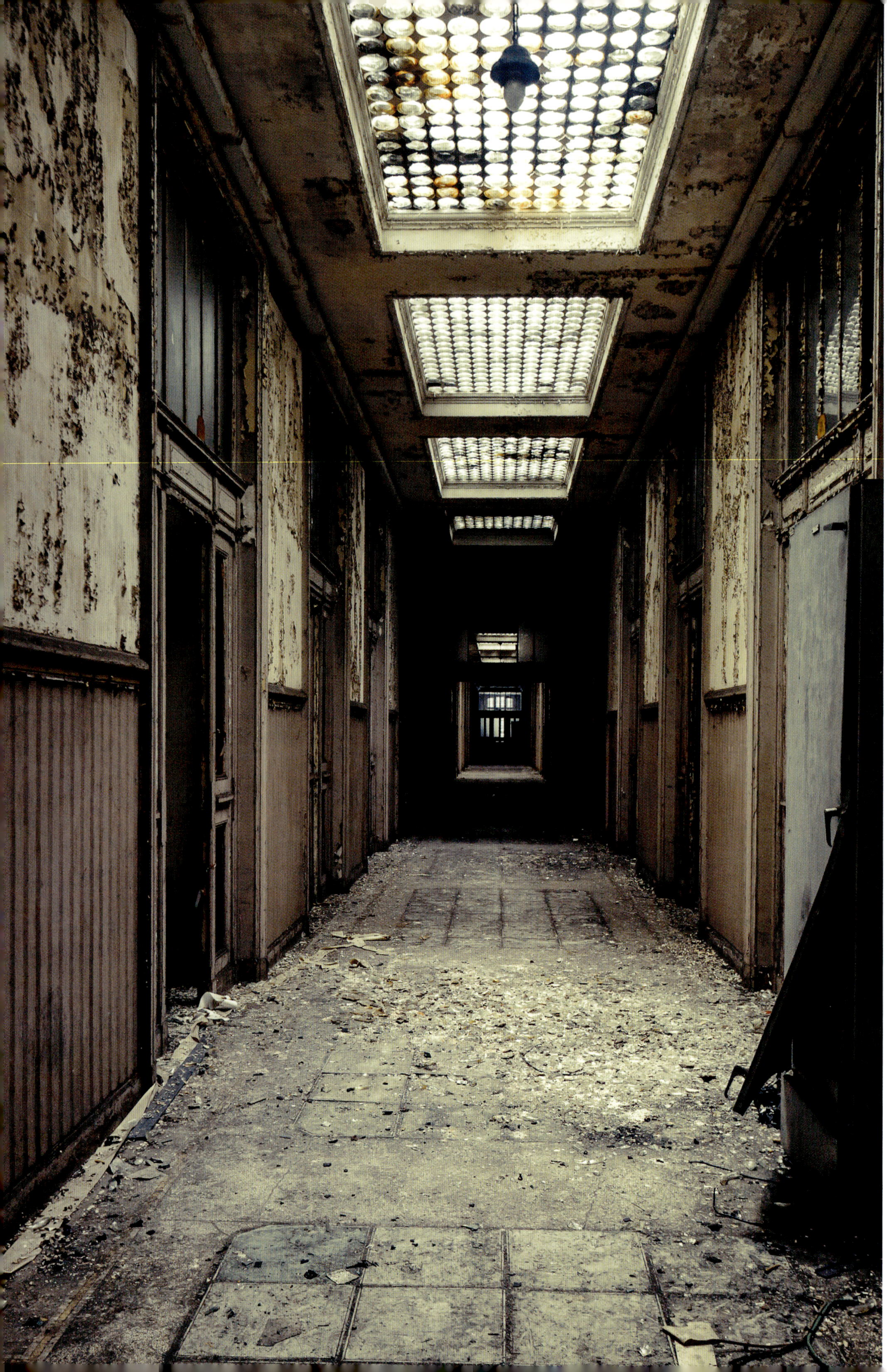

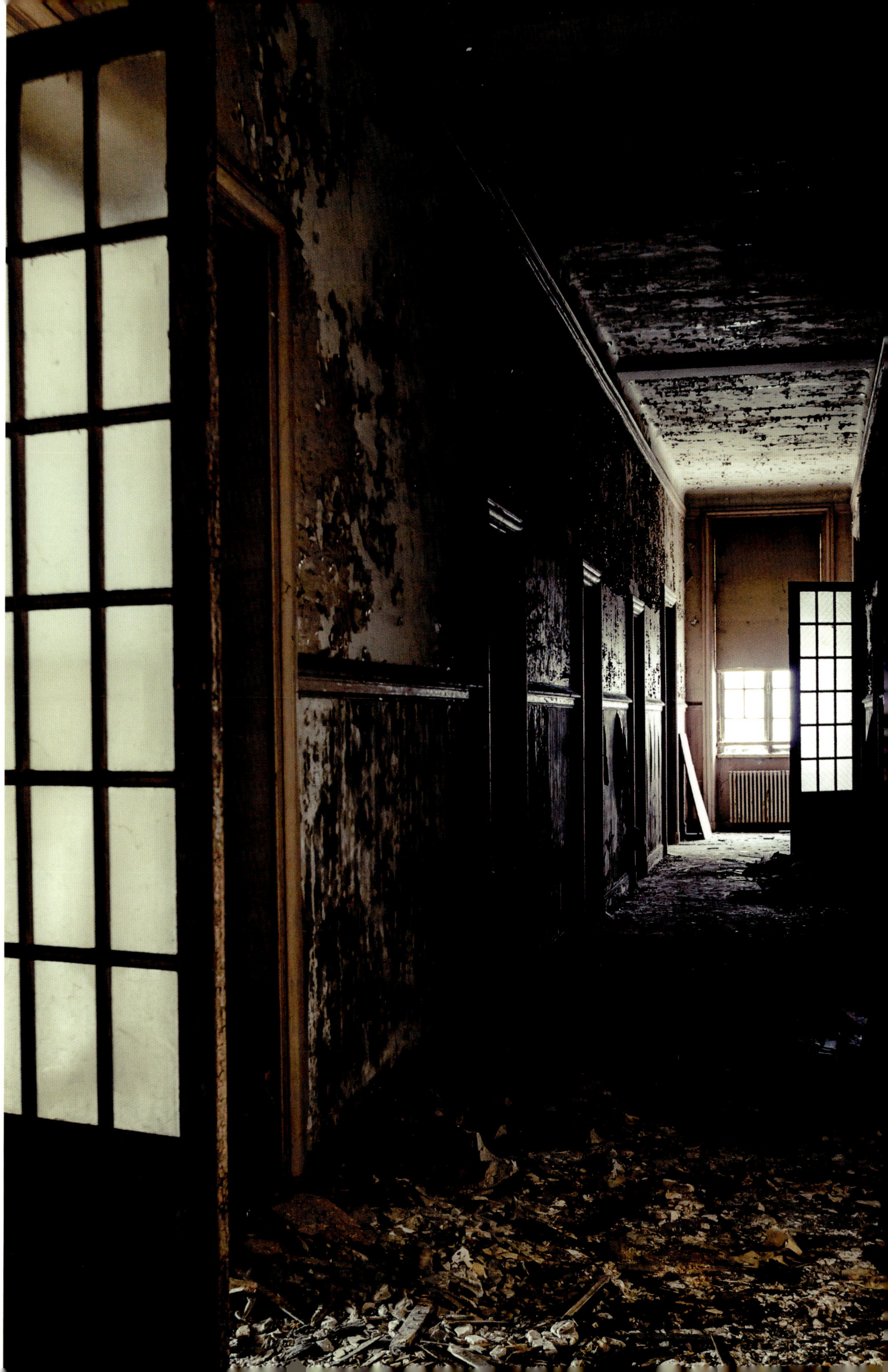

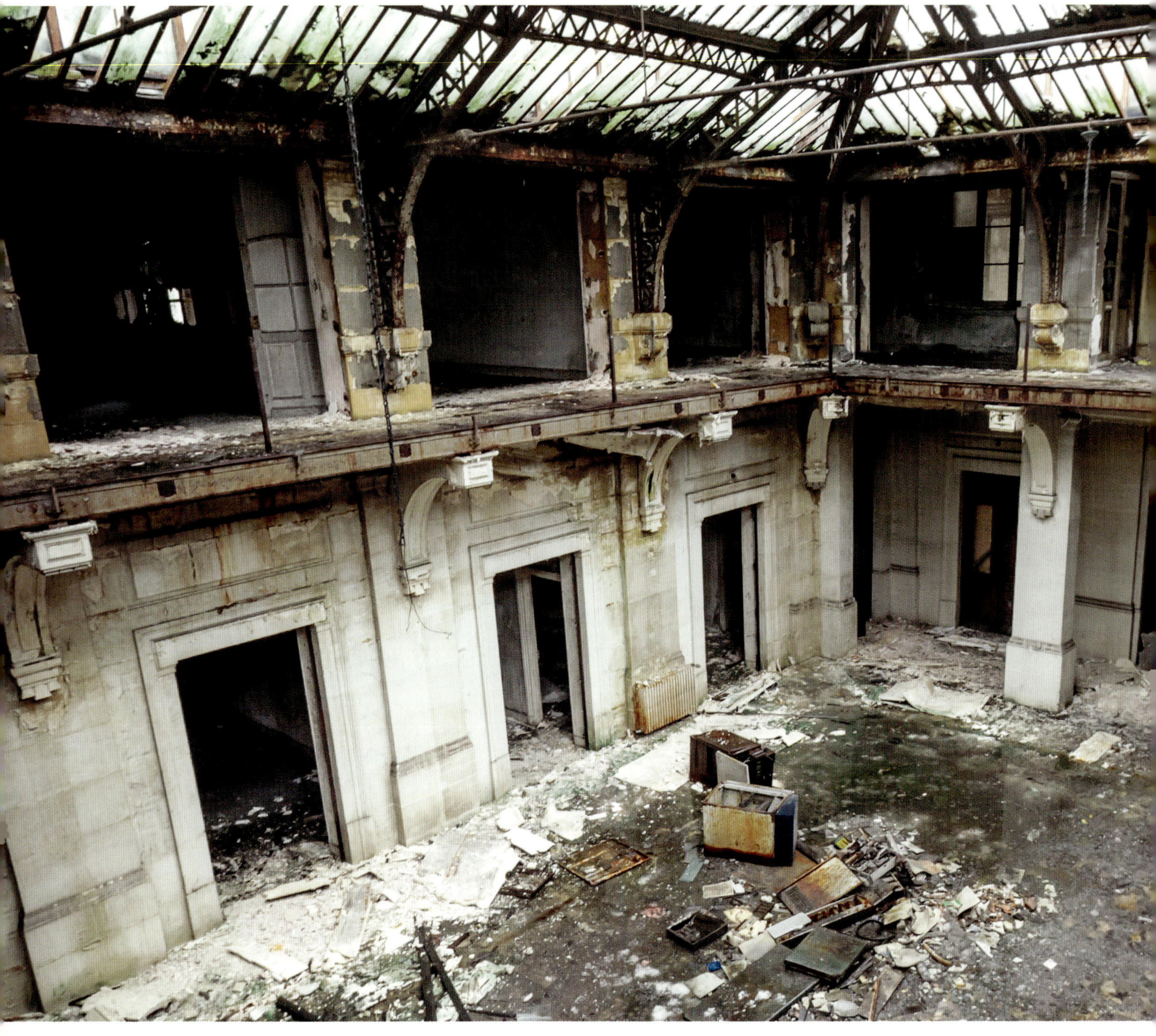

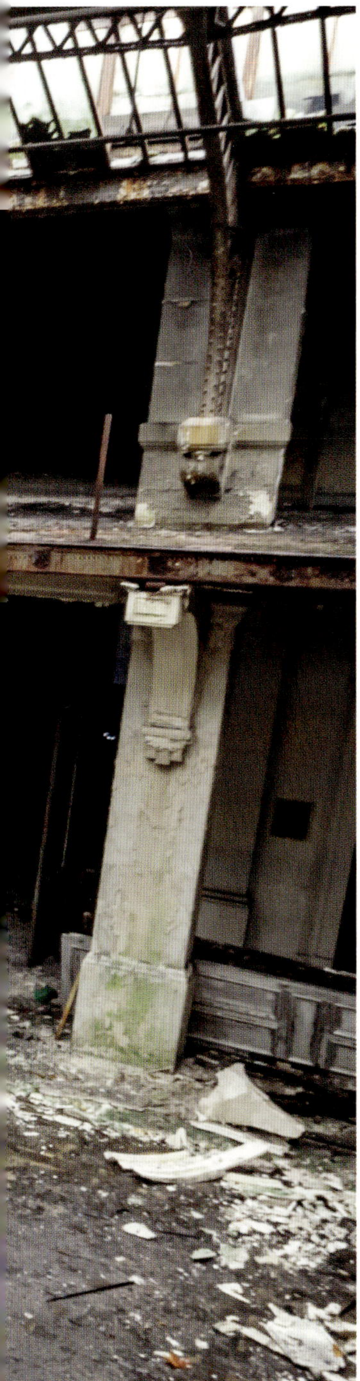

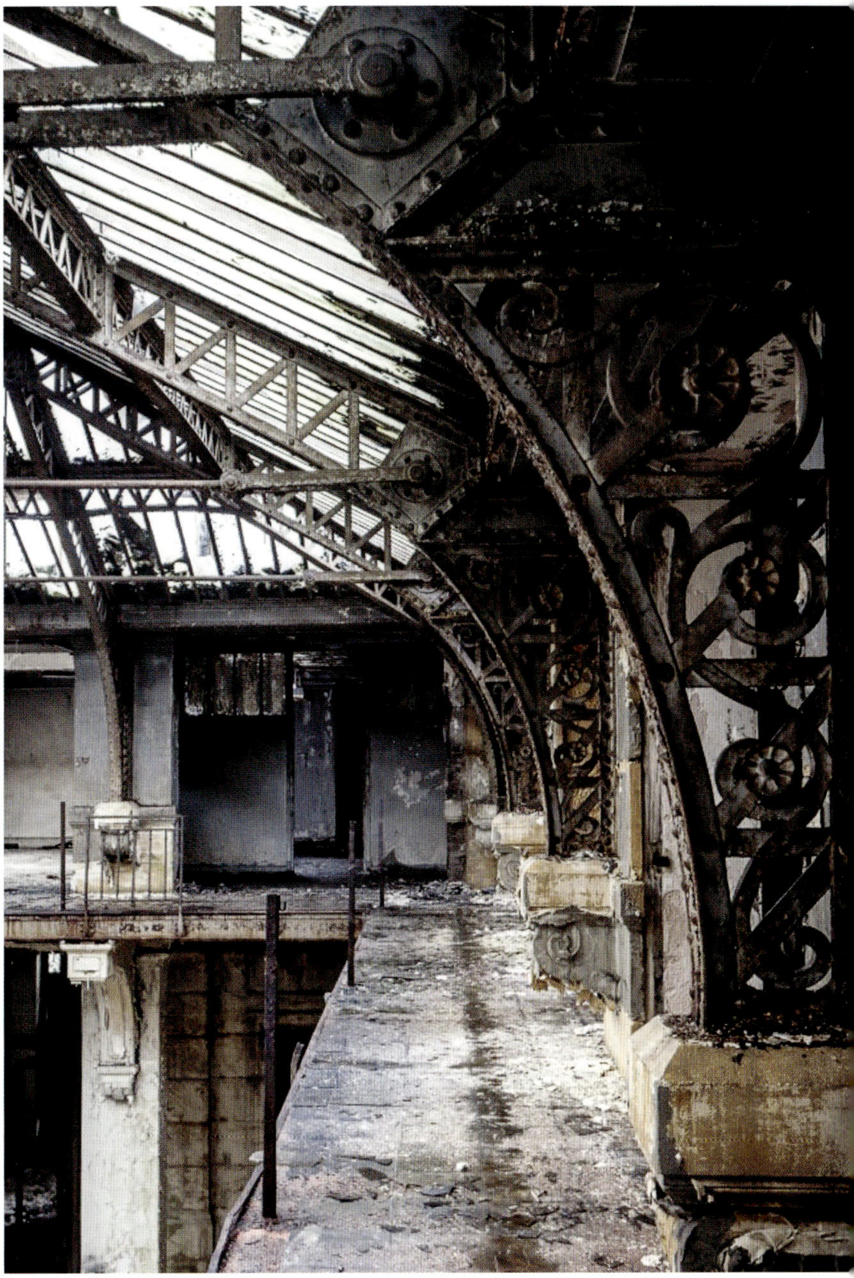

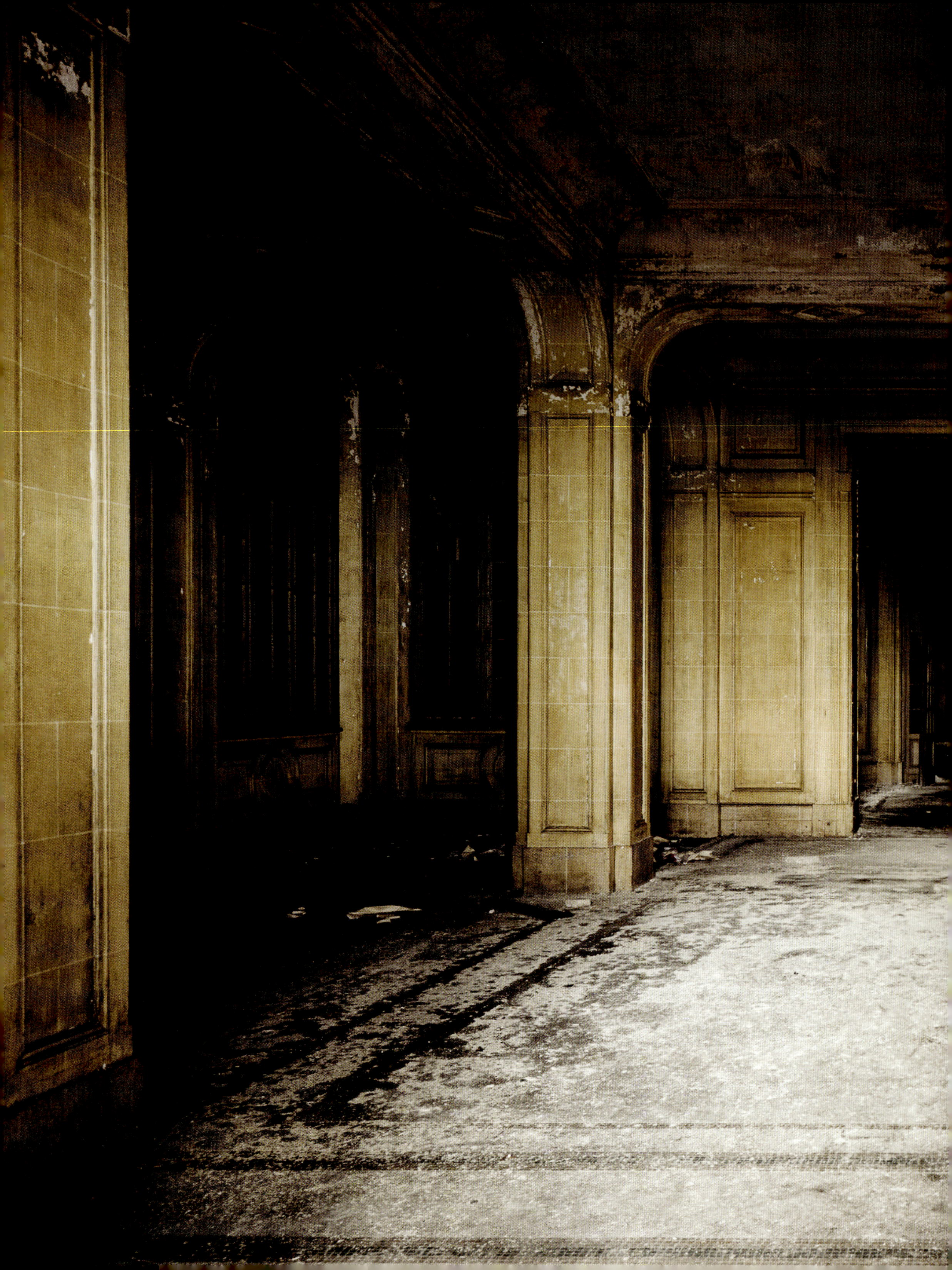

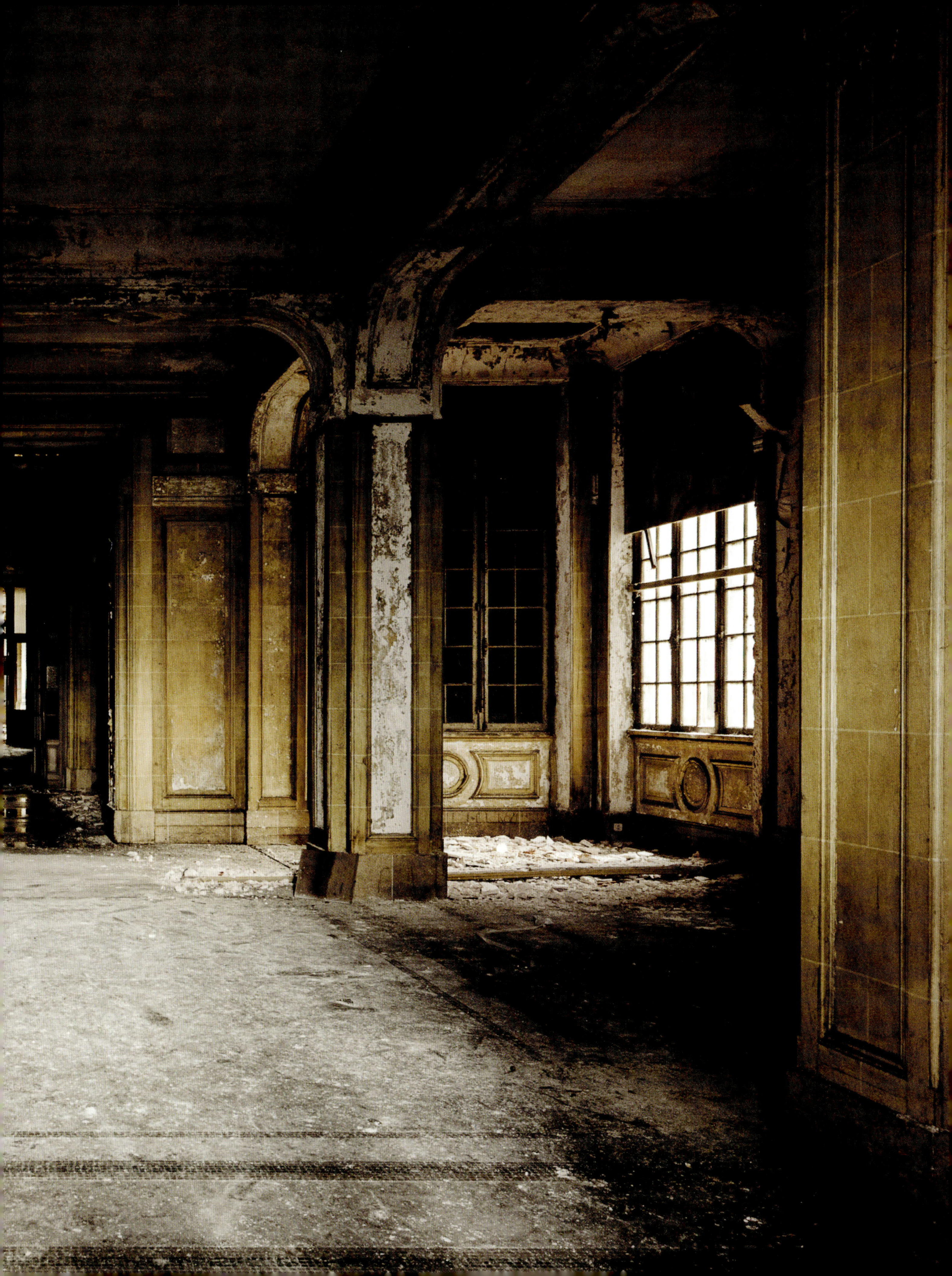

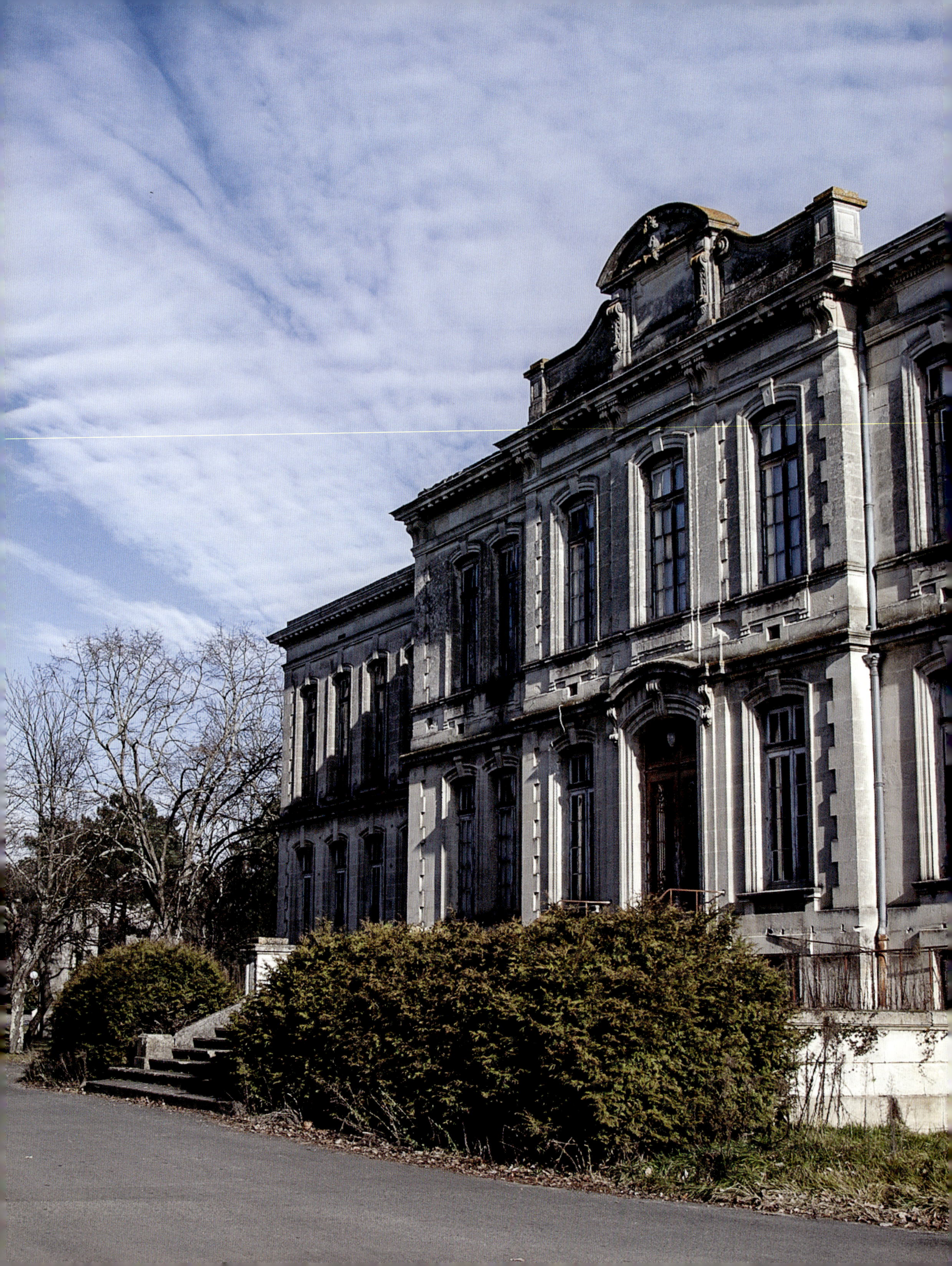

Sanatorium Xavier Arnozan, Bordeaux

When German bacteriologist Robert Koch discovered the bacillus responsible for tuberculosis in 1882, he demonstrated that this disease (believed to be hereditary) was in fact highly contagious. The fight to stop it spreading then turned to isolating sick people in sanatoriums that sprang up all over Europe.

In Bordeaux, the hospital facilities in the city centre were inadequate and an epidemic risk. In 1889, thirty years before the Honnorat law that provided for the establishment of sanatoriums all over France, two Bordeaux doctors set up the charitable organisation, Œuvre du Sanatorium Girondin pour le Traitement de la Tuberculose. The doctors required a well-ventilated site, which was both accessible and isolated, and which could receive and treat TB cases – they finally chose the 14-hectare estate of Feuillas, ideally located in the neighbouring municipality of Pessac.

The construction work, which was financed by private subscription, took two years.

The adult pavilion was opened on 14 October 1902.

The sanatorium, consisting of high-ceilinged rooms on two floors, was designed to admit air and light. It had its own central heating and electric lighting. It soon reached full capacity, and was extended several times until 1914, when it was requisitioned by the army. At the end of the war, the Girondin charitable organisation no longer had the means to carry on. In early 1919, Bordeaux municipality took over the building on the initiative of Prof. Xavier Arnozan.

Extension and modernisation work resumed, creating one of the most modern specialist care centres in the country. In 1928, it was renamed Sanatorium Xavier Arnozan in tribute to the person responsible for its development (the professor had died a few months earlier).

The 20-hectare complex had a capacity of 270 beds. It could accommodate up to 500 patients in three different pavilions, depending on age, gender and prognosis. There were also several treatment rooms, a laboratory, central kitchen, chapel, laundry room, water-treatment plant and staff accommodation.

The sanatorium, later renamed Hôpital Xavier Arnozan, was further extended until antibiotics became available. Combined with advances in surgery, they dramatically reduced the number of TB patients.

From the early 1960s to the 1980s, the oldest buildings were closed, and others were converted. Specialist medical services were transferred to the neighbouring site of Haut-Lévèque, a private sanatorium acquired by Hôpitaux de Bordeaux in 1962.

The Xavier Arnozan hospital is now the Bordeaux geriatric centre.

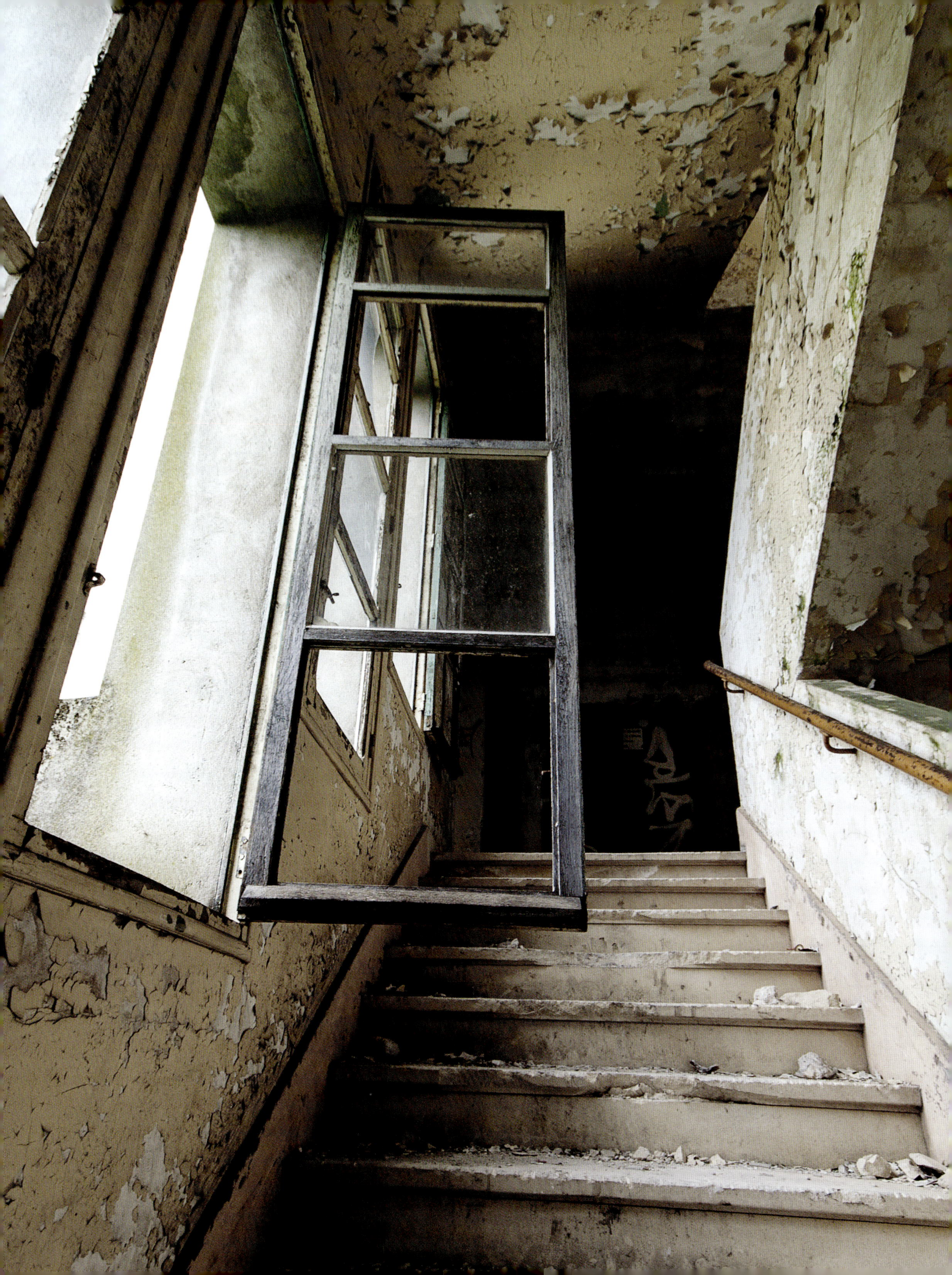

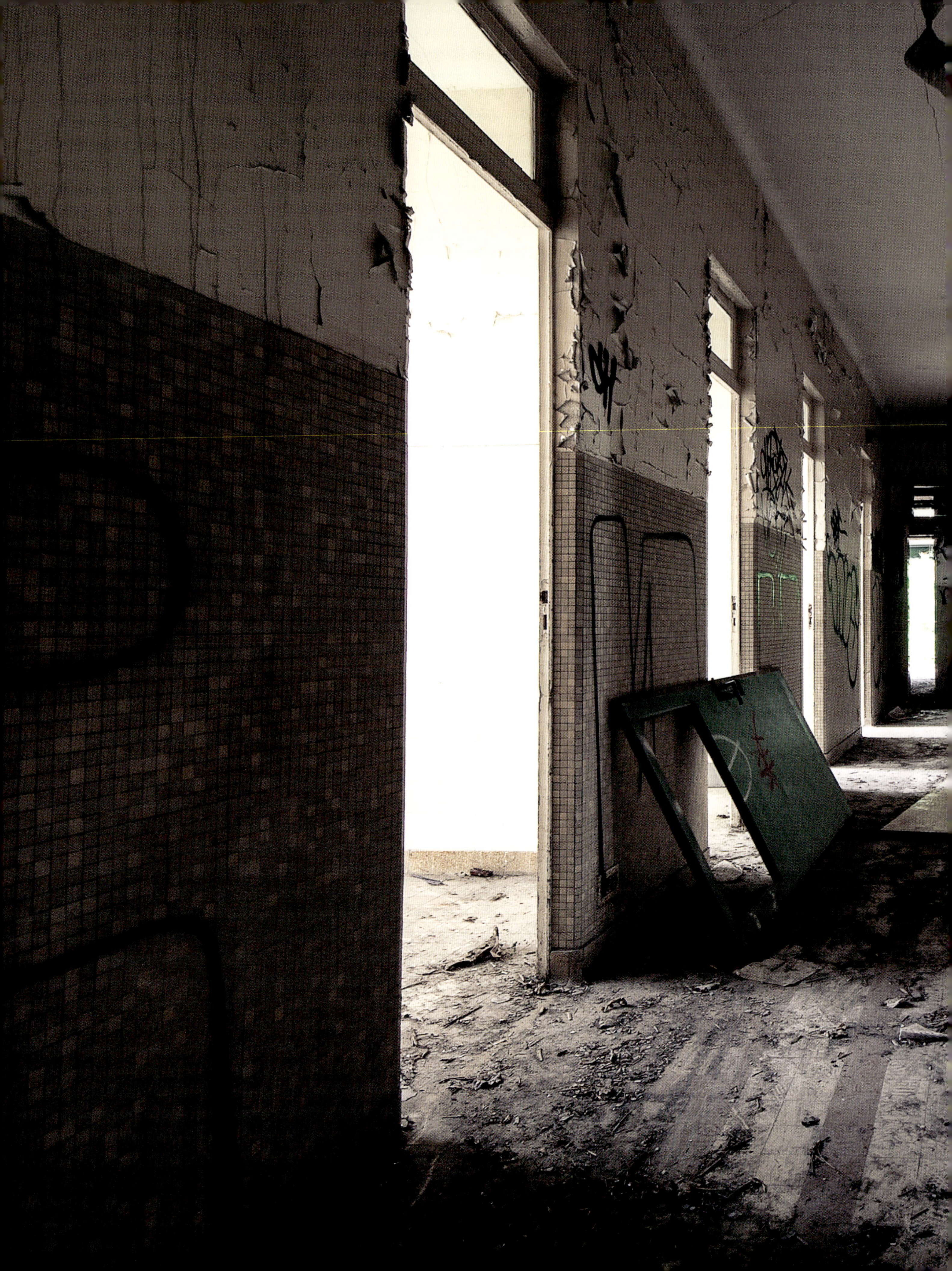

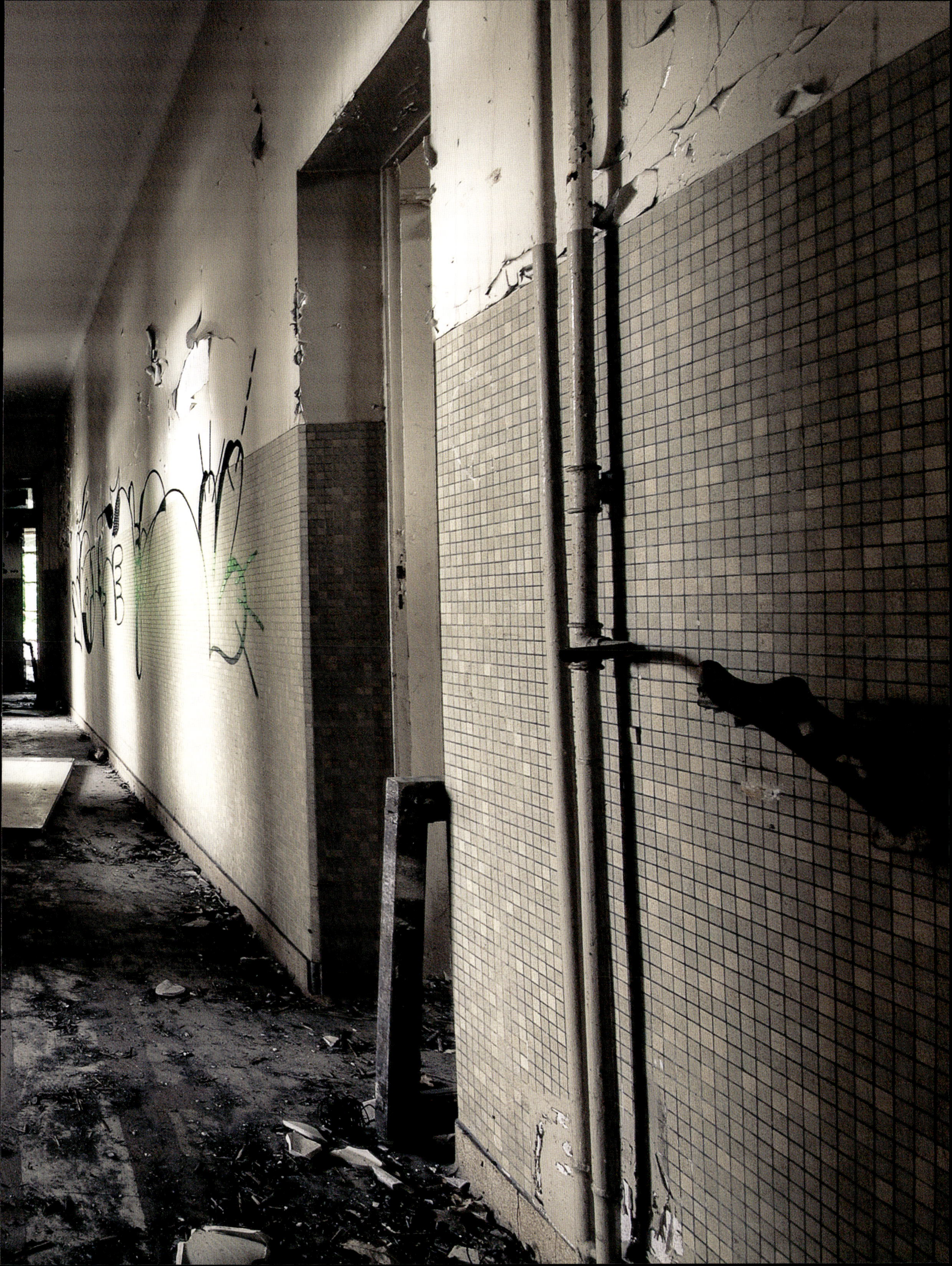

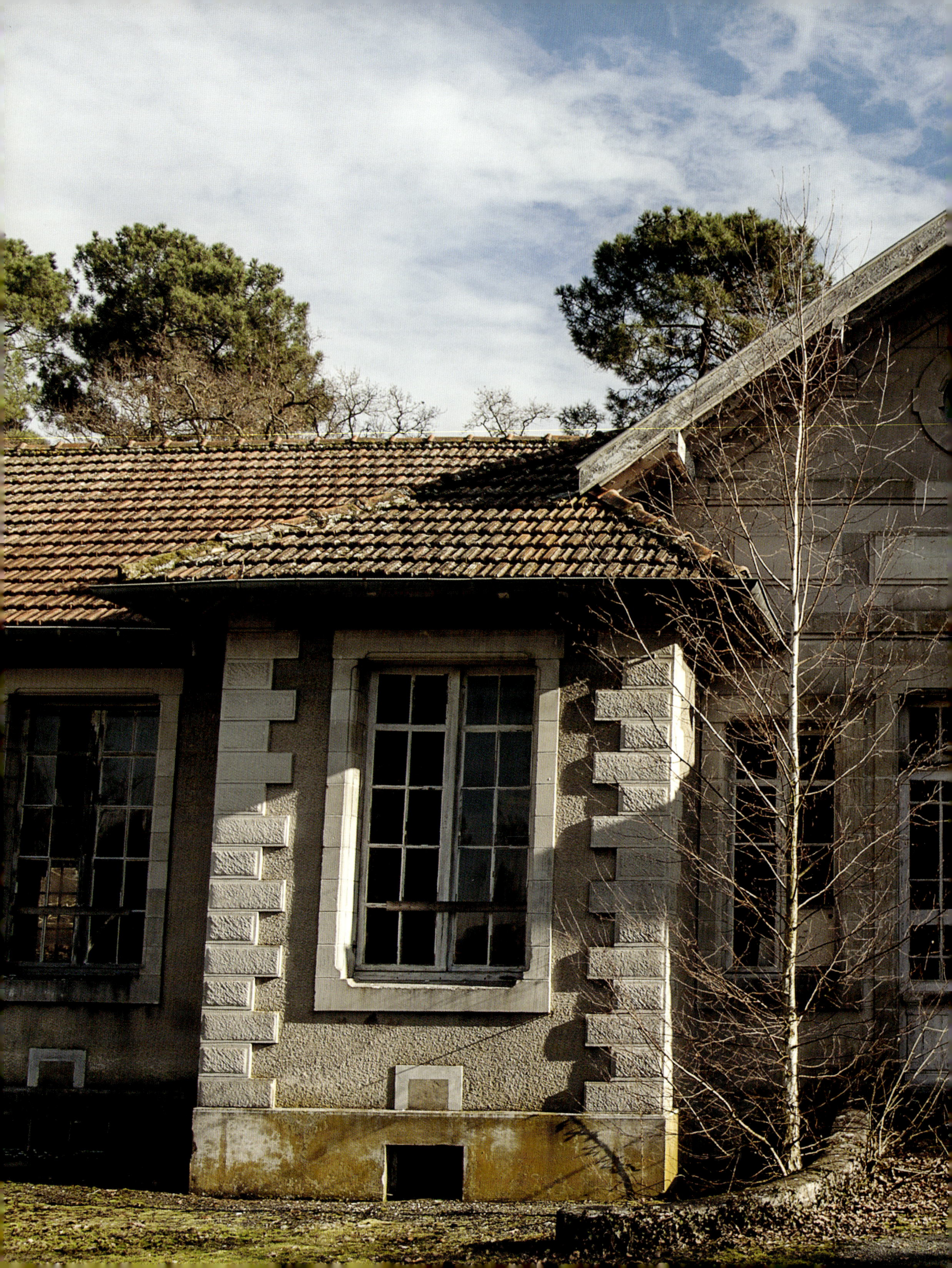

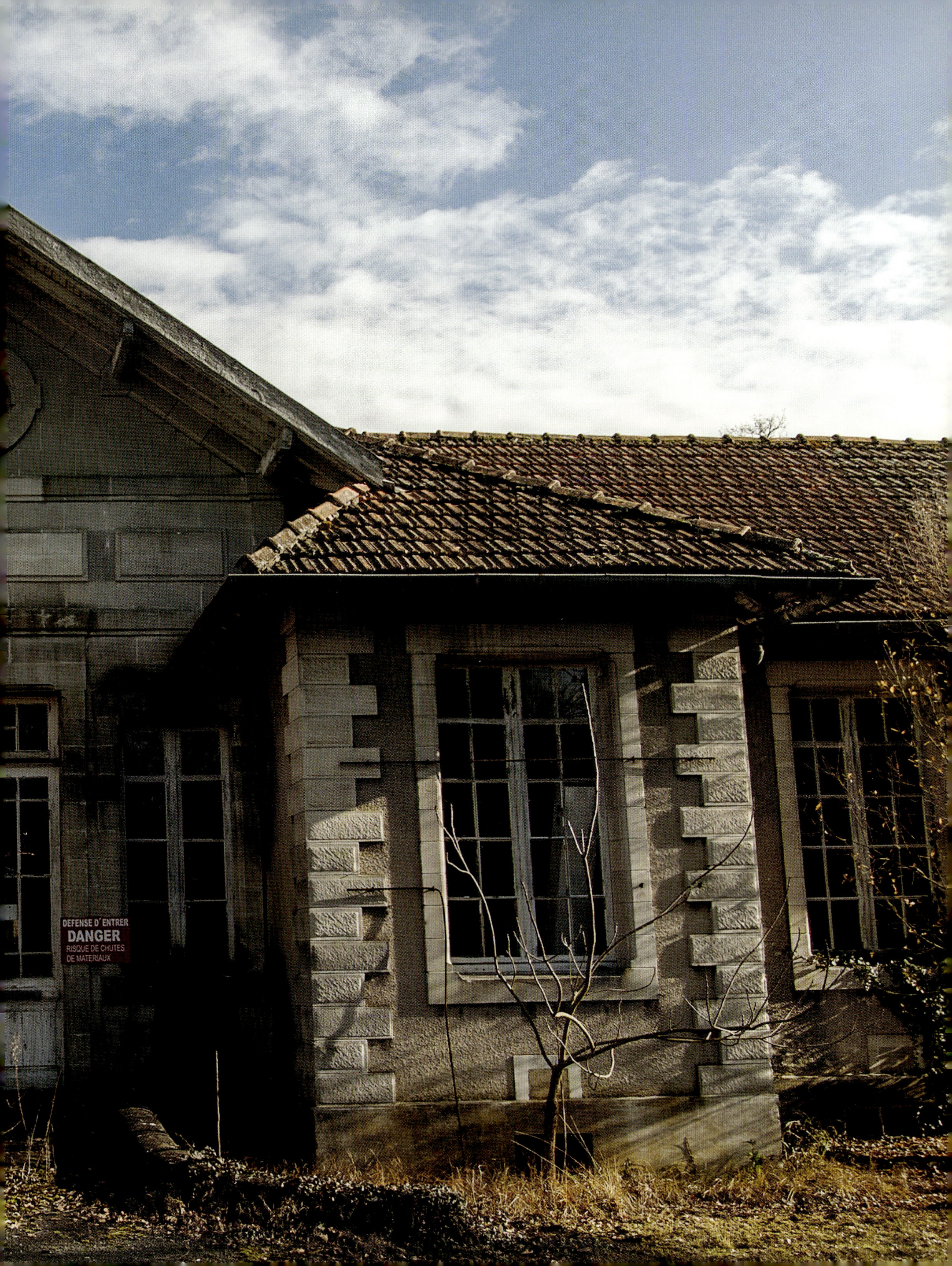
DEFENSE D'ENTRER
DANGER
RISQUE DE CHUTES
DE MATERIAUX

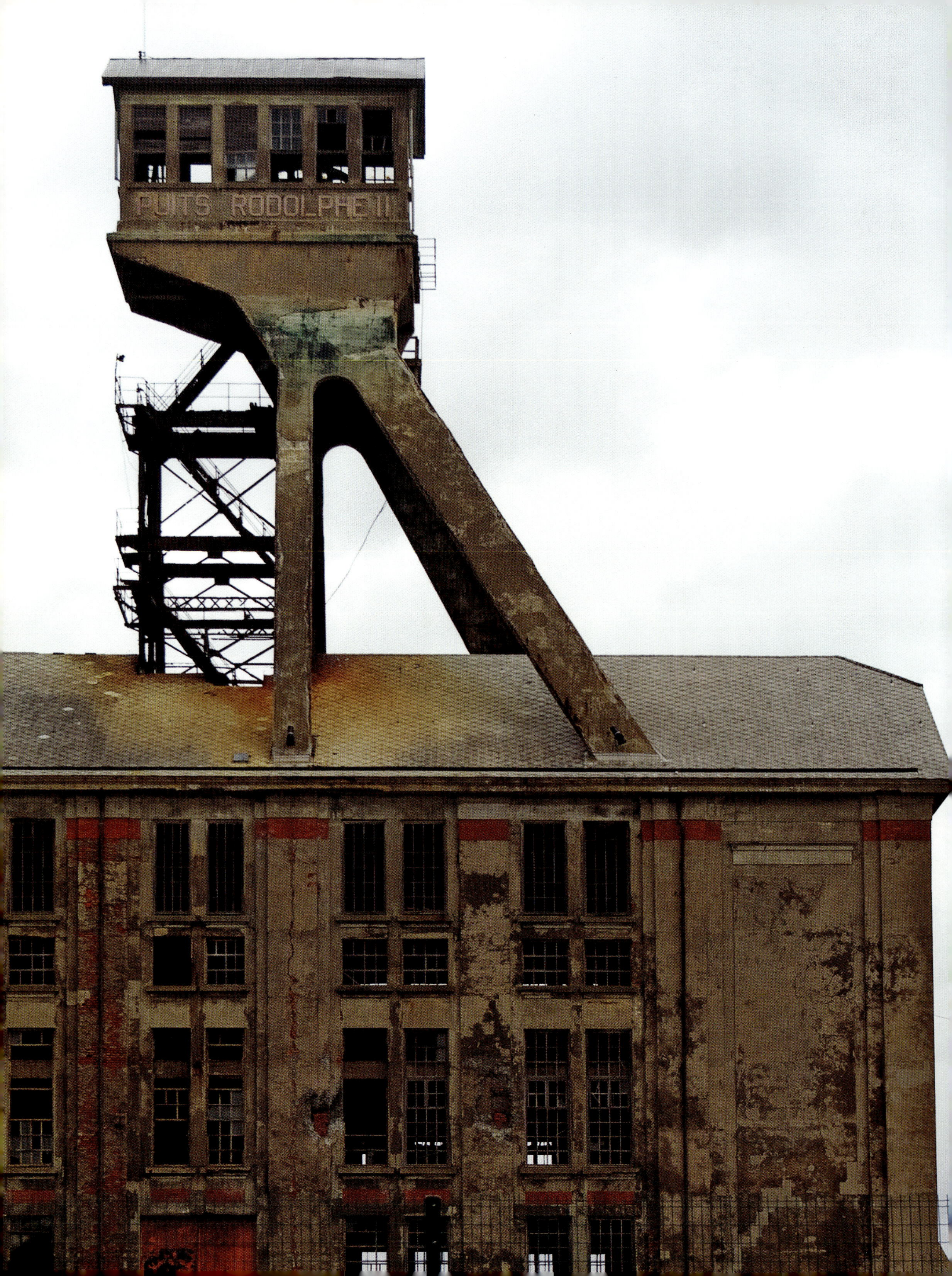
PUITS RODOLPHE II

Rodolphe mines, Alsace

When drought affected parts of Europe in 1893, Amélie Zurcher, owner of a farm in southern Alsace, watched her harvest shrivel. She sought an escape from impending ruin. She knew the wealth of coal buried underground in the neighbouring Vosges. In 1904, she convinced borehole specialist Joseph Vogt to use his equipment to try and detect the valuable ore. Instead of the expected grey-black colour, his samples had an orange-pink tint, typical of potash salts.

Subsequent surveys confirmed the extensive presence of potassium chloride, associated with sodium chloride, in two layers between 400m and 1,000m deep. The multiple uses for potash, both in chemistry and agriculture, make its mining a lucrative business.

The first mine was dug in 1906 and naturally it was named after Amélie. To manage his holdings, Vogt founded the Kali Sainte-Thérèse (KST) company, headed by his son Fernand. The Rodolphe mine that opened in 1913 belonged to him. The galleries descend 711 metres below the communes of Ungersheim and Pulversheim.

When war broke out the following year, there were already thirteen mines in operation. During the First World War, which temporarily halted any expansion, all the potassium mines came under German control.

A bomb dropped on Pulversheim hit an ammunition depot next to the plant and caused serious damage. Only the steel headframe above the main mineshaft was spared.

The mines were confiscated at the Armistice, but were reacquired by the French state in 1924. They were then nationalised under the authority of Mines Domaniales de Potasse d'Alsace (MDPA). The KST company, on the other hand, reverted to Fernand.

The prewar expansion restarted until a first crisis hit in the early 1930s. A wide-ranging social programme had accompanied the boom, to meet the medical, nutritional, educational, religious and cultural needs of the industry's 10,000-plus employees.

Demand for labour was such that many of the miners were recruited from abroad, especially Poland.

The Rodolphe II mine was dug around this time, about 100 metres from its predecessor. It was equipped with a concrete headframe, a first in the potash fields. Vast constructions arose to cater for the storage, crystallisation, mixing and preparation of chlorides.

The financial crisis of 1929 led to unemployment and cutbacks, despite which production had reached 3.5 million tonnes a year on the brink of the Second World War.

On 23 July 1940, a firedamp explosion in the Rodolphe galleries killed twenty-five workers. This incident was to be the deadliest in the history of the mines.

At Liberation, the occupied mines were returned to French control, and a year later production had risen to prewar levels. Despite modernisation and constant growth, however, the exhaustion of the deposits led to the gradual closure of the mines.

1976 saw the last days of the Rodolphe site. Over the following years, the mining superstructure disappeared from the landscape.

The MDPA was responsible for the conversion. Some sites were cleared for green spaces; others were turned into business parks.

In 1987, the Écomusée d'Alsace bought the Rodolphe mines in partnership with the Haut-Rhin regional council and decided to preserve all structures still standing. These consisted of the two headframes, the extraction machinery and several large buildings. Groupe Rodolphe, a former miners' association created in 1994, aims to restore the machines and rehabilitate the site.

Thanks to the association's efforts, a mining site in good condition can now be opened to the public – testimony to the powerful heritage of an industry that shaped the region for a century.

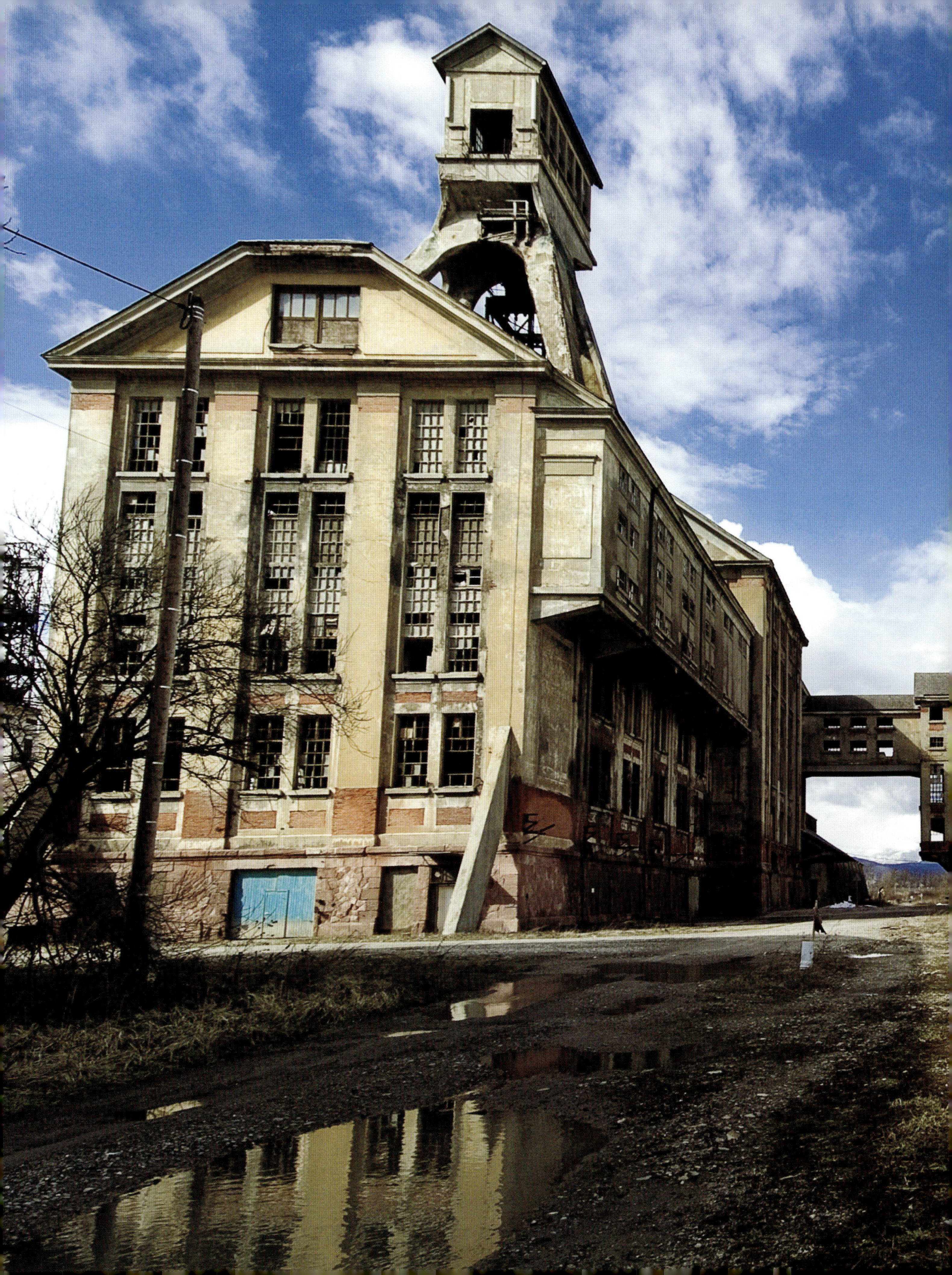

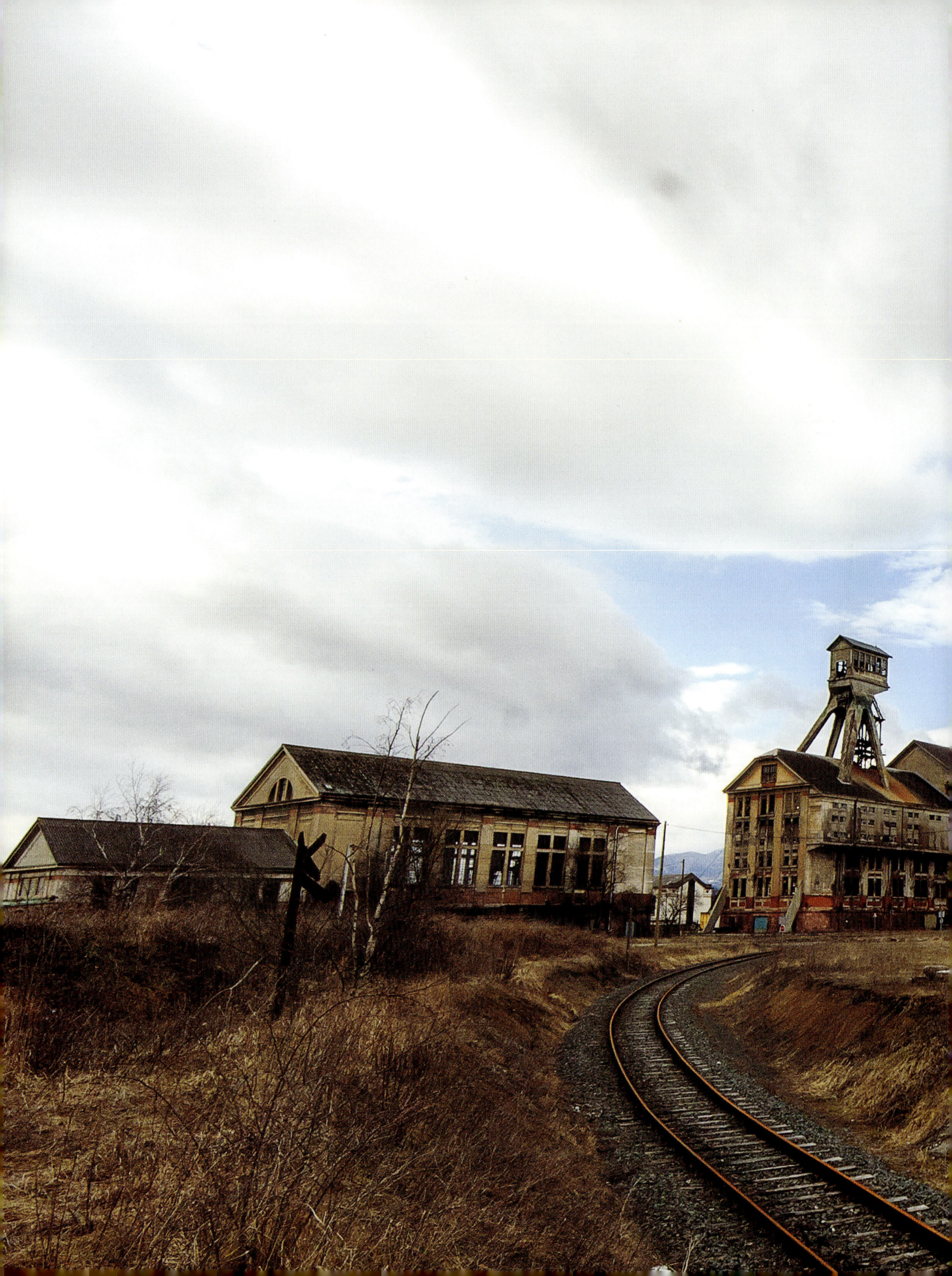

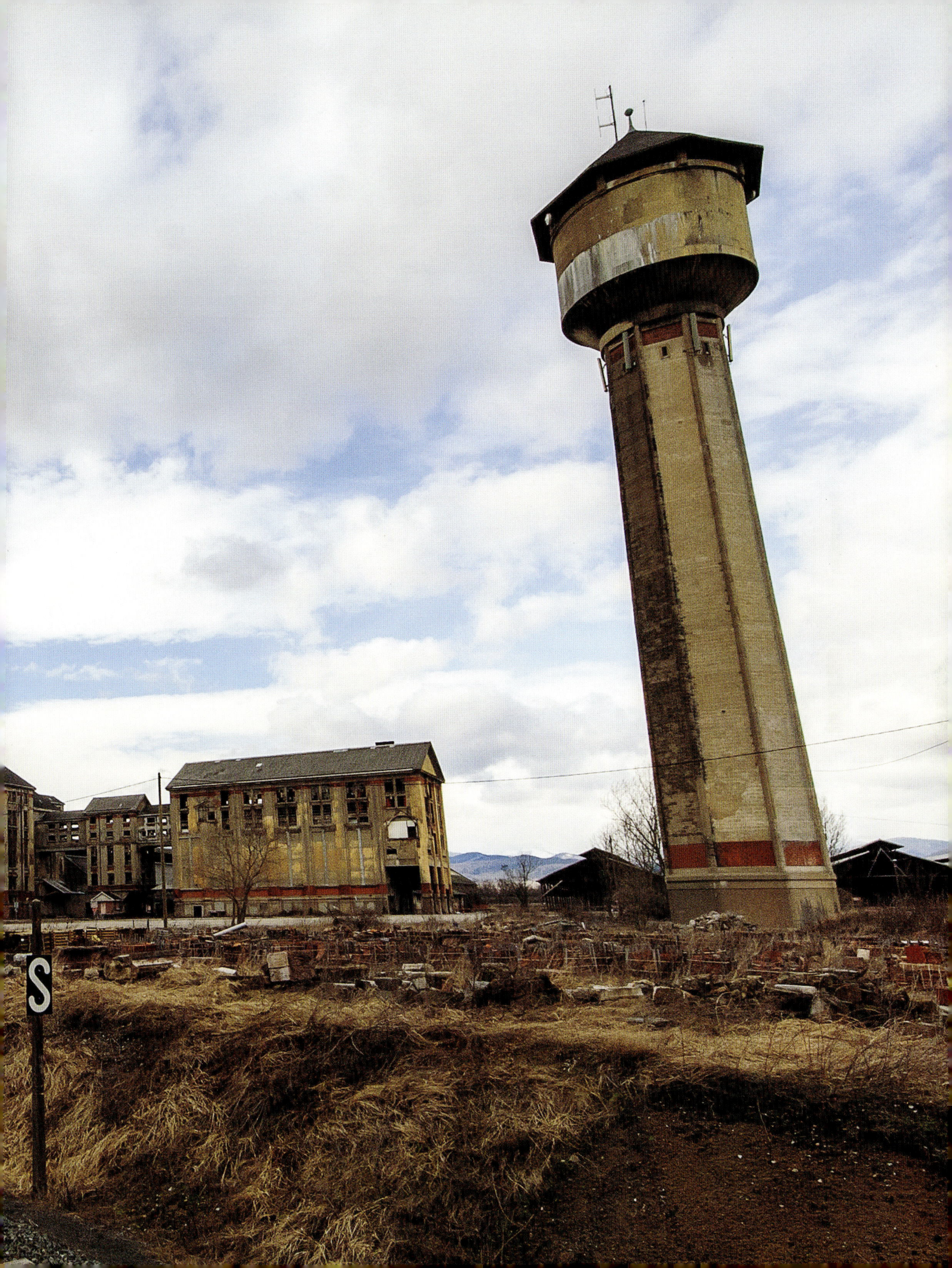
S

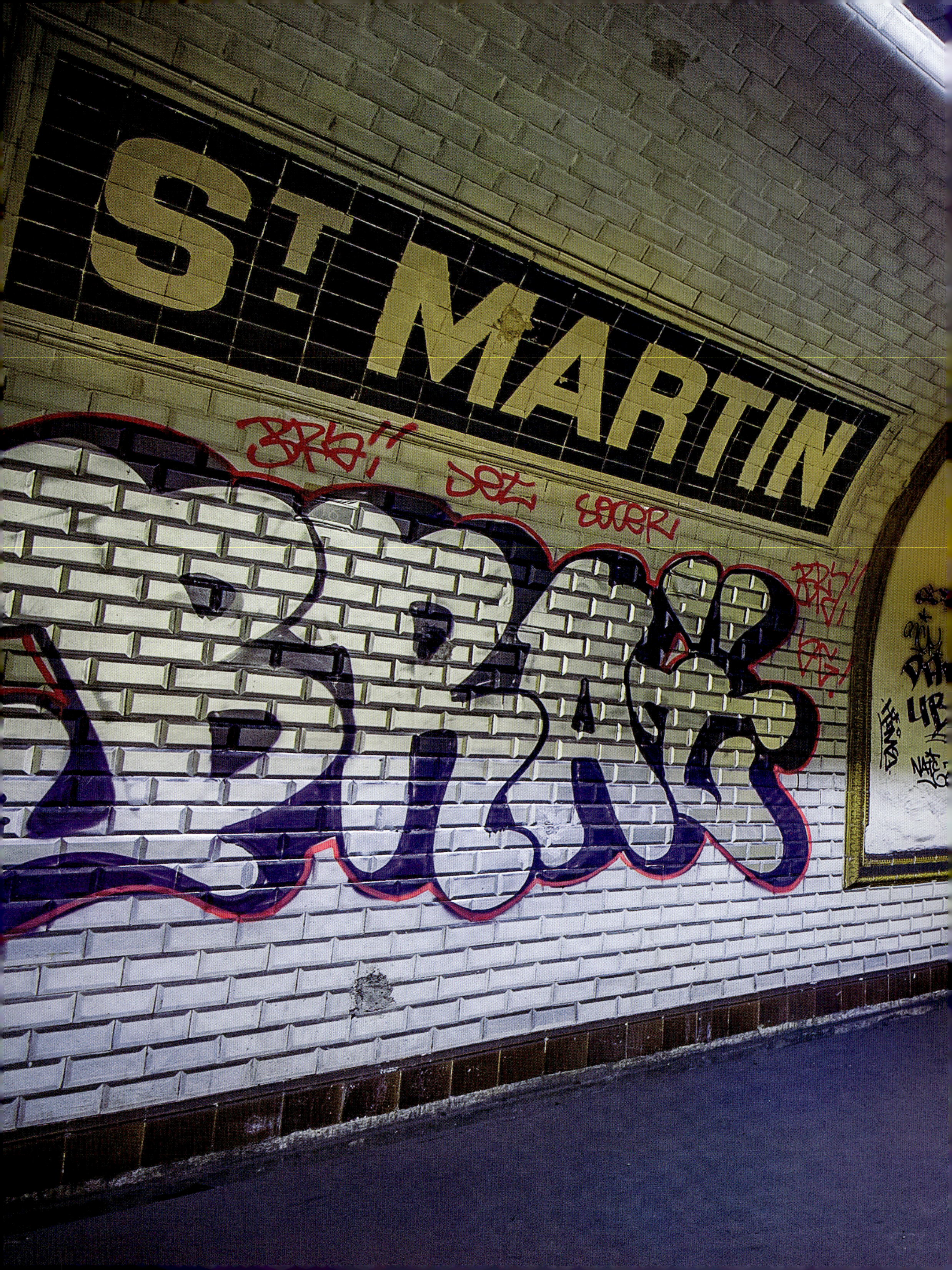
ST. MARTIN

Métro Saint-Martin, Paris

At the outbreak of the 1939–1945 war, men of military age were called up.

Entire sectors of industry faced a labour shortage.

To compensate for this, the Compagnie du Chemin de Fer Métropolitain de Paris, in charge of the city's metro network since it opened in 1900, decided to close a number of stations.

Trains no longer stopped at Saint-Martin, between the 3rd and 10th arrondissements, after September 1939.

Although the station was briefly brought back into service again after the Liberation, its location only a hundred metres from the next stop ultimately sealed its fate.

The Paris metro now has about fifteen unused stations.

Some have merged, others have been moved or reused for other purposes.

This is what happened to Saint-Martin, whose tiled walls became a test ground for advertisements in the 1950s.

Although these publicity campaigns had no outside influence, the station was hired a few decades later by the MediaTransports company, working with the Publicis advertising agency and partner of the state-owned public transport operator RATP (Régie Autonome des Transports Parisiens).

In the 2000s, clothing brands, sports shoe manufacturers and even film director Ridley Scott would plaster the quays with posters advertising their products.

Metro passengers travelling through the station at full speed could spot these installations for a few seconds only.

The premises themselves are partly used as a homeless shelter (Espace Solidarité Insertion) by the Salvation Army.

The rest is given over to RATP Partners of Art, some 40 people responsible for installing artworks over the 360-kilometre network.

In the near future, the station may have reason to change: a follow-up to the "Reinventing Paris" call for projects was launched on 23 May 2017. This new competition, which aims to transform exceptional forgotten sites within the city to offer the public innovative cultural venues or events, gives pride of place to Les Dessous (The Underworld) of Paris. Métro Saint-Martin is among the thirty-four sites selected.

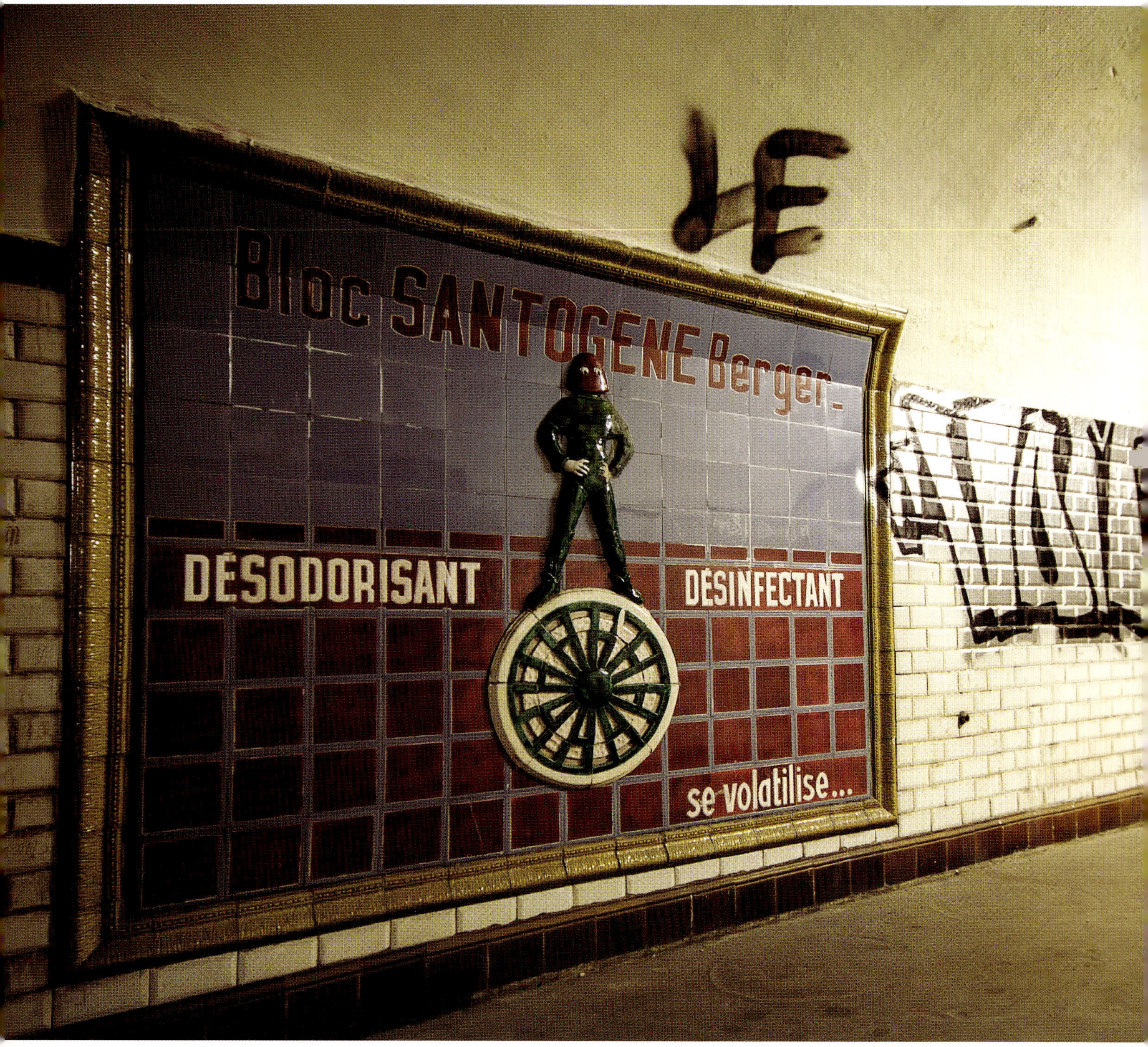
Bloc SANTOGÈNE Berger.
DÉSODORISANT
DÉSINFECTANT
se volatilise...

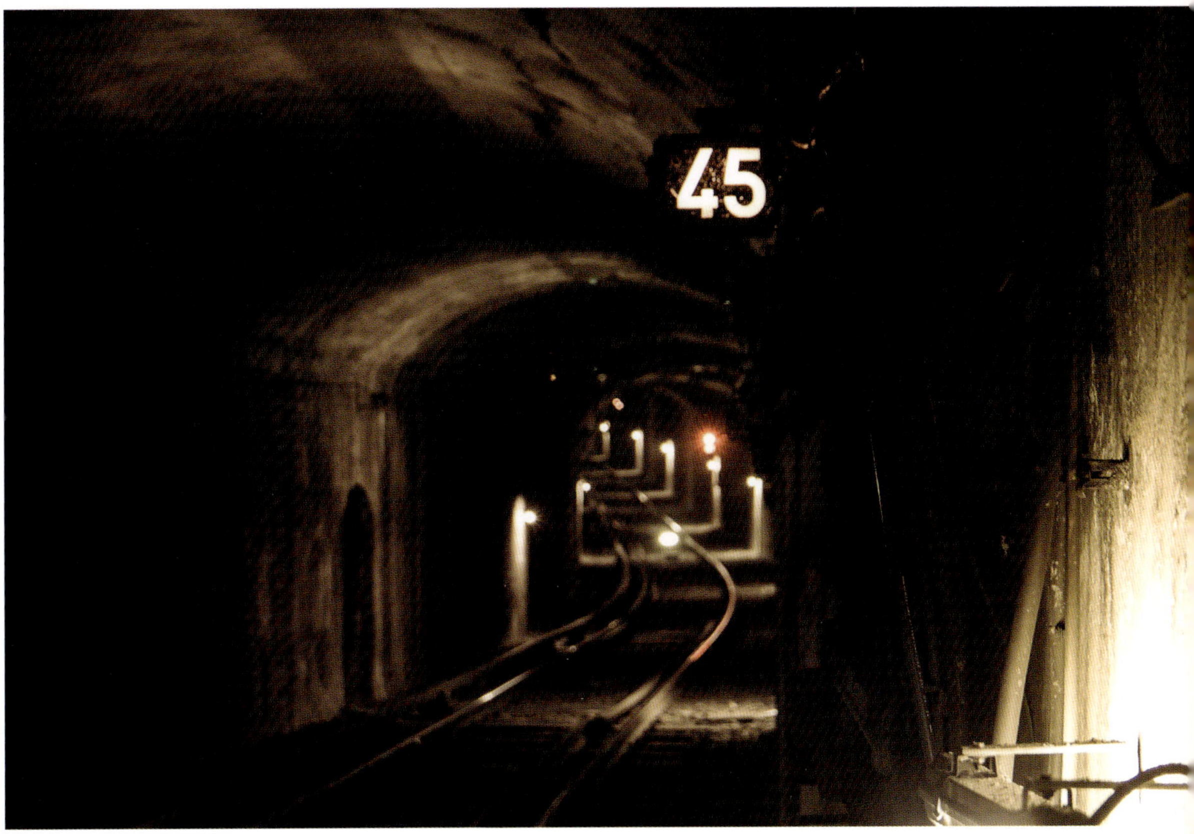
45

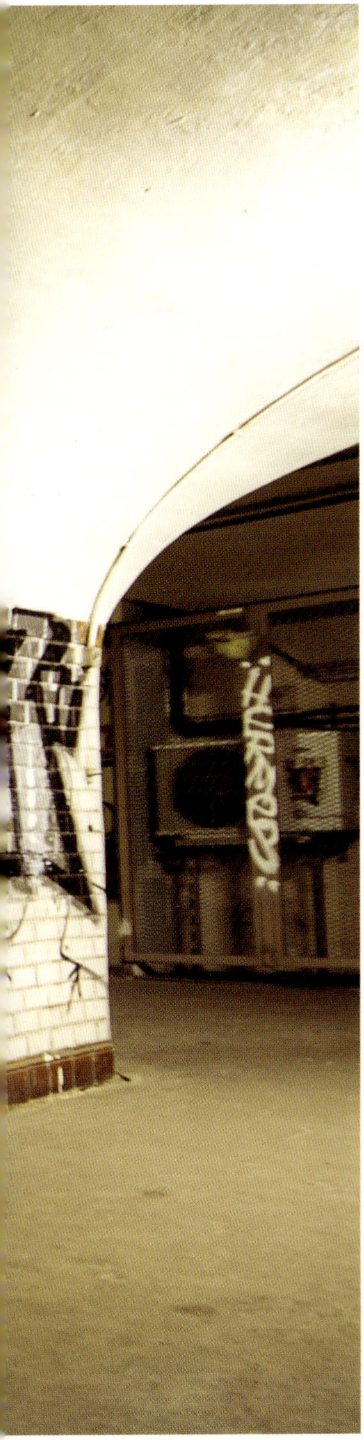

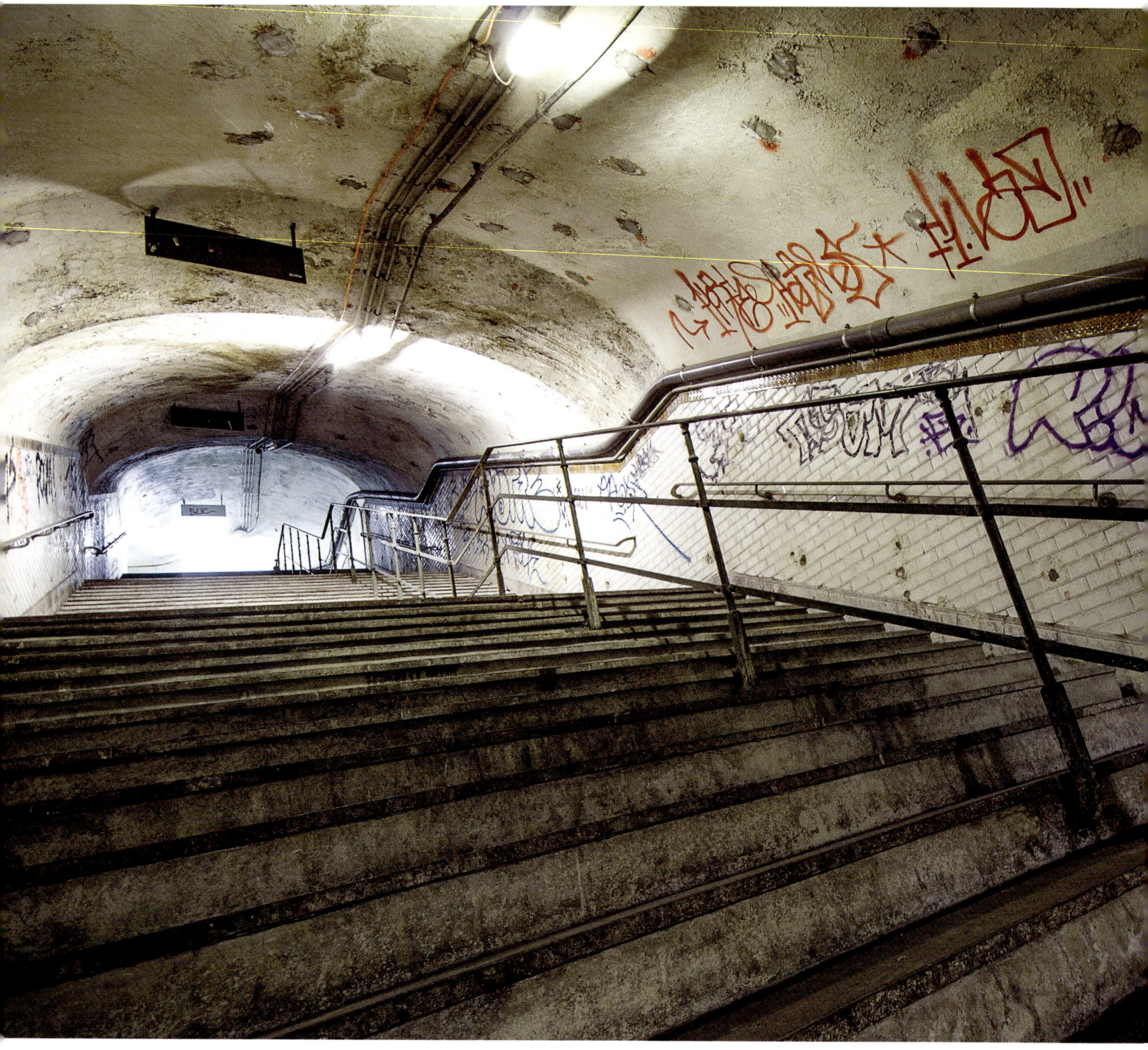

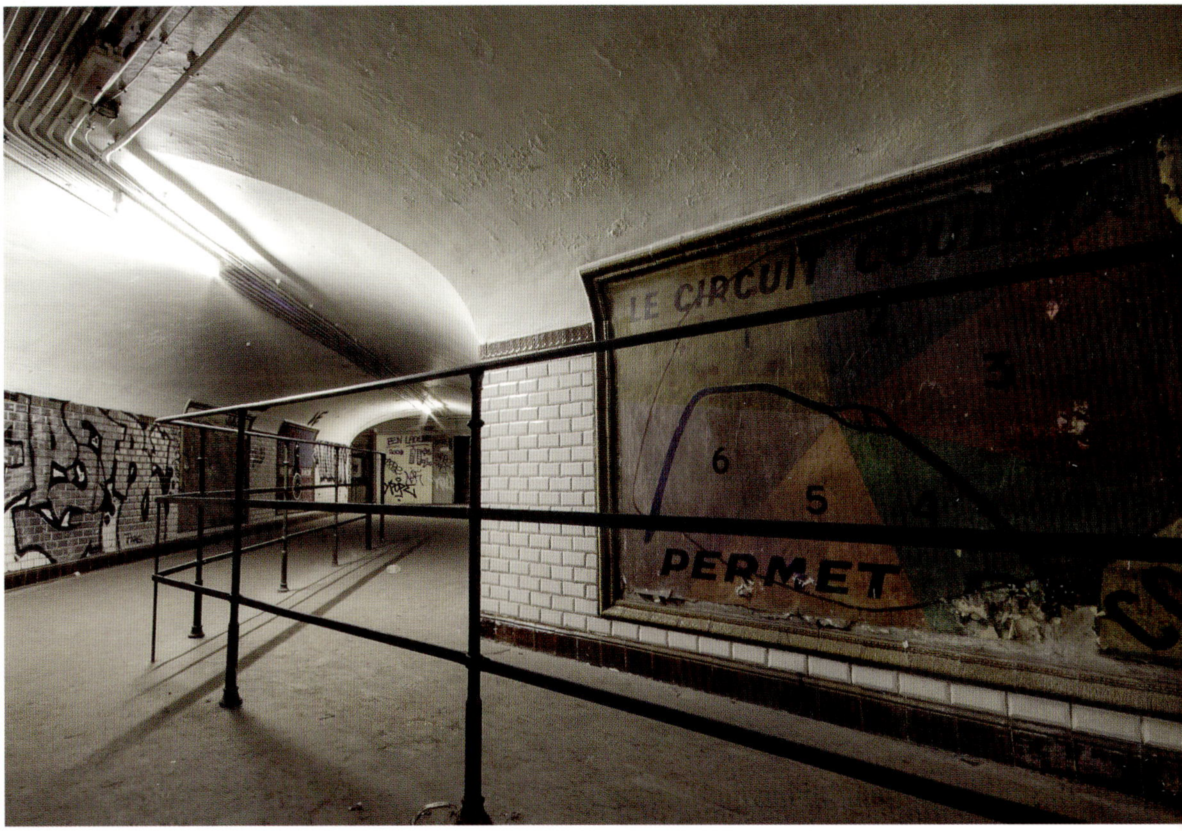
LE CIRCUIT
PERMET

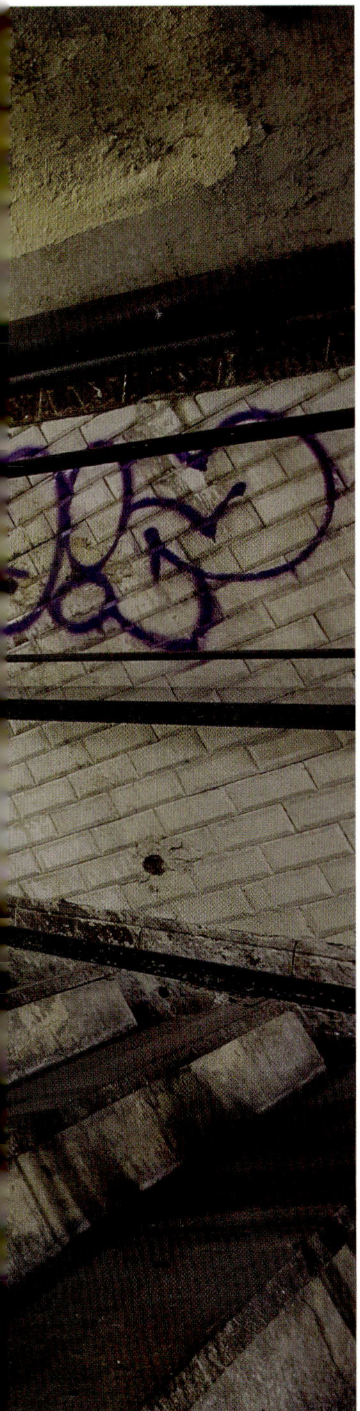

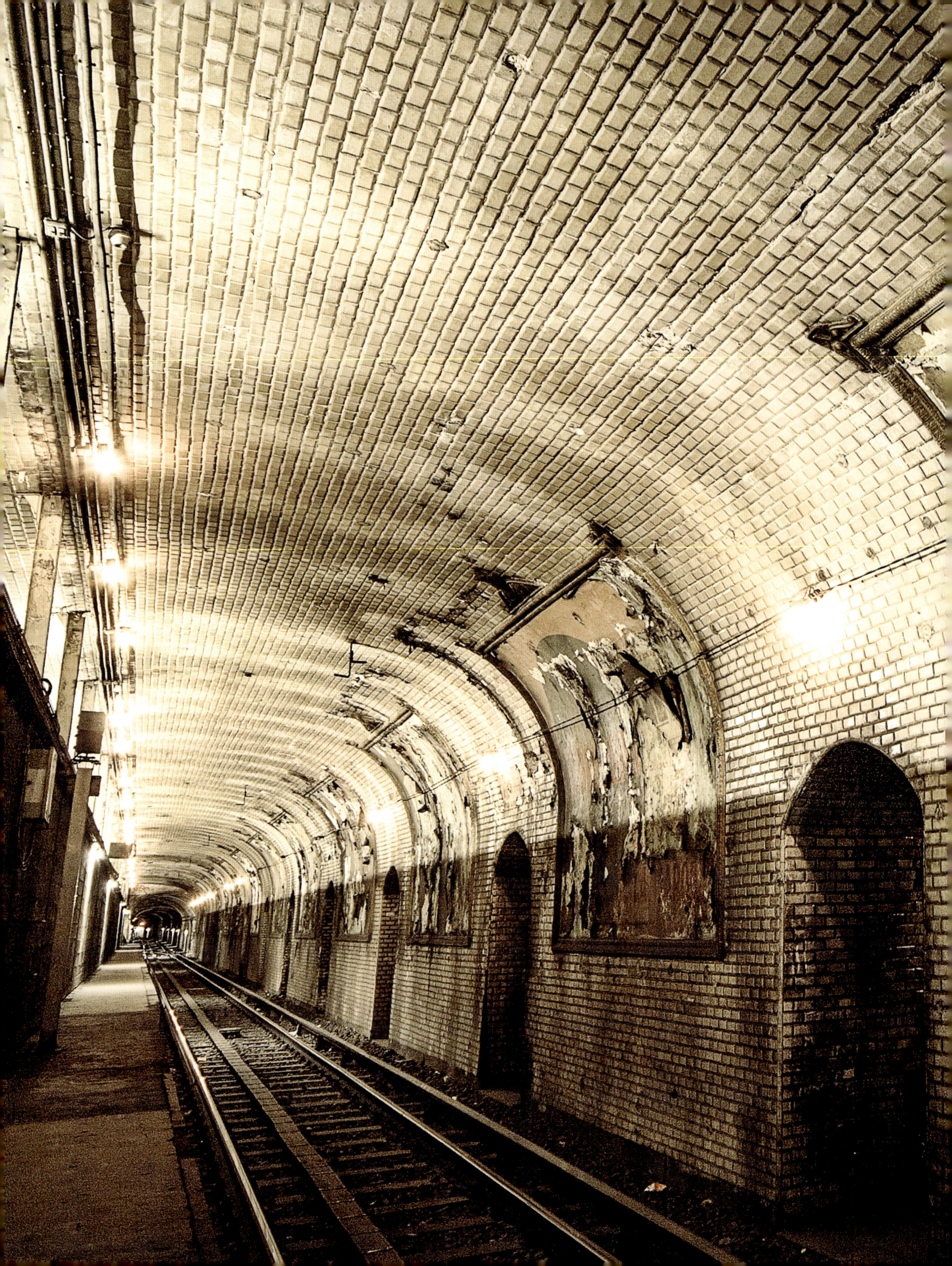

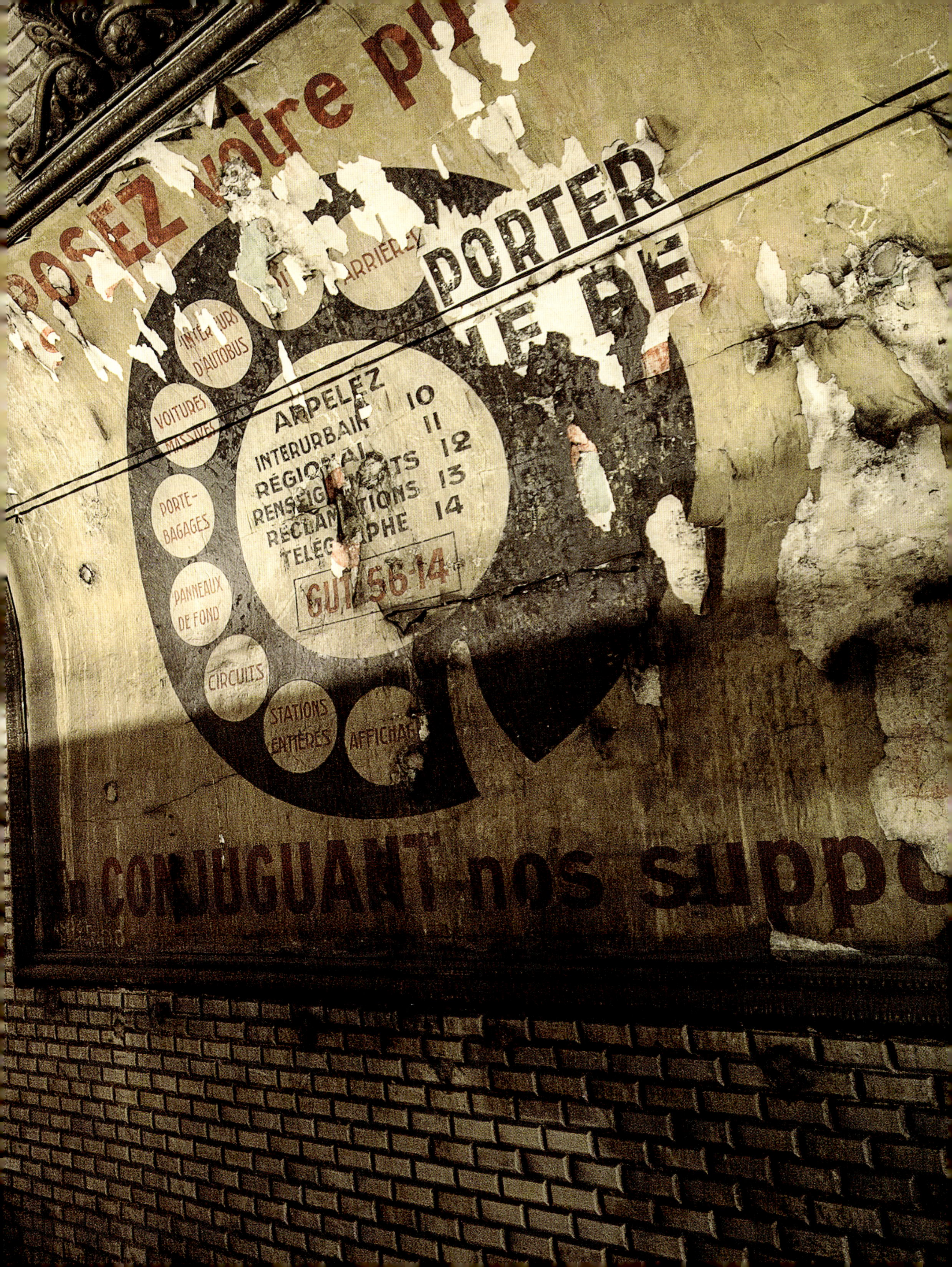
votre
PORTER
D'AUTOBUS
VOITURES
PORTE-BAGAGES
PANNEAUX DE FOND
CIRCUITS
STATIONS ENTIÈRES
APPELEZ 10
GUT. 56-14
CONJUGUANT nos

The authors

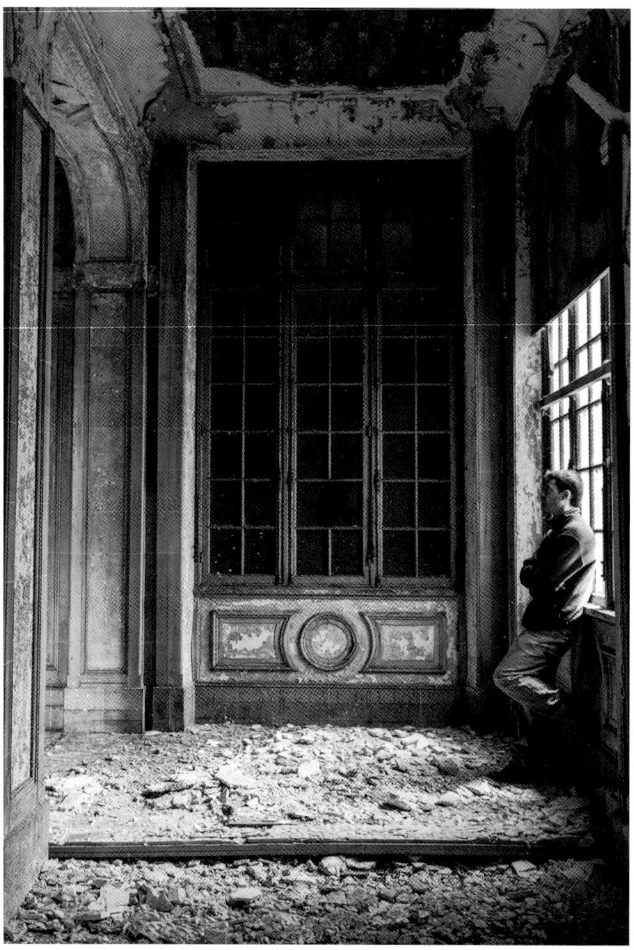

Sylvain Margaine : born in 1977, is an engineer. Since 1998 he has been identifying and photographing the world's forgotten heritage and publishing these urban explorations on his website: www.forbidden-places.net.

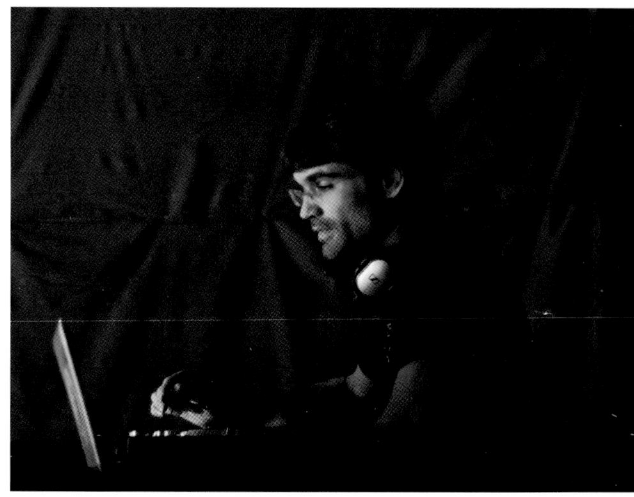

David Margaine : born in 1980, is a pharmacist by trade. For the past twelve years he has been working as a writer, composer and performer with several groups of musicians from the Bordeaux alternative scene.

Acknowledgements

Sylvain would like to thank his fellow explorers, travelling companions and long-term friends.

He also greatly appreciates the backing of Thomas Jonglez and Stéphanie Jonglez in this project, which has meant so much to him over many years.

David is ever grateful to the publishers for their confidence in his work.

He also thanks Martine Azŏulai, steadfast roving proofreader; and Chinese Man, Dvorák, the EZ3kiel band and Grorr for their supportive sounds.

And finally a special mention of Marielle Glouchko for her always invaluable companionship.

Credits

Editor
Thomas Jonglez

Photography
Sylvain Margaine

Texts
David Margaine

Designer
Maria Lago (FAMILIA STUDIO)

Translation
Caroline Lawrence

Proofreading
Jana Gough

Registration of copyright: November 2017
ISBN : 978-2-36195-216-7
Printed in China by TOPPAN